REGNUM EDINBURGH CENTENARY SERIES
Volume 15

A Century of Catholic Mission

The Centenary of the World Missionary Conference of 1910, held in Edinburgh, was a suggestive moment for many people seeking direction for Christian mission in the twenty-first century. Several different constituencies within world Christianity held significant events around 2010. From 2005, an international group worked collaboratively to develop an intercontinental and multi-denominational project, known as Edinburgh 2010, and based at New College, University of Edinburgh. This initiative brought together representatives of twenty different global Christian bodies, representing all major Christian denominations and confessions, and many different strands of mission and church life, to mark the Centenary.

Essential to the work of the Edinburgh 1910 Conference, and of abiding value, were the findings of the eight think-tanks or 'commissions'. These inspired the idea of a new round of collaborative reflection on Christian mission – but now focused on nine themes identified as being key to mission in the twenty-first century. The study process was polycentric, open-ended, and as inclusive as possible of the different genders, regions of the world, and theological and confessional perspectives in today's church. It was overseen by the Study Process Monitoring Group: Dr Maria Aranzazu Aguado (Spain, The Vatican), Dr Daryl Balia (South Africa, Edinburgh 2010), Mrs Rosemary Dowsett (UK, World Evangelical Alliance), Dr Knud Jørgensen (Norway, Areopagos), Rev. John Kafwanka (Zambia, Anglican Communion), Rev. Dr Jooseop Keum (Korea, World Council of Churches), Dr Wonsuk Ma (Korea, Oxford Centre for Mission Studies), Rev. Dr Kenneth R. Ross (UK, Church of Scotland), Dr Petros Vassiliadis (Greece, Aristotle University of Thessalonikki), and coordinated by Dr Kirsteen Kim (UK, Edinburgh 2010).

These publications reflect the ethos of Edinburgh 2010 and will make a significant contribution to ongoing studies in mission. It should be clear that material published in this series will inevitably reflect a diverse range of views and positions. These will not necessarily represent those of the series' editors or of the Edinburgh 2010 General Council, but in publishing them the leadership of Edinburgh 2010 hopes to encourage conversation between Christians and collaboration in mission. All the series' volumes are commended for study and reflection in both church and academy.

Series Editors

Knud Jørgensen	Areopagos, Norway, MF Norwegian School of Theology & the Lutheran School of Theology, Hong Kong. Former Chair of Edinburgh 2010 Study Process Monitoring Group
Kirsteen Kim	Leeds Trinity University College and former Edinburgh 2010 Research Coordinator, UK
Wonsuk Ma	Oxford Centre for Mission Studies, Oxford, UK
Tony Gray	Words by Design, Bicester, UK

REGNUM EDINBURGH CENTENARY SERIES
Volume 15

A Century of Catholic Mission

Roman Catholic Missiology 1910 to the Present

Edited by Stephen B. Bevans, SVD

First published 2013 by Regnum Books International

Regnum is an imprint of the Oxford Centre for Mission Studies
St. Philip and St. James Church, Woodstock Road
Oxford OX2 6HR, UK
www.ocms.ac.uk/regnum

09 08 07 06 05 04 03 7 6 5 4 3 2 1

British Library Cataloguing in Publication Data
A catalogue record for this book is available from the British Library

ISBN: 978-1-908355-14-0

Typeset by Words by Design
Printed and bound in Great Britain
for Regnum Books International
by TJ International LTD, Padstow, Cornwall

*The paper used for the text of this book is manufactured to ISO 14001 and EMAS
(Eco-Management & Audit Scheme) international standards, minimising negative
impacts on the environment. It contains material sourced from responsibly managed forests,
certified in accordance with the FSC.*

FSC

The publication of this title is made possible by the generous financial assistance
of the Pontifical Council for the Promotion of Christian Unity, facilitated by its
Secretary, Bishop Brian Farrell.
Additional funding for distribution of the book to theological libraries in the Global South
was provided by Stephen Bevans, SVD and Roger Schroeder, SVD,
both at Catholic Theological Union, Chicago.

To

Rev. Lawrence Nemer, SVD

Always an inspiration

CONTENTS

INTRODUCTION

Stephen B. Bevans, SVD

The origins of this book lie in a lunch engagement to which I was invited by Drs Wonsuk and Julie Ma of the Oxford Center for Mission Studies in 2009. It was then that Wonsuk Ma asked if I would be willing to edit a volume that would trace the development of Catholic mission practice and thinking from 1910 – the year of the Edinburgh World Mission Conference – to the present day. Dr Ma said that Regnum Books International – of which he was publisher – was planning to publish a series around the Edinburgh Conference, and he was convinced that any series that did not include the immense Catholic contribution of mission in the last century would be incomplete. I heartily agreed with him, and, after some consideration agreed to take on what I knew would be an immense project, and yet one worthy of the effort.

Just *how* immense, however, I did not completely realize. In order to offer as complete a picture as possible of a century of Catholic mission I had to engage the help of a large number of authors, and contacting them and encouraging them to write was to take a good bit of time. An even more immense task was editing the twenty-six chapters as they came in. While the authors who agreed to submit chapters were all relatively prompt in their submissions, I found myself swamped with many other projects and found very little time to devote myself to reading, revising, formatting, and in a few cases shortening their work. The fact that I was so busy about many things in the last three years is the principal reason why this volume has taken so long to see the light of day.

What has finally been published, however, is a volume that I believe has been well worth waiting for. It is the product of twenty-six authors from every continent, from several generations, of both genders. It is a volume that is truly Catholic: geographically, content-wise, and theologically. It is the work of both scholars and practitioners – practitioners who are scholars and scholars who are practitioners – all of whom are deeply committed to God's mission and many of whom have themselves shaped the disciplines of missiology and mission theology in the last quarter of the century about which they write.

A Century of Catholic Mission

This volume is, as its title indicates, a book about *Catholic* mission – mission done and reflected upon in the context of the Roman Catholic Church – in the last century – roughly from 1910 until the present day.

A Century *of Catholic Mission*

The time span of this book is extremely significant, for it marks an era of monumental transition in the understanding of mission and the way it is carried out. The year 1910, of course, was the year in which the monumental Edinburgh World Mission Conference was held, a truly landmark event for Protestant and Anglican church communities in mission, and, as it turned out, a moment to which can be traced back the origins of the Ecumenical Movement. For Roman Catholics, their presence at Edinburgh was confined to a letter from Bishop Bonomelli of Cremona that was read to the Conference by Baptist Silas McBee (see Delaney 2000). However, like other Christian churches and communities, the Roman Catholic Church in 1910 was experiencing what would later be recognized as the height of the modern missionary movement. For Protestant communities the origin of this movement is usually traced back to 1793, when William Carey wrote a short treatise that inspired mission among churches that had not, since the Reformation, been much engaged in mission at all. For Catholics, a renewed missionary spirit can traced back to the second decade of the nineteenth century, when Europe had regained some semblance of order after the terror of the French Revolution and the final defeat of Napoleon, and when the church began to find new vigor as it experienced a virtual explosion of religious and missionary communities of both women and men. The missionary movement was flourishing in 1910.

The optimism of that period, however, would be forever shattered in the next several decades by two World Wars that brought in their wakes both the end of the European colonialism that served in many ways as a foundation for the missionary expansion of the previous century, and by the independence of the colonies that had been the places where missionary work had flourished and had been basically successful in establishing educated local leaders and local churches. Such new independence, together with a renaissance of local religious sensibility, worked to bring about a new understanding of mission marked by the documents of the International Missionary Council, the Second Vatican Council, the World Council of Churches, and the Lausanne Committee for World Evangelization.

At the same time, this new era of independence brought about a crisis regarding mission itself, a crisis that is only being resolved in our own day with an expanded understanding of mission to include work for justice, reconciliation, dialogue, and reconciliation. A new missionary attitude has begun to emerge as well among women and men in mission. Pope Paul VI and the Asian Bishops have described this attitude as one of openness for dialogue (ES 1963; FABC I 1992; FABC II 1997; Eilers, ed. 2002, 2007). Recently, inspired by our own missionary congregation, the Society of the Divine Word, Roger Schroeder and I have spoken of it as 'prophetic dialogue' (e.g. Bevans and Schroeder 2011). Moreover, mission today is beginning to flourish once more due to growing recognition that some of the great mission-sending countries are now receiving missionaries from Asia, Latin America, Africa, and Oceania. Mission today is indeed, in the often-quoted words of Michael Nazir-Ali, 'from everywhere to everywhere' (Nazir-Ali 2009). Particularly because our age is an 'Age of Migration' (see Castles and Miller 2009), migrants – whether Filipina maids in Hong Kong, Nigerian students in the UK, Vietnamese sisters in the USA, or Mexican migrants in Canada, like migrants and refugees from the beginning of the Christian era, are themselves becoming missionaries. In these first decades of the third millennium we are seeing a totally new missionary era.

A Century of Catholic *Mission*

In reading and editing the twenty-six chapters of this book, I have become aware of, if not the *uniqueness* of Catholic mission, certainly its *distinctiveness*. I would describe such distinctiveness as possessing at least six qualities.

First, Catholic mission is distinguished by its *ecumenical* nature. Only a glance at the extensive bibliography at the end of the book will show that Catholic scholars depend greatly on the wealth of scholarship of many other Christians. While the authors here quote one another, and scholars like Joan Delaney, Walbert Bühlmann, William R. Burrows, José de Mesa, Jesús López-Gay, Teresa Okure, Adam Wolanin, they also have recourse to Protestant writers like David Bosch, Mercy Odoyoye, Wilbert Shenk, and Andrew Walls. Catholic missiology is unabashedly Catholic, not only in the sense that it finds expression within the parameters of Catholic doctrine, but in the wider sense as well of drawing on any truth that can help deepen an understanding of the *entire* church's great commission to proclaim and witness to Jesus Christ to all creation. One could say that Catholic (capital 'C') missiology is deeply catholic (small 'c')!

Second, and perhaps more narrowly Catholic, Catholic missiology and mission practice relies on the wealth of the Catholic Magisterium, the church's official teaching office, whether papal or episcopal. Catholic mission is deeply rooted in the scriptural witness, of course, and in the tradition that finds expression in the church's history and doctrinal tradition. Included in that tradition, however, is the great number of documents, going back in the period covered in this book to 1919, when the first of the five pre-Vatican II Mission Encyclicals, Benedict XV's *Maximum Illud* (MI), through the Council's ground-breaking Decree on Missionary Activity *Ad Gentes* (AG), and culminating in documents like

Paul VI's *Evangelii Nuntiandi* (EN) and John Paul II's *Redemptoris Missio* (RM), and episcopal documents issued by Asian, African, Latin American episcopal conferences and papal documents resulting from Synods of the African, Asian, European, Latin American, and Oceanian bishops. This book includes three chapters that focus on developments in the Magisterium before, during, and after the Second Vatican Council, but almost every other chapter in the book has recourse to this rich heritage of Catholic teaching.

Third, and closely connected to this emphasis on the Magisterium's teaching, is the fact that Catholic missiology as it has developed in the last fifty years is deeply rooted in the documents and, if I might use the controversial expression, the 'spirit' of the Second Vatican Council. The Council was indeed the most important moment in Catholicism in these last one hundred years, and the documents well express both the continuity and new directions that Catholic thinking on mission have taken in this past century. As I point out in my own chapter on mission at the Council, missiological thinking was not confined to the official document on mission alone. The documents on Liturgy, the church, non-Christian religions, the church in the modern world – to mention only a few – were imbued with a strong missionary spirit.

Fourth, and once more connected with the two previous points, is the Catholic conviction that mission cannot be reduced to any one of its manifold elements. Mission, as Pope John Paul expressed it, is a 'single, complex reality', and so is composed of a number of constitutive elements. One cannot, in other words, reduce mission to proclamation of the gospel on the one hand, or to working for justice and liberation on the other. Authenticity of life, commitment to ecology and eco-justice, prayer for the world and celebration of liturgy, patient inter-religious dialogue or constructing of local theologies are all integral parts of the church's engagement in the mission entrusted to it by Christ's Spirit.

Fifth, Catholic thinking and practice is convinced that mission is indeed *entrusted* to the church. It is not in any way something the church possesses on its own. Catholic mission, both in expressions of the Magisterium and in theological reflection, is founded on the principle that what calls for the church is its call to participate in the mission that is first and foremost God's. It is in this radical sense that the church is 'missionary by its very nature' (AG 2). Indeed, as it is common to say in these days, the church does not so much have a mission as the mission has a church. In this context it is important to say as well that *every* Catholic Christian, by virtue of his or her baptism, is called to mission. Mission is not something 'extra' that the church does or that certain people in the church do in the church's name. To be a Christian, rather, is to be in mission. Catholic missiology has its foundation in faith in a missionary God who endows Jesus of Nazareth with the Holy Spirit, the same Spirit that anoints the church to continue that mission. Christian faith is commitment to mission.

Sixth, and finally – although there may indeed be other particularly distinguishing traits – Catholic mission in practice and reflection takes the world seriously. What this means in particular is that women's and men's historical, social, and cultural contexts are acknowledged and honored as sources that reveal God's will and action. Mission, therefore, is *never* about destruction of the human. It is rather about its cultivation, perfection, and healing. While this has always been the case in mission (think of Justin Martyr, Origen, *The Heliand*, Cyril and Methodius, Matteo Ricci), even though not always practiced, since the earliest Mission Encyclicals of the twentieth century it has been very much the church's official policy. As a result, for Catholics, mission always involves a 'sincere and patient dialogue' (see AG 11) to discover God's presence in every situation in which the gospel is preached and witnessed to. Catholic mission, while it can be profoundly *counter*-cultural or *counter*-contextual, is never *anti*-cultural or *anti*-contextual.

The Plan of the Book

This book, then, surveys Catholic mission as it has been practiced and reflected upon in the last century, a century of momentous changes both in the church and the world, and so demanding significant changes in the way the church makes God's mission in the world concrete as the Universal Sacrament of Salvation (see AG 1, 48). The book begins with an overview of how mission has been lived out and thought about in the various continents of our world: in Africa, Asia, the Americas, Europe, and Oceania; in various mission movements of the last century; and in the lives of women, often neglected in earlier accounts of mission. Then, in a second major part, it reflects on how mission has been conceived in the half-century before the watershed moment of the Second Vatican Council (1962-65), and in the half-century since. A third part focuses on Catholic missiology as such, examining its biblical foundation, its major developments in the last century, the theology of mission that it has generated, and its ecumenical dimensions. Then, in Part IV, the book moves to reflect on the various constitutive elements of mission today. These are divided according to the six 'elements' that Roger Schroeder and I propose in *Constants in Context* (2004), with inclusion of reflections on mission and education and mission and migration. In a fifth and final part the book offers two reflections on mission spirituality, spirituality in general, and the rich spirituality of accompaniment.

All of the authors of this volume are Catholic, with one exception. In the final chapter I asked my colleagues Eleanor Doidge and Claude-Marie Barbour to author the chapter on mission as accompaniment. Claude-Marie is an ordained minister in the Presbyterian Church USA, but no one else to my mind, is as qualified to write a chapter on mission as accompaniment as she and Eleanor. For more than three decades she and Eleanor have accompanied women and men from the inner city of Gary, Indiana and the Lakota People on the Pine Ridge and Rosebud Reservations in North Dakota as they have struggled for better lives on the one hand and have generously shared their wisdom with thousands of students on over a thousand visits to their neighborhoods and homes.

Acknowledgements

As in every work of this size, my debt to colleagues and friends is enormous. I extend my gratitude in the first place to Dr Wonsuk Ma who first invited me to undertake this project, and for his enthusiasm and patience when the project was not proceeding at full speed. Second, I am deeply grateful to Dr Kirsteen Kim, the editor of the series in which this volume is a part, for her guidance, trust, and patience as well. I am no less grateful to my friends and colleagues Roger Schroeder and Robert Schreiter – to both of them for their wisdom in helping me plan this volume, and to Bob Schreiter in particular for translating three of the chapters that appear here.

I can only stammer my thanks to the twenty-five authors who have contributed to this volume – for their willingness to share their wisdom and expertise, for their punctuality in submitting their chapters, for their promptness in answering my queries, and for their patience with me when many other commitments meant that this collection was delayed in its final editing. There are many more people that need thanking, among whom are the staff of the Paul Bechtold Library at Catholic Theological Union, especially Melody Layton McMahon, library director; my colleagues Sheila McLaughlin and Birgit Oberhofer at the Bernardin Center at Catholic Theological Union; my friends Bill and Linda Burrows, Barbara Reid, Judy and Ed Logue, Gary Riebe-Estrella, Mark Schramm, Jim Bergin, Stan Uroda, Cathy and Steve Ross, and the wonderful people of my worshipping community and spiritual home, St Giles Family Mass Community in Oak Park, IL.

Without the financial support of the Pontifical Council for the Promotion of Christian Unity in Rome, this volume would never have seen the light of day. I am indebted especially to Bishop Brian Farrell, secretary of the Council, and to Ms Maria Arantxa Aguado, former liason of the Vatican to the Commission on World Mission and Evangelization at the World Council of Churches in Geneva, Switzerland for the generous subsidy with which publication has been made possible. This has been a truly amazing ecumenical gesture!

This book is dedicated to Fr Lawrence Nemer, SVD, one of the contributors to this volume, my former professor of Church History, my mentor, and my friend for over forty years. If there is anyone who deserves the credit – or responsibility – for turning me into a systematic theologian who sees theology and Christian life through the lens of mission, Larry is the one. Larry celebrated his golden jubilee of presbyteral ordination in 2010. I offer this volume to him as a belated jubilee gift.

Stephen Bevans, SVD
July 17, 2012

PART ONE

HISTORICAL STUDIES

CATHOLIC MISSION IN AFRICA 1910-2010

Francis Anekwe Oborji

Introduction

Any discussion of Catholic mission in Africa carries with it a reference to various phases of evangelization of the continent. A person would have to be blind not to see in Africa the long presence of Christianity before the two missionary expansions in the fifteenth and nineteenth centuries. The history of Christianity in Africa is as old as Christianity itself. However, this does not imply that the whole of Africa encountered the Christian faith at the same time. Hence, one is led to ask: how did the evangelization of Africa start? What inspiration could one get from the early efforts so as to understand the reasons for the present one? Finally, what is the Catholic mission contribution in the evangelization of Africa? In order to answer these questions, the present study will concentrate only on the phases of evangelization of Africa, with particular focus on the role of the Catholic mission toward the end of the nineteenth century, just prior to the Edinburgh Conference of 1910, and its development through the twentieth century, up to the present day.

Allowing for some overlapping, the evangelization of Africa could be divided into five phases. The first phase began with the founding of the church in North Africa; the second phase covers the fifteenth and sixteenth centuries' Christian expansions in sub-Saharan Africa, while the third phase is the period of the great missions, from the nineteenth century up to Vatican Council II. The fourth phase is from Vatican Council II to the celebration of the First Synod of Bishops, Special Assembly for Africa (1994); and the fifth phase is Post-Synod Africa, leading to the Second Synod of Bishops, Special Assembly for Africa (2009). Since the history of these phases of evangelization of Africa is so vast and varied, I shall present only an outline here, and focus particularly on the last three phases.

Phases One and Two: Christian Origins and Fifteenth Century Colonial Expansion

Christianity began in Africa along the Mediterranean Coast of the continent, starting from Egypt, the North Africa Maghreb region (Algeria, Libya, Morocco, Tunisia), and reaching Ethiopia, which shared almost the same history of Christianity with Egypt and ancient Nubia. The history of Christianity in modern Africa cannot be adequately grasped without linking it to this early phase of Christian mission in the continent. In other words, Christianity came to Africa in its early centuries through Mediterranean Coasts and Trans-Saharan routes. It was only from the fifteenth century European expansion that Catholic mission began to reach the other parts of Africa through the coasts of the Atlantic Ocean, thanks to the newly discovered transatlantic trade routes and the papal privileges (*padroado*) granted to the Portuguese sovereign by the Popes.

From its origins in Egypt and the north, Christianity spread down the Nile to Kush and Nubia, and many dioceses were founded. But the strength of the church at this era is not limited to the number of bishops and bishoprics. Indeed it was an active, strong and productive church. For instance, this phase produced the first African martyrs (e.g. Felicity and Perpetua of Carthage), and holy women (e.g. Monica and Thecla). The church in North Africa also gave Christianity its first theological institutes at Alexandria and Carthage.

However, the vibrant church of North Africa did not last long before it began to encounter many difficulties that weakened it and quickened its decline in the seventh century, and almost total disappearance in the eighth. The church was destabilized by internal conflicts provoked by doctrinal controversies. There were also external factors, such as the invasions of the Vandals from AD 429 to 439, and the Muslim occupation of North Africa between seventh and eleventh centuries, both of which contributed to Christianity's disappearance. With the Muslim conquest of North Africa, the organized life of the churches disintegrated and could not hold their faithful against the stimulating effects of the new and vigorous Islam (Spencer 1962: 17).

The Coptic Church survived in Egypt as a minority, reduced to a state of protected minority (*dhimmi*), for which it had to pay tax (Brett 1982: 499). Christianity survived in Ethiopia, in spite of the poor education of its clergy and many years of isolation from the rest of the Christian world (caused by the Arab-Muslim occupation of trans-Saharan routes), because it appropriated local cultural elements congenial to African religiosity (Mbiti 1990: 230; Shenk 1993: 131-54).

The second phase of Africa's contact with the Christian faith began with the arrival of Portuguese navigators in sub-Saharan Africa in the fifteenth century. After the fall of the church in North Africa, there were some attempts by some religious missionaries like the Franciscans, the Trinitarians and the Mercedarians, along the Mediterranean coast to save the situation. However, the heroic efforts of these religious missionaries could not do much. Hence, Africa had to wait until the fifteenth century for the 'second missionary journey' of the Christian faith. This time, unlike the first, which concentrated on Roman Africa, Ethiopia and their neighbors, the inhabitants of the tropical and sub-tropical Africa received the Christian message, that is, the Christians of Africa, south of the Sahara (see Nwachukwu 1994: 18).

The great king of the Congo, Nzinga a Nkuwu, asked for missionaries to proclaim the gospel to his people. The missionaries did arrive. The first group to make this event possible, as we have noted earlier on, were the Portuguese. The Portuguese explorers brought with them priests who became the first missionaries along the West African coasts. Many more missionaries came later, with the approval of the Portuguese kings, as was stipulated on the privileges of patronage (*padroado*) granted them by the popes over the new missions in Africa (Baur 1994: 48).

However, the newly founded missions began to decline. Neither the erection of an Apostolic Prefecture of the Congo in 1640 and the consequent arrival of the (Italian) Capuchins in 1645, nor the advent of the French also in seventeenth century could help in salvaging the situation. Such that by the beginning of the nineteenth century, the second phase of the missionary enterprise in Africa had failed practically (see Bouchaud 1967: 172-86; Baur 1994: 55-99; Nwachukwu 1994: 18-20).

Phase Three: The Nineteenth Century to Vatican II

The third phase of the effort to evangelize Africa is historically linked with the second phase. It covers the period of the great missionary expansions, from the nineteenth century to Vatican Council II. This period coincided with the abolition of the trans-Atlantic slave trade, the colonization of Africa, and the independence of many African countries. The period witnessed attempts among nations of the world towards reaching better understanding after the two World Wars. Major missionary impetus in the years after the Edinburgh Conference in 1910 came from Benedict XV's apostolic letter *Maximum Illud* (1919) and Pius XI's encyclical letter *Rerum Ecclesiae* (1926 – see James Kroeger's chapter in this volume).

Many missionary institutes were founded in France during the first half of this period, specifically for the *conversion* of Africans to Christianity. Among these are the Holy Ghost Congregation, the Sisters of St Joseph of Cluny, the Society of African Missions, the Missionaries of Africa (commonly known as White Fathers), and the Comboni Missionaries (see Obi 1985: 7).

Consequently, Portugal was virtually replaced by France in the missions in Africa. It was also during this period that the *Congregation de Propaganda Fide* issued the *ius commissionis* by which mission territories were allocated to particular missionary institutes to evangelize and administer (Oborji 1998: 53; AAS 1930: 11-15). In principle, the pope himself, represented by *Propaganda Fide*, had the primary responsibility for evangelization, and not a monarch, as it was the practice in earlier times (Ela 1986: 11). The missionary institutes were therefore responsible to the pope and not to their national sovereigns in matters concerning the mission territories. Nevertheless, some missionaries had to collaborate with the colonial administrators representing their nations in Africa, and the latter

helped in financing mission projects such as, schools, hospitals, church
buildings, and so forth (see Bouchaud 1967: 177 and Mosman 1961: 69-
70). But this was not the case in all the places. There were places where the
colonial masters impeded missionary activities, either because of
anticlericalism of the colonizing nation, or because the Christian gospel and
the education of Africans by missionaries undermined the colonial ideology
(see Charles 1938: 386).

One remarkable feature of this phase was the gradual move from the
understanding of the goal of mission as saving of souls to that of planting
of churches, which included building of schools and hospitals, and other
forms of social services. However, many missionaries interpreted the
planting of churches literally, and tried to reproduce in Africa carbon
copies of the churches in Europe, especially in terms of architecture,
organizations and devotions. Again, some missionaries tended to judge the
cultures of the 'mission land' according to the criteria of their own cultural
traditions. In most cases, such judgments were very negative; so much so
that the *Congregation de Propaganda Fide* had to intervene in 1939, to
warn against negative and distorted interpretations of the traditions of the
peoples of the mission lands (AAS 1939: 269).

During this phase also, the Bible and catechetical books were translated
into some African languages. Apart from that, there was not much effort to
carry on theological investigations into various aspects of African cultural
elements and religiosity as a necessary step towards inculturation (see Baur
1994: 107-109).

Furthermore, this phase witnessed unfortunate inter-denominational
rivalries among missionaries. Christian missionaries of different
denominations were competing to outdo one another with regard to
winning converts and establishing social services. This type of attitude
made some Africans question the motive of the missionaries. In addition, it
made Africans confused about which denomination to follow. It was really
a scandal in the face of the new converts. Moreover, the competition caused
unnecessary duplications in the establishment of social services as each
group often tried to outdo the other. On a more serious note, the rivalries
aggravated ethnic divisions among the local populace (see Mbiti 1990: 232-
33).

Indeed, a good number of African authors are very critical of the
missionary efforts of this phase (see Parrat 1995: 7). Such critiques include
the missionaries' involvement in colonial rule, denigration of traditional
rites and customs, attitudes of superiority based on skin pigmentation and
of paternalism, and unhappy desire to keep the African Church for as long
as possible under European control (see Parrat 1995: 7ff; Fassholé-Luke et
al. 1978: 357ff; Torres and Fabella, ed. 1976: 222-66).

However, many Africans regard the missionaries of this phase as the real
founders of Christianity in modern Africa and are remembered with deep
gratitude and admiration (see Synod of Bishops 1994c: 6). Evidences of the

success of the missionary efforts of this phase could be seen both in the numerical strength and geographical distribution of the faithful. For instance, before the official opening of the Vatican Council II in 1962, the church was present almost everywhere on the continent and on the islands. J. Bouchaud writes that by 1964, when the Vatican Council II was in session, Africa had a total population of 230 million. Out of this figure, African Christians numbered 50 million (26 million Catholics, 19 million Protestants, 5 million Orthodox); Muslims, 95 million; African traditional religionists, 85 million. Catholics represented about 12 percent of the population (Bouchaud 1967: 41).

In addition, it could be said that the efforts of the missionaries produced good Christians, among these were: the Ugandan martyrs, Blessed Clementine Anwarite (virgin and martyr from Congo), Blessed Victoria Rasoamanarivo of Madagascar, St Josephine Bakhita of the Sudan, Blessed Bakanja Isidore (the Zairean martyr beatified on April 1994), and Blessed Michael Cyprian Tansi of Aguleri, Nigeria (a Cistercian monk). Other causes are reaching their final stages (see EAf 34).

Within this phase also, some Africans were accepted for the priesthood and religious life. These were to continue the work begun by the missionaries. The pastoral methods in vogue during this phase include outstations, Christian villages, and the school and hospital apostolate. Very significantly, by the mid-twentieth century, missionaries of this era, together with the newly evangelized Africans (theologians) began talking of the possibility of local theologies and pastoral methods for the African churches. These were to mature to what we call today 'African theology'. That was the general situation up to the Vatican II (see Baur 1994: 290-93).

Fourth Phase: From Vatican II (1962-1965) to the African Synod (1994)

The fourth phase of evangelization of Africa is the period from Vatican Council II to the first Synod of Bishops, Special Assembly for Africa (1994). This phase has been described as a dynamic period of missionary commitment in the African churches, a period during which the whole world has started to benefit from the efforts of evangelization in the young churches of Africa. The missionary impetus of this phase naturally, is from the Vatican Council II's teaching, especially its missionary theology of local churches as agents of mission in their territories. This led to the consolidation of the local hierarchy initiated by Pope Paul VI with his apostolic letter *Africae terrarum* (1967) and inauguration of SECAM (Symposium for Episcopal Conferences of Africa and Madagascar) during his historic visit to Kampala, Uganda in 1969 (see Hickey 1982: 198ff).

Again, the main impetus for this phase came from the Council's missionary decree *Ad Gentes*, which defines mission in its two-fold aims of evangelization and church formation (AG 6). The Council's missionary juridical system of *mandatum*, which replaced the *ius commissionis*, also empowered the local bishops as fully responsible for evangelization in their dioceses. The missionaries are to enter into contract with bishops in whose dioceses they wish to serve (AG 26; CIC 1983: no. 790). This new approach is centered on the Council's theology of mission as reciprocal activity among sister churches. In other words, the Council developed a theology of co-responsibility in evangelization and of trust of the local churches. This is a rediscovery of the local churches as the primary agents of mission (see Oborji 2001: 116).

But how have the African local churches been carrying out this role of being agents of mission? Cardinal Hyacinte Thiandoum of Dakar, in his capacity as the General Relator of the Synod Bishops for Africa (1994) presents the African churches' approach to the mission of evangelization. According to Cardinal Thiandoum, evangelization is at the center of the missionary activity of the African churches today. It is first of all 'Good News', as the very word connotes. It is the proclamation to the world of the good and joyful news that God, who loves us, has redeemed and is redeeming his world through Christ. In its method and aim, therefore, evangelization must seek to give Good News to the world, and in particular, to peoples of Africa and Madagascar:

> In a continent full of bad news, how is the Christian message 'Good News' for our people? In the midst of an all-pervading despair, where lies the hope and optimism which the gospel brings? Evangelization stands for many of those essential values which our continent very much lacks: hope, joy, peace, love, unity and harmony. Africa is in dire need of the gospel message for through the gospel God builds up his family. (Synod of Bishops 1994: 2)

In this regard therefore, the African local churches operate with a positive and *integral concept* of evangelization as clearly set forth in the relevant official documents of the church. It involves, no doubt, the preaching of the Word, inviting hearers to accept Jesus and his saving message and to enter into his church. But it is wider and deeper than that. It includes the transformation of human society through the message and living witness of the church and her members. What the gospels refer to as the 'reign of God', therefore, is what is witnessed to: promoting peace and justice, restoring human dignity, and bringing this world as close to God's designs as possible. Evangelization touches all human beings and every human person, as also every aspect of human life. In the encyclical letter *Redemptoris Missio*, John Paul II considers evangelization in its three different situations: mission *ad gentes*, pastoral care, and new evangelization, all of which are realities of major importance (RM 33). In the African context, however, one often speaks of aspects of evangelization that sometimes overlap. These are: primary evangelization whereby the gospel is brought to those who have never received it, and the pastoral care of those already in the church and witness of Christian living as a necessary implication of our faith. Moreover, the Catholic Church has, in recent years been calling for a new evangelization, and so there is need to work out what this means in the context of the different local churches of Africa.

A remarkable feature of this phase is the birth of an indigenous hierarchy, indigenous missionary institutes and religious congregations, as well as a formidable lay faithful. Though there are still patches of foreign missionaries in many parts of Africa (which demonstrates the universality of the church), during this phase Africans have started to take responsibility for the churches in their own land. Addressing the Fathers of the Synod of Bishops, Special Assembly for Africa, Cardinal Josef Tomko, the then Prefect of the Congregation for the Evangelization of Peoples (to whom almost all the African local churches are still dependent), gave the following statistics: 'in Africa today there are 412 ecclesial jurisdictions, excluding 18 circumstances dependent on other Vatican Curia offices; 66 of these are under missionary Bishops or other missionary orders; 327 are governed by African Bishops (to which must be added 15 auxiliaries). In all Africans constitute 90% of the total number of Bishops in Africa today' (Tomko 1994: 18).

The reality of indigenous hierarchy in the African churches is a result of increase in priestly and religious vocations on the continent. In addition to the formation houses, there are numerous catechetical centers, and higher ecclesiastical institutes have been also founded in different regions and countries of Africa.

Another fact about this phase is the founding of many religious institutes in the African churches. Some of these are: the Congregation of Our Lady of Kilimanjaro (Moshi, Tanzania); institute of the Handmaids of the Child Jesus (Calabar, Nigeria); the Benetereziva Institute (Burundi); the Benibikira Congregation (Rwanda); the Bannabikira Congregation (Uganda); the Congregation of the Sisters of the Immaculate Heart of Mary, Mother of Christ (Nigeria); institute of Apostles of Jesus (Moroto, Uganda); the institute of the Evangelizing Sisters of Mary (female wing of the Apostles of Jesus, Moshi, Uganda); institute of the Brothers of St Stephen (Onitsha, Nigeria); Missionary Society of St Paul (Nigeria), and so forth (see Oborji 2008: 158).

However, the increase in the numerical strength of the local hierarchy, priests, and religious, and the lay faithful does not mean that African churches have achieved the needed adulthood in their growth. African churches are yet to utilize the autonomy granted them as particular or local churches, for the development of acceptable local liturgies, theologies, spiritualities and morals. They are yet to develop African structures for church organization. Generally speaking, church structures in Africa are still as at the earlier phases, modeled on the mother churches of the pioneer missionaries. Basically, this type of situation renders the local churches in Africa very dependent on the mother churches on which they were modeled.

Nevertheless, some efforts have been made in some of the local churches towards inculturation. An example is the Zairean (Congolese) local church, which developed its 'form for the celebration of Mass' (*Notitiae* 1988: 454-72). There are also the Cameroonian Mass (which enjoys the approval of the local bishop), the Eucharistic Prayers of East Africa, and the ritual for the consecration of virgins in Zaire (Democratic Republic of Congo). Apart from these, similar efforts are emerging in other parts of Africa. For instance, in West Africa, there are particular ways in which the Eucharistic celebration is turning native among the Ashanti, Yoruba, and the Igbo groups. But the emerging liturgical contribution of this region to African Christianity and to the universal church is in developing Christian passage or transition rites. This region has consequently produced a very well-developed adaptation of traditional initiation rites to the received Christian rites (the Moore ritual in the diocese of Diebougou, Bourkina Faso); a Christianization of traditional naming ceremony (as distinct from baptism) among the Yoruba of Nigeria; and the Christianization of Igbo (Nigeria) patterns of passing through crises in life with adequate rites that heal or enhance relationship (*igba ndu*, ritual covenanting). Also in Central and East Africa afflictions by witches, evil men, and spirits may be resolved by participation in charismatic prayer that is widely diffused in this region and indeed all over Africa (Oborji 2008: 158ff).

However, the emergent liturgies of these areas are concentrating on the Eucharistic celebration and consecration of virgins. In West Africa, experiments geared towards celebration of the feasts of Corpus Christi and Christ the King are emerging. For instance, among the Ashanti of Ghana the Corpus Christi celebration is adapted to the *Odwira* festival (the yearly outing of the *Asantehene*, the Ashanti king). It is a ceremony suffused with color and meaning. The same emergence of the king has been integrated into rituals surrounding the words of institution during the Eucharistic Prayer. Among the Igbo of Nigeria, the same Corpus Christi festival is celebrated as *Ofala Jesu* (Jesus' annual outing as king) with fanfare, cannon shots, and song and dance. Another rather striking adaptation among the Igbo is the introduction of patterns of cooperative development or improvement unions into the rite of the 'presentation of gifts' during the Eucharistic celebration. The most dramatic display of this kind of presentation of gifts is on Holy Thursday (Chrism Mass). It has become a fundraising strategy to ensure a self-reliant church. Offertory hymns are carefully worked to inspire participation (Uzukwu 1997: 270ff.).

All these efforts are accompanied also by theological reflections in the African local churches. The emergent theological concepts in Africa are expressions of the way in which Christians of the continent are trying to interpret the Christian message and to provide models taken from their own situation, their own culture, and their own experience as a people for an African reading of the Christian mystery. The theological reflections are therefore efforts of evangelization. They reflect the commitment of African

Christian theologians to relate the Christian message to the socio-cultural, religious political and economic reality of the continent. The main currents of African theology are inculturation and liberation (human promotion), each with its own currents and cross-currents. In this context inculturation concerns discussion on the encounter of the gospel with African cultures. The theology dwells on the role of cultures in evangelization and studies ways of deepening the Christian faith in Africa. Liberation theology in Africa develops in its three main currents: 1) an African liberation theology developed in the early independent African countries; 2) African women's liberation theology, developed as a reaction against the injustices women are subjected to in traditional society; and 3) South African liberation theology, born as a protest against racial ideology, concentrates on problems of poverty and social realities, on structures for creating political and economic stability and on the self-reliant of African local churches and society. This theology is attentive to the oppressive cultural effects of traditional and modern Africa, and to elements of racial and color discrimination.

To the credit of African theologians it must be said that among all aspects, Christology is the area that has received most attention, since the decisive element of every Christian life lies in the response that must be given to the question Christ asked: 'Who do you (African Christians) say that I am?' (Mt. 16:15). It is a well-known fact that Christology is the most fundamental aspect of Christian theology. Therefore, every particular church must give its own explicit answer to this question, in a real contextual manner. A correct understanding of the person of Christ, of his nature, of his significance, and of his message addressed to the human race, will help to make Christianity authentically planted in the African soil. Therefore, in recent times there have been many Christological models that come from the pens of African theologians. Christ is called, to give a few examples, the liberator, the ancestor, the firstborn son, the master of initiation, the healer, the African king, the African chief, the mediator, the savior, the giver-of-life, the African lover, the all-powerful redeemer (Oborji 2006: 196-203).

Fifth Phase: Post-Synod Africa and the Synod of 2009

The fifth phase is the 'post-Synod Africa'. It is a period of hope that has also seen the celebration of the Second Synod of Bishops, Special Assembly for Africa in 2009. This phase presents challenges and prospects for the young churches of Africa. At the first Synod in 1994, the African Bishops considered as realities of major concern the present situation of things in the continent and from there put forward a missionary ecclesiology of the 'Church as Family of God' as a possibly guiding model of evangelization in the continent.

Therefore, in this phase of African mission, we meet a striking characteristic of the local churches in the continent, the attempt to view evangelization from the perspective of a missionary activity that aims at building up the church as the *family of God* on earth. This is an effort of the Africans to define the Christian community in terms which are perceptible to them and which are rooted in the gospel, Christian tradition and the cultural ingenuity of the people. The concern is about founding local churches that would express the profound Christian and African values of communion, fraternity, solidarity and peace. For in a truly African community or family, joys, difficulties, and trials are shared in a trusting communitarian spirit and dialogue. The missionary activity *ad gentes* aims at formation and solidification of local churches. With the erection of many dioceses in different parts of the continent, the African local churches are occupied with deepening the faith already received and of expounding its areas of influence and ministry throughout the local territory (EAf 47). Thus, in the teaching of the African Bishops at the Synod, the relevant image of what evangelization is all about in the African context is seen in the building-up of the church as the family of God on earth. Evangelization invites humanity to participate in the very life of the Trinity, calling it to return, through the Son, in the Spirit, back to the Father 'so that God may be all in all' (1 Cor. 15:28) (Synod of Bishops 1994c: 25).

Therefore, one of the most acclaimed achievements of the First Synod is this evaluation of the image of the church-as-family of God (an extended or universal 'Family of God'). It is the key for understanding and evaluating the documents of the Synod. It is an ecclesiology developed in the context of proclamation and evangelization with its inspiration generally from St Paul the great missionary. The inspiration is specifically from Paul's letter to the Ephesians on reconciliation of the Jews and the gentiles with one another and with God (see Eph. 2:11-22). The image of the church-as-family is a concept, which Africans can easily appreciate and identify with, because of its African value of extended family, bound together by ancestral blood and community life. The communitarian accentuation of the family makes the new model a real African reading of Vatican II concept of the church as communion or as the people of God (see LG Ch. II). It is an African cultural heritage that, if properly studied and applied, has many pastoral advantages, especially for the African local churches. The bishops invited African theologians to work out the theology of the church-as-family of God with all the riches contained in this concept, showing its complementarity with other images of the church.

Then comes the Second Synod of Bishops, Special Assembly for Africa in 2009. The full title of the Second Synod is: 'The Church in Africa in Service to Reconciliation, Justice, and Peace: 'You are the salt of the earth ... You are the light of the world' (Mt. 5:13-14).' Drawing from this title and the documents of the synod itself, the bishops at the Synod sessions held in Rome in 2009 discussed the theme of 'Reconciliation, Justice, and

Peace' in the wider context of the present-day geopolitics, neo-colonialism, globalization, and the socio-economic and ethno-religious political factors that shape the contemporary African society. If the 1994 Synod provided the church in Africa an opportunity for self-definition (of the church-as-family of God in Africa) and the self-awareness of its evangelizing mission as a church, the Second Synod of 2009 offered the same African Church another avenue for critical self-examination, to articulate in concrete terms, the scope and strategies of that mission of the church family in the areas of promoting reconciliation, justice, and peace which are the most cogent challenges facing the continent today. Again, if the First Synod gave more attention to the question of inculturation, the Second Synod devoted most of its attention to social issues from the perspective of the social doctrines of the church. In other words, the Second Synod has proved to be a creative assembly of the African Bishops during which reflections were offered on the many ways the church can contribute to promoting reconciliation, justice and peace in a continent devastated by conflict of different forms and dimensions. The deliberations at the Second Synod provide a unique insight into the prospects and challenges for the church in Africa today.

Put together, the two Synods (1994 and 2009) have one thing in common. They both show the attention African local churches have started to give to the question of forging relationships between Africans of different ethnic groups, religious and cultural backgrounds sharing one community or nation. There is a pressing concern for the local churches to help in the strengthening and deepening the relationships among Africans of different groups and origins living in the same Christian community or parish and nation, and between them and people of other religions living in the same society. It is disturbing that Africans of diverse ethnic groups cannot stay together in one parish church or organization without rancor and suspicion of one another. In Africa, exaggerated ethnocentrism and intra-religious disturbances have continued to frustrate the ongoing work of evangelization and church formation in the continent. This situation affects both ecclesial and civil communities in Africa. The two Synods have all addressed this problem.

In his teaching at the end of the Second Synod, Benedict XVI emphasized the importance of conversion of heart as an essential path for building a society of reconciliation, peace and justice. In his post-Synodal exhortation *Africae Munus*, Benedict XVI speaks of a spirituality of reconciliation and communion for the African churches:

> Reconciliation is not an isolated act but a lengthy process by which all parties are reestablished in love – a love that heals through the working of God's word. Reconciliation then becomes at once a way of life and a mission. In order to arrive at genuine reconciliation and to live out the spirituality of communion that flows from it, the Church needs witnesses who are profoundly rooted in Christ and find nourishment in his word and the sacraments. (AM: 34)

Therefore, one of the privileged areas of concern in missionary efforts in Africa today is about building relationships in Christian communities in various local churches. It is creating Christian communities that are pluralistic, non-discriminating, loving and welcoming. In this way African local churches would become models for deepening the relationship in a mixed environment. To achieve this, the two synods seemed to agree on one fact, namely, that missionary activity in Africa today is challenged to encourage authentic formation of agents of evangelization and church formations that have the common goal of assisting African Christians towards becoming witnesses of authentic Christian conversion, reconciliation, justice and peace, and of overcoming the menace of exaggerated ethnicity and intra-religious hatred (see AM: 163).

Conclusion

Our analysis of the phases of evangelization of Africa has revealed two obvious facts. Firstly, we noticed that Africa is full of hopes and promises for Christianity. For example, at a time when some parts of the world are experiencing rapid de-Christianization under the influence of secularization, the African churches are growing annually in numerical strength. Besides, there is a noticeable development among Africans to assume responsibility for the work of evangelization in their local churches.

Secondly, we discovered that apart from the Alexandrian school, that veritable power house of theologies and theologians (of the early church in North Africa), the church in Africa has had to wait until mid-twentieth century before we could talk of renewed theological reflection from an African perspective. While the former was the affair of African Christians from the Mediterranean zone, the latter consists in the pre-occupations and labors of the newly evangelized sub-Saharan Africans.

Finally, the state of mission in Africa as presented here may appear very simplistic to an outsider. However, for the African Christians, particularly pastors and theologians, it is not as simple as that. The whole issue of salvation and God's love for God's children is involved (see Kalilombe 1981: 66). In fact, today, the church in Africa is faced with different problems from those which face most churches in Europe, America or elsewhere; problems which foreign theology or missionary models can provide no relevant ready-made answers. Africans are attempting to grapple with these problems, and to relate the gospel to the practical issues, whether social and political, or cultural and liturgical, which confront them.

Furthermore, as the last two Synods on the continent have shown, building a self-reliant church in Africa also rests principally, on liberating the people from the incident of primitive ethnicity, religious and cultural hatred that disturb them in their various situations in different African nations. To be true disciples of Christ, African Christians have to outgrow exaggerated ethnicity and hatred. It is only in this way that they can credibly launch out to the task of evangelization of their people and others. Thus, as Pope John Paul II said, in the African context, the new evangelization will aim at building up the church-as-family, avoiding all ethnocentrism and excessive particularism, trying instead to encourage reconciliation and true communion between ethnic groups, favoring solidarity and sharing of personnel and resources among the particular churches, without undue ethnic considerations (EAf 63). Making the same point, Pope Benedict XVI, in the post-Synodal exhortation, *Africae Munus,* says:

> Since the vocation of all men and women is one, we must not lose our zest for the reconciliation of humanity with God through the mystery of our salvation in Christ. Our redemption is the reason for the confidence and the firmness of our hope, 'by virtue of which we can face our present: the present, even if it is arduous, can be loved and accepted if it leads towards a goal, if we can be sure of this goal, and if this goal is great enough to justify the effort of the journey'. (AM: 172)

CATHOLIC MISSION IN ASIA 1910-2010

Joseph Putenpurakal, SDB

Introduction

Asia is a huge continent! In fact, it is the earth's largest one, and is home to nearly two thirds of the world's population, that is, 4.4 billion, the total world population being 6.7 billion according to the World Bank, World Development Indicators, 2008. China and India alone account for nearly half of the world population. Were we to shrink the earth's population into a village of 100 people, then 58 persons would be Asians, 33 Christians and 17.5 of them would be Catholic. Christians form 5 per cent of Asia's total population. The total number of Catholics would be some 106 million or 2.7 per cent of the total population of Asia. When we realize that 70 per cent of the world's Catholics live outside Europe and North America, the demands of mission in terms of first proclamation and pastoral care in Asia and elsewhere in the world can be easily assessed.

In Asia some 1.3 billion are living in what is called 'absolute' poverty, existing on less than $1 a day, among them some, certainly, having not even that! Seventy per cent of these hungry people of planet earth live in Asia! Here we can already see that Asia is potentially the biggest market and the largest labour force in the world. Fifty per cent of the Asian population is below 25 years of age.

Asia is the cradle of the world's great religious traditions: India for Hinduism, Buddhism and Jainism; Arabia for Islam; Palestine for Judaism and Christianity; China for Confucianism and Taoism; Japan for Shintoism; Iran for Zoroastrianism, and different parts of Asia accounting for the nearly 200 million indigenous/tribal religious beliefs.

Asia is the confluence of the world's great civilizations: Mesopotamian (Iraq), Persian (Iran), Indian, and Chinese. It was the destination for navigators and colonizers: British (India, Myanmar, Malaysia, Sri Lanka), Portuguese (Goa, Timor), French (Laos, Cambodia, Vietnam), Dutch (Indonesia) and Spain/North America (the Philippines).

In Asia the sacred and the secular compenetrate. Everything has a spiritual dimension. Asia is known for its sense of the divine and the mysterious, of harmony and balance, of community and belongingness. As we read in Pope John Paul II's Apostolic Exhortation *Ecclesia in Asia* (EAs):

> The people of Asia take pride in their religious and cultural values, such as love of silence and contemplation, simplicity, harmony, detachment, non-violence, the spirit of hard work, discipline, frugal living, the thirst for

learning and philosophical enquiry. They hold dear the values of respect for life, compassion for all beings, closeness to nature, filial piety towards parents, elders and ancestors, and a highly developed sense of community. In particular, they hold the family to be a vital source of strength, a closely knit community with a powerful sense of solidarity. Asian people are known for their spirit of religious tolerance and peaceful co-existence ... Asia has often demonstrated a remarkable capacity for accommodation and a natural openness to the mutual enrichment of peoples in the midst of plurality of religions and cultures ... All this indicates an innate spiritual insight and moral wisdom in the Asian soul, and it is the core around which a growing sense of 'being Asian' is built. This 'being Asian' is best discovered and affirmed not in confrontation and opposition, but in the spirit of complementarily and harmony. (EAs 6)

Presently, 'Asian religions are showing signs of great vitality and capacity for renewal ... Many people, especially the young, experience a deep thirst for spiritual values ... [It is in Asia's capacity for] 'complementarity and harmony, the Church [read Churches] can communicate the Gospel in a way which is faithful both to her own tradition and to the Asian soul.' (EAs 6)

Summing up the Past

Ecclesia in Asia succinctly sums up the past and the present of the Church in Asia (see EAs 9). It affirms that Christianity in Asia is as old as Christianity itself. Asia is the birthplace of the Saviour, Jesus Christ. The first Apostles are of Asia. So too are the first disciples. Asia is mentioned in the first Pentecost narrative (see Acts 2:9). People from the then Roman province of Asia (Asia Minor or the present day Turkey) were present when Paul was preaching in the hall of Tyrannus (see Acts 19:10). Following the Lord's command the Apostles shared with people the good news about Jesus of Nazareth, and founded churches. A few snapshots of the 'fascinating and complex' history of the impact of Jesus of Nazareth, the God and man, across the centuries before we move to the period 1910-2010 may be in order.

From Jerusalem to Antioch and then to Rome and Beyond is that captivating and compelling history in a single line. Ethiopia in the south, Scythia in the north and India in the east are important points in the trajectory. The strong and unassailable tradition of the coming of St Thomas, one of the Apostles of Jesus, to South India in AD 52 is like a lamp for our journey in Asia. Cranganor in South India is considered the place where the saint arrived. He founded several churches. Tradition and early documentary evidence show that Saint Thomas was martyred and buried in India.

In the third and fourth centuries the East Syrian community at Edessa was known for its missionary spirit. From the third century onwards, the ascetic communities of Syria proved to be 'a major force of evangelization in Asia' (EAs 9). At the end of the third century Armenia had the distinction of becoming the first nation as a whole to become Christian. By the end of the fifth century the good news reached the Arab kingdoms. However, it is said that perhaps due to division among Christians, the good news did not take root there. In the fifth century itself the Persian merchants were instrumental in bringing the gospel to China. The churches flourished there during the T'ang dynasty (AD 618-907). The ardent missionary spirit of the Persian Church, the inner strength that came from its monastic life, the arrival of a Syrian Nestorian Monk Alopen, the use of Buddhist, Confucianist and Taoist symbols in conveying the gospel teachings, and the use of the Chinese language to express the Christian faith may have contributed to the church's success there at that period of history. But by the end of the first millennium the church in China lost its vibrancy mainly due to persecution of Christians. The persecution began in 845, making what happened there in the following decades 'one of the sadder chapters in the history of God's People' in Asia (EAs 9). The gospel reached the Mongols and the Turks in the thirteenth century. Once again it reached the Chinese people in the same century. But for reasons which are several, by the end of the fourteenth century Christianity in Asia experienced a 'drastic diminution' (EAs 9) except for the isolated (Saint Thomas) Christians in South India.

With the coming of the missionaries from the West, especially Jordan Catalany, the first Latin diocese in India was erected at Quilon in South India in 1329. The arrival of the Portuguese Vasco de Gama who opened the sea route to India/Asia in 1498 and others after him was the beginning of church expansion and transplantation along with colonization. The *Padroado* arrangement by which the popes of the time placed mission work under the kings of Spain and Portugal, the work of many religious congregations for the spread of the gospel, the role of the Jesuits in particular, the missionary zeal of Saint Francis Xavier (1506-1552), Matteo Ricci (1552-1620), Robert de Nobili (1577-1656), Alexander,Valignano (1539-1606), Alexander Rhodes (1591-1660), John de Britto (1647-1693), Constant Beschi (1680-1746), Rudolf Aquaviva (1550-1583), Ferdinand Verbiest (1623-1688), Joseph Vaz (1651-1711), etc. are the outstanding contributors to the growth of Catholic mission in Asia. In spite of the clear instruction of 1659 from Rome asking missionaries not to transplant the Church of Europe in Asian countries, but to respect the cultural values and symbols of people in sharing with them the Catholic Christian faith, the Malabar Rites, Chinese Rites and Japanese Rites controversies impeded very much mission work in Asia. The church in Asia had to wait from 1744 (the year in which Benedict XIV suspended all accommodation experiments) until 1941 (when the controversy was officially resolved under Pope Pius XII). Disunity and jealousy among evangelizers themselves were major causes of the shameful Rite Controversies. With the suppression of the Jesuits in 1773, the loss of missionary vitality of Spain and Portugal, the passing of the missionary responsibility to the Catholic nation of France, did not save the dismal picture of Asian Catholic Mission. Rather, the situation became worse with the outbreak of the French Revolution of 1789, the wars of Napoleon, the loss of freedom the pope and the Sacred Congregation for the Propagation of the Faith experienced (for they were literally under 'house arrest') affected not only Europe, but mission all over the world, especially in Asia towards the end of the eighteenth century and the beginning of the nineteenth century.

The revival of Catholic Mission during the nineteenth and well into the twentieth centuries is attributed especially to the numerous missionary congregations of men and women from Europe and their opting to serve in Asia. The return of the Jesuits to their mission in Asia also contributed in no small measure to the revival of the Catholic Mission in Asia. The Paris Foreign Mission Society (MEP), which had come into existence in the seventeenth century, greatly supported the revival of the mission in Asia. The hope of a flourishing mission in Asia disappeared before the rising fear of a World War. In fact, World War I (1914-1918) cut off the flow of missionaries from Europe. Benedict XV's encyclical *Maximum Illud* (1919) with a subtitle 'On spreading the Catholic Faith throughout the World' was meant to rekindle missionary enthusiasm. The economic depression in the aftermath of World War I, the rise of Hitler and Mussolini, and the horror of millions of deaths perpetrated in Stalin's Russia, in Nazi Germany, in America's bombing of Hiroshima and Nagasaki during World War II changed forever 'the shape of the world and of mission' (Schroeder 2008:81). In addition, Christianity and its mission received a stunning blow with the entry of Marxist communism following the Russian Bolshevik Revolution of 1917 which spread also to Central Asian countries, North Korea and China with its soulless and Godless atheistic teachings.

Besides the missionary encyclical *Maximum Illud*, four other 'mission encyclicals' (see James Kroeger's contribution in this volume) appeared in succession before the Second Vatican Council to strengthen the church's missionary involvement. Still, the concept and reality of mission needed a fresh thinking and new inspirations of the Holy Spirit to meet the demands of a fast changing world where new challenges were facing the church and society in mid twentieth century. A focusing on mission was the requirement also for Asia.

Major Events of Mission in Asia 1910-2010: A Glimpse

The Second Vatican Council (1962-1965) is without a doubt the most impactful event of the century for the church universal and for the church in Asia in particular. As far as the church in Asia is concerned, the Federation of Asian Bishops' Conferences (FABC) with its various offices is certainly Asia's continuing Vatican II. The influence its insights had on the shaping of the Synod of Bishops, Special Assembly for Asia (1998), and consequently on the Post-Synodal Apostolic Exhortation *Ecclesia in Asia* is indeed vast.

Improved relationships among Catholic-Non-Catholic churches during 1910-2010

Looking at Asia region by region, here are some of the highlights showing improved relationship among churches. In South Asia, *Nepal* became a *sui iuris* mission and was subsequently raised to Prefecture Apostolic in 1997. Since the opening of Nepal in 1951 several religious groups reached Nepal. *India* had the rare joy of receiving Paul VI for the Eucharist Congress in Bombay in 1964. Pope John Paul II, who released the historic Post-Synodal Apostolic Exhortation *Ecclesia in* Asia in New Delhi in November 1999, offered a road map for mission in Asia. The evolving dialogue between Roman Catholic theologians and other great religions in India is poised for a more fruitful result. Though the vast majority is Muslim, North Asia is experiencing the ferment of the gospel in all its different countries: Afghanistan, and the five Republics of Central Asia.

Among the countries of South East Asia, 85 per cent of *the Philippines'* population of 92 million people are Catholic, and about 90 per cent are Christian. Without it the presence of the Catholic Church in Asia would be like a drop in a mighty ocean *statistically*, but a *drop* that really matters. The most significant event for the church in Asia was the meeting of Paul VI in Manila in 1970, with 180 bishops from the various countries of the continent.

East Asia comprises China, Japan, Taiwan, North and South Korea. *China*, one of the largest countries of the world in terms of area, has a population of 1.2 billion or one fifth of the world's inhabitants. And China occupies the first place in Christian population today in Asia. The great Cultural Revolution (1966-76), organized by Mao Zedong, turned out to be the most tumultuous social movement in the modern history of China. It was also the most traumatic experience for all Chinese. An important decision of the Holy See that greatly facilitated mission work in China was the 1939 decree of Propaganda Fide (now known as the Congregation for the Evangelization of Peoples) declaring the veneration of Confucius, ceremonies in honour of deceased ancestors and other national customs to be purely civil in character, and therefore, permissible to Chinese/Catholics. The effort that the Vatican is making to regularize the status of the Chinese Catholic Patriotic Association (CCPA) helped the church to maintain almost continuous link even during the Cultural Revolution. The future of the church in China is as bright as the promises of God.

A word on West Asian countries: The population of the West Asian countries may be put at 266 million. The establishment of the state of Israel in 1948 introduced new factors into the struggle for survival of the Arab

Palestinian Christian communities. Because of constant friction between Israel and Palestine many Christians have been forced to flee from the West Bank and Gaza. Some of them later on have emigrated too. In 1994 full diplomatic relations were established between Israel and the Holy See reflecting an improvement in the relationship between the two faiths (Catholics and Jews).

Allow me to close this aspect of improved relationship by placing on record the formation of the World Council of Churches (WCC) 1948 and the establishment of National Councils of Churches (NCC) in most parts of Asia. The Roman Catholic Church and the NCCs have worked together in several issues in Asia.

The FABC: Asia's continuing Vatican II

The Federation of Asian Bishops Conferences (FABC) has its roots in the historic visit Pope Paul VI made to Manila in November 1970. His visit set in motion a 'dynamic process' (Kroeger 2010:1) that impacted and continues to influence the church's mission in Asia. On that historic occasion Paul VI met 180 Asian bishops and said, 'You have before you an immense field for your apostolate' (Kroeger 2010:1). Yes, the evangelizing mission in Asia is immense in every sense: having enormous challenges and unlimitled possibilities. The final message of the Asian Bishops Meeting in Manila 1970 confirmed their desire to pledge themselves 'in an open, sincere, and continuing dialogue' with the rich cultural heritage of Asia and with the adherents of other religions and religious traditions of the continent. Of particular emphasis was their resolve to be more truly the church of the poor. These resolves became more concrete with the official establishment of the FABC when on November 16, 1972 the Statutes of the FABC were approved by Paul VI. The FABC's refreshing breeze, we may say, is the continuation of the cool and at the same time energizing and uplifting breeze which the saintly Pope John XXIII let into the church when he convoked the Second Vatican Council. Moreover the FABC has made its own the Council's insights.

Snapshots from the Council: a background to FABC

In the Council the church looking into herself saw the Spirit that guided her through history with all its vicissitudes, with all its ups and downs. In it the church experienced a power which is none other than the power of the Father, the Son and the Holy Spirit. A breakthrough that took place at that moment is the realization that 'mission' is God's mission. We are only his instruments! The Trinitarian love became central. It became the source and at the same time the goal of mission. From this love and because of this love, the church experienced a *courage*, a courage that came from the Spirit of God. The consequence was to see fear vanishing. The church in that courage found *strength* to face the world. The result is known as *dialogue*: the courage to dialogue with peoples, religions and cultures. The scope of this dialogue is best seen in no other part of the world as in the continent of Asia. The FABC is the best proof of it, for dialogue has emerged as the 'interpretive' key to the church's life in the multi-cultural and multi-religious context of Asia. The strength, the courage and the dialogue we have mentioned above have been seen in various forms and degrees by missionaries all over Asia.

Vatican II, by affirming the Trinitarian love as the source and goal of mission, puts mission in its correct and only valid perspective, and at the same time made mission somewhat vague. The self-understanding of the church in Vatican II as *Pilgrim People of God* renders the church not the goal of mission, but what the church and Jesus Christ point to, becomes the goal of mission, namely, the kingdom or the reign of God. In this connection, a breakthrough statement on salvation in the Council is LG 8. In it we read that the true church of Christ '... *subsists* in the Catholic Church, which is governed by the successor of Peter and by the bishops in union with that successor ...'. By *subsists* is meant that even though the fullness of the church founded by Christ abides in the Roman Catholic Church, '... many elements of sanctification and of truth can be found outside her [Roman Catholic Church's] visible structure ... [which] possess an inner dynamism toward Catholic unity'. Another breakthrough in mission is the church's attitude to non-Christian religions. 'The Catholic Church rejects nothing which is true and holy in these [non-Christian] religions ...' (NA 2). Yet another point linked with the evangelizing mission particularly in the multi-religious context of Asia is that all people 'are to be immune from coercion ... in such wise that in matters religious, no one is to be forced to act in a manner contrary to his/her own belief. Nor is anyone to be restrained from acting in accordance with his/her own beliefs ...' (DH 2). A very pertinent statement in this regard which appears in GS is that, '... we ought to believe that the Holy Spirit in a manner known only to God offers every person the possibility of being associated with [the] paschal mystery' (GS 22).

Insights from the FABC

The last forty years of the FABC can be summed as instilling a new way of being church in Asia through the life and practice of the 'triple-dialogue', namely, dialogue with the poor, with cultures and with religions. As a result, the words of James Thoppil, the church in Asia today can be envisioned as a 'communion of communities, a credible sign and witness to the life and mission of Jesus in Asia' (Thoppil, 2005: xii). The FABC does this not without affirming the uniqueness of Jesus Christ and the inseparable link that exists between him, the church and her evangelizing mission (see EN 20). The church's effort to be in Asia as 'an incultured community, a liberative community, a dialogue community, a kingdom-centred community, a community of harmony and a *koinonia*' (Thoppil, 2005: 9) is clear, and the process for it is still being intensified year after year. The focus is to create a *local church* in its full and integral meaning.

The themes of the FABC Plenary Assemblies (convened approximately every four years) may provide us some idea of the areas of emphasis in building *local* churches, fully rooted in the universal communion and at the same time truly inserted in the different contexts. They are:

- Evangelization in Modern Day Asia (Taipei, Taiwan, 1974)
- Prayer, the Life of the Church in Asia (Calcutta, India, 1978)
- The Church, Community of Faith in Asia (Bangkok, Thailand, 1982)
- The Vocation and Mission of the Laity in the Church and in the World of Asia (Tokyo, Japan, 1986)
- Journeying Together Towards the Third Millennium (Bandung, Indonesia, 1990)
- Christian Discipleship in Asia Today: Service to Life (Manila, Philippines, 1995)
- A Renewed Church in Asia: A Mission of Love and Service (Samphran, Thailand, 2000)
- The Asian Family Toward a Culture of Integral Life (Daejeon, Korea, 2004)
- Living the Eucharist in Asia (Manila, Philippines, 2009).
- Renewed Evangelizers for New Evangelization in Asia (Xuan Loc, Vietnam, 2012)

Faith and culture integration lived concretely and pastorally, an inculturated and inculturizing (stressing the need and attitude) evangelization, careful analysis of social situations leading to a contemplative and prayerful dimension of life, pastoral planning and regular evaluation are part of the Asian method of evangelization. The church in Asia is committed to evangelization. She repeats joyfully, 'Woe to me if I do not preach the gospel' (I Cor. 9:16). Evangelization has to be understood in its holistic and integral meaning to bring the good news into all the strata of humanity, transforming humanity from within. It is sharing the Word, witnessing to it in life and getting involved in the lives of people through human development works. Dialogue is the interpretive key for it. For the FABC, evangelization in Asia is Jesus continuing his mission in today's Asia, with a preferential option for Asia's poor. It is possible only if the whole church in Asia and everyone in it is missionary.

It is the firm conviction of the FABC that evangelization in Asia assumes an 'urgency and magnitude' as never before in the history of our faith. The preparation of the evangelizer – spiritual and intellectual – is crucial. This reminds us of an unfulfilled hope of John Paul II, 'I hoped', the Holy Father writes in *Ecclesia in Asia*, citing *Tertio Millennio Adveniente*, 'that the Synod might 'illustrate and explain more fully the truth that Christ is the one Mediator between God and man and the sole Redeemer of the world, to be clearly distinguished from the founders of other great religions' ' (EAs 2). This leads us to the main highlights of *Ecclesia in Asia*, the Magna Carta for evangelization in Asia.

Insights from Ecclesia in Asia

Whereas *Redemptoris Missio* (RM – see the contribution of Roger Schroeder in this volume) is a powerful answer to *why* Christian mission should be carried out throughout the world, *Ecclesia in Asia* is an equally potent answer to *how* mission in Asia is to be carried out. Asia needs Jesus Christ just as the whole world needs him. He is the best gift for the continent. He is a gift not only to be received, but above all, to be shared. This receiving and sharing is possible only in the strength of the Spirit of God, the Spirit of the Father and of the Son. No wonder, chapter II and chapter IV are linked with chapter III on the 'The Holy Spirit: Lord and Giver of Life'. Jesus is the best gift for Asia, because in him, 'through the power of the Holy Spirit, we come to know that God is not distant, above and apart from man, but is very near, indeed united to every person and all humanity in all of life's situations ...' (EAs 12). And again, in Jesus Christ, 'by his Incarnation, he, the Son of God, in a certain way united himself with each individual' (EAs 13). God so close to us, God so one with us: this is Jesus Christ. No news can be better than this for humankind, and especially for Asia with its pluri-cultural and pluri-religious world. It is for love of this Jesus that the saints and martyrs of Asia offered their lives (see EAs 9). The same thought appears also towards end of the Apostolic Exhortation (see EAs 49) as if to make an inclusion so as to bind together the whole content of EAs, leaving us a message that the love of the saints and martyrs in Asia is a key to effective mission in Asia.

    The uniqueness and universality of Jesus in Chapter II is a beautiful Christological catechesis in *Ecclesia in Asia*. It continues into Chapter III and forms a profound meditation on the Holy Spirit. In it the false separation between the work of Jesus and that of the Spirit is healed (EAs 16). Jesus as the *only* manifestation of the Divine creates problems in Asia. EAs without mincing words clearly but gently states that, 'Even for those who do not explicitly profess faith in him as the Saviour, salvation comes as a grace from Jesus Christ through the communication of the Holy Spirit' (EAs 14). It reminds us of the only single quotation which occurs three times in *Redemptoris Missio,* thus linking the *why* and the *how* of mission (see RM 6, 10, 28). This is an inseparable link for mission: To know why Jesus should lead to share him with creative *how*. And that is perhaps one of the main highlights of EAs by proposing certain methodological helps: an attitude of loving respect and esteem for our listeners; a gradual pedagogy; narrative sharing in presenting Jesus complemented by more relational; historical and even cosmic perspectives; use of evocative pedagogy; and the common sense to adapt oneself to the sensibilities of Asian peoples. This leads us to the theme of inculturation. Culture, EAs defines, as 'the vital space within which the human person comes face to face with the Gospel' (EAs 21). The implications of this short description of culture are many. But this brief paper cannot go into it here. Understood deeply it would lead us to affirm that a truly cultured person is a compassionate person. The three key words in EAs that take us into a 'mission' of compassion are *communion, mission* and *dialogue* which the Exhortation highlights. Involvement of the laity, basic ecclesial communities, solidarity among churches, ecumenical and all other forms of dialogue as a characteristic mode of mission in Asia, willingness to cooperate, fidelity to Catholic heritage, desire for purification and renewal as a result of a discerning and sincere heart, the service of human promotion, facing contemporary challenges in Christian mission and genuine holiness of life. This last mentioned, EAs tell us is very important, because people today put their trust 'in witness than in teachers, in experience than in teaching and in life and action than in theories' (EAs 42). I must confess that what we have mentioned above on EAs is only an invitation to read it personally, perhaps again and again, as a marvelous masterpiece from the heart of John Paul II. It was from the same missionary heart that the church has received also *Redemptoris Missio* for evangelizing mission in Asia.

Conclusion

Asia is a huge continent in terms of geography and human and natural resources. The presence of the Catholic Church though very small, has impact beyond measure. Many things have happened in Asia in the hundred years 1910-2010. Asia, FABC (Asia's continuing Vatican II) and *Ecclesia in Asia* are all huge realities. To do justice to them is an impossible task in few pages.

CATHOLIC MISSION IN EUROPE 1910-2010

Martin Üffing, SVD

This article will mainly deal with mission *ad intra*, i.e. the question of Europe as a 'mission continent', not mission *ad extra*, i.e. missionary activities of European churches or Christians outside Europe. And because mission in Europe is still controversial, developments in the understanding of mission and a reading of church documents from a European missionary perspective will be presented.

Changes in Europe 1910-2010

Comparing maps of Europe from 1910 and 2010 indicates significant changes in the continent. Some countries or empires disappeared, others evolved, borders were moved. The twentieth century was the time of two world wars, both started in Europe, and the rise and fall of Nazism and communism. Political systems and nations have changed as well as worldviews and ways of thinking. The twentieth century also marks the end of European colonialism.

Europe is a diverse and multicultural continent flowing out of several very distinct traditions, resulting in a complex weave of political, social and religious currents. Latin, Orthodox and Protestant Christianity are part of Europe, as are Judaism and Islam, both historically and in the contemporary setting. In addition to these elements we find the secular humanism that was a direct result of the Enlightenment. While its achievements are somewhat haltingly acknowledged, it still remains the object of great suspicion for the church, as it is accused of having 'weakened the faith and often, tragically, led to its complete abandonment' (EE:47). As Europe becomes more pluralistic, it is becoming increasingly difficult to speak in precise terms of religion in Europe – though it is impossible to deny a decline in religious adherence and the rise of 'the spirit of an immanentist humanism' (EE:47). Even where church membership may be high, practice can be low. As a result, the Catholic Church in Europe has become aware that there are 'missionary situations' in the continent today.

Religious affiliations in Europe have changed significantly over the past 100 years. In 1910 almost 95% of Europeans were Christians; by 2010 this figure has fallen to about 80%. The number of agnostics and atheists together increased from about 0.5% in 1910 to more than 13% today. In 1910 there were about 10 million Muslims in Europe. Today they are more than 41 million. Due to the Holocaust and emigration the number of Jews declined from 2.4% to 0.3%. There is, however, a new increase of the number of Jews in Western Europe because of recent immigration of Eastern European Jews to Germany. The numbers of Hindus and Buddhists in Europe are also increasing (see Johnson and Ross, ed. 2009: 156).

Immigration has had a strong influence on the Christian community. There are Christians from Africa, Asia and Latin America in today's Europe – both in traditional Catholic parishes and in special national groups. The future of European Christianity seems to be largely in the hands of immigrants.

Missiology

The development of the understanding of mission is related to a number of developments in Europe over the past 100 years. Joseph Schmidlin (1876-1944) the 'father' of Catholic missiology was influenced by developments in mission in the nineteenth century and by Gustav Warneck, the inaugural holder of the first chair in Protestant missiology that was established in 1896. Mission, for Schmidlin, was an activity of the church in the non-Christian world (the world outside Europe), aimed at the conversion of non-Christians (culminating in their baptism and the establishment of local churches). Catholic missionaries were mainly members of European religious congregations that were founded for the purpose of mission *ad extra* and supported by the Catholic population in Europe. The nineteenth century was considered the 'missionary century' (Schmidlin 1931: 114), because during that period a large number of Protestant as well as Catholic missionary societies emerged. In addition, different lay movements in support of the 'missions' came into being.

Contemporary concept of mission

According to Warneck, Protestants used the term mission in various ways in his day. It could mean (1) mission among Catholics or other (rival) Protestant groups; (2) *'innere Mission'* (in German), that is, social service for the needy; (3) pastoral work among German Protestants who had migrated to countries outside Europe; and, finally, (4) mission among non-Christians (Ommerborn 2008: 242-43).

Among Catholics the situation was similar. There were the so-called *'Northern Missions'*, that is to say the predominantly Protestant Scandinavian countries and the territories in Northern Germany, with their very sparse Catholic populations – no more than 10,000 in all in the nineteenth century. They were subject to the central missionary organization of the Catholic Church, the *Congregatio de Propaganda Fide* in Rome. The parishes in this territory – which fluctuated in the course of time – were called *missions* or *mission stations* and the priests serving there, mostly religious, were styled *missionaries*. In Germany their support during the nineteenth century was primarily assured by the St Boniface Association, founded in 1849. Then there is the *mission among non-Catholics*, since Catholics were convinced they had the right to convert non-Catholic Christians to the Catholic faith. *Home mission* aims at renewal and revitalization of the Catholic flock. There was the *mission among migrants*, especially in America, which was considered a mission territory not only by mission societies, but also the propaganda, to whom the United States were subject until the curial reform of 1908. And finally there was the mission among non-Christians or foreign mission (Ommerborn 2008: 242-43).

Although the term 'mission' was thus sometimes used in a wider sense, mission proper meant Christian activity among 'pagans'.

With special interest Schmidlin observed whatever happened in the field of support for the missions in Germany at the beginning of the twentieth century. The reports 'Aus dem heimatlichen Missionswesen' that were regularly published in his *Zeitschrift für Missionswissenschaft* (ZM) give a lot of information about developments in that area. Schmidlin writes about his lectures at Münster University, and informs his readers about diverse mission-relevant topics (see Üffing 1994: 117ff).

Such articles are important, because they give some insight into mission thinking and ideas of that time. In addition, we see the new interest in mission that in the course of the twentieth century grew into an important force in Germany. While the main focus of mission and of missiology was *ad extra*, there have already been some who started thinking about the need of mission also *ad intra*, i.e., inside Europe. There was a – still controversial – development considering the re-Christianization of formerly Christian areas as a challenge also to missiological thinking. In 1935 Schmidlin published an article on 'Heidenmission und Neuheidentum' (pagan mission and neo-paganism) in the ZM. He developed the idea of mission in Europe on the basis of what he calls 'neo-paganism', looking at the increasing number of former Christians who had lost their faith and were not Christians anymore.

Mission in Europe for centuries was understood as concluded, an affair of the distant past. There were some exceptions, for example in looking at Germany in a missionary perspective since the end of the First World War. The Catholic home missions started with laypeople, who worked in pastoral care and care for families to support the growing demands in parishes that were caused by urbanization and industrialization. The use of the term 'mission' here and elsewhere was influenced by Protestant vocabulary, as, for instance, in 'city mission'. Two female religious congregations, understanding their charism as social apostolate, evolved from this: in 1921 the 'Sisters of Catholic Home Missions of Our Lady', and in 1922 the 'Catholic Home Mission Munich'. Areas of special mission developed, in the sense of social apostolate or apostolate among certain groups of people, like city mission, mission at train stations (*Bahnhofsmission*) or mission among seamen.

Mission in Europe

Before Vatican II

Since the 1930s, and especially immediately before and after World War II, there have been a number of church thinkers who spoke about mission in Europe, saying that in the center of Christian Europe there were two mission countries: Germany and France. For Germany, the philosopher Josef Pieper as well as the Jesuits Alfred Delp and Ivo Zeiger need to be mentioned. For France, there is Etienne Gilson, who in 1935 wrote that France has turned into a 'mission country' again, and the well-known book by Yves Daniel and Henry Godin *La France pays de mission* of 1943. Although their ideas were not generally accepted, we need to take a look at them.

Josef Pieper (1904-1997) was at the forefront of the Neo-Thomistic wave in twentieth-century Catholic philosophy. Reflections about the need for a modern Catholic mission in Germany started in the mid-1930s, in relation to the challenge of a new self-understanding of church and Christianity in Nazi Germany. Pieper takes position and uses the term mission. He relates his reflections to an article about Etienne Gilson's book, in which challenges Catholics in France to relate in a new way to the world around them (see Bünker 2004: 229-30). The task of the church in France, he says, is to find ways for a re-Christianization. Pieper takes up the idea and sees similar challenges in Germany. 'The mission of the Church for the German people is far from being finished, the process of the Christianization of the German people is not yet concluded; the situation of the Church in Germany is the situation of mission' (Pieper 2000: 1). Mission for Pieper is a basic task of the church sent to all peoples with the goal to win them for Christ. Because of the situation of the 1930s, he sees Germany again in such a missionary situation.

The German Jesuit Alfred Delp spoke in 1941 about the missionary challenges for Germany (see Bünker 2004: 235ff). His urgent call for 'a missionary dialogue with the time' is related to the accusation that the church is using a foreign language in her contact with the people of her own time. Delp says: 'We have become a mission country. The environment and the factors determining all life are not Christian anymore. A mission country can only be entered with a truly missionary will, that is, the determination to approach the other person to win him for God, who is the Lord ...' (Bünker 2004: 235ff). Delp talks about real dialogue of the church with the people of the time as an important first missionary step. This has to happen in a context (Nazi Germany) that is clearly opposed to Christianity and church.

Ivo Zeiger, another German Jesuit, claimed in 1948 that 'Germany lies in front of us as a mission country calling out to us' (see Bünker 244ff). The basis for this statement is the post-war situation in Germany – the end of clearly defined Catholic or Protestant milieus, the population being mixed with refugees from former Eastern parts of Germany, the difficult material and the weak inner situation of church communities. Ziegler understands mission in a clearly geographic sense, often related to the minority situation of Catholics ('Diaspora'). This new situation becomes a clear challenge to individual Catholics – each responsible for mission in their own context.

Finally, *France, pays de mission?* (France, a mission country?) – the book by Daniel and Godin of 1943, in which they describe France as a country with large regions without religion. Such a statement shattered the geographical understanding of mission and Christianity. How was the traditional 'sender' of mission to become a 'receiver'? (Bevans and Schroeder 2004: 248-49). The book presents a basic and differentiated new understanding of mission for a European context. Their perspective is sociological, mission for them is not related to a certain territory, but to clearly defined groups in society, in this case the proletariat, which is compared with the 'pagan indigenous people' of the classical mission territories. Daniel and Godin understand mission as the building up of an incarnated Christianity. They stress that it cannot be the task of a missionary to make the Chinese French or German, but to make them Christian. It is his task, rather, to build a Chinese Church in China. And it is not only about making individuals Christians, but to Christianize the whole environment, institutions, customs, and habits. Mission for them is not the renewal of Catholicism, but building Christianity (Bünker 2004: 254).

We must also mention Madeleine Delbrêl, who since 1941 served as a lay advisor of the French bishops' *Mission de France*, a seminary whose main apostolate was to re-evangelize the country. In 1943 Cardinal Suhard founded the *Mission de Paris*, an effort to form bonds of lay and clerical solidarity with the urban working class ('worker priests'). These activities fueled M. Delbrêls conviction that Christians today are called to be 'missionaries without a boat' (see Delbrêl 2000).

Vatican II and Evangelii Nuntiandi

These insights and reflections, however, remained isolated and were not widely accepted, until the church started looking from a new theological and global perspective at its situation and task including in Europe. The foundation for a new understanding of mission was laid by the Second Vatican Council. *Ad Gentes* (AG 1965), the Decree on the Church's Missionary Activity, represents a milestone in the formulation of the modern concept of mission. The document offers a new theological foundation of mission and is to be understood in relation to the Council's ecclesiology (see *Lumen Gentium* LG 1964), to the pastoral constitution on the church in the modern world *Gaudium et Spes* (GS 1965), and other documents, like *Nostra Aetate* (on the relation of the church to non-Christian religions NA 1965), *Dei Verbum* (on divine revelation DV 1965) or *Dignitatis Humanae* (on religious liberty DH 1965).

The Council is the point of departure and background of the new evangelization of Europe. Mission now is no longer understood in a merely geographic sense as proclamation outside Europe, but was brought back into the heart of theology and the church. The classical statement of this understanding can be found in AG 2: 'The Church on earth is by its very nature missionary since, according to the plan of the Father, it has its origin in the mission of the Son and the Holy Spirit ...' This statement was the beginning of a paradigm shift in mission theology: mission is not an appendix to the church that is delegated to one Roman congregation in charge of the church's missionary activities. Neither is it an activity that concerns only some specialists (missionaries, mainly members of religious congregations), who are sent by the 'real church' (mainly existing in 'Christian' Europe) to the 'missions' (mission countries or territories), mainly outside Europe (and North America). Mission is essential, the church is missionary by nature, the church itself is already the result of the mission that originates in God the Father. Therefore, *the* church as a whole, wherever it exists, participates in the mission of God and is responsible for mission. It was also recognized that mission has to take place as inculturation (as it was called later) and dialogue (see also Paul VI's *Ecclesiam Suam* ES 1964) within modern culture (see AG 10, GS 53-62).

In *Evangelii Nuntiandi* (EN 1975) Paul VI deepens the terminological, theological and strategic basis for the mission of the church in the modern world, based on the insights of Vatican II, using the term evangelization. The essence of evangelization is the transmission of the all-embracing and Christocentric salvation that starts with personal conversion (EN 10) and leads, through the evangelization of cultures (EN 20), to the eschatological fulfillment (EN 27). Jesus Christ is the center of the message. Evangelization is addressed to the 'world of today', to today's humanity (EN 18): atheists, non-practicing Catholics, simple people and intellectuals, members of non-Christian religions, the faithful and those who are not living in full communion with the Catholic Church (EN 52-54). EN 19 states: 'Strata of humanity which are transformed: for the Church it is a question not only of preaching the Gospel in ever wider geographic areas or to ever greater numbers of people, but also of affecting and as it were upsetting, through the power of the Gospel, mankind's criteria of judgment, determining values, points of interest, lines of thought, sources of inspiration and models of life, which are in contrast with the Word of God and the plan of salvation.' This statement, and the challenge to 'evangelize cultures ... in a vital way, in depth and to their very roots ...' gives up a geographic definition of the evangelizing mission of the church and can be applied as a challenge to the church in Europe. EN becomes the most important theological basis for the concept of new evangelization of John Paul II as well as for the understanding of mission in Europe.

After Vatican II

After Vatican II, local churches worldwide started reflecting on their identity and their responsibility for mission in their respective continents. For Europe, the collaboration of bishops in the CCEE (Council of Catholic Episcopal Conferences in Europe) was an important step for the development of the concept of new evangelization. As early as 1965 questions about collaboration in Europe were raised and Europe was identified as a special context for church action. The reality of an increasing alienation from Catholic (Christian) faith and the growing presence of other religions in Europe were understood as special challenges (Walldorf 2002: 42). After symposia in 1967 and 1969, the CCEE was founded in Rome in March 1971. The main documents of the symposia up to 1989 are available in a publication entitled 'The Bishops of Europe and new Evangelization' (CCEE 1991). Questions of new evangelization and mission in Europe were of utmost importance for the CCEE since its beginnings. The third symposium of the European bishops in 1975 dealt with missionary questions explicitly under the topic 'Mission of the Bishop in the Service of Faith'. In his presentation, the Archbishop of Krakow and future Pope John Paul II, Cardinal Wojtyla, stressed the missionary priority of the proclamation of the gospel. 'The *kerygma* has a missionary task, with which the bishops together with their priests and deacons bring new disciples to Jesus by calling people to the faith or by strengthening their faith' (Walldorf 2002: 44). Wojtyla stresses that the content of the proclamation must be the gospel – the message with the mystery of Jesus Christ as its center, with the goal of showing people the ways of salvation and the fulfillment of the God's salvific plan in Christ. 'Proclamation must make faith relevant and fruitful for the listeners ... by giving due space to human experiences and the authentic questions of people of today' (Walldorf 2002: 44). In a way, the meeting of 1975 was the origin of the future – controversial – program of Europe's new evangelization. While today many talk about mission in Europe (although not all would agree, as stated at the beginning), the concept of new or re-evangelization as a response to missionary challenges remains controversial. Pastoral theologian Ottmar Fuchs states: 'The term new evangelization of Europe presupposes a relationship of Church on the one hand and society, culture and world on the other, that since Vatican II has to be rejected ... Talking about the new evangelization of Europe suggests an evangelized Church that should lead the terribly secularized Europe back to the faith, with the Church possessing what Europe is lacking' (quoted in Walldorf 2002: 46). For Fuchs 'the challenge of evangelization in Europe is not that those who are distant should come back to the Church, but that they, wherever they are and most probably would remain, should be encouraged in their ability for hope and humanism ...' (Walldorf 2002: 46).

For John Paul II the new evangelization of Europe was a central project from the very beginning of his pontificate. For the 'discovery' of Europe as a mission context the global perspective was important. Looking at Europe from another, for example a Latin American, reality and comparing the situation here with others made it even clearer for John Paul II that there were genuine missionary challenges and situations here. So, Europe is both, a mission continent and a Catholic and Christian continent. The importance of this discovery of Europe as mission continent becomes even clearer if we look at the understanding of mission before Vatican II and also at statements like that of Walbert Bühlmann, who writes 'that in Catholic, especially in Roman circles there was a lot of opposition' against accepting the expression 'mission in six continents' that was coined in 1963 in Mexico City, and therefore also against recognizing Europe as a mission continent (Bühlmann 1984: 12ff). Until recently, such a concept of mission was controversial. Not only missiology, i.e. reflection on mission, but also the practice of mission has to adapt to the idea. Local churches as well as religious congregations in Europe are struggling to this day with mission and ways, goals, etc. of mission in Europe. Is mission here more to be understood in the sense of a re- or new evangelization, or are the challenges going much deeper, demanding radically new ways of being church and Christian in this continent? What are the characteristics of mission in Europe? (see Walldorf 2002: 48ff).

New evangelization of Europe is a project of the whole church. It is theologically oriented inculturation and therefore has to begin with cultural analysis: understanding the signs of the times, the question of God's presence and action in modern culture is the condition for an adequate, culturally relevant transmission of the gospel. It also is to be understood as self-evangelization – 'The Church is an evangelizer, but she begins by being evangelized herself...' (EN 15) – and in the era of ecumenism it has to take place in collaboration with all Christians.

In 1990 John Paul II published *Redemptoris Missio* (RM) on the permanent validity of the church's missionary mandate. For John Paul II mission is universal, 'one which knows no boundaries, which involves the communication of salvation in its integrity' (RM 31). 'The ... return of the missions into the Church's mission, the insertion of missiology into ecclesiology, and the integration of both areas into the Trinitarian plan of salvation, have given a fresh impetus to missionary activity itself, which is not considered a marginal task for the Church, but is situated at the center of her life, as a fundamental commitment of the whole People of God' (RM 32). In this one mission and task of evangelization three situations can be distinguished: (1) mission *ad gentes* in the proper sense of the term, (2) pastoral care for the faithful, and (3) new evangelization or re-evangelization (RM 33; see AG 6). These three types of mission are 'not intrinsic to that mission, but arise from the variety of circumstances in which that mission is carried out' (RM 33), and the boundaries between them 'are not clearly definable, and it is unthinkable to create barriers between them or to put them into watertight compartments' (RM 34).

Mission *ad gentes* in the proper sense of the term is directed to the non-Christian world, the world outside the church, 'to 'peoples or groups who do not yet believe in Christ', 'who are far from Christ', in whom the Church 'has not yet taken root' and whose culture has not yet been influenced by the Gospel' (RM 34). As such, mission *ad gentes* can be distinguished according to geographic, social and cultural circumstances into three areas.

First, there is the geographic orientation. Mission *ad gentes* is necessary mainly in Asia, but also in Africa, in Latin America and Oceania, because there are vast non-evangelized zones. But, 'even in traditionally Christian countries there are regions that are under the special structures of the mission *ad gentes*, with groups and areas not yet evangelized. Thus, in these countries too there is a need not only for a new evangelization, but also, in some cases, for an initial evangelization' (RM 37).

Furthermore, mission *ad gentes* is directed towards new worlds and new social phenomena. The massive growth of cities, young people, who in many countries comprise more than half the population, and the global phenomenon of migration are mentioned here.

Finally, there are cultural sectors, the modern equivalents of the Areopagus, challenging the mission of the church to proclaim the gospel in a language appropriate to and understandable in those surroundings. The world of communication (including mass media); commitment to peace, development and the liberation of peoples; rights of individuals and peoples, especially those of minorities; the advancement of women and children; safeguarding the created world – all areas that need to be considered in the mission of the church.

New evangelization is directed mainly to those in countries with ancient Christian roots, but occasionally also to people in the younger churches, where entire groups of the baptized have lost a living sense of the faith, or even no longer consider themselves members of the church and live a life far removed from Christ and his gospel.

Mission in Europe Today

Most of the groups or phenomena mentioned in RM can be found in contemporary Europe. There are, for instance, people who have not been evangelized and who understand themselves as agnostics or atheists. They may live in countries with ancient Christian roots, their ancestors may have been Christians, but they themselves have not been baptized and never seriously consider Christianity as an option for themselves. More numerous still, there are those who have been baptized, but who are not practicing their Christian faith or who have left the church. There are people of other religions and religious and cultural pluralism has become a reality in numerous European nations.

Secularization and religious pluralism have become challenges to local churches in Europe, as well as migration, poverty, questions of justice and peace, etc. From a missiological perspective, the Catholic Church in Europe finds itself in a new situation: it is no longer only a mission-sending church, but has become a receiving church as well: missionaries from Africa and Asia are numerous, they are working not only with migrants from their own nations or in special apostolates, but are also assigned to local parishes, working in the pastoral care of the faithful. In the prologue to a document of the German Episcopal Conference with the telling title 'Time for Sowing: Being a Missionary Church', Cardinal Lehmann writes: '*All ecclesial activity is to be understood against the background of the missionary dimension of the Church and strengthened thereby*' (Die deutchen Bischöfe 2000).

Europe is a difficult mission continent. Mission or evangelization cannot function today with what the German bishops called an 'ecclesial ... mentality of conquest', which would go to show that Christians have learned nothing from their own mission history. Europe might learn from the missionary activities of the church in other continents and apply what has been stressed for some time already: mission has to take place in the mode of dialogue.

In 2000, the French bishops wrote a letter to the Catholics of France: 'Offering the Faith in Today's Society' ('*Proposer la foi*'), in which they describe the mission of Catholics in the following way. These words can serve as an apt conclusion for this chapter:

1. We do not permit ourselves to put up with the complete privatization of our faith as if the Christian experience in our hearts must remain buried without having any effect on the reality of the world and society. Our Church is not a sect. We do not build ghettos. We oppose any attempt to enclose the Church into herself [...].

2. Even if we dismiss any marginalization, we must be realistic. The Catholic Church does not cover the entire French society. She does not allow herself to dream of acquiring a more or less established and privileged position through the State [...].

3. But even if the Catholic Church [...] has renounced any kind of domineering position, she remains nevertheless true to her missionary duty: this means she addresses herself to all and is open to everyone [...] In a word: the presence of the Catholic Church in France remains [...] a sacrament of presence. We are in our society a 'sign and instrument both of a very closely knit union with God and of the unity of the whole human race' (cf. Lumen Gentium, n. 1). (Les Evêques de France 1996: Premier Partie, II, 6).

CATHOLIC MISSION IN LATIN AMERICA AND THE CARIBBEAN 1910-2010

Paulo Suess

There are three ways of writing history: that of the fisherman, that of the sailor, and that of the domestic servant. The piranha the fisherman caught turns into a manatee (*Peixe-Boi*), that was stolen by a jaguar that stealthily was waiting for him. The fisherman is the apologetic historian and one is well advised to mistrust his stories.

The sailor tells of trips he has taken over the sea – trips he actually made as well as others of which he has only dreamed, although he reports them with distance both in time and in geography as though they are real. The sailor is the macro-historian. There is much in his stories that is not verifiable.

The domestic servant tells many small stories that she heard in the bus on the way to her workplace or has heard from her neighbors. She tells them in such a lively manner that the listener has the impression that she was actually there. The domestic servant is the micro-historian who has story-telling talent.

We encounter all of these 'fantastic' ways of writing history in Latin American church history, and we must read all these 'big and little' stories 'against the grain'. Those who know the dangers will be able to withstand them in an appropriate fashion. The watershed of the time frame taken into consideration (1910-2010) is also for Latin America the time of the Second Vatican Council (1962-1965) that tried to come to terms with questions that had been left unaddressed for centuries.

Preconciliar Latin America in the Twentieth Century

After the colonial period and the wars of independence at the beginning of the nineteenth century, there followed in almost every land of Latin America the declaration of a republic by Creole elites (i.e. people of European decent born in Latin America). After the heir apparent to the Portuguese throne declared independence in 1822, Brazil went through a period as an empire until 1889. The Catholic Church, especially during the pontificate of Pius IX (1846-1878), energetically opposed the liberal and socialist movements that were being established in Latin America. One has to imagine this time of 'hard and radical' ecclesiastical condemnations ranting against modernity in the encyclical *Quanta Cura* (1864) and its appendix, the so-called *Syllabus of Errors* with its eighty propositions. The

First Vatican Council (1869-1870) lent these attempts to distance the church from modernity special weight through the dogma of infallibility and the claim to universal jurisdiction of the pope.

For Brazil, the time of the republic, with its separation of church and state (a laicist state without patronage for the church), was a completely new situation of anxiety-ridden freedom without privileges (Lustosa 1991: 17ff). Within the church two different tendencies manifested themselves at the same time: a backward-looking ultramontanism and a critical republicanism. Ultramontanism considered the ecclesiastical privileges of the colonial period and of the empire as historically achieved rights. It found its home in the anti-modernism of the *Syllabus* and the strengthened papacy that developed after the First Vatican Council. Until the Second Vatican Council, it was church doctrine that error had no rights. The image of the church as *societas perfecta* was not reconcilable with the republican laicism that was marked by the laicism of the French Revolution. The church took a long time to accept the modern, religiously neutral state. The religious monopoly of 'Catholic Brazil' came officially to an end with the letting in of other religious cults, creeds, and churches. But one was still far away from an ecumenism among the various Christian confessions or a macro-ecumenism among the various religions.

The World Mission Conference of 1910 (in Edinburgh) – which hardly went beyond the colonialist concept of the conversion of the pagans by a Christian West – was hardly noticed in what was still Catholic Brazil. As the movement around Blessed Antonio Conselheiro (1830-1897) showed, anti-republican catechesis had roots in the religiosity of the simple folk. In the course of time – especially through Leo XIII's (1878-1903) acceptance of the republican state as one possible form of government among others – a critical republicanism was accepted in Brazil as well. However, the ideological debate with the republican state that was carried by liberals, freemasons, positivists and atheists was not yet resolved by any means.

A special bone of contention was religious instruction in the schools. The Catholic Church was finally able in 1931 during the authoritarian rule of Vargas to make it an option in the official school curriculum, as well as 'catechesis' and aid for the indigenous peoples. Until the declaration of the republic the indigenous peoples were consigned to the care of Catholic religious orders. Now the state took them in hand. The Indios Protection Agency (*Servico de Protecao aos Indios* or SPI), founded in 1910, was dissolved in 1967 because of corruption and replaced by the *Fundacao Nacional do Indio* (*Funai*). The military, marked by Comtean positivism, had taken the rule of a laicist catechesis for the indigenous peoples to itself. But it did have a basic sympathy for the affairs of the Indios, albeit in an evolutionistic perspective of integrating them into the general population. Through this, the anthropological status of the indigenous peoples with their religions was explained officially as a model that would eventually exhaust itself and expire.

As far as mission was concerned in this preconciliar period, the attempts to give some organizational and internal unity to the regionalism of diocesan pluralism were of a certain importance. This happened through the founding of the National Bishops' Conference (*Conferencia nacional dos bispos do Brasil* – CNBB) in 1952, and through the common pastoral goals (*Pastoral de Conjunto*) that it brought about. The founding of a conference of religious orders (*Conferencia dos religiosos do Brasil* – CRB) in 1954 was in this regard an important instrument for giving a prophetic edge to catechesis and mission. Especially important was the founding of the Latin American Bishops' Conference (*Conselho Episcopal Latino-Americano* – CELAM) in 1955, prepared for by the First General Assembly of Latin American Bishops' Conferences that took place that same year in Rio de Janeiro. It proved to be an important tool for evangelization, mission, and transnational pastoral-theological independence, precisely in the time of military governments.

Also in this preconciliar period of the 1960s came the beginnings of the Brazilian base communities (found also throughout all of Latin America) with their rootedness in popular catechesis and the grassroots education movement (*Movimento de Educacao de Base*). The base communities were promoted by many bishops, because of the chronic absence of clergy in these lay-led communities. Added to this was the dissemination of Catholic Action and the Young Christian Workers (JOC), founded by Joseph Cardijn (1882-1967), and lay movements introduced by Belgian missionaries working in Brazil. Their social analysis of 'see-judge-act' was affirmed in John XXIII's encyclical *Mater et Magistra* (1961), and nourished the base communities. A theology of the laity adopted by the Second Vatican Council confirmed them and initiated a pastoral ministry of liberation of all the baptized.

Missiological Renewal by the Second Vatican Council

We can understand the missionary renewal of the Council only if we keep before us what the missionary standard of the concept of 'mission' was in the first half of the twentieth century in the so-called mission lands. What the Second Vatican Council had to deal with is well summed up in a sentence from the Decree for the Copts of the Council of Florence (1442):

> (The Holy Roman Church) ... firmly believes, professes and preaches that 'no one remaining outside the Catholic Church, not only pagans', but also Jews, heretics or schismatics, can become partakers of eternal life; but they will go to the 'eternal fire prepared for the devil and his angels' (Mt. 25:41), unless before the end of their life they are joined to it. (DS 1351)

The missionaries since the sixteenth century preached in this way, not out of their own invention but as authorized by the church. Error has no public rights – so it was in the textbooks of canon law right up to the beginning of the Council. Error could rely only on the 'tolerance' of the state under very specific conditions. The official documents of the church in Latin America, up to the middle of the twentieth century, speak of a church that insisted on its monopoly of the truth in order to realize ultimately the civilization of those 'tribes that remain still in unbelief' (see Suess 2011: ch. 5.1). The Second Vatican Council, with its decree of religious liberty, recognized an essential axiom of the modern state.

Also within the church (and that was important for the further unfolding of missionary praxis and reflection in Latin America) the church renewed itself within an interplay of continuity and discontinuity. In many new missiological initiatives the Council drew selectively on those Fathers of the Church who attempted – as did the Council itself – to build a bridge for the gospel in a new era: thus the philosopher and martyr Justin (d. 165) who spoke of the 'seeds of the Word of God' (*logoi spermatikoi*) in pagan cultures (see AG 11; LG 17; GS 57); or Irenaeus of Lyons (d. 202) and Eusebius of Caesarea (d. 339) who tried to characterize pagan cultures as being a divine pedagogy of '*preparatio evangelica*' (AG 3).

The Council followed in broad lines Thomas Aquinas, who held (in opposition to Augustine) that there existed no breech between the order of creation and the order of redemption as a result of original sin. Today of course, fifty years since the Council, a pessimism carrying the burden of Augustinian theology is gaining ground regarding earthly realities. Divine law – that has its origin in grace according to Thomas – does not suspend human law – that has its origin in the natural order (see ST II.II.104.10; Suess 1988: 21-44). Nature, which in essence belongs to creation, cannot be substantially changed or corrupted. Only with this background can we understand the Pastoral Constitution on the Church in the Modern World when it says:

> The Church learned early in its history to express the Christian message in the concepts and language of different people and tried to clarify it in light of the wisdom of their philosophers ... Indeed, this kind of adaptation and preaching of the Revealed Word must ever be the law of all evangelization. (GS 44).

In the first step, cultures have to be accepted as they are in order to speak to them of the offer of redemption and the renewing power of the gospel. At a central place the 'Document of Puebla' (Puebla 1979), in reaching back to AG 3, cites a phrase of the father of the church Irenaeus as the principle of the Incarnation: 'What has not been assumed cannot be redeemed' (Puebla 1979: 400). Thus the *aggiornamento* of John XXIII led to a fundamentally positive view of the world as well as to a recognition of the otherness of cultures, even if this was to be effectively withdrawn in the declaration *Dominus Iesus* (DI 2002) by the Congregation for the Doctrine of the Faith, when religious pluralism within the church was accorded a right to exist only *de facto*, but not *de jure* (DI 4).

More precisely, the Council brought out two 'adaptations' (*aggiornamenti*), one of which is the presupposition for the other: the first, a gesture back toward indigenous cultures, something very important to mission; and second, a magisterial development in which salvation, redemption, and the rescue of souls is not longer limited to the inner court of the Catholic Church. The most important statements of the Council supporting them are as follows:

a) 'The Savior wishes all peoples to be saved' (LG 16; see 1 Tim. 2:4).

b) 'Those who have not yet received the Gospel are related to the People of God in various ways' (LG 16)

c) 'But the plan of salvation also includes those who acknowledge the Creator' (LG 16)

d) 'The Catholic Church rejects nothing of what is true and holy in these religions.' Whose commandments, teachings, and ways of life 'nevertheless often reflect a ray of that truth which enlightens all men' (NA 2)

e) 'Nor shall divine providence deny the assistance necessary for salvation to those who, without any fault of theirs, have not arrived at an explicit knowledge of God, and who, not without grace, strive to lead a good life. Whatever good or truth is found amongst them is considered by the Church to be a preparation for the Gospel and given by him who enlightens all men that they may at length have life' (LG 16; see AG 7).

f) Finally, the Council anchors religious liberty 'in the dignity of the human person' and on the level of human rights. By doing so the preconciliar thinking of primacy and a juridical entitlement claim to truth over against freedom and error is superseded. In so doing, an abstract prohibition against error is removed from religious liberty. As the Declaration on Religious Liberty (DH) puts it, 'nobody is forced to act against his convictions nor is anyone to be restrained from acting in accordance with his convictions in religious matters' (DH 2). The varying use of religious liberty is proof that this freedom actually exists.

The decisions of the Council posed a great challenge for a Church still committed to its civilizing impulse, its privileges, and its monopoly on salvation. But there was a majority at the Council who, with the slogan 'back to the gospel', were prepared to shake off the yoke of alienation and paternalism.

Postconciliar Magisterial Teaching

When we trace the heritage of Council in Latin America and the Caribbean up to 2010, five major themes can focus our attention.

1) The church possesses a *missionary nature* on the basis of the baptism of all Christians (AG 2, 6, 35; Aparecida 2007: 347). The state of grace is a 'state of mission' (Aparecida 2007: 213) and the

'state of mission' is a state of freedom and responsibility. The
missionary nature of the church became the leitmotif of Aparecida.

2) The church is not merely the sum of individuals, but is the *People of
God* (LG 9-17) under the *Word of God* (DV), that through the
ministries of service is structured for the salvation of human beings.
The laity participate in this 'salvific mission of the Church' (LG 33).
The proposition of the right *sensus fidei*, proper to the People of
God in their entirety on the basis of the Word of God that is theirs,
i.e., 'from the bishops to the last faithful layperson' (LG 12) has
empowered Latin American base communities. To be sure, the
relation of word and sacrament has to be rethought here. In
Aparecida, the Latin American church brought its concern about this
to expression in a very concrete fashion: 'If we think that the
Eucharist is the constitutive principle of the church, we are
concerned about the many thousand communities that have to
forego the Sunday Eucharist for long periods of time' (Aparecida
2007: 100e). The empty altar has been for centuries a pastorally
enervating and theologically solvable problem.

3) The goal and the service of the church as a 'messianic people' is the
reign of God and its historical manifestation until the day the Lord
returns (LG 9; 36; Aparecida 2007: 190, 223). In the service of this
task the church has the responsibility of 'reading the signs of the
times and interpreting them in light of the gospel. In language
intelligible to every generation ....' (GS 4) This gave the possibility
to reel in the historically developed ecclesiocentrism that gave
belonging to the church priority over its function of service. Only in
this service can it be a means of redemption, sign of justice, and
image of hope.

4) At Medellín the Latin American magisterium took a decisive step
from the abstract option for humankind to the concrete *option for
the poor*. There was already a certain sensibility at the Council
toward *paupertas* and *pauperes* (GS 1, 88; AG 24). But an option of
the Council for the poor – which runs like a red thread through Latin
American documents and pastoral practice – can nonetheless not be
read from them. The final document of the Fifth General Assembly
of the Bishops' Conferences of Latin America and the Caribbean
(Aparecida 2007) emphasized this option once again. 'To recognize
and to encounter Jesus Christ in the poor and the suffering as well as
defense of the rights of those excluded: it is by these that the Church
measures its loyalty to Jesus Christ' (Aparecida 2007: 533). The
church is the 'house of the poor' (Aparecida 2007: 524). It does not
understand itself as the adjudicator between rich and poor, but as
advocate for the poor (Aparecida 2007: 533). The pre-eminent
'option for the poor' is not one option among others, but an

imperative that 'is to permeate all our pastoral priorities and structures' (Aparecida 2007, 396; see Suess 2010: 111ff.).

5) Whereas at the Council many discussions justifiably were about the *freedom* of human beings and the *autonomy* of earthly realities, about *dialogue* and *aggiornamento*, in Latin America related but not coextensive key terms crystallized in the discussion: *liberation* as the struggle for freedom and autonomy for previously colonized and now majority-poor human beings; *participation* as dialogue in action in processes of transformation; and inculturation as becoming rooted in different cultural contexts that extended much deeper than mere adapation (*aggiornamento*) to strange or new customs. By articulating God's becoming human and the redemption of all human beings, of inculturation and liberation – thus by universal contextuality and a fundamental openness to salvation and readiness to dialogue with all confessions, religions, cultures, and modernity, the catholicity of the church received a quite new face (GS 22). The Council invited the church to see ecumenical work as a sign of the times and to find creative ways to participate in it (see UR 4).

Emphases in a Pastoral Practice of Liberation

The church of Latin America and the Caribbean took up this impulse from the Council creatively and at different levels of its magisterium, its theology, and its pastoral practice and developed it further. Each of the five postconciliar General Assemblies of the Bishops' Conferences of Latin America and the Caribbean can be summarized with a keyword that inspired and renewed pastoral practice. At Medellín in 1968 'liberation' and 'option for the poor' stood in the central point of evangelization. Liberation, as it was first thought about at Medellín, proved to be a too narrow approach without inculturation. But Medellín opened the door to think anew about not only liberation of the poor and the redistribution and justice of goods, but also to focus on questions of otherness. The annual Lenten appeals of the Brazilian Bishops' Conference, the *Campanhas da Fraternidade*, have since 1964 stood under the banner of a pastoral practice of liberation and have been devoted to themes relevant to the poor and to the 'others': equality, participation, reconciliation, redistribution, work, health, violence, justice, human dignity, women's issues, Afro-Americans, and the indigenous.

Puebla (1979) was concerned with 'Community and Participation' (*comunhao e participacao*). At Santo Domingo (1992) evangelization in the colonial period and inculturation were treated: 'Any kind of evangelization must therefore be an inculturation of the Gospel .... The inculturation of the Gospel is indispensible for following Jesus; it is required for the restoration of the disfigured visage of the world' (SD 1992: 13; see LG 8). The final document of Aparecida (2007) took all these points of emphasis and put them together in the concept of mission and the pastoral imperative of 'back to the missionary nature of all the baptized'.

Out of these keywords that were enlarged in their mutual interplay, pastoral organizations, movements, theologies, and magisterial documents appeared that took as their themes a consistent pastoral practice of liberation, the option for the poor and the 'others', the articulation of basic social problems and evangelization, but also had at its base an anti-systemic praxis. It had to do with a praxis of faith that had been given voice in the Lenten Campaign of the CNBB in 1968: 'Believe with your hands.' Small farmers and indigenous people who were fighting for their land, street people and all those sectors who were pushed to the margins by the model of development, have a hard time under current social conditions to struggle for participation, autonomy and becoming subjects. Base communities were helpful with this as a new model for being church. All of this required a long period of conscientization and organization. The poor and the 'others' are not in the first instance enlightened or people of broad vision. It was precisely to these sectors and processes that a pastoral policy of liberation was devoted. Legal assistance is here part of integral mission. The 'Ecumenical Center for Service to Evangelization and Popular Education,' founded in 1992 (*Centro Ecuménico de Servicos à Evangelizacao e Educacao Popular* – CESEP) had in grassroots ecumenical service disseminated these inspirations to young managers and social movements of Latin America and the Caribbean.

Base communities

The ecclesial base communities (*Comunidades Eclesiais de Base* – CEB), as it says in a 1982 document of the CNBB, 'bring to expression today one of the most dynamic characteristics in the life of the Church.' They originated in the 1960s and spread rapidly. In 1975 the first national meeting of base communities took place. Three characteristic traits of base communities are its reading of the Bible, the celebration of liturgies very close to the people, and socially organized solidarity. The celebration of their liturgies is a continuous reference to the Eucharistic fast to which they are subjected. They are church, 'and at their place God's called new people in the Holy Spirit and in great fullness' (see 1 Thess. 1:5 and LG 26). Laity and priestless communities come to speak, so that they represent, in their consciousness of being the People of God, a new way of ecclesial existence.

In all the postconciliar documents of the General Assemblies of the Latin American Bishops' Conferences they are acknowledged. They have become 'the focal point of evangelization and the motors of liberation and development' (Puebla 1979: 96). Aparecida has maintained this line as well:

The ecclesial base communities ... commit themselves with their evangelizing-missionary engagement and with the people living at the margins of society; they make the preferential option for the poor visible. Various services and ministries have emanated from them for the life of the Church and of Society. (Aparecida 2007: 179)

To be sure, 'other recognized forms of small communities' and 'movements' are set alongside the CEBs. The local church has farmed out to these the responsibility for formation of people in management positions and for spirituality of the various interest groups and special interest groups. While in the CEBs it has been about a deep integration of simple and poor people, who through this have found access to ecclesial ministries and services. The pastoral ministry of the CEBs calls into question on the basis of the gospel through its simplicity of speech and nearness to the concrete life traditional parish ministry. It represents what Aparecida has now emphasized again: pastoral conversion (Aparecida 2007: 365, 366, 368, 370) and missionary prophecy.

The Natal Movement

The Council gave ecclesial impetus to many things, but it did not invent the Brazilian Pastoral Wheel. The 'Natal Movement' in the northeast of Brazil was a pastoral movement that already in the pre- and postconciliar period brought together evangelization and social engagement. It was brought to life in the 1940s by Eugenio Sales, the future cardinal of Rio de Janeiro. The heyday of this movement was from 1960 to 1964. Conscientization, countless educational radio broadcasts, pastoral ministry on land issues, education of the managerial class, basic health services, cooperativism and trade unions were brought together with catechesis, evangelization, popular missions, Catholic Action and pastoral ministry to workers. The *Movimento de Natal* educated young managers, strengthened the self confidence of the less significant people, and convinced both clergy and laity of the necessity of socially organized action in line with Catholic social teaching as it also came to expression in *Mater et Magistra* in 1961. It was suspected by the big landowners and ridiculed by revolutionary sectors such as the *Ligas Camponesas* of Francisco Juliao. The military coup in 1964 brought many of these activities to an abrupt end (Lustosa 1991: 154-56).

Ministry on land issues and work with the Bible

During a meeting of those working in ministry to the Amazon region in 1975, the 'Natal Movement' became the '*Comissao Pastoral da Terra – CPT*' on the basis of many fundamental inspirations. Today it is an organization connected with the Brazilian Bishops' Conference. Since its beginnings it has had an ecumenical character in regard to the accompaniment of those who live on the land and the pastoral agents who accompany them. They advise and network small-scale farmers, those who are landless, and seasonal farm workers and help them find their voice on issues such as having lost land to the hydroelectric dams that produce electricity. This often involves extended juridical cases, the legal guarantee of land ownership or getting land back. The CPT tries to assure the production and sale of the products of small-scale farmers on an ecologically defensible basis over against the large-scale agricultural monoculture directed toward export. The authoritarian logic that is exploiting people is also exploiting the land and the planet. Often it is these farm workers, who live far away from the urban centers, who are victims of elementary labor- and human rights violations and see themselves subjected to slave-like working conditions. In such situations a lawyer can become a catechist and bearer of hope. Even good laws (which often are not absent) mean nothing if the judicial system is both expensive and complicated and takes so much time to complete that simple people hardly get what is due them.

Being driven from the land has a long history in Latin America. Land has become scarce for the small-scale farmer and the indigenous, because land has been expropriated in large-scale land accumulation that has gone on for centuries. Contrary to what happened in other Latin American countries, there was no land reform in Brazil. When the slaves were emancipated in 1888, they were denied access to land and property by land legislation from 1850. Large-scale land holdings, being driven from the land, migration to the large cities, starvation wages, unemployment, and urban neglect are the two sides of one and the same coin of social injustice. Brazil is a rich, but unjust, land.

What does 'missionary responsibility' mean in this situation? What can pastoral agents call upon, without having themselves accused at the same time of mixing church and politics? The church of Latin America tries to ground the charge to intervention in situations of social injustice in scripture and the magisterium (see CNBB 2010).

In the biblical tradition ideally conceived, the Year of Jubilee (Lev. 25:10) should correct social inequality every fifty years: the emancipation of slaves, the cancellation of debts, and the giving back of land. Israel understood justice as protection of the weak and liberation of the poor. Land – like the sun and the sea – should not be private property, but common possession of the entirety of humankind. The Year of Jubilee served to restore justice, freedom, and equality.

In the synagogue at Nazareth Jesus concerns himself with this unrealized ideal of the Year of Jubilee, and declares it to be his program for his life (Lk. 4:16-18). Anointed by the Holy Spirit, that is, as the Messiah, he came to proclaim a year of grace as good news for the poor, liberation of prisoners, and healing for the blind. This opens a new reckoning of time. Such a Year of Grace was the promise of the Israelite Year of Jubilee, of being liberated from the coils of the legislators, the hair-splitting of the temple elite, and from the boundary markers of the big landowners. His listeners were so speechless after such unheard-of words that they drove him out of town to make him mute and to toss him off a cliff.

The good news for the poor always leads into conflicts. New life according to the gospel is a birthing procedure with high risks. The way to 'eternal life' leads through the resolving of damages in favor of the victim (see Matt. 19:16; Lk. 10:29-37). Christians are not referees in the conflict between rich and poor. They take sides, without being beholden to parties or government systems. Their actions are only reasonable when they see the world with the eyes of the poor. 'Discovering the visage of the Lord in the suffering visage of the poor – marked by hunger, being despised, fear and suffering – is a challenge to all Christians to personal and ecclesial conversion' (SD 1992: 178).

Time and again the Catholic Church of Latin America has taken a position on questions of land: 'It is unthinkable the work of evangelization would dare to neglect the extremely grave problems that above all agitate us today: such as those that concern justice, liberation, development and world peace' (EN 31). The final document of Puebla makes it clear: 'Unproductive land hides the bread that so many people do not have' (Puebla 1979: 1245). The document of Santo Domingo admonishes as well: a 'more just distribution of land' through land reform, a 'genuine presence of pastoral agents in the communities of farmers' and a 'theological reflection on the problematic of land' (SD 1992: 177). 'The organization of farmers and the indigenous population' is to be supported in solidarity in the struggle 'to hold on to their land or to get it back' (SD 1992: 177).

Pastoral work among the indigenous peoples

In the pastoral work for the defense of indigenous peoples it is about land questions as well, although in a completely specific way. First it had to be clarified whether it would be possible to defend within Latin American countries an indigenous life project of its own, or rather whether the future of indigenous peoples was to be along the two rails of assimilation and physical survival on the one hand, and Western civilization and conversion to Christianity on the other. The issue of a life project of the natives on their own, first in the church and then over against state interventions, had to be clarified and carried out. Wide sectors of Brazilian society and of the local churches did not believe in a separate future for the indigenous peoples. In general, the Indio-question was considered a 'lost cause'. The prospect of integration meant expropriating the land of the Indios into those of the big landowners.

In the postconciliar period this perspective, from the side of the church, was rubbed against the grain, especially by the Council for Mission among the Indigenous (*Conselho Indigenista Missionário* – CIMI). From CIMI's point of view, it should be possible that indigenous peoples could have their own (and on the basis of their cultural pluralism, differing) life projects in Latin American countries, receiving protection and experiencing promotion from state and Church.

CIMI has today a forty-year history. In April 1972 the CNBB called together a group of bishops and missionaries to consult and advise on the Indio Law that was going to be treated in the Chamber of Deputies. The Brazilian Bishops' Conference had been alarmed by the charges made by anthropologists who, in 1971 in Barbados, had accused the church's missionary activity of ethnocentrism and racial discrimination (Declaration of Barbados 1980: 16-18). They held the mission stations to be enterprises for 'recolonization and acts of domination'.

In May of 1970 thirty-two bishops of the Amazon region had described the reports of the massacres of Indios in Brazil as 'exaggerated' and in so doing gave expression to their support of the integration policy of the military regime of General Medici (1969-1974). The building of the Amazonian highway, which was to cross the Amazon region from east to west, had begun casting a shadow on twenty-nine indigenous peoples who were directly affected by it.

Seven years after the Vatican Council and four years after Medellín a coordinating council for missionary activity among the indigenous people of Brazil came into being out of the small advisory group. According to its own statutes, all pastoral agents who are directly or indirectly involved with pastoral work among the indigenous belong to CIMI.

CIMI was founded too late to influence the text of the Indio Law in any decision way. The article in the law that would have made possible ecclesial and academic institutions' right to provide services to the indigenous peoples fell victim to a veto by President Medici on December 19, 1973. In his statement justifying the veto, the president declared that 'the central goals of the law' were 'the speedy and wholesome integration of the Indios into civilization.'

The exclusive claim of the state to provide aid to the indigenous peoples and its goal of 'integration' – which meant the destruction of indigenous cultures – was the root of the later conflicts between the state and its Indio Authority (*Fundacao Nacional do Índio – Funai*) on the one hand, and the church and the rest of civil society on the other. *Funai* understood itself on the basis of the law to be the 'Guardian Agency' of the indigenous peoples.

In accord with the pastoral guidelines of Medellín and knowledge of postcolonial anthropology, and disturbed by the authoritarian regime directed against the people, a significant part of the missionaries adopted their 'option for the indigenous peoples'. Since then, CIMI has promoted meetings between representatives of the indigenous peoples – not only in Brazil, but for all of indigenous America. From this have come autonomous organizations that have opened new political and theological horizons.

Of course, this option has led to conflicts. To the history of bloody deeds against the Indios have now come murders of missionaries, both men and women. Salesian Father Rodolfo Lunkenbein, one of the missionaries in the newly founded CIMI from the first hour, was also the first murder victim in the struggle around the surveying of the land of 'his' people, the Bororo. He died on July 15, 1976 (see Suess 1982: 142-46; see CIMI 2001: 203-40; see CIMI 2011). He was one of the many who struggled and died for a world in which there is to be a place for everyone. In pastoral work among the indigenous the mysteries of the incarnation of Jesus of Nazareth and his paschal liberation on the cross articulate the cause of the crucified of history in the struggle for the recognition of the 'others' and for the distribution of the gifts and goods intended for all (GS 29).

CIMI has responded to the challenges to the cause of the indigenous peoples with a specific, holistic, and networked plan of pastoral action. This has to be distinguished from a traditional 'pastoral program on land issues'. The autonomous indigenous societies with their culture of subsistence are distinguished essentially from Brazilian society on the question of land. This is the case with regard to the way land is possessed (primal possession, not purchase), the way and manner in which it is used (subsistence and common possession), and how it is seen religiously (the sacral character of land). This land is not 'a means of production'. It is the site of the collective memory of a people, its history, its leisure and its labor, where the rites of life and death are carried out. If one realizes that for the indigenous peoples all the separate questions of liberation and resistance are ultimately bundled together in the single question of the land, then the struggle for the land is also the privileged site of an integral evangelization.

But integral evangelization must also be networked – socially, interethnically, and inter-religiously. At this time, more than thirty confessions or churches are present among indigenous peoples with very different tendencies. In order to defend their land, their culture, and their lives, many indigenous peoples have two religions today: Christianity, to come to agreement 'politically' with the surrounding society; and their own religion, for the celebration of their concrete lives.

The globalization of relations requires today – alongside the perfection of any specific life-world (cultures) – common codes for mutual understanding and common action in order to fight against the scourges of humanity such as hunger, violence, unemployment, and the accumulation of land and capital. Thus the defense of indigenous people cannot be successful within the framework of a political project that is settled in the pre-modern, postmodern, or beyond modernity. The life perspective of the indigenous peoples opens new horizons within and via the achievements of modernity itself. Indigenous projects make suit for these achievements, e.g., self-determination and autonomy, human rights, and democratic participation in the decisions of the nation, participation in the process of becoming subjects that at the same time maintains their otherness, and the inclusion of future generations in their own horizon of action. The indigenous peoples have made the demands of modernity their own, but criticize at the same time the hegemonic appropriation of these achievements of modernity by media empires and economic elites.

In indigenous cultures today, the Stone Age and modernity, mythological explanation and historical visions of resistance and struggle, are mixed. Even modernity cannot explain reality without reaching back to myths (Oedipus, the Big Bang). How things are ordered in the indigenous world can be at once an enlarged and an alternative ordering for humanity. Indigenous peoples remind us of the essentials in life, that 'the 'this side' of thinking and the 'other side' of society lies hidden in mystery' (Lévi-Strauss 1992).

(Translated from German by Robert J. Schreiter)

CATHOLIC MISSION IN NORTH AMERICA 1910-2010

Angelyn Dries, OSF

Two factors heavily influenced twentieth century mission in North America. The first was a constant stream of immigration/migration from all parts of the world. The second was the contiguous land mass of the Americas. Their physical connection influenced the cross-continent, as well as trans-oceanic paths of mission. Mission issues affecting one part of the continent did not stop at national borders. The patterns of North American Catholic mission activity in the twentieth century further reveal an evolving mission theology.

Immigration/Migration in Relation to Mission

An experience that characterized much of twentieth century mission and evangelization in North America was the continuous immigration or migration of diverse ethnic/racial groups, as had been the case from the beginning of the Americas. This phenomenon shaped the mission and evangelization response of bishops, laity, clergy, and religious orders across the socio-economic and ethnic spectrum. With astute pastoral observation, the U.S. bishops, who gathered at the Third Plenary Council of Baltimore, laid out the wide-ranging mission and evangelical field in 1883. They identified the need to respond to Native Americans, African Americans, and immigrants – the latter largely from Ireland, Germany, Italy, Austria-Hungary, Belgium and the Netherlands at the time. Though not specifically mentioned by the bishops, internal migration from Mexico and people of Hispanic heritage in Texas, California and the southwest represented either new populations or existing Hispanic and Amerindian communities in those areas. When the bishops met, thirty-seven states comprised the United States with most of that land in the frontier West. A large amount of the energy of the American Catholic Church went toward immigrant populations, to make sure a vigorous pastoral presence and evangelical outreach assisted in maintaining and developing Catholic faith and 'regular' parish life in a land, thought by Europeans to be a 'Protestant' country. To renew and recommit the faith of Catholics, religious orders, especially the Jesuits and Redemptorists, traversed the country preaching one or two week 'missions' in parishes, a practice they continue to the present.

In 1908, the United States and Canada were removed from the jurisdiction of Propaganda Fide and placed within the regular jurisdiction of the Holy See. The bulk of personnel and financial resources were given to the burgeoning immigrant population, who often settled in cities. Many of the needs of new arrivals in North America were filled by a plethora of women's religious communities who responded to the varied situations of immigrant communities. Religious sisters engaged in mission or evangelization through education, social work, medicine, and catechetical instruction, often as pioneers in the fields. Frances Xavier Cabrini (1850-1917) was among the notable sisters in her mission to Italian immigrants in medical and education ministries through the community she founded, the Missionary Sisters of the Sacred Heart. Between 1872 and 1922, 167 new congregations or provinces of women religious were formed, significantly affecting the direction of the North American Catholic Church's mission and evangelization, both for the 'Americanized' and for new immigrants from the Mediterranean and Eastern Europe in the late nineteenth and early twentieth centuries. The growth of a Catholic school system through much of the United States played a key role in the evangelization of hundreds of thousands of grade and high school students. These schools, as well as seminaries, became the locus for the success of the Catholic Students Mission Crusade, with membership of almost a million young people at its height.

National ecclesiastical structures to minister to new immigrants or refugees to the United States began in 1920, when the National Catholic Welfare Conference established a Department of Immigration after the First World War. Following the Second World War, Catholic Relief Services and the Catholic Committee for Refugees assisted in the resettlement of Europeans. Since 1965, Migration and Refugee Services, established by the U.S. Catholic Conference, have provided a number of services to those arriving in the United States because of war or persecution in their home countries. After the Vietnam War, refugees arrived in numbers from Southeast Asia and more recently, immigrants and refugees have come from Central and South America and Africa. Within the last decade, the United States Catholic Mission Association (USCMA), which compiles annual statistics on U.S. Catholics in overseas mission, has included the category of 'cross-cultural' missionary in the United States.

Mission Among Native and African Americans

In Canada, between the mid-1860s and the 1960s, Oblates of Mary Immaculate, who had a strong presence among First Nations, operated many residential schools in Canada, an experience that had conflicting results, according to the Native Americans, the Oblates themselves, and the Canadian government (see Fay 2003). In the United States, the Bureau of Catholic Indian Missions (1848) continued its work, financed to a great extent by Katharine Drexel (1858-1955), who also founded the Sisters of the Blessed Sacrament for Negroes and Indians, with the idea that education was a key to social and economic improvement for people whose lives had been impaired on both counts. While most of the North American Catholic communities were on government reservations, a few urban communities arose, with the one in Milwaukee, Wisconsin being the largest. Begun informally between 1939 and 1946, the Kateri Tekakwitha Conference has strengthened Native American Catholic identity and works toward the evangelization of Native Americans.

The mission to and evangelization of African Americans was the goal of two communities of black women religious founded in the nineteenth century – the Oblates of Providence and the Holy Family Sisters – and the Franciscan Handmaids of Mary founded in 1916 in Savannah, Georgia. Against great odds, these women taught and assisted the poor, and in the case of the Holy Family Sisters, sent their Sisters to minister in the Caribbean.

Discrimination against blacks by Catholics and others prevented black men from entering most North American seminaries. The problem had been addressed in the lay-organized African American Congresses and again by Howard University professor, Thomas Wyatt Turner (1877-1978), a leader among educated black Catholics in Baltimore. As an organizer of the Federated Colored Catholics in 1925, he spoke eloquently for entrance of African American men into seminaries. Two men's communities who particularly identified with this group were the Josephite Fathers, who served African American parishes, and the Society of the Divine Word, who began a preparatory seminary in Bay St Louis, Mississippi for black young men (1923). The first ordained priests from that seminary served in Lafayette, Louisiana parishes, and after World War II some African American Divine Word Fathers and Brothers were sent to Ghana.

In the turmoil of the mid to late 1960s, The Black Catholic Clergy Caucus (1968) and the Black Sisters' Conference (1969) expressed a greater national self-definition, addressed issues related to racism and pledged themselves to the liberation of blacks. The March to Selma, Alabama (1965), by hundreds of Sisters, clergy and laity under the leadership of Martin Luther King, Jr was a watershed for American Catholicism in terms of a strong public and ecumenical witness against racism.

Hispanic Americans

After the Spanish American War (1899), the United States had responsibilities toward Cuba, Puerto Rico, Guam, and the Philippines. Puerto Rico, with a Catholic culture, but not well organized in its Catholicism, went through a process of 'Americanization'. Several U.S. men and women's communities were sent there particularly to establish a Catholic school system. With a large number of Protestants applying to teach in the Philippines, Bishop John Ireland (1838-1918) urged Catholics to do likewise. The Mexican Revolution of 1910 with its subsequent persecution of the Catholic Church resulted in barrio churches north of the Mexican border, exiled clergy, and the opening of the Montezuma Seminary in Las Vegas, New Mexico (1936), for exiled Mexicans to study for the priesthood.

The largest Hispanic immigrant group in the United States before 1965 came from Mexico, Puerto Rico, Cuba, and the Caribbean. While men generally had less of a connection to the parish church, women took responsibility to educate their children in faith. A strong devotional life was a key to Hispanic identity, especially prayer to Our Lady of Guadalupe, a portable image that could be taken along during migratory work as they followed the harvest of vegetables and fruit. The people's mobility made mission/evangelization of Hispanic families more difficult because they remained in an area for a few months and then moved on. The introduction of the *Cursillo* movement from Spain in 1965 energized Hispanic leadership, especially among the men. As was true for many other immigrant groups, the formation of mutual aid societies, *mutualistas,* played an important associational role in Mexican and Catholic identity and as economic and labor forces in the Midwest. In the mid-1960s, leadership among migrant groups, especially through United Farm Worker founders Cesar Chavez (1927-1993) and Delores Huerta (b. 1930), drew the attention of Catholics to the socio-economic and religious plight of migrants. A successful boycott was organized against large California companies that grew grapes and lettuce. While the companies benefitted from the labor and sweat of Hispanics, the migrants lived in substandard housing and suffered from the effects of chemical sprays on crops.

The first Mexican-American ordained bishop, Patricio Flores, and Father Virgilio Elizondo founded the Mexican American Cultural Center (1972), an important gathering place for teaching and research on Hispanic Catholicism and culture. Three pastoral *Encuentros*, or Encounters (1972, 1977, 1985), addressed the needs of Hispanics and subsequently, the U.S. bishops adopted a National Pastoral Plan for Hispanic Ministry (1987). Another level of mission and evangelization with the Hispanic community took place in 2006, when over 2,000 youth gathered at the University of Notre Dame for the first National *Encuentro* of Hispanic Youth Ministry.

Home Missions

Francis Clement Kelley (1870-1948), originally from Prince Edward Island, Canada, had been a pastor in a small, predominantly Protestant town in Michigan. He was impressed with the large churches they built, thinking that imposing buildings marked a stable parish community. Without a church wherein to worship, Kelley maintained, there would not be faith, and 'Christian pride would surely die' (Kelley 1922: 16). He founded the Catholic Church Extension Society in 1906 to raise money to fund missions in heavily Protestant or unchurched areas. He spearheaded two American

Catholic Missionary Congresses (Chicago, 1909; Boston, 1913) that drew together bishops, missionaries, and laity to discuss and act on behalf of all types of mission. The society continues its goal to strengthen Catholic presence in isolated or underserved areas of the United States. A Catholic Church Extension Society formed in 1908 in Canada, though with somewhat different purposes: to assist Ukrainian Catholic and other Eastern European immigrants in building churches, meet their various needs and to anglicize them (Fay 2003:166-169).

The Glenmary Home Missioners were founded by Father Howard Bishop (1886-1953) in 1939 to establish the Catholic Church in rural areas. In addition to the services provided by the Glenmary Fathers and Sisters, the Glenmary Research Center has conducted sociological analysis for the southern and rural United States, where Catholic presence was minimal. Many Catholics remember seeing Glenmary's 'No Priest-land' maps of the United States. Glenmary experience and research was important background in the pastoral letter, *This Land is Home to Me* (1975), written by bishops who served in the Appalachian mountain region. The document addressed justice issues related to coal mining, workers, the misuse of land and subsequent impoverishment of local communities.

National ecclesiastical groups formed to draw together representatives of mission sending and mission funding organizations, individual missionaries, bishops and others interested in mission. After a successful national collaboration during World War I, the U.S. Catholic bishops formed the U.S. Catholic Welfare Council, under whose auspices the American Board of Catholic Missions was begun (1925). Further national configurations worked for mission collaboration and to keep mission before the minds of American Catholics: a Mission Secretariat (1949/50-1969), the U.S. Catholic Mission Council (1969-1981), and the United States Catholic Missionary Association (1981-present). The membership of the latter includes the leadership of mission communities, mission fundraisers, and missionaries, with a goal to foster cross-cultural and global mission.

In 1986 the U.S. bishops' pastoral, *To the Ends of the Earth*, provided an overview of the history of missions in the U.S., a brief theology of mission using the insights of the Second Vatican Council, and encouragement for dioceses to develop mission committees. Local involvement in mission awareness would provide a wider base of education and financial support for missions and would assist the bishops in effecting a greater realization of the essential missionary nature of the Church. Currently, the office of the United States Catholic Conference of Bishops Committee on World Mission is charged with oversight to promote mission *ad gentes* through education and mission animation and to be a liaison with pontifical mission societies.

Mission Education and Formation

Many mission congregations published their own magazines to inform Catholics about their missionaries and to raise money for their support, reflective of the earlier *Jesuit Relations*. By 1930, U.S. Catholics could choose from over forty-five mission magazines available to them. In the first half of the twentieth century, local and national offices of the Society for the Propagation of the Faith (SPF) provided solid mission reading for American Catholics. Joseph McGlinchey in the Boston SPF office translated Paulo Manna, *The Workers are Few* (1911) and *The Conversion of the Pagan World* (1921). Between 1945 and 1950, the National SPF, along with the Missionary Union of the Clergy, published seven volumes of *Missionary Academia* to infuse seminary curricula with mission knowledge. The articles covered a range of mission topics, including a theology of accommodation, laity and overseas missions, interracial justice, world religions, and a geographic perspective on comparative mission approaches around the world. The periodical intended to involve seminarians in the work of the SPF, to provide specific familiarity with missions and to develop a 'mission mindedness'. The furtherance of this academic study was the publication of *Worldmission* (1970-1982), sponsored by the National SPF.

Between 1920 and the late 1960s, the Catholic Students Mission Crusade provided mission education materials in a range of media – study books, pamphlets, radio programs, and plays for high schools, colleges and seminaries. Current creative and dynamic mission education programs in English and Spanish include those produced by the Society of Saint Columban and the Maryknoll Society. Other groups focused on education of adults toward current understandings of mission and ecumenism. The Paulist Fathers' innovative *Living Room Dialogues* (1965) was a popular forum for Catholic adults to discuss practical and theological elements of post-Vatican II mission and ecumenism in the comfort of their homes.

As seminaries sought ways to reform their education and formation programs for future priests in the 1960s, the Servite Fathers, the Order of Friars Minor (Sacred Heart Province), and the Passionists collaborated to form the Catholic Theological Union (CTU) in Chicago, Illinois, in 1968. Shortly thereafter, other men's groups joined them, including several mission congregations. This mission emphasis led to CTU having perhaps the strongest missiology and cross-cultural curriculum among comparable Catholic schools of theology in the United States. Currently twenty-four communities of men provide their seminarians graduate education for priesthood and/or mission in an international and multi-ethnic student body that includes laity. The Dominicans, Jesuits, and Franciscan Friars collaborated in an ecumenical endeavor to coordinate theological programs at the Graduate Theological Union, formed in 1968 in Berkeley, California.

Lay Mission

Many lay missioners both within North America and those going overseas were influenced by Pope Pius XII's encyclical, *Mystici Corporis* (MC 1943), that infused many types of lay mission, including Catholic Action. A particular model of mission – observe, judge, act – undergird the approach of several groups from the 1930s through the 1960s, including the Young Christian Workers, Young Christian Students, and Christian Family Movement. The model reflected the influence of Belgian Canon Joseph Cardijn (1882-1967). His concept emphasized that laity could and should have an influence in their milieu to effect changes for a more just and 'Christian' public sphere. Several lay mission groups, such as the Grail, the Papal Volunteers for Latin America, the Lay Mission Helpers of Los Angeles, and the Women Volunteers for Africa represented the mid-twentieth century numerical growth of lay missioners going overseas. In the last twenty-five years, short-term overseas missions for laity (anywhere from six months to one year) have increased noticeably among U.S. Catholics, as they realize the call to mission through baptism. The USCMA suggests the number to be in the hundreds of thousands, who serve anywhere from a few weeks to a year. Diocesan and parish 'twinning' missions, connecting one diocese or parish in North America with one usually in South America, have also grown more numerous. A recent study indicated that over 330 U.S. parishes have a 'relationship of support' with parishes in Central and South America (McGlone 1997).

Missions Abroad

Prior to the twentieth century, few religious congregations in the United States sent missionaries overseas. World War I, however, created disorder in the European-sponsored missions, and North American Catholics saw the time to be ripe for their involvement in overseas mission. In 1909, the Society of the Divine Word opened a preparatory seminary outside of Chicago to prepare men for missions overseas. In 1911, the Catholic Foreign Mission Society of America (Maryknoll) was founded outside of Ossining, New York, to send missionaries to Asia. In 1918, John Mary Fraser (1877-1962), a priest from the Archdiocese of Toronto, founded the Scarboro Fathers, initially for work in China. A comprehensive pastoral letter of the U.S. Catholic bishops (1919) called for continued work in home and 'foreign' missions. An innovative dimension in mission came in 1925, when medical Doctor Anna Dengel (1892-1980), against great odds in gaining ecclesiastical approval, founded the Medical Mission Sisters, the first women's community dedicated to professional health care to meets the needs of women and children in cultures that did not provide adequate care for them, first in India and then elsewhere.

The geographic focus from the 1920s until the 1950s highlighted Asia, particularly China. Mission emphasized the importance of saving souls, lest they be 'lost forever,' and the establishment of the Catholic Church, because without baptism one would not be saved. Conversion or 'planting' the Church, involved cultural, economic and religious 'elevation'. The assumption was that the missionary was a priest, while religious brothers and sisters were 'auxiliary' to mission work.

Pope Pius XII urged North American Catholics in 1959 to send missioners to South America, against a background of increased Protestant evangelization and the threat of communism gaining structural influence in traditionally Catholic countries. The U.S. bishops created a Latin America Bureau (1960) with John J. Considine, MM (1897-1982) as director. The Bureau played a critical, authoritative role in advising American laity and religious congregations, some of which took on overseas missions for the first time. The Bureau sponsored five Catholic Inter-American Cooperation Program (CICOP) meetings between 1964 and 1972, wherein North Americans learned from progressive Latin American bishops and others of the needs and realities of that part of the world, with the idea to influence public opinion about the connection between social, economic and religious issues.

Theologically, in the last three decades of the twentieth century the mission emphasis moved from re-evangelization to development and then to liberation. The founding of Orbis Books by the Maryknoll Society in 1970 brought theologians from around the world to the attention of North American audiences. The Orbis Book publication of Gustavo Gutiérrez, *A Theology of Liberation: History, Politics, and Salvation* (1973), alerted North Americans to the relationship between unjust socio-economic circumstances and a mission ecclesiology. In the 1990s, particularly in Latin America where thousands had disappeared, were tortured or murdered, North American missioners, along with their South American counterparts, stressed reconciliation as a needed value in mission. In 2004, Stephen Bevans and Roger Schroeder published *Constants in Context: A Theology of Mission for Today* (2004), in which the understanding of mission was developed as an action of 'prophetic dialogue', constituted by the elements of witness and proclamation; liturgy, prayer, and contemplation; justice, peace, and the integrity of creation; inter-religious dialogue, inculturation, and reconciliation.

Conclusion

From the beginning of missions to and within the Americas, there was an intercontinental relationship through linked cultures, geography, history, religion and commerce. Even though North American Catholics dealt with constantly changing demographic patterns, they also sent men and women in mission overseas. The greatest number of U.S. missionaries are in Latin America. The inter-relationship of the two continents and the common problems, needs, and proposed responses to migration were highlighted in a pastoral issued jointly by the Mexican and U.S. bishops, *Strangers No Longer: Together on the Journey of Hope* (2003). Women have been and remain by far the majority of missionaries, whether in the U.S. or abroad.

The experience of Roman Catholics, probably the most ethnically diverse group of religious adherents in twentieth century North America, reflected the startling changes in global Catholicism and a concomitant change in the church's self-understanding. While the Catholic Church has long thought of itself as 'universal,' the concept tended to center upon a somewhat disembodied 'substance' that appeared in the church around the world in the accidents of race, ethnicity, and social locations. More recently, a world Catholicism embodied in multiple cultures reflected nuances in the appropriation and expression of the faith and a practice of mission to and from six continents. As expressed at the USCMA sponsored *Mission Congress 2000*, mission had expanded to include a 'global endeavor that reaches not only areas where a small percentage of the population is Christian, but also traditionally Christian areas such as Europe and the United States where secularization is challenging and displacing religion in urbanized communities' (USCMA 2000).

CATHOLIC MISSION IN OCEANIA AND THE PACIFIC 1910-2010

Lawrence Nemer, SVD

The Synod of Bishops of Oceania was held in Rome from November 22 until December 12, 1998. Eighty-two of the eighty-five bishops who headed dioceses in Australia, New Zealand, and the Polynesian, Micronesian, and Melanesian Pacific Island Nations were present. The fact that they were for the most part indigenous people representing not missions but local churches clearly indicated the significant change that had taken place in course of the twentieth century.

John Paul II, in his post-synodal apostolic exhortation *Ecclesia in Oceania* (EO) published in November 2001, recognized Oceania as 'a unique area spanning almost one-third of the earth's surface' with 'a large number of Indigenous peoples' who had accepted the gospel. 'These peoples form a unique part of humanity in a unique region of the world.' He acknowledged that while Oceania was geographically very large, much of it being water, its population was relatively small (EO 6). While in Australia the population grew from three million plus in 1900 to twenty-two million plus in 2010, and in New Zealand from 823,000 in 1900 to four million plus in 2010, in all of the island nations combined the total population in 1900 was only about two million people and in 2000 only between four and six million.

In this study, after some initial remarks about the local churches of Australia and New Zealand and their 'missions' to the indigenous peoples, the development from mission to church in the various Pacific Island Nations can only be noted since its history is still to be written. By the end of the nineteenth century the overwhelming majority of Pacific Islanders were Christians, either Protestant or Catholic, depending on whose missionaries arrived first. Evangelization was done both by European and Pacific Islander missionaries. The one exception to this pattern were the Melanesian Islands where the evangelization of the peoples for the most part took place in the twentieth century. Finally reference will be made to some of the significant institutions that have been developed in this part of the world to further Catholic living as well as ecumenical cooperation.

Australia

Since the end of the eighteenth century European convicts and immigrants arrived in Australia. In the course of the nineteenth century they began to form a distinctive identity, calling themselves Australians. These were for the most part Europeans. They brought their faith and their ministers with them. Australia was seen by the Propaganda Fide in Rome to be the mission of the Catholic English and Irish Churches. The English Benedictines had an impact on the early development of the Australian Catholic Church, but it was the Irish clergy and religious that dominated the growth and institutional development of the church in the nineteenth and twentieth centuries.

There was a missionary consciousness among Australian Catholics even as they were forming their own church. The Columban Mission Calendar, Maytime Fairs, Jackie Mite Boxes and publications such as *Catholic Missions, Word,* and *The Far East* all contributed to it. However, it was the destruction of the many overseas missions in the Pacific during World War II, especially in New Guinea, that made Australian Catholics deeply aware of these missions and brought recruits to the various missionary orders in Australia. The peak period in this missionary movement was the mid-1970s. In 1972 alone there were over 1250 Australian Catholics involved in overseas mission work full-time. (D'Orsa: 2000: 35-36.) Most were priests, brothers, and sisters; however a large number of lay missionaries were sent to New Guinea by the Paulian Australian Lay Missionary Society (PALMS). The Religious Congregations with Australian members who were being sent out at this time were: Franciscan Missionaries of Mary, Missionaries of the Sacred Heart, Our Lady of the Sacred Heart Society, Marist Fathers and Brothers, Divine Word Missionaries, Marist Missionary Sisters, Salesians, Little Company of Mary, Mercy Sisters, Sisters of St Joseph, Christian Brothers, Sisters of St Joseph of Cluny, and Sisters and Brothers of St John of God. The Columbans set up a Pacific Mission Institute in 1972 to train these departing missionaries. Fr Cyril Hally, SSC, played a significant role in their training and in the development of the institute.

Immediately after Vatican II the Australian bishops set up a National Missionary Council (NMC) to coordinate the national missionary effort in the late 1960s, but it proved not to be very effective. A national conference held in 1972 resulted in the establishment of a permanent NMC Secretariat to facilitate dialogue among mission congregations and to coordinate mission education nationally. For reasons that are not clear to this day the Australian bishops disbanded the NMC in 1986. (D'Orsa 2000: 7)

As John Paul II noted: 'The largest country of Oceania in both size and population is Australia, where the Aboriginal people have lived for thousands of years, moving over large tracts of land and living in deep harmony with nature' (EO 6). He goes on to say:

> The relationship of the Church to the Aboriginal peoples and the Torres Strait Islanders remains important and difficult because of past and present injustices and cultural differences ... Whenever the truth has been suppressed by governments and their agencies or even by Christian communities, the

wrongs done to the indigenous peoples need to be honestly acknowledged ... The past cannot be undone, but honest recognition of past injustices can lead to measures and attitudes which will help to rectify the damaging effects for both the indigenous community and the wider society. The Church expresses deep regret and asks forgiveness where her children have been or still are party to these wrongs. Aware of the shameful injustices done to indigenous peoples in Oceania, the Synod Fathers apologized unreservedly for the part played in these by members of the Church, especially where children were forcibly separated from their families (EO 6).

The Aboriginal members of the 'Stolen Generation' welcomed this apology.

The Catholic Church from its arrival in the early nineteenth century was concerned about the Aboriginals. There were repeated attempts to reach out to them. The activity of Polding and the Passionists at Stradbroke Island, the enterprise of Dom Salvador in New Norcia, the mission of the Trappists and Pallottines in the Kimbeleys, and the attempts made by the Jesuits in the Northern Territory each deserve a chapter in the history of the Catholic Church in Australia. And yet there was little lasting success. The Catholic Church has found difficulty in recognizing and empowering Aboriginal Christian leaders.

The history of the Catholic Church's involvement in Aboriginal Ministry in the twentieth century still needs to be written. The Missionaries of the Sacred Heart, the Jesuits, and the Divine Word Missionaries, among the male congregations have taken an active role in this ministry. Mercy Sisters, Loreto Sisters, Sisters of St John of God, Sisters of St Joseph of Cluny and Sisters of Our Lady of the Sacred Heart have also made significant contributions to the mission outreach to the Aboriginals.

New Zealand

John Paul II wrote: 'The original inhabitants of New Zealand, an island nation, were the Maori people who called their country *Aotearoa, 'Land of the Great White Cloud.'* Colonization and later immigration have shaped the nation into a bi-cultural society, where integration of Maori and Western culture remains a pressing challenge. Foreign missionaries first proclaimed the gospel to the Maori people. Then when the European settlers came in greater numbers, priests and religious came as well and helped to maintain and develop the Church.' (EO 6). He went on to say: 'When the missionaries first brought the Gospel to Aboriginal or Maori people, or to the island nations, they found peoples who already possessed an ancient and profound sense of the sacred. Religious practices and rituals were very much part of their daily lives and thoroughly permeated their cultures' (EO 7).

Europeans appeared in the early nineteenth century and by the time it was made a British Colony in 1840 there were at least 5,000 Europeans living in the islands, about 500 of them Catholic. That year 46 Maori head chiefs signed the Treaty of Waitangi; it recognized the suzerainty of Queen Victoria in return for the preservation of land and tribal rights.

In the nineteenth century the Marists and Mill Hill Missionaries were evangelizing the Maori while the white settlers were engaged in a series of wars with them over land rights. After the wars many Irish soldiers settled in New Zealand. The early pioneers in the development of the Catholic Church were Bishop Jean Pompallier who arrived in 1839 and later Bishop Patrick Moran. Already in the nineteenth century the church was engaged in education and building cathedrals. By 1910 the church was already established among the immigrants since it numbered 126,995 Catholics out of a total European settler population of 888,578.

During the first half of the twentieth century the church had a friendly relationship with the government. This improved after World War II when the government agreed to help the Catholics in their educational program. By 1950 there was one archdiocese (Wellington) and five dioceses. As in Australia the 1970s saw an increase of missionary vocations among the religious congregations destined for the South Pacific.

The principal male religious orders serving in New Zealand were the Marist Fathers, Marist Brothers, Redemptorists and Trappists. The women religious included the Sisters of Mercy, Congregation of Our Lady of the Missions, and Sisters of St Joseph of the Sacred Heart. (Broadbent 2003: 328*)*. According to the census of 2006 there were 508,437 Catholics – 12.3% of the total population of 4,143,279 people.

The Maoris are thought to have arrived in New Zealand around AD 800. The first missionaries to arrive were Protestant in the early 1800s; later in 1839 Bishop Jean Pompallier arrived. While there was some outreach to the Maoris it was only after the wars with the settlers were ended that the Marists and Mill Hill Missionaries revived the Maori Mission.

After World War II the Maori moved into the cities and took advantage of the education made available to them. The injustices committed after The Treaty of Waitangi began to be addressed, often at the urging of the Catholic bishops. The bishops too encouraged the appointment of the first Maori bishop, Takuira Mariu of the Society of Mary, in 1988. 'The bishops also established a national Maori *runanga*, or council, with representatives of Maori lay, religious and clergy. The council supported and advised the New Zealand Catholic Bishops' Conference on all matters relating to the pastoral care of Maori people' (Broadbent 2003: 328).

Polynesia and Micronesia

John Paul II pointed out: 'The island nations of Polynesia and Micronesia are relatively small, each with its own indigenous language and culture. They too are facing the pressures and challenges of a contemporary world ... some of which are facing a very uncertain future, not only because of large-scale emigration but also because of rising sea levels caused by global warming. For them, climate change is very much more than a question of economics' (EO 6).

Polynesia

The inhabitants of the Polynesian islands were organized in family structures with certain rituals. They tended to have kings/queens; and so when the kings/queens were converted, the whole island was converted. Thus by the beginning of the twentieth century, most of these islands were Christian.

The development of the local church in these islands in the twentieth century during which indigenous leadership and forms of religious life were developed still needs to be written. Here we can only make some observations about some of the island nations.

Tahiti (French Polynesia), first evangelized by Protestants, is today predominantly Protestant. However, some individual islands, e.g. Mangareva and Tuamotou, converted by French missionaries in the nineteenth century, to this day remain totally Catholic. Catholics in all of French Polynesia make up about 30% of an estimated population of 266,300 in 2010.

The Cook Islands began to be evangelized by Catholics in 1894 by which time the Protestant churches were solidly established. Catholics made up only a small percentage of the population throughout the twentieth century and to this day (2010) make up only about 10% in a population of about 21,200.

Wallis and Futuna are 99% Catholic in an estimated population of 15,900 in 2010. The Marists arrived in the early 1840s, and the success of the Catholic Church is attributed to the martyrdom of Peter Chanel in 1841 and the support of the Catholic royalty.

The Wesleyans arrived in Tonga in the early nineteenth century and sparked a mass movement into the church. Catholics could not enter until the middle of that century. By 1900 the islands were 100% Christian. It is estimated that Roman Catholics make up about 20% of a population of about 110,000 in 2010.

The Marists arrived in the Samoan Islands in 1845. The Catholic population remained small. In 1962 some of the islands proclaimed their independence and thus Samoa is now divided between American Samoa and the Independent State of Samoa. In 2010 Catholics in American Samoa made up 20% of the population estimated at 57,900, while Catholics in the Independent State made up a much smaller percentage in an estimated population of 177,700.

Micronesia

The Northern Marianas, a Spanish possession until the end of the nineteenth century, sold Guam to the United States and the other islands to Germany. By 2010 the overwhelming majority of the 78,300 inhabitants of the islands were Catholics.

Guam, which had already been evangelized in the seventeenth and eighteenth centuries by the Spanish Jesuits, was in the twentieth century guided in its church development first from Cebu and then from the Marianas. Since in 1965 it was made a suffragan of the archdiocese of San Francisco, many North American religious came to work there after World War II. In 2010 Catholics made up about 85% of a population estimated at 166,100.

The Federated States of Micronesia, which includes the Caroline Islands, had been evangelized by the Spanish, and in 2010 in a population of 108,200 Catholics numbered about 50%. In the Marshall Islands, there is just a very small Catholic population among the 57,500 people present in the islands in 2010.

The islands of Kiribati were almost totally Christian by the end of the nineteenth century. Some islands are totally Catholic, and some totally Protestant. In 2010 in a total population of 100,800, 52% were Catholic.

Melanesia

The southwest area of the Pacific consists of larger islands with more varied peoples and languages. They are suspicious of outsiders. Their division into tribes and villages was for their protection, and so they needed to be converted village by village.

Wesleyans arrived in Fiji in the 1800s and persuaded the chief to resist the entry of Catholics. During the twentieth century, however, the Marists and Columbans arrived. In 2010 in a population of 880,900 only 9% were Catholic.

Both British and French settled the island of New Caledonia in the nineteenth century, driving the original inhabitants into the mountains. Catholics arrived first but the mission developed slowly. In 2010 there was an estimated mixed black and white population of 213,700, 60% being Catholic.

Both British and French also settled in New Hebrides (Vanuatu) in the nineteenth century. Wesleyans and Presbyterians arrived first; Catholic Marists appeared late in that century. Of the 202,600 inhabitants only 15% were Catholic in 2010.

The Solomon Islands, a chain of islands, were evangelized by the Marists in the nineteenth century. In 2010 the population was 523,600, about 18% of them Catholic.

Papua New Guinea, which became an independent state in 1975, included some islands that formerly belonged to the Solomons (e.g.

Bougainville) and some to the German protectorate (New Britain and New Ireland). It also combined the southern part of the island, Papua, which had been under Australia, with the northern part that had been under Germany until 1918 and afterwards under Australia. The evangelization in each of these territories has its own story to tell. Most of the mission work was done during the twentieth century. It began on the coasts and only in the 1930s moved into the highlands. The missions suffered greatly during the time of the Japanese occupation. After the war there was a resurgence of missionary activity. In 2010 of the 5,420,000 people on the island about 22% was Catholic.

Some Significant Institutional Developments

Seminaries

The first major regional seminary was established at Vunapope in 1937 and its first intake of twenty-four seminarians were from the Vicariates of Rabaul, North Solomons and Papua. Five of these students were later ordained, among them the future bishops Herman To Paivu and George Bata (both of Rabaul). Minor seminaries were set up after the war and the students completed their theological studies at Holy Spirit Regional Seminary at Kap, near Madang, staffed by the Divine Word Missionaries. In 1968 the seminary was transferred to Bomana where the Missionaries of the Sacred Heart had already opened de Boismenu Seminary and the two were joined. Later other congregations moved to Bomana, resulting in seven affiliate colleges whose students were being trained at Holy Spirit Seminary. In 1994 the institution was divided into Holy Spirit Seminary which provides for the spiritual dimension of priestly formation and the Catholic Theological Institute of Port Moresby which looks after the intellectual formation of the candidates.

The Pacific Regional Seminary in Fiji was set up by the Episcopal Conference of the Pacific in 1972, supported by some of the religious congregations working in the Pacific: the Marists, the Vincentians, the Missionaries of the Sacred Heart, the Columbans, and the Salesians. A new campus was established in 1973. In the 1980s the various religious congregations set up their own houses of formation. Since its beginning the seminary has had between 100 and 140 students each year. The Pacific Regional Seminary is a member of the South Pacific Association of Theological Schools, an ecumenical association established by the Pacific churches in 1969.

Hierarchy and Episcopal conferences

In 1966, after Vatican II, the hierarchy was officially established in most of
the island states of the South Pacific, thus bringing the official structure of
the church into line with that in Australia and New Zealand and most of the
Catholic world.

The Catholic Conference of Australian Bishops was first organized in
1958; the New Zealand Catholic Conference of Bishops appeared in 1967.
That same year the Catholic Bishops' Conference of Papua New Guinea
and Solomon Islands was established and in 1970 the *Conferentia
Episcopalis Pacifici* (CEPAC) was formed which included American
Samoa, Cook Islands, Fiji, French Polynesia, Guam, Kiribati, Marshall
Islands, Micronesia, New Caledonia, Northern Mariana Islands, Samoa,
Tonga, Tuvalu, Vanuatu, and Wallis and Futuna. The Federation of
Catholic Bishops' Conferences of Oceania (FCBCO) composed of the
above four conferences came about in 1992. The periodic gatherings of
these conferences have played an important role in the development of the
local Church in the late twentieth century.

Melanesian Institute for Pastoral and Socio-Economic Service

The Association of Clerical Religious Superiors of Papua New Guinea and
the British Solomon Islands Protectorate brought this institute into
existence. Fr Herman Janssens, MSC, was appointed the first director and
the first orientation course was held in January 1970 in Vunapope.
According to its Constitution: 'The Melanesian Institute will serve the local
Churches and the peoples of Melanesia. It will assist missionaries or full
time church workers, both Melanesian and overseas, in Papua New Guinea
and the British Solomon Islands, to be better equipped for pastoral and
socio-economic service.' It does this through orientation and in-service
courses and seminars while also pursing research. The Institute publishes a
quarterly magazine *CATALYST* and occasional reports with the title *POINT*
followed by a number. In 1973 staff quarters, a library and an office were
built in the central town of Goroka. Since 1971, the Lutheran, United and
Anglican Churches joined in the various courses, publications and research
projects. (Janssen 1994: 30-33). The institute has played a significant role
in the development of the local church in the Melanesian Islands.

CATHOLIC MISSIONARY MOVEMENTS OF THE TWENTIETH CENTURY

Mary Motte, FMM

Introduction

Unfolding insights into the transformative process of twentieth century missiology point to the dynamic creativity of the gospel-propelling mission (Bevans and Schroeder 2004). The colonial perspective in the first half of the century framed missionary concerns with the expansion of Christianity throughout the world. As the century progressed, the right of every person to hear the gospel (see RM 46), as well as the missionary responsibility of every baptized person (LG 17, AG 28, 35-38) triggered motivation for changes. The Western-dominated church gave way to a global church with local leadership on every continent, and appearance of new approaches.

Moving forward from 1900, missionaries challenged static understandings and practices. Contributions from the world church gradually changed mission theology and praxis by developing new insights, enriched with multiple cultural perspectives.

Expansion of Christianity

In 1908 the American Catholic Church transitioned from a mission church made up of immigrants and ministered to by mainly European immigrants to a church assuming its responsibility for world mission. Catholic participation in the missionary movement was also strongly influenced by the American Protestant John R. Mott and the Student Volunteer Movement for Foreign Missions. The energy, enthusiasm, spirit of sacrifice that characterized these young men and women fired generations to evangelize the world in their lifetime. This awakening among Protestants birthed a new missionary vision in James Anthony Walsh and Thomas Frederick Price, a vision that became the Catholic Foreign Mission Society of the United States (Maryknoll Fathers and Brothers). Very soon, Josephine Rogers began the Maryknoll Sisters of St Dominic (*www.maryknoll.org*). Maryknoll communicated the gospel to those who had not heard the Word of God from within the ethos of American culture.

New missionary societies of men and women advanced the Catholic Missionary Movement in Europe. For example, the Society of the Divine Word (SVD) started mission houses and mission days in Germany.

Growing Catholic commitment to foreign mission accompanied the continuing Protestant surge.

In 1910 the World Mission Conference was held in Edinburgh, and was credited with beginning the modern ecumenical and mission movements. Brian Stanley, in his noted book on the conference, quotes the Boston *Missionary Herald* proclaiming that it was 'the most important ecclesiastical assembly since Nicea' – an opinion, perhaps a bit exaggerated (!) that was common at the time (Stanley 2009: 16). There was no official Roman Catholic representation at Edinburgh 1910. However, an elderly Italian Catholic Bishop, Geremia Bonomelli of Cremona, Italy reached well beyond both Catholic and Protestant understanding of the time, writing to the gathering to encourage further growth in ecumenical collaboration (Delaney 2000: 418-31).

Roman Catholic participation in the Commission on World Mission and Evangelism (CWME) of the World Council of Churches (WCC) began in 1963 and continues, with full-time consultants on the WCC Program staffs of CWME, Justice Peace and the Integrity of Creation (JPIC) and the Bossey Institute. There are also twelve Catholic theologians appointed to the international Faith and Order Commission, and consultants are officially appointed by the Holy See to major meetings of the WCC and CWME (Rausch and Gross 1998: 516).

As American commitment to mission grew, a crusade-like image *to capture the world for Christ,* captivated the minds of Catholics. Two SVD seminarians, Clifford J. King and Robert B. Clark, inspired by the Protestant students as well as by the SVD German 'Mission Days', founded the Catholic Students Mission Crusade (CSMC) in 1918. Its purpose was mission education. The organization grew rapidly to over one million youth, supporting missionaries in the field, promoting missionary vocations, and educating youth about the needs of the church throughout the world. Large numbers of Catholic youth grew to savor enthusiasm for world mission (Endres 2010: 37-46). The CSMC ended in 1969, following Vatican II, which had opened new vistas for mission with a more relational approach towards the world. Yet the visions of the Protestant Mott and the Catholics King and Clark imbued Christians with a lively spirit that continues to challenge many imaginations.

In 1962 John XXIII, carrying forward an idea of Maryknoll Missioner John R. Considine, called for religious congregations to send ten percent of their personnel to the church in Latin America. This proposal included Canada, United States and eventually Europe. A generous response came from the newly founded Missionary Society of St James the Apostle, Maryknoll, and international congregations who eventually wrote a memorable chapter in the history of both missiology and inter-American relations (Quigley 2009: 20). Collaborations with Latin American counterparts accompanied a deepening awareness of the significance of the incarnation. These partnerships were strengthened through faith stretched by experiences among the poor, the painful realization of underlying injustices, and theological reflection. Missionaries and their partners began to see in new ways helped by liberation theology, the practice of which also spread to other continents. Many institutions experienced profound restructuring through theological visioning embedded in the incarnation. A new era of martyrdom emerged in the world as thousands were arrested, tortured, or assassinated by oppressive regimes or wealthy landowners.

Well past the half-century mark, missionary orders of men and women especially from Europe and North America dominated the mission field in Asia, Africa and Latin America. Occasionally some lay missionaries worked with them. The Society for the Propagation of the Faith and the Holy Childhood Association, both of which continue today exerted great effort to raise consciousness and support for mission throughout Europe and North America.

Rights and Responsibilities

A rush of missiological chaos burst in the aftermath of Vatican II. In addition to raising serious theological considerations, the Council affirmed the missionary nature of the church and the missionary responsibility of every baptized person. The Council provided the immediate context for this chaos, but there was a contributing factor in the emerging post-colonial world as its newly independent countries sought confirmation for ancient but debilitated cultural identities.

A number of clerical or religious missionary societies, recognizing the missionary responsibility of all the baptized, initiated lay mission groups. The Latin American Bishops Conferences (CELAM), met in Medellin in 1968, gifting mission theology with insights and questions drawn from liberation theology. Concerns about poverty, injustice, identity, and just relationships accompanied efforts to communicate the gospel. The Synod of Bishops in 1971 indicated clearly that action on behalf of justice is constitutive of evangelization. Mission became more concisely expressed as evangelization after the Synod of Bishops in 1974. *Evangelii Nuntiandi* (EN 1975), the papal document issued after the Synod, examined various situations in modern society as challenges to evangelization. John Paul II, 1978-2005, frequently called for a New Evangelization. In *Redemptoris Missio* (1990) he, reiterated the right of all to hear the gospel (RM 46), and introduced the idea of the *areopagi* (RM 37) as challenges to evangelization. Missionary practices expressing this understanding had already surfaced in various parts of the world. John Paul II's missionary travels and outreach to ordinary people and the poor, witnessed the missionary fiber of a global church. New insights and practices forged innovative ways of missiological thinking and training. While missionary societies of women and men continued as important contributors to this

thinking and action, very meaningful inputs were coming from lay groups
and episcopal conferences throughout the world.

Lay Missionaries

Lay mission groups increased rapidly after Vatican II, and provide insights
into the vigorous, growing image of mission activity. The trajectory of
many of these groups illustrates their effective assuming of missionary
responsibility in various local churches throughout the world. Mission
societies sponsoring lay missionaries include the Society of African
Missions, Combonis, Maryknoll, Missionaries of Africa, Colombans, and
Scarboro Missions along with several others. A number of episcopal
conferences and dioceses on each of the continents have lay missionary
groups. At times a lay mission group, begun initially by a missionary
society, eventually became associated with a national bishops' conference
in a specific country. This was the case of the Philippine Catholic Lay
Mission (*www.philcatholiclaymission.com*), begun by Maryknoll and the
Japan Lay Missionary Movement (*www.jlmm.net*), begun by Fr Michael
Siegel, SVD and associated initially with the Volunteer Missionary
Movement, treated below. The Episcopal Conference of Mexico began the
Evangelizadores de Tiempo Completo, fully trained catechists who are sent
as evangelizers to different parishes in four countries (*www.
evangelizadores.org*).

Edwina Gateley began the Volunteer Missionary Movement (VMM) in
England in 1969. This independent lay community which is now
international, receives members of all Christian faith traditions. Both
women and men, single and married, and families are included. They serve
in Central America, Africa and the United States (*www.vmmusa.org*).

Among volunteer groups in the United States are The Catholic Volunteer
Network (1963 – *www.ncnvs.org*), and St Vincent Pallotti Center (1984 –
www.pallotticenter.org). They promote lay volunteer service and support
faith-based programs that sponsor volunteers through training, networking
and advocacy. In 1956 the Jesuits of Oregon Province (United States)
started the Jesuit Volunteers. The volunteers live together in apostolic
communities. Every year there are approximately three hundred volunteers
working in the United States and in six other countries
(*www.jesuitvolunteers.org*).

While hardly complete, these few glimpses hold new missiological
insights. In the second half of the century there has been a burgeoning of
groups concerned with communicating the gospel. Many of them share
these significant elements:

- lay persons predominate even though some include religious men
  and women among their members;
- activities present a wide variety of activities through which
  members are committed to live and communicate the gospel;

- their dedication and activities illustrate how fidelity to the gospel leads them into new *areopagi* and/or how new *areopagi* challenge them to discover new expressions of fidelity to the gospel (RM 37c);
- just relationships across boundaries take on a new importance in globalization and this includes collaboration with a network of partners;
- incarnational theology has taken greater hold of Christian consciousness, and increasingly provides insights about how to approach those still unreached by the gospel;
- they are generally international in scope.

Ecclesial Movments

The post-conciliar period in the world church discloses a continual emergence of lay ecclesial movements and new communities. The Vatican lists these groups as *International Associations of the Faithful.* They are also frequently referred to as ecclesial movements. These groups are generally composed of laity, and while having diverse purposes, a number are international with ministerial focus on the poor and evangelization. They bear the common characteristic of 'the newness which baptismal grace brings to life', and that: 'give rise to a renewed missionary zeal which reaches out to the men and women of our era in the concrete situations where they find themselves, and turns its loving attention to the dignity, needs and destiny of each individual' (John Paul II 1998). Their purpose is: '... to proclaim the joy of believing in Jesus Christ and to renew the commitment to be faithful disciples in our time ... They are one of the most important innovations inspired by the Holy Spirit in the Church for the implementation of the Second Vatican Council' (Benedict XVI 2008). These movements have not always been spoken of as *missionary* movements. However, their characteristics of *renewed missionary zeal* and being *faithful disciples in our time*, suggest a commitment to evangelization that warrants inclusion of those which are motivated by the right of every person to hear to gospel

The International Conference of Catholic Organizations (CICO) brings together different Catholic international associations in a forum for reflection, dialogue and concerted action. They are committed to making their own contribution to international initiatives by responding to challenges from contemporary political, economic, social, cultural and religious contexts. Today the member organizations of the CICO choose to fully live their faith in Jesus Christ by being a Christian presence in the world. While begun in the first half of the century, this ecclesial movement illustrates the developmental model directing members to serve the improvement of all humanity. They commit themselves to interfaith listening and dialogue; and give priority, in the light of the gospel, to the poorest. They work for peace, fellowship and justice, emphasizing respect, promotion of human rights and dignity, and the safeguarding of creation.

Maximilian Kolbe, a Polish Conventual Franciscan, began the Militia of the Immaculata in 1922. Its purpose was to promote expansion of the kingdom of God throughout the world by means of Our Lady of the Immaculate Conception. This movement continues to grow through the efforts of the Conventual Franciscans; it is international with more than three million members today and exists in 48 countries. Members can be priests, religious (men and women), lay persons.

The Focolare Movement, began in Italy in 1944, continues today. John Paul II referred to the charism of Chiara Lubich, foundress of the Focolare Movement, as '*a radicalism of love*' and saw in the Movement influences from Vatican II through its openness to various dialogues (1984). The Focolare 'share with *humanity the painful birth of a new civilization* that is globalised, interdependent, and made up of many faiths and cultures.' Similar to the Militia of the Immaculata, Focolare membership is inclusive; it also extends beyond denominational and faith boundaries (*www. focolare.org*).

A further brief note about some other associations suggests how they share a missionary purpose:

- ADSIS (Associación de Servicios Iniciativa Social [Association of Social Services Initiative]) Community, begun in Spain, working in Europe and Latin America with the poor;
- Bread of Life Community, begun in France, now in twenty-five countries on all continents for evangelization and the poor;
- Christian Life Movement, begun in Peru, now in twenty-one countries, four continents with special focus on announcing and witnessing to faith in Jesus Christ;
- Community of the Beatitudes, begun in France, now in twenty-nine countries, seven continents, works for evangelization and in service to the poor;
- Couples for Christ, begun in Manila, now in seventy-six countries, six continents, committed to the work of evangelization and with the poor;
- Emmanuel Community, begun in France, in fifty-seven countries, seven continents, with attention to reconciliation, building a fraternal life and evangelization;
- Encounters of Youth Promotion, begun in Colombia, now in fourteen countries, three continents for the service of evangelization;
- Institute for World Evangelization, begun in Malta, now in ten countries on four continents for the service of evangelization.
- the Community of San Egidio, of Italian origin, is especially known for its commitment to peacemaking and conflict mediation.

There are several additional groups not included here. With very few exceptions, these groups have begun after Vatican II. There are also various evangelization movements working under the bishops' conferences.

During the last years of John Paul II's pontificate the episcopal conferences met concerning the mission of the church in their specific continent. The entire process indicates how churches have assumed responsibility for evangelization and mission within their cultural contexts. They are seeking deeper rootedness of their experiences of the gospel through the ethos of their people. For example, the Aparecida Conference of the Latin American Episcopal Conferences (CELAM 2007), after extensive preparation and participation, shows how being missionary disciples of Jesus is at the heart of all aspects of evangelization. An important missiological vision is in the process of being realized through these developments.

An Emerging Future

Mission in the twentieth century has moved from an awakening imbued with a powerful hope to bring the whole world to Christ towards a deepening insight about the incarnation, commitment to evangelization, and a growing convergence of concern about the environment and the universe. This movement of mission has been crafted with input from ecumenism, cultural diversity, globalization and especially by lay persons assuming responsibility for mission. New theological insights with roots in Vatican II and the experience of so many peoples have brought further development through deepening awareness of scripture, prophecy, reconciliation and witness.

As the twentieth century approached its close, images from the Hubble Telescope led many scientists to recognize the evolutionary nature of the universe which continues to unfold (Haught 2007: 105-6, 128-31). Scientific discovery has been deepening our awareness of the devastation on earth and in the universe (Edwards 2008: 2-4; McFague 2008: 9-40). Further scientific studies have indicated that all of life is interrelated, emergent and evolving (Stoeger 2007: 229-47). These facts confront theologians with questions about what kind of God creates an unfinished universe (Delio 2010: 8-9). Theologian Ilia Delio states that 'Newness is what defines the revelation of God in Jesus Christ', and suggests that we need to revisit the God of the New Testament as the God who does new things. (Delio 2010: 9). Further insights about the God of the Absolute Future who calls us into the communion of relationship with the Trinity, challenge us to rethink our understanding of God (Delio 2010: 3-22; Edwards 2009: 159-195; 2010:1-8; Haught 2007: 43; see also Edwards's essay in this volume). We are theologically required to discern the implications of new scientific discoveries for our understanding of God and the meaning of discipleship. How does this agenda of newness push us to reshape our self-understanding as missionaries who are disciples?

We are confronted with the rapidly increasing number of lay persons committed to the ministry of evangelization, especially to the poor. Many of them, through collaboration and dialogue, seek ways of bringing the gospel to all who have the right to hear the Word of God. Missionary orders of men and women continue to explore new avenues in mission, collaborate with lay partners, and network with others in various ways. A globalized world is urging us to discover just relationships with everyone, including those who are different, who are *other*. We believe in a Trinitarian God who invites us into a communion of relationship. God who is God of the Future and God of the New, is calling us into the future by provoking us to contemplate a humble God (Haught 2007:44; 2010: 64-65; Edwards 2010: 185-186; Delio 2010: 15, 2005: 49-67).

Many of the transformations in mission in the past century can be recognized as new ways of seeing, and many of them are still in process. God who creates an unfinished universe and who is God of the New invites us to explore insights about how to be an evangelizing, missionary disciple. Twentieth century contributions to theoretical missiology, missionary practice, and the new impulses from the various ways in which mission has evolved point to a fresh approach to discipleship. Innovative ways of seeing leads into unexplored territory and new challenges.

CATHOLIC WOMEN IN MISSION 1910-2010

Susan Smith, RNDM

The opportunity to reflect on the role of Catholic missionary women in the decades since 1910 is indeed welcome, as the issues raised at the Edinburgh Conference of that year provide a benchmark against which Catholic missionary practice since 1910 can be measured. Three issues highlighted by the Conference – indigenization of Christianity, inter-religious dialogue, the emergence of a world church – would not have been perceived as significant for most Catholic missionaries before Vatican II (see Phan 2010: 105-108). However, in the last century, Catholic missionary women have experienced and initiated significant changes in their exercise of mission. Such changes should not be attributed to the Edinburgh Conference but rather to influences within Catholicism that pre-dated Edinburgh and to Vatican II (1962-1965), which transformed the way in which Catholics often thought of mission and missionaries.

Catholic Women and Mission Prior to Vatican II

A number of factors that influenced Catholic missionary activity in general and the role of women in particular in the sixty years before Vatican II had their origins in the first decades of the nineteenth century, that is, several decades before Edinburgh. Nevertheless, their importance continued through to Vatican II, almost sixty years after Edinburgh. These included the French Revolution as its persecution of Catholics seemed to spell the collapse of the institutional church in France. However, far from causing the disappearance of religion, the nineteenth century church emerged as an important missionary force.

Secondly, the dominant Ultramontanist ecclesiology associated with the post-revolutionary church was often 'good news' for many newly founded congregations of Catholic Sisters in Europe and North America. These congregations were established as pontifical institutes. This allowed them a qualified autonomy in respect of governance and lifestyle though they were responsible to the local bishop in respect of apostolic works. Furthermore pontifical status did not encourage new congregations of women being under the authority of a male superior general. Although Vatican policy should not be regarded as an early expression of feminism, being beholden to the Vatican was often a better option in a pre-Vatican II church than being beholden to the local bishop.

Thirdly, the missionary work of Catholic women was welcomed by Europe's imperial powers and the United States who recognized the important contribution that missionary congregations could make in their newly acquired lands or spheres of influence. Older and newly founded religious congregations of Catholic Sisters were essential actors in the extraordinary missionary outreach that was supported by and which in turn often supported the colonizing powers. This is apparent in the involvement of sisters in English and French medium schools in pre-colonial India or Vietnam.

The missionary activity of Catholic women expressed itself in different ways. The Judaeo-Christian tradition had always identified care of the poor as a priority (see Is. 61:1-4; Lk. 4:16-19), but ministry to the poor became even more urgent in the modern age on at least three fronts: first in Europe's industrialized cities; second, in the colonies where it was presumed that the indigenous populations lived in sin and poverty, and finally in the rapidly expanding immigrant communities in North America, Australia and New Zealand. Thus, the Mercy Sisters founded by Catherine McAuley (1778-1841) in Dublin offer an important example of a congregation founded to work among the poor in Ireland and also to minister to Irish immigrant communities in the United States, Australia, New Zealand and elsewhere.

But the most significant development in the first half of the twentieth century was the commitment to the foreign missions. An extraordinary number of women's congregations were founded primarily for the 'foreign missions'. Mission was understood in expansionist categories so *missio ad gentes* with its emphasis on conversion of pagans was emphasized, as was mission understood as *plantatio ecclesiae*. It is not difficult to see how imperialist ideologies were influencing the way in which mission was exercised. Although the Edinburgh Conference highlighted the need for an indigenized Christianity, most Catholic and Protestant missionaries believed in the superiority of Western culture. John 10:10, 'I have come that they may have life and have it more abundantly', mandated encouraging in local people an uncritical acceptance of Western educational, health and agricultural practices. That 'West was best' seemed apparent to most missionaries. Not that this was necessarily always bad and there is little doubt that educational and health institutions established by the missionaries offered emancipatory possibilities to the local people.

Examples of Catholic women who understood mission as something that happened in distant colonies include the Holy Spirit Missionary Sisters founded by Arnold Janssen, Maria Helena Stollenwerk and Hendrina Stenmans in Holland in 1889. Janssen saw the Sisters' primary role as providing domestic service for the male order he founded, the Society of the Divine Word, an understanding of the role of women's missionary activity that suited the needs of a patriarchal and clerical church. By 1910, a year after Janssen's death, the Sisters assumed responsibility for their own governance and financial arrangements, and were soon involved in health, social and educational work in the United States, Brazil, Papua New Guinea, China and Japan.

Just as important as the movement of women from Western nations to Asia, Africa, Latin America and Oceania were the early twentieth century foundations in those continents. These foundations included the Daughters of Mary of Bannabikira founded for work in East Africa in 1910, the Associates of Mary Queen of the Apostles, usually referred to as the Toomilia Sisters, founded in Bangladesh in 1933, or the Rosary Sisters founded in Wewak, Papua New Guinea in 1952. Such foundations, unlike European foundations, were often diocesan congregations, and therefore under the authority of the bishop. Bishops throughout Asia, Africa and Oceania were enthusiastically founding communities of indigenous sisters for mission directed to women and children, or in some instances to the domestic care of expatriate priests.

In the 1920s growing numbers of Catholic foreign missionaries recognized they needed to match Protestant missionary efforts in health work. Dana Robert writes that in 1889 that 'there were 61 Protestant missionary hospitals and 44 dispensaries in China but only 5 Catholic hospitals and 7 dispensaries' (Robert 1996: 372). Canon Law forbade religious, women or men, from working as physicians, surgeons and obstetricians, although general nursing and simple dispensary work were tolerated. In 1936, Canon Law was changed and women religious could train for such positions. Anna Dengel's Society of Catholic Medical Missionaries and the Medical Missionaries of Mary, founded in Nigeria by the Irish woman Mary Martin, soon were training their personnel for health work in Africa and Asia.

Other twentieth century developments prior to Vatican II include the approach to mission of the Little Sisters of Jesus founded in 1939 by French woman Madeleine Hutin (1898-1989). She was profoundly influenced by the radically new model of mission provided by the Frenchman Charles de Foucauld (1858-1916). Former French legionnaire de Foucauld believed that mission required him to live a deeply contemplative and hidden life among the Tuaregs in southern Algeria. The Little Sisters' approach to mission meant that they opted for a similar non-institutional way of life that allowed them to live among the poorest of the poor. Usually one community member was in paid manual employment similar to that of other women in their neighborhood. The Little Sisters' decision to live among the poor anticipated what a post-Vatican II church called an option for the poor. Their de-institutionalized and inculturated approach to mission anticipated other post-Vatican II approaches to mission.

Another important pre-Vatican II development was the involvement of lay women in mission. Lay women had always sought to involve themselves in mission, but often a patriarchal church opposed the idea of

unmarried or widowed women, non-cloistered, who often enjoyed a
measure of economic independence, being able to engage in missionary
activity. As the lives of Angela Merici or Jeanne Frances de Chantal
demonstrate, a patriarchal church believed that missionary women should
be professed religious whose activities were most suitably guided by
bishops or parish priests.

The American lay woman, Dorothy Day (1897-1980) offered another
radically different way of being missionary. In response to Pope Pius XI's
1930 encyclical *Quadragesimo Anno* which asked that lay people respond
to situations of economic deprivation, Day and the French-born Peter
Maurin (1877-1949) founded the Catholic Worker movement. The
movement was acclaimed for its outreach to the poor and dispossessed but
often criticized for its pacifist and socialist philosophies. Day's opposition
to the Spanish Civil War (1936-1939), and then to World War II did not
initially win her too many admirers in the upper echelons of American
Catholicism, but more recently her beatification process was initiated by
the former archbishop of New York, John Cardinal O'Connor.

The involvement of lay women in the mission of the church was also
seen in the emergence of lay groups such as the Grail Movement founded
in 1921 by the Dutch Jesuit, Jacques van Ginneken. Although he intended
Grail members to provide a Christian witness in an increasingly secularized
Europe, after World War II the movement directed its energies to
cooperation with people of good will for the sake of all, particularly the
poor.

Lay women's involvement was evident too in the work of the Lay
Auxiliaries of the Missions in the China mission. The Auxiliaries were
founded in 1937 by the Belgian Vincentian missionary, Vincent Lebbe,
who was committed to bringing about 'a Catholic Church rooted in the
culture and society of China' (Wiest 1999: 35-37). Like the Grail
Movement, the Auxiliaries understood that their call to mission flowed
from baptism, not religious profession.

We can see that the three issues identified by Peter Phan (2010) as
significant at Edinburgh – indigenization of Christianity, inter-religious
dialogue, the emergence of a world church – did not significantly affect
women's exercise of mission prior to Vatican II. But shifts were
discernible. It was recognized that the institutional approach to mission
demonstrated by large educational and health institutes could be and indeed
should be complemented by a non-institutionalized solidarity with the poor.
A non-institutionalized approach to mission such as that of the Little Sisters
of Jesus also represents an early attempt at inculturation although there was
little emphasis on inculturation at that time. Given that Hutin was French, it
is hard to see that she would have been influenced by the Edinburgh
Conference statements, nevertheless her efforts indicate that prophetic
voices in both the Catholic and Protestant communities were speaking out
against the Eurocentrism of the age.

Nor did a pre-conciliar ecclesiology and missiology encourage inter-religious dialogue. A monological rather than a dialogical approach to other religions was affirmed given that most Catholics subscribed to an *extra ecclesiam nulla salus* ideology. This explains the prophetic character of groups and the movement of groups like the Little Sisters or the Catholic Worker Movement which advocated greater openness to other religions.

Finally, the arrival of organized groups of lay missionary women anticipated Vatican II's teaching that it is through baptism that the faithful are called to mission. A pre-Vatican church that looked back to the presumed dangers of Luther's insistence on the priesthood of all the faithful instead of looking forward to the compelling missionary needs of the twentieth century was always going to prioritize the missionary significance of ordination over that of baptism.

Vatican II and Changes in Catholic Missionary Practice

On the eve of Vatican II, the world was changing rapidly. World War II had alerted people to human inhumanity to other human beings, and to the enormous loss of life that modern technology meant. The war had led to the emergence of two superpowers, the Soviet Union and the United States of America whose competing ideologies – communism and capitalism – shaped the way in which contemporary people understood the world. Political independence for former colonies and their wish to be the agents of their own development posed enormous questions for missionaries who previously had often uncritically acquiesced to much of the imperial agenda. The growing economic disparities between the north and south were concerning, and one of the factors that lead to the United Nations declaring that the 1960s should be the first Development Decade.

Even more significant for women was the impact of Vatican II. The Council mandated Catholic Sisters to reclaim the vision that had inspired their foundation and to reinterpret it in ways that reflected their fidelity to their particular founder's dream, and their ability to discern the 'signs of the times'. The decades preceding Vatican II had often meant the development of large institutional works which had met a real need at the time but which had sometimes evolved into operations that met the needs of the middle classes rather than the poorer sectors of society. The growing realization that that such a growth represented a development that founders would not have encouraged meant a certain de-institutionalization of apostolic works particularly in the more liberal congregations.

Pre-conciliar understandings concerning the relationship of the church to the world, to other Christian churches and to other religions were critiqued and found wanting by the Council. In the first six decades of the twentieth century, most Catholic Sisters followed a monastic way of life in so far as their busy apostolic lives permitted. 'The world' was to be avoided. Contact with Protestant and other world religions was problematic unless it had as its goal conversion. Missionary activity was about church growth, an understanding that prioritized the sacramental ministry of the priest. The work of the Sisters – school teaching, caring for orphans or nursing the sick – was a means to an end, the growth of the institutional church. The conciliar emphasis on the church in the world, on ecumenism and inter-religious dialogue pointed to a changing context in which women could exercise their mission.

Catholic social teaching began to change Catholic sisters' thinking about mission. As the nineteenth century drew to a close, Pope Leo XIII's social encyclical *Rerum Novarum* (1891) was the first of great modern encyclicals that alerted Catholics to their vocation of creating a more just world. Prior to Vatican II, these encyclicals did not receive the attention they warranted, but after Vatican II, the church's social teachings meant many Catholic Sisters acknowledged that their traditional works of charity needed to be complemented by social action or works of justice.

But Vatican II had significance for Catholic lay women too. The call to mission was rooted in baptism, not in ordination or in religious profession. As Richard McBrien notes, this represented an advance on the belief that priests and bishops had 'to shoulder the whole mission themselves' (McBrien 1980: 672). The Council taught that through baptism and confirmation, 'all are commissioned to that apostolate by the Lord himself ... Now the laity are called in a special way to make the Church present and operative in those places and circumstances where only through them can she become the salt of the earth' (LG 33).

This was liberating for women and perhaps one of the most exciting developments of the post-Vatican II decades has been the ever-growing involvement of lay women in the mission of the church. As one of the better know lay groups, the Volunteer Missionary Movement, founded in 1969 by English woman Edwina Gately stated: 'Imagine what it was like to be a layperson in 1969 who wanted to be a missionary. Your choices were pretty much limited to becoming a priest or minister, a religious sister or a brother. While many people felt the call to mission, they didn't always feel called to one of these other ministries' (http://www.vmmusa.org/spiritandlifestyle.html, 2006). Today lay women are increasingly involved in missionary activity as members of lay organizations such as the Maryknoll Lay Missioners, as associate members of religious congregations such as the Mercy Sisters' Mercy Volunteer Corps or through NGOs such as the Jesuit Refugee Service or the Edmund Rice Volunteer Scheme. Their involvement may be short-term or long-term but most lay people commit themselves for a minimum of three years, although some are involved for longer.

Women's missionary activity in the last three decades of the second millennium was profoundly influenced by liberation theology (LT). LT's methodology required that oppressed groups become 'doers' of theology, not simply 'receivers' of the theology of others. Latin American religious and priests, indigenous and foreign, recognized that LT empowered the traditionally economically and politically disenfranchised masses to become subjects of change rather than objects of change. Women were among the first to realize the importance of LT for the poor among whom they worked and lived. LT's insistence on the necessity of the church making an option for the poor had led numbers of Sisters to forsake the security of institutional living and apostolic activity in favor of living among the people in solidarity with them in their daily struggles.

Although LT had come to birth in the context of extreme economic disparities, the importance of its methodology for other groups, such as women or ethnic minority groups was soon recognized. A liberationist methodology allowed women to better appreciate how a patriarchal culture not only oppressed the poor but also oppressed women both in society and in the institutional church. This led many women missionaries to focus attention on other women in an effort to overcome the gender oppression they so often suffered. Such a focus obliged the institutional church to affirm the role of women. Thus in 1988 Pope John Paul II's apostolic letter *Mulieris Dignitatem* (MD) offered a more positive understanding of women's role in the church.

As the second millennium drew to a close, further developments affecting the way in which Catholic women understood their call to mission emerged. Just as the poor and women were oppressed by patriarchal culture, so too was creation. Although both the Magisterium and different bishops' conferences have issued important statements on care of creation as an emerging missionary imperative, women in particular seem to have attempted in a more experiential way to see what this might entail. In *Gaia and God*, Rosemary Radford Ruether argued that 'domination of women has provided a key link, both socially and symbolically, to the domination of the earth, matter, and nature, while identifying males with sky, intellect, and transcendent spirit' (Ruether 1992: 3).

This type of theology allows women to make the connection between ecological degradation and the oppression of the poor, especially poor women. There is little doubt that ecological degradation widens the gap between rich and poor in our global community. Furthermore the rich are more likely to be the perpetrators of ecological degradation than the poor. Thus the carbon footprint of a United States citizen is almost twenty tons per year, while that of a Bangladeshi citizen is less than two tons, and yet Bangladesh is suffering and is going to suffer more from environmental devastation than is the United States.

Edinburgh 1910 named inter-religious dialogue as an important missionary task, a goal confirmed by Vatican II's *Nostra Aetate*. Today Catholics are invited to participate in different types of dialogue: the dialogue of life; dialogue which has as its goal the resolution of a problem; dialogue between theologians of different faith communities; and, finally a type of spiritual dialogue in which believers meet with the other in 'the cave of the heart'. Dialogue between theologians of different faiths, usually male, often seems to receive more public attention than the other three, but women, whatever their particular religious affiliation are often in dialogue about mutual concerns that have as their starting point social or gender issues that diminish women. Dialogue and action about issues that impact negatively on family life succeed in bringing women together in important ways. Consciously and unconsciously women are important facilitators of inter-religious dialogue.

Postconciliar developments in Catholic women's exercise of mission should not considered in isolation from theological shifts. Vatican II's invitation that people be involved in the joys and sufferings of humankind and recognize that God spoke through these realities has assumed increasing significance for Catholic women in determining mission priorities. Liberation theology invited people to hear and respond to the cry of the poor whether they were in India or in the United States. Mission was no longer understood primarily in geographical categories but in socio-economic realities. This insight reflected a real continuity with the Judaeo-Christian tradition, not the radical discontinuity that some critics of liberation theology claim.

Perhaps most important theological development concerned the Holy Spirit. After Vatican II, pneumatological developments complemented or balanced an earlier emphasis on the particularity of the Spirit's presence in church authorities or religious superiors. They did this by directing attention to the universal nature of the Spirit's presence in human history, in cultures and in creation. To believe in this made it more difficult to hold fast to *missio ad gentes* or *plantatio ecclesiae* as the privileged ways of being missionary. Instead of women's missionary activity being regarded as subordinate to that of the priest, it too was acknowledged that women were central to the church's major missionary goal of hastening the reign of God a task in which women were now key players. As the third millennium dawned we can see that important goals, announced in Edinburgh a century ago, have been recognized by Catholic women as essential in their mission today. It is more difficult to argue that women were directly influenced by Edinburgh. Rather the Holy Spirit, whose 'presence and activity are universal, and limited neither by space nor time' (Burrows 1993: 19; see RM 28 and AG 10) is bringing about a wonderful convergence of hopes and dreams that are motivating the disciples of Jesus to work for a better world, one in which the gospel's values associated with the reign of God are ever more real.

PART TWO

CATHOLIC TEACHING
ON MISSION

PAPAL MISSION WISDOM: FIVE MISSION ENCYCLICALS 1919-1959

James Kroeger, MM

The flowering of the church's vision of her mission of evangelization in the Second Vatican Council (1962-1965) is preceded by decades of continuous mission experience and reflection. This cumulative 'wisdom' which coalesces into the church's vision on a particular subject is subsequently often articulated in certain landmark documents. Thus, for the church's 'mission perspectives' in the first half of the twentieth century one can look to five papal encyclicals: *Maximum Illud* (1919), *Rerum Ecclesiae* (1926), *Evangelii Praecones* (1951), *Fidei Donum* (1957), and *Princeps Pastorum* (1959).

The church has continued to reflect on her missionary identity ever since Jesus told his disciples: 'As the Father has sent me, so am I sending you' (Jn. 20:21). The papal mission encyclicals, important sources of mission reflection, are 'papal circulars dealing with missionary themes, ... whatever their exact title may be, provided that they are directed to the entire episcopate' (Glazik 1971: 406).

While acknowledging the pivotal role of encyclicals, one must keep in mind that papal teaching is set within a wider church context. Thus, a full presentation of mission reflection in the first half of the twentieth century (beyond the purview of this chapter) would necessarily include a treatment of major schools of mission thought (Belgian, French, Spanish), influential publications (*Bibliographia Missionaria, Bibliotheca Missionum*), as well as important theologians such as: Robert Streit, Joseph Schmidlin, Pierre Charles, Jose Zameza, Olegario Domingues, Andre Glorieux, Henri de Lubac, and Thomas Ohm (see Murphy 1962, Nemer 2003, and Vadakumpanan 1992 and 2006; see Francis Oborji's chapter in this volume).

Even the papal encyclicals themselves are better appreciated when seen within the entire corpus of papal mission thought. An important study by Francis X. Clark locates the encyclicals within the many documents (instructions, letters, homilies, Mission Sunday messages, radio broadcasts, etc.) issued by these same popes. Clark made an exhaustive study of all papal mission documents from the *Acta Apostolicae Sedis* from 1909 (first AAS volume) until 1946 (Clark 1948: 1-65). Much papal insight and wisdom is revealed in Clark's fine contribution.

The five papal encyclicals that form the central subject of this presentation frequently reflect 'the development in the Church's teaching at any moment in history ... [and they] should also be related to the events in history' (Murphy 1962: II-3; see Burke, ed. 1957: 3). In a word, the mission encyclicals often reflect the particular period of history in which they appeared – both in their theology and current world events (Coleman 1967: 936). And yet, these same encyclicals present many new and creative insights that prove fruitful in mission theology and praxis in subsequent decades (Glazik 1971: 406). A short overview presentation that identifies the pivotal insights of each encyclical now follows.

I. Maximum Illud

The first great missionary document of modern times, *Maximum Illud* (MI 1919) ('Spreading the Catholic Faith'), was issued by Pope Benedict XV on November 30, 1919 (Burke 1957: 9-23). This document 'broke a forty-year silence from the papacy in regard to a missionary encyclical' (DuBose 1979: 381; Glazik 1971: 406). MI has been called the 'Magna Carta' of modern missions, and its directives have had far-reaching ramifications. 'The importance of this encyclical is shown by the fact that all subsequent missionary encyclicals quote *Maximum Illud*' ('Before Vatican II' 1978: 297).

The context in which the document was written is significant. The First World War (1914-1918) had just ended; it had brought great destruction on several levels – including the church's missionary endeavors. The encyclical sought to revive missionary initiatives affected by the catastrophe of the war. In addition, the post-war period saw significant development in the world of social communications (De Letter 1961: 23).

Benedict XV stated two purposes for his letter: to encourage missionary leadership and to recommend mission methods. Speaking to those directly involved in mission, the pope notes that heads of missions must act with 'prudence and charity', always seeking to expand mission efforts. They should be open to accept the help of various apostles, even those who do not belong to their religious order. The work of religious women needs recognition and promotion.

Missionaries are encouraged to grow in 'sanctity of life', following 'the example of Christ our Lord and of the Apostles.' They should frequently recall 'the lofty and splendid character' of their vocation. The pope recognizes 'the stupendous hardships our missionaries have undergone in extending the Faith.' He also has strong words that direct the missionary to avoid 'serving the interests of his homeland ... the true missionary is always aware that he is not working as an agent of his country, but as an ambassador of Christ.' Missionaries must have careful and profound training, especially in 'the science of missiology'; they 'should not be content with a smattering of the language, but should be able to speak it readily and competently.'

A pivotal emphasis of MI is the development of the indigenous clergy; there must be 'special concern to secure and train local candidates for the sacred ministry.' Benedict XV asserts: 'In this policy lies the greatest hope of the new churches.' Why? 'For the local priest, one with his people by birth, by nature, by his sympathies and his aspirations, is remarkably effective in appealing to their mentality and thus attracting them to the Faith.'

The local clergy are to be 'well trained and well prepared.' They are 'not to be trained merely to perform the humbler duties of the ministry, acting as the assistants of foreign priests.' Every effort must be taken to avoid having 'a local clergy that is of inferior quality.' Mission superiors should have the founding of seminaries as a main concern.

The encyclical invites the entire church to assist the missions through prayer, personnel, and finances. The diverse works of the Society for the Propagation of the Faith deserve support and cooperation. The pope's 'mission theology' would reflect that of the times; his vision would be based on the traditional conviction *extra ecclesiam nulla salus*. Benedict XV also commends the church's missionary efforts to 'the great Mother of God, the Queen of Apostles.'

II. Rerum Ecclesiae

Seven years after *Maximum Illud*, Pope Pius XI issued *Rerum Ecclesiae* (RE 1926) ('Fostering Missionary Zeal') on February 28, 1926 (Burke 1957: 26-38; Carlen 1990: III, 281-291). Pius XI follows quite closely the thought of his predecessor, though some points are developed in greater detail.

The pope begins by affirming his zeal for mission; he declares that he will 'leave nothing undone in bringing the light of the Gospel ... to more and more pagans.' To achieve this goal he sees that 'a much larger force of missionaries' is needed and that the lay faithful need to become more aware of their responsibilities in mission.

Pius XI makes a clear point of identifying the objective of missionary work. He writes: 'What, we may ask, is the purpose of these missions, if not building an establishment of the Church of Christ in so vast a number of places?' He is promoting 'the establishment of a fully-organized Church', 'the establishment of the Church among non-Christians'. In short, 'Pope Pius XI regards the planting of the visible organization of the Church and the erection of seminaries as the first duty of missionaries' (Culhane 1950: 390).

In light of this central focus, the pope vigorously promotes the native clergy, often quoting the words of *Maximum Illud*. Local youth are not to be refused admission to the priesthood; local priests are not to be regarded as 'inferior to the foreign clergy or employed in only the more humble ministries'; 'let there be no discrimination or caste distinction between

European and local clergy.' Native religious communities and the contemplative vocation are to be fostered.

Pius XI also offers practical advice (Metzler 1993: 221-222). The pope asserts the need of 'better management of the missions'; missionary witnessing is very effective, since 'men's hearts are easily captivated by deeds of love'. Missionaries should refrain from 'erecting ornate or costly edifices'. It is appropriate to build 'orphanages, hospitals, and medical dispensaries.' Religious orders 'should remember that they possess no exclusive or permanent title to their mission areas.'

Known as the 'Pope of the Missions,' (Tan 2003: 681), Pius XI took several important initiatives: promotion of the Universal Missionary Exhibition (1925) which became permanent in 1927 with the establishment of the Ethnographical Missionary Museum, now in the Vatican (see Considine 1925); establishment of World Mission Sunday (1926); recognition of two faculties of missiology in Rome (Gregorian University in 1932 and Urban University in 1933). Pius XI is also remembered as the first pope who fostered the indigenous hierarchy by 'personally consecrating Chinese, Indian, and Japanese bishops' (Coleman 1967: 937).

III. Evangelii Praecones

This missionary encyclical, the third in thirty-five years, was issued in commemoration of the twenty-fifth anniversary of *Rerum Ecclesiae* by Pope Pius XII. *Evangelii Praecones* (EP 1951) ('Development of the Missions') 'reiterates and completes the missionary teaching' of the two previous popes, Benedict XV and Pius XI ('New Encyclical' 1951: 321). Pius XII chose to issue EP (Burke 1957: 40-61; Carlen 1990: IV, 189-202) on the same day (June 2, 1951) he made a pastoral visit to a parish church in Rome ('Pope' 1952: 373). During his lengthy pontificate, Pius XII (1939-1958) issued ten mission-related letters; EP is his principal mission document (Coleman 1967: 937).

Fulton J. Sheen, the famous director of the Propagation of the Faith in the U.S. at the time, noted that the encyclical has three major divisions (Sheen 1951: 3). Section One is given to the present status of the missions; Section Two provides seven principles and norms of missionary activity; Section Three outlines seven forms of mission aid. Similar themes are emphasized by various commentators on the document (Considine 1952, Metzler 1993, O'Connell 1952).

Pius XII begins by reflecting on 'the giant strides' and 'recent progress' of the church's missionary activity. He provides a variety of statistics, including the number of Catholics worldwide, the number of priests, and the growing number of 'native-born bishops.' Along with this growth, there are new challenges to be faced, e.g. emergence of newly independent nations and the rise of Communism.

As noted earlier, the pope lists seven principles and norms of missionary activity: (1) the missionary's home is to be a foreign land, and the foreign land is to be his home; (2) missionaries must have specialized training; (3) missionaries must work for the establishment of a native clergy and hierarchy; (4) missionaries must utilize lay activity; (5) the initiation of social reforms demanded by justice and charity; (6) the necessity of cooperation between missionary societies; and, (7) the sanctification of pagan truths (Sheen 1951: 6-8; see Considine 1952: 422).

Perhaps, the greatest novelty in EP is the emphasis on preserving the positive elements found in 'the special customs and time-honored observances of pagan peoples.' Pius XII specifically mentions indigenous learning, fine arts, and liberal studies. Thus, 'the Church does not wish to eradicate any good tradition, artistic production or custom of any people. Its mission is to preserve, elevate and sanctify these things in the spirit of the Gospel' ('Pius XII' 1951: 321).

The seven 'mission aids' noted by Sheen (1951: 9-13) are: (1) Prayers by the Faithful; (2) Adoption of Native Priests; (3) Zeal by the Clergy; (4) Prayers and Sacrifices of Children; (5) Women in Altar Societies; (6) Fostering Vocations; and, (7) General Alms. Other topics mentioned include: persecutions in China and Korea, the role of Catholic Action, and the importance of various institutions of service and mercy. Theologically, 'the doctrine of the Mystical Body is the basic idea in the encyclical' (O'Connell 1952: 411); in addition, the dogma of the 'communion of saints' informs the vision of the pope ('New Encyclical' 1951: 329).

IV. Fidei Donum

Pope Pius XII, one year before his death, signed his second mission encyclical on April 21, 1957. By promulgating his encyclical on Easter Sunday (a remarkable action), the pope wished to emphasize the links between mission and Easter-Pentecost. *Fidei Donum* (FD 1957) ('Gift of Faith') is of modest length (Burke 1957: 64-79; Carlen 1990: IV, 321-32) and focuses the church's attention on the urgent missionary needs of Africa.

The encyclical falls into four parts. Part One presents an overview of the 'condition of the Church in Africa with a reference to its great expansion in recent years' (Coonan 1957: 534). Most territories were facing social, economic and political changes that deeply affected their future as young and emerging nations. Pius XII notes that 85 million Africans 'are still attached to pagan beliefs.' There is the advance of Islam as well as a technological revolution. The pope notes that 'the number of priests compared to that of the faithful is decreasing in Africa.'

In this context Pius XII seeks the cooperation of the entire church (Parts Two and Three). The pope expresses his conviction clearly: 'The missionary spirit and the Catholic spirit ... are one and the same thing.

Catholicity is an essential note of the true Church.' Indeed, 'the assistance of the whole Church is required' (Ilundain 2005: 343). In Part Four, Pius XII concludes his exhortation by expressing his 'gratitude and hope' to missionaries; he urges the entire church to follow her Divine Founder's mandate: 'Put out into the deep'! (Lk. 5:4).

The pope identifies seven specific areas needing attention by the Church in Africa ('Future' 1957: 427): (1) promotion of missionary vocations in schools and through Catholic Action; (2) bishops must recruit more vocations; (3) bishops should meet to address common challenges; (4) collaboration among mission entities is needed; (5) pastoral care for students is urgent; (6) priests should volunteer for service in Africa; and, (7) lay involvement is an important contribution.

An enduring effect of *Fidei Donum* has been the sending of diocesan priests to serve in mission, one of the 'new forms of aid' for mission (Scalzotto 1977: 10; Pacelli 2007). Known as *Fidei Donum* priests, they have partially addressed the scarcity of missionaries. These exchanges have resulted in strengthening the bonds between local churches as well as promoting creative thinking and pastoral approaches, both in Africa and in the missionary's church of origin. This initiative has been beneficial; it follows a key principle enunciated by Pius XII: 'A Christian community which gives its sons and daughters to the Church cannot die.'

V. Princeps Pastorum

Pope John XXIII, elected at the age of seventy-seven, was expected to be a 'care-taker' pope. However, in the five years of his pontificate (1958-1963) he made a great impact on the church. Seizing on the fortieth anniversary of *Maximum Illud,* John XXIII issued his mission encyclical *Princeps Pastorum* (PP 1959) ('Prince of the Shepherds') (Carlen 1990: V, 43-57) on November 28, 1959.

John XXIII takes for granted as the starting point of his encyclical 'the outcome of the forty years of missionary endeavor: 'the establishment of the hierarchy and clergy in regions that were confided to missionaries'' (De Letter 1961: 26; for a partial chronological list of the establishment of hierarchies in mission lands, see: 29-30). The pope even provides some statistics regarding the growth of the local clergy and hierarchy. He notes that the consecration of the first East Asian bishop was in 1923 and the first African bishop in 1939; he adds: 'By 1959, we count 68 Asian and 25 African bishops.'

In this context, John XXIII provides directives for the local clergy and the missionaries who remain in the emerging young churches. Some brief items may be noted: fraternal collaboration between local clergy and expatriate missionaries; solid training to priestly holiness; the need that all clergy study missiology; the importance of schools and cultural centers; the employment of modern techniques to spread the faith; the role of the laity;

and, the avoidance of ultra-nationalism within the young, local churches (cf. Metzler 1993: 223-24; Putenpurakal 1997: 10-11; Vadakumpadan 2006: 30-31).

The changes that had taken place in the mission field over a four-decade period (1919-1959) were significant, since they showed the church's growth toward an adult status. Also, 'the very change in the political status of the ex-colonies, now independent countries... commands the change in the status of the Church in those countries' (De Letter 1961: 29). Clearly, in the mind of John XXIII the time of any attitudes or approaches reminiscent of 'colonial mission' is definitely passed.

Princeps Pastorum was issued in November 1959; John XXIII had already announced his convocation of the Second Vatican Council in January, 1959. This encyclical contains seeds of renewal; it 'preceded Vatican II and helped to pave the way for the significant pronouncements it would make on the mission of the Church' (DuBose 1979: 390-91).

Overview and Synthesis

The five papal encyclicals highlighted in this chapter reach well over a total of one hundred pages in their official Latin publication in the *Acta Apostolicae Sedis;* thus, to attempt a comprehensive synthesis would be a daunting task. This final section is but a modest presentation of selected pivotal topics arising from an appreciation of the pre-Vatican II papal mission teaching.

Based on a close reading of the material as well as indices to the published encyclicals, a list of the ten most notable themes can be presented; they are arranged according to the prominence they receive. Papal emphasis is given to the following items: (1) the missionary nature of the church; (2) the purpose of the missions; (3) the person of the missionary; (4) local churches and local clergy; (5) role of the pope and bishops; (6) the role of mission superiors; (7) types of mission work; (8) missionary virtues; (9) the pontifical mission aid societies; and, (10) laity in mission.

Viewed from an evolutionary viewpoint, one could assert that 'the decree of Vatican II on the Church's missionary activity is in many respects a logical consequence of the missionary documents we have studied so far' (Vadakumpanan 1992: 11). Some few examples, found both in the pre-Vatican II papal mission teaching as well as in *Ad Gentes,* can illustrate this point. The goal of establishing the church is a primary task of mission (AG 5) and this is often expressed in terms of 'planting of the Church' (AG 6, 19). The obligations of the missionary are outlined, especially the call to holiness (AG 23-27). Missionary cooperation is essential for a fruitful outcome of diverse mission endeavors (AG 35-41). Lay participation in mission is promoted (AG 41).

In some specific areas of mission reflection, one notes that it would be unrealistic to look for a fully developed vision in the pre-Vatican II mission encyclicals. Thus, a full understanding of such themes as inculturation, inter-religious dialogue, justice issues, and Christian unity as they relate to mission only emerges in the Vatican II era. A developed Trinitarian theology of mission is only found in the *Ad Gentes* document. However, tracing the path of the church's 'wisdom' on mission through the earlier papal encyclicals and into the renewal fostered by the Council allows one to appreciate the positive, incremental growth that has definitely occurred under the inspiration of the Holy Spirit.

One commentator on the impact of papal mission encyclicals notes that unfortunately they 'have never attracted the attention due to them, and in consequence many demands which are rightly made in them have never been carried into effect' (Glazik 1971: 406). While this observation is true, it can best be understood within the contemporary theological category of 'reception.' Reception is that process whereby the Christian community acknowledges, accepts, and integrates the insights of a church teaching or experience. This is an ongoing process and to achieve it often demands long-term concerted efforts. Thus, the church today continues to struggle to integrate both the papal mission wisdom of the early encyclicals, the insights of Vatican II, and important post-conciliar documents such as *Evangelii Nuntiandi* of Paul VI and *Redemptoris Missio* of John Paul II. The church fervently prays: *Veni, Sancte Spiritus!*

To conclude this chapter this writer refers to the 'mission motivation' with which Pius XII insightfully began *Fidei Donum* (1957). The pope wisely notes that mission springs from 'the gift of faith'. Thus, a profound recognition of God's 'incomparable riches' becomes 'the motive for immense gratitude'; one rejoices and desires to sing a 'hymn of gratitude'. Though written in 1957, this is a very contemporary insight; it will resonate with anyone who has had experience in Asia: one becomes missionary out of gratitude for the gift of faith received. Paraphrasing Asia's bishops, one can assert: we evangelize from a deep sense of gratitude to God; mission, above all else, overflows from grateful hearts.

MISSION AT THE
SECOND VATICAN COUNCIL: 1962-1965

Stephen B. Bevans

The Second Vatican Council (1962-1965), held at the virtual midpoint of the years that this volume studies – has often been called the most significant theological and religious event of the twentieth century (Schreiter 1999: 158; O'Malley 2008: 1). For the Catholic Church, as many essays in this volume point out, the Council was a watershed moment of reform and renewal, a moment toward which much of the church's energies had moved in the fifty years that preceded it, and from which the church has been nourished and challenged in the half century since the Council took place.

Despite much controversy and even movements of 'restoration' in the last several decades, after Vatican II the Catholic Church – and, indeed, many other Christian churches and communities – would never be the same. In 1864 Pope Pius IX boldly condemned any thought that the Roman Pontiff could reconcile himself with progress and the 'modern world' (DS 1967: 2980). Just one hundred years later Pope John XXIII called for *aggiornamento* – literally, updating – and the church issued a document on the Church in the Modern World. In 1928 Pope Pius XI forbade any Catholic to become involved in the growing ecumenical movement in the encyclical *Mortalium Animos* (MA 1928). Some three decades later Christian unity was held up by Pope John XXIII as one of major goals of the Council (John XXIII 1961: 706).

When one thinks of how the Council treated the church's mission at the Council, one naturally looks to its 'Decree on Missionary Activity', entitled *Ad Gentes* (AG 1965) after its first two words. This would be correct, of course, but it is also important to note that 'mission' or 'evangelization' is really at the heart of everything that the Council was about (for more extensive treatment of this topic, see Bevans and Gros 2009). In its deepest intent, in fact, Vatican II was a missionary council. Its central theme, as it turned out, was the mystery of the church, in its interior reality as a community that is a sacramental sign to the world, but also in its reality as an instrument of the grace and wholeness it signified in the midst of the world (see LG 1).

Vatican II, unlike many if not all previous ecumenical councils, was not called to attend to any particular crisis in is doctrinal system or governing structure. At least on the surface, during the reign of Pius XII from 1939 until 1958 the papacy had never been stronger, and the church was growing vigorously throughout the world. Nevertheless, in a move of prophetic insight, John XXIII's reason for calling the Council was to help the church preserve and teach Christian doctrine in a more effective way in the light of major political and cultural changes in the twentieth century. *Aggiornamento* was not a call for change for change's sake, but a call to mission. Mission is what gave the Council its basic direction (see Schütte 1967b: 7 and 1967: 120).

Each of the Council's four main 'Constitutions' – on the church, the church in the modern world, the liturgy, and divine revelation – which, said the Special Synod of Bishops in 1981, are the main documents by which the Council can best be interpreted, contain elements that illumine the church's evangelizing mission, and which provide a firm theological foundation for the document on missions proper. The seminal idea that the church is a 'sign and instrument' of God's salvation being worked out in the world (LG 1); the truly radical notion that all Christians have a different but equal share in the church's mission (LG, ch. II; LG 32); the recognition that the 'joys and hopes, the griefs and anxieties' of humanity are those also of the 'followers of Christ' (GS 1); the move from an understanding of revelation as a set of propositions to a personal call to friendship (DV 2); and the great sensitivity to culture that inspired much of the reform of the liturgy (SC 37-40) – all of these and more are motivated by a spirit of evangelization and mission.

In addition, to single out only two other documents, those on religious freedom and non-Christian religions, the Council provided a vision that has challenged traditional understandings of mission to the core, and yet has offered a new, basically more evangelical, motive for the preaching of and witnessing to the gospel among all peoples. The Council's declaration that all peoples have a right to religious freedom has forever cut the ground from under any effort of proselytism in the name of the church or the gospel (DH 1). In addition, the Council's recognition that every religion contains 'rays of that Truth that enlightens all women and men' (NA 2) opens up mission not only to a clear proclamation of the gospel message, but a proclamation in the context of dialogue and an effort to understand the sincere beliefs of those to whom the gospel is presented.

From another perspective, as church historian John W. O'Malley has explained in several significant works, not only did the Council offer a different *content* on many issues, it also offered a new *form* or style. The Council eschewed the usual canonical, legal language of Roman documents, studded with 'power words' or words 'of threat and intimidation, words of surveillance and punishment, words of a superior speaking to inferiors, or, just as often, to an enemy' (O'Malley 2006: 20; see O'Malley 2008), and chose the language of persuasion, more pastoral and positive in tone. Such a change in tone was emblematic of the change in the church's entire missionary commitment: the church is missionary by its very nature, not only or even primarily because Christ commanded it to 'make disciples of all nations' (Mt. 28:19), but because it is rooted in the missionary life of the Trinity (AG 2); Christians on mission respect and cherish the cultures of the people that the evangelize, as well as their religious beliefs (AG 11; NA 2); Christians not only have something precious to share with the world, but can learn as well from its struggles, its sincerity, its progress (GS 43-44). If Vatican II was a missionary Council, it also set a new tone to what mission was all about.

The Decree on Missionary Activity

The development of the decree

Except for a virtual hiatus in explicit foreign missionary activity at the end of the eighteenth century (see Bevans and Schroeder 2004: 194; Latourette 1975: 1012), the church has always engaged in what Pope John Paul II called mission *ad gentes* (see Roger Schroeder's chapter in this volume). Because of such a long and constant history of missionary commitment, therefore, it may come as a surprise that the Council's Decree on Missionary Activity (*Ad Gentes*) represents the first time in history that an ecumenical council had issued a document dedicated explicitly to the church's evangelizing mission in the world (see Corboy 1968: 9; Brechter 1969: 87).

Interestingly, however, the document was almost abandoned during the course of the Council, as pressures mounted to end its deliberations with the third session in 1964. The path of *Ad Gentes* was, as one historian of the decree put it, 'strewn with ambushes' (Grootaers 1997: 455). What follows is a brief summary of a very complex process. For a fuller development see Bevans and Gros 2009, Paventi 1967, or Brechter 1969.

In June 1969 it was announced that Cardinal Gregory Peter Agagianian, prefect of the Congregation for the Propagation of the Faith (Propaganda Fide), would head the commission that would draft a document on the church's missionary activity. The fifty-four member commission was almost entirely European in makeup, and although there were several fine theologians and missiologists on it, it was dominated by churchmen who, in the words of commission member André Seumois, were 'stuck ... in the old canonical schema ... and unable to conceive a new authentically missionary schema that would really and frankly address the major missionary problems that face the church today ...' (see Komonchak 1995: 195, see note 120).

A first draft of a document was produced that was strongly canonical, hardly theological, and took into little account suggestions submitted from bishops in Asia and Africa. It had seven chapters, beginning with the governance of the missions, and moving through chapters on clergy and lay formation, questions around the sacraments and liturgy, and a final chapter dealing with missionary cooperation. Since there was so much material that overlapped other schemas submitted to the council, the Central Preparatory

Commission (CPC) decided that only two of the chapters – on governance and on missionary cooperation, along with a rather inadequate preface (see Bevans and Gros 2009: 13) – would be submitted for consideration of the Council.

This rather inadequate schema never made it to the Council floor, however. The first session of the Council was marked by a strong reaction of the bishops against the legal, triumphalistic, and canonical tone of the documents presented for discussion, and of the four drafts discussed in 1962, three of them – the document on the church, on Mary, and on Revelation, were rejected outright and sent back to the drawing board. Only the schema on the liturgy had a positive reception and was assured of passage during the next session in 1963. There was a strong anti-curial atmosphere among the bishops, and – relevant to any discussion on mission – the Francophone bishops actually circulated a petition calling for the Propaganda Fide to be deprived of all power and be reduced to a fund-raising body (see Paventi 1967: 157). The bishops from missionary areas demanded that they themselves have an active role to play in the governance of the missions, not Roman bureaucrats.

In the intersession from December 1962 until October 1963 the commission preparing the document on mission met again, but with very unprofitable results. It did manage to submit a document to the CPC entitled *De Missionibus* (On the Missions), but it was basically rejected and sent back for more revisions during the second session of the Council in 1963, with the hope that a document could be discussed at a third session in 1964.

In the meantime, however, it was announced in April, 1964 that all documents not yet discussed on the Council floor were to be reduced to a number of propositions. In this way, time would be saved, and the Council would be able to close at the end of the 1964 session. In May of 1964, therefore, although a longer revision had been written, a new document was drafted entitled 'On the Church's Missionary Activity'. It consisted of six pages containing thirteen – eventually fourteen – propositions. Commentator Evangelista Villanova writes that, compared to the previous schema, this new set of propositions 'was even more feeble from the standpoint of theology and as a reading of the historical moment: decolonization, the globalizing of problems, and poverty remained outside its scope, as did the ecclesiological criteria recognized in the schema on the Church' (Villanova 2000: 392).

In this intersession period, however, a very significant move had been made. The Commission on Mission had been expanded to include more African, Asian, and North American participation, and, most significantly, Fr Johannes Schütte, superior general of the Society of the Divine Word, had been appointed as well, eventually to serve as vicepresident. Under his leadership, together with members of the Commission of the caliber of

Yves Congar and Joseph Ratzinger, a new, more adequate, schema would be developed.

Such a schema, however, only came about after the rejection of the set of propositions when they were presented on the Council floor. Even though Paul VI had explicitly spoken in their favor, the bishops, after several strong speeches calling for a full schema once again, called for a revision of the fourteen propositions in favor of a more adequate document on missionary activity (see Bevans and Gros 2009: 18-22). Under the leadership of the 'tireless German' Johannes Schütte (Villanova 2000: 391), the Commission drafted during the remaining days of the third session and in the intersession of 1964-1965, the document that was to become *Ad Gentes*.

The final editing of the document on mission took place at the Society of the Divine Word's continuing formation house in Nemi, just outside Rome. After a brief introduction of the text by Cardinal Agagianian on October 7, 1965, Fr Schütte gave a long presentation on the schema, concluding that he considered the document the 'Magna Carta' for the church's missionary activity and that it 'would shape the universal church into a truly missionary church' (AS 1977: IV, III: 707).

From October 7 to 13, forty-nine speeches were given and many applications to speak were denied for lack of time. On October 12, the day's moderator, Cardinal Pericle Felici, called for a vote, and the results, made public the next day, were 2,070 in favor and only 15 against. Speeches continued the next day, but the schema had made it safely through the Council. The Commission members scrambled the next several weeks to incorporate what seemed like countless suggestions of the bishops who spoke or who submitted ideas in writing, but the schema was ready for the final vote on December 7, 1965. The Decree on Missionary Activity was the last document that the Council approved, and it was approved by a vote of 2,394 in favor and only 5 against – the highest number of 'yes' votes of any document approved by the Council. A new age of missionary activity had begun.

The Content of the Decree

Chapter I

Ad Gentes contains a brief introductory statement, six chapters, and a short conclusion. Perhaps its most important and enduring chapter is Chapter I, entitled 'Doctrinal Principles', and the first line is perhaps the most significant statement in the entire document, although there are several other wonderful passages. The line reads: 'The pilgrim Church is missionary by its very nature, for it is from the mission of the Son and the mission of the Spirit that it takes its origin, in accordance with the decree of the Father' (AG 2). With this sentence, inspired both by Protestant missiological thinking going back to Karl Barth and by elements somewhat forgotten in the Catholic tradition, the Council roots the reality of mission not in an extrinsic command of Jesus (the 'Great Commission' of Mt. 28) but in the very 'fountain of love' (AG 2) that is God as such. In a reflection rich in scriptural quotations and patristic references, the Council speaks of creation as God's first act of mission, made explicit in the incarnation (for some reason the history of Israel is not mentioned, although it is alluded to), and handed on to the church (AG 2-5).

From this general reflection on the missionary nature of the church, the document takes a crucial turn in paragraph 6, which focuses on mission in the strict sense of 'preaching the Gospel and planting the Church among peoples and group who do not yet believe in Christ.' In this sentence the Council settled the debate – laid out in this volume by Francis Oborji – between the Louvain and Münster schools of thought. Mission is not 'either-or'. It is 'both-and'.

The theology of mission in the decree takes another step forward in the sense that mission is not spoken of in a strictly territorial way – although the document vacillates on this in several places – but as an outreach to persons. In this way, mission is not simply confined to particular *places* – the 'West to rest' as was the common understanding of mission, for example, at the 1910 Edinburgh Conference and among Catholics as well. Mission might be carried out in European or Australian cities among immigrants, or among unbelievers in a secularized North America, with the same integrity as in the African bush or the highlands of Papua New Guinea.

Another noteworthy section of Chapter I is paragraph 9, where the Council comes as close as it could to defining the missionary endeavor: 'Missionary activity is nothing else and nothing less than a manifestation of God's will, and the fulfillment of that will in the world and in world history.' God 'works out the history of salvation by means of mission', and its goal is to bring about 'the presence of Christ, the Author of salvation.'

Nevertheless, in words that sound a recurring theme of the document, Christ's presence does not destroy a culture, but brings it to perfection. This is because in each culture there is 'a sort of secret presence of God' that the gospel makes manifest as that culture is healed and ennobled. Mission, paragraph 9 and Chapter I says in conclusion, has an ultimately eschatological goal. It works toward that unity of the world and humanity that 'will come at the end of time'.

Chapter II

Chapter II is entitled 'Mission Work Itself', and lays down several important principles in the way that mission is to be carried out among the peoples of the world. Paragraphs 11 to 12 reflect on Christian witness; paragraphs 13-14 speak of the actual preaching of the gospel; and paragraphs 15-18 deal with the dynamics of forming a Christian community, as women and men respond to the gospel and commit themselves to Christ. These three activities are engaged in within three contexts, as paragraph 10 points out: among adherents to the world's great religions, among people with no religious faith whatsoever, and among people who are actually hostile to religion and belief in God.

Paragraph 11 is one of the more eloquent passages in the document. It speaks of the need for Christians to witness to the gospel by their very life, lived in full participation with the culture and values of the people. As they 'become familiar with their national and religious traditions', they 'gladly and reverently' lay 'bare the seeds of the Word which lie hidden in them'. The phrase 'seeds of the Word' is from Justin Martyr and has been often cited after the Council. It points to the fact that mission is not done in a vacuum, but in the context of the already-present Spirit and mysterious presence of Christ. This is why missionaries must engage 'in a sincere and patient dialogue' in order to discover 'what treasures a bountiful God has distributed among the nations of the earth.'

It is this basic holiness of peoples, their history, and their cultures that grounds the Council's strong and clear prohibition of any kind of proselytism that would force people to embrace the faith or would entice people 'by unworthy techniques' (AG 13). We see echoes of the Council's discussion of religious freedom here, as well as in its insistence that all persons have a 'right not to be deterred from the faith by unjust vexation on the part of others' (AG 13).

A major goal of missionary activity is the establishment of a vibrant and vital Christian community that is – as Paul VI would say ten years later in *Evangelii Nuntiandi* – in its turn evangelizing (EN 15). In paragraphs 15-18 the document addresses itself to the formation of such a community. It focuses on the importance of the lay vocation, and then turns to the vocation of women and men to religious life, to ordained ministry, and to training for ordained ministry. In paragraph 16 it echoes the Constitution on the Church by calling for the restoration of the permanent diaconate if episcopal conferences deem it opportune. Finally, in paragraph 17 it focuses on the important role of catechists and their proper training.

Chapter III

This chapter on 'Particular Churches' focuses on local churches that are still 'missions' in the sense that they are not quite ready to stand on their own in terms of the numbers of Christians, local clergy, or material resources. Nevertheless, the members of the Council insisted, these are *churches* in their own right, and should be treated as such. This is a move away from the word 'mission church' as somehow signifying a community that is not complete. This chapter, therefore, is firmly established on the foundation of a vigorous theology of the local church.

Paragraph 20 speaks of the bishop and his clergy. The bishop should be 'a herald of the Faith', and clergy should not only be engaged in pastoral work but also involved in the preaching of the gospel among peoples of the diocese who have not yet accepted Christ. Paragraph 21 is a powerful reflection on the laity, insisting that 'the church has not been really founded, and is not yet fully alive, nor is it a perfect sign of Christ among humanity, unless there is a laity worthy of the name working along with the hierarchy.' The laity's main task is to bear witness in their daily lives, and the document places particular emphasis on the fact that this must be done in the context of their cultures. The Christian community, *Ad Gentes* asserts again and again, is not to be removed from the midst of the world, but a full participant in it, and a contributor to it.

The final paragraph of the chapter is devoted to the encouragement of local, contextual, or inculturated theologies, although the text does not use these terms that would be developed in the decades since. It uses rather the term 'adaptation'. Nevertheless, in one of those beautiful phrases, echoing wording often used in the liturgy of the Christmas season, local churches are encouraged to 'take to themselves in a wonderful exchange all the riches of the nations which were given to Christ as an inheritance (cf. Ps. 2:8)' (AG 22). In this way, 'it will be more clearly seen in what ways faith may seek understanding' (AG 22) in the context of the philosophy, the wisdom, the customs, and the worldviews of local peoples.

Chapter IV

This chapter is entitled 'Missionaries', and, as missiologist William R. Burrows judges, it 'is an excellent, balanced and far-sighted chapter designed to help prepare future missionaries' – whether they are priests, brothers, women religious, or lay people, or whether they are foreign or indigenous' (Burrows 1986: 189). Once again the text implicitly acknowledges that missionary activity is based not on geography but on particular needs of particular peoples, and includes all Christians.

However, while every Christian is called to do his or her part in spreading the faith in word and especially in deed (AG 23), there exists in the church a particular missionary calling by which Christians leave the countries or environments in which they were born and nurtured and cross cultures for the sake of spreading the gospel. This vocation is a gift of the Holy Spirit, but the presence of such a charism is not enough. Future missionaries also need 'special spiritual and moral training' (AG 25) to develop their generosity, their sense of dedication, their openness, and their willingness to sacrifice. Missionaries also need training in theology, a training that 'takes into account both the universality of the Church and the diversity of the world's nations' (AG 26). 'Above all' (AG 26), the future missionary should be trained in missiology, both in terms of what the church teaches regarding missionary work, and the history of that work. While the words are not explicitly used, the theology recommended, as well as the missiology, should be imbued with the social sciences, especially anthropology. 'For anyone who is going to encounter another people should have a great esteem for the patrimony and their language and their customs' (AG 26).

Chapter V

Entitled simply 'Planning Missionary Activity', Chapter V is the chapter about which there was the most discussion during the preparation of the final schema. This is because the chapter deals particularly with the restructuring of the Congregation of the Propagation of the Faith, and aims to give local bishops in areas under its jurisdiction a greater say in their churches' development.

Such restructuring of the Propaganda Fide is placed in the context of a theologically based understanding of the direction of the church's mission. Paragraph 28 begins the chapter by stating that all the Christian faithful, according to the gifts bestowed on them, are called to participate in the church's mission. But this missionary activity of all the faithful needs to have direction so that (quoting 1 Cor. 14:40) 'all may be done in order.' That direction is provided primarily by the entire body or college of bishops, as LG 23 teaches. And so, as a way of exercising that collegial responsibility, the Council directs that the 'stable Council of bishops for the entire Church', the Synod of Bishops, should give special consideration to the church's missionary activity. The Propaganda Fide, therefore, directs the church's missionary work, but as the agent of the entire church in general and the episcopal college in particular.

At the end of paragraph 29 there appears the passage that caused so much controversy during the drafting of the schema as well as on the Council floor. This paragraph states that as part of the direction of the Congregation, there should be representatives of the world's bishops, moderators of pontifical institutes that support missionary work (e.g. the Holy Childhood Association), missionary congregations of men and women, and lay organizations. An earlier draft had spoken of these as 'members' of the Congregation, but this was not accepted by the Council. Nevertheless it is clear that the Council intended these groups to play an active part with a deliberative vote in the Congregations decision-making processes.

This is quite a radical restructuring, but it must be noted that, sadly, this crucial directive of *Ad Gentes* was never put into practice. Over the years after the Council, a series of documents gradually lessened the role of these non-curial groups, and in John Paul II's *Redemptoris Mission* we read that the world's bishops, major superiors, etc. should only 'cooperate fully with this Dicastery' (RM 75). Ultimately, as missiologist Josef Glazik has written, practically nothing has changed from what the congregation was before Vatican II. A truly unfortunate development (see Glazik 1970: 13-15).

Chapter VI

The final chapter on 'Missionary Cooperation', or how various Christians contribute to the missionary activity of the church, begins with an affirmation once more of the entire church's role in its mission. The text then goes on to outline how bishops and priests, various types of religious – active and contemplative – and then the laity participate in missionary activity. There is, however, a great distance between this chapter and the strong statement about the missionary nature of the local church in Chapter II. Here 'misisons' basically means 'foreign missions'. There are 'home countries' and 'mission countries'.

Two things might be highlighted in the chapter. First, paragraph 39 offers reflections on the intrinsic missionary dimension of the priesthood. Because priests collaborate with bishops in ordering the church, they are also in some way responsible for the worldwide mission of the church. Part of their ministry, therefore, should be involved in raising missionary awareness among the faithful, fostering missionary vocations, and asking for alms for missionary work.

Second, the document emphasizes the missionary nature of contemplative orders of religious. While it is often thought that missionary work is the purview of active congregations, the Council insists that contemplatives are also an essential part of missionary activity. Because it is *God* who ultimately touches human hearts to open up to the gospel message, the prayers, sufferings, and acts of penance offered by groups of contemplative men and women contribute immensely to the conversion of non-Christians. The text then encourages contemplative communities to establish houses in the lands of Asia, Africa, Latin America, and Oceania, so that 'living out their lives in a way accommodated to the truly religious traditions of the people, they can bear excellent witness among non-Christians to the majesty and love of God, as well as our union with Christ' (AG 40).

Ad Gentes concludes with a salutation to all missionaries, especially those who are suffering persecution. The Council once more affirms the importance of the church's participation in mission, but acknowledges once again as well – as it did in the beginning of the document – that mission is ultimately the work of God. The bishops pray for the conversion of the world to the gospel, through the intercession of Mary, Queen of Apostles. Any changes of law that the decree provides for, the document says in its last lines, will take effect on June 29, 1966, and that the pope will issue norms for the implementation in due time.

Conclusion

As Roger Schroeder outlines in the essay to follow this chapter, citing Robert J. Schreiter, Vatican II inaugurated a 'period of ferment' in the thinking and practice of Christian mission, followed soon after – ironically largely because of the Council's stance on religious freedom, its respect for local cultures, and on the possibility of salvation outside the church – by a 'period of crisis' in which the very idea of mission was questioned. While that period of crisis persists in some way, it co-exists with a 'period of rebirth', in which mission has taken on less of a triumphalistic character, and has expanded to include elements of dialogue, justice, peacemaking, ecological sensitivity, inculturation, ministry among migrants, and reconciliation. Many things have changed in the fifty years since the end of the Council, perhaps most radically the fact that mission is done much more in short-term commitments, more by laity, and more by women and men from traditional 'mission lands' in the majority world. Mission looks very different today than it did in 1965 when *Ad Gentes* was formally promulgated. And yet there is continuity, all of which has its origins in the amazing event that was the Second Vatican Council.

CATHOLIC TEACHING ON MISSION
AFTER VATICAN II: 1975-2007

Roger P. Schroeder, SVD

In a seminal article, 'Changes in Roman Catholic Attitudes toward Proselytism and Mission', Robert Schreiter (1994) described the development of the Catholic understanding and practice of mission through the twentieth century in terms of four stages – certainty, ferment, crisis and rebirth. The first stage of certainty covered the nineteenth through the first part of the twentieth century. The Second Vatican Council stands as the turning point of ferment. The previous two chapters of this volume treated church teachings during the certainty stage of the twentieth century (1919-1959) and the ferment stage of Vatican II (1959-1965).

Transitional Decade after Vatican II

Schreiter identified the ten-year period after the Council (1965-1975) as the stage of crisis for mission. The world itself was overflowing with change: the civil rights movement in the United States, the Cultural Revolution in China, the Six-Day War in the Middle East, the 'Prague Spring' in Czechoslovakia, and youth uprisings in Mexico. Other factors within the church contributed to a sense of crisis. The exodus of many priests and religious began to deplete the numbers of missionaries. The end of colonialism, to which mission had been so closely aligned, led many to call for the end of mission, at least an end to what mission had been. Furthermore, the theological shifts of the Second Vatican Council – in explicitly recognizing 'the missionary nature' of the entire church (AG 2), God's presence in the world as the 'signs of the times' (GS 4), the need for 'discussion and collaboration with members of other religions' (NA 2) and the possibility of salvation without baptism (LG 16) – undercut the pre-Vatican II mission motivations for the salvation of souls and the establishment of the visible church.

A new theology and practice of mission needed to be developed. Schreiter identified the beginning of the fourth stage, the rebirth of mission, with the year 1975 and the apostolic exhortation of Paul VI, *Evangelii Nuntiandi* (EN). However, it is necessary to note that a number of new life-generating movements during the 'decade of crisis' contributed to this birth. In 1968, the Conference of Latin American Bishops (CELAM) in

Medellín, Columbia in did an analysis of and reflection upon the reality (*realidad*) of Latin America and developed an agenda for moving beyond development and revolution to transformation of unjust structures. This impacted the global church as the 1971 Synod of Bishops in Rome spelled out the integral relationship between justice and evangelization. New developments emerged as well in other parts of the world: Catholics in Asia focused on inter-religious relationships; in Africa on faith and culture; in Europe, North America and Australia on Christianity and secularization; and in the Pacific Islands on the impact of rapid social change. Basic Christian Communities developed and Catholics began studying the Bible around the world.

The post-Vatican II decade was a transitional time marked with its share of breaking down and building up (see Eccl. 3:3). We shall now trace the subsequent 'rebirth' phase of the understanding of mission as seen in official church documents, starting with *Evangelii Nuntiandi* in 1975 and ending with the document 'Doctrinal Note on Some Aspects of Evangelization' in 2007. This chapter is the third installment of Part II on 'Church Teaching on Mission' during the hundred years since Edinburgh 1910.

Evangelii Nuntiandi (1975)

Paul VI convoked the 1974 Synod of Bishops with the theme 'Evangelization in the Modern World'. Drawing upon the deliberations of the synod, which included a much larger percentage of bishops from the majority world than the Second Vatican Council, the pope produced and released his apostolic exhortation *Evangelii Nuntiandi* in 1975. Probably in an effort to avoid identifying mission with colonization, the term 'evangelization' was used rather than 'mission'. While evangelization can be identified more narrowly with its principal form of proclamation by word and witness, Paul VI preferred to understand it here more broadly as inclusive of all the forms evangelization can take. With this latter sense, the terms 'evangelization' and 'mission' are basically interchangeable. We now highlight the three most significant contributions of the apostolic exhortation to rebirthing the Catholic understanding of mission.

The Church continues the mission of Jesus

In the opening chapter, EN affirms the fundamental missionary nature of the church, rediscovered in Vatican II. However, rather than building this on the Trinity (*missio Dei*), as done in *Ad Gentes* [AG], Paul VI centers the church and mission theologically on the reign of God. 'As an evangelizer, Christ first of all proclaims a kingdom, the kingdom of God; and this is so important that, by comparison, everything else becomes 'the rest,' which is 'given in addition.' Only the Kingdom, therefore is absolute, and it makes everything else relative' (EN 8). The kingdom of God was central to Jesus' mission in his words (particularly parables), actions (particularly healings and exorcisms) and behavior (particularly table fellowship). Those who accept the good news and seek this kingdom 'make up a community which is in its turn evangelizing' (13). In this way, 'Evangelizing is in fact the grace and vocation proper to the Church, her deepest identity' (14).

The pope insists on several key consequences of this missional nature of the church. First of all, the church 'begins by being evangelized herself ... by constant conversion and renewal, in order to evangelize the world with credibility' (15). Secondly, there is a strong link and continuity between Jesus' mission of the reign of God and the church, which is 'the normal, desired, most immediate and most visible fruit' of Jesus' work. In response to those who separate the love of Christ from the church, EN states that the two cannot be separated. In this way, evangelization is an ecclesial work that is 'not accomplished without her [the church], and still less against her' (16). Thirdly, since the entire church is missionary by nature, everyone in the church is to participate in its mission, and 'the work of each individual member is important for the whole' (15). In this way, although not stated explicitly in the document, it implies that baptism like the church is missionary by nature.

The multi-faceted reality of evangelization

The second major impact of EN was its expanded understanding of mission to include not only direct proclamation and planting the church, but also, a variety of other activities. While AG hinted at this broader intention, EN goes further. In response to the tendency to reduce evangelization to only proclaiming Christ to those who do not yet know him, Paul VI states that 'any partial and fragmentary definition which attempts to render the reality of evangelization in all its richness, complexity and dynamism does so only at the risk of impoverishing it and even of distorting it. It is impossible to grasp the concept of evangelization unless one tries to keep in view all its essential elements' (17).

While explicit proclamation is essential, 'it is only one aspect of evangelization' (22). The second chapter describes the other 'essential elements'. Evangelization 'means bringing the Good News into all the strata of humanity', that would hopefully lead to the conversion of 'both the personal and collective consciences of people ... and the lives and concrete milieus which are theirs' (18). Paul VI described the latter as an evangelization of cultures, 'not in a purely decorative way as it were by applying a thin veneer, but in a vital way, in depth and right to their very roots' (20). Furthermore, EN insists on the absolute necessity of the witness of Christian communities and individuals as 'a silent proclamation of the Good News' (21).

Evangelization and liberation

The development of this expanded understanding of mission leads to the third principal contribution from EN – evangelization also includes a commitment to full human advancement and liberation (31). Building upon the conclusion of the Synod of Bishops four years earlier that justice is a 'constitutive dimension of the preaching of the gospel', Paul VI states that 'evangelization involves an explicit message ... about the rights and duties of every human being, about family life without which personal growth and development is hardly possible, about life in society, about international life, peace, justice and development – a message especially energetic today about liberation' (29). 'This is the first appearance of the word *liberation* in an official Catholic document, and it clearly reflects the influence of the theology of liberation that was so important in the 1970s' (Bevans and Schroeder 2004: 306).

The apostolic exhortation insists on a balance between evangelization and liberation. First of all, mission is not to be reduced 'to the dimensions of a simply temporal project' (32). The spiritual dimension of the good news is the source of the deepest liberation for humanity. Secondly, the church is against violence since 'violence always provokes violence and irresistibly engenders new forms of oppression and enslavement which are often harder to bear than those from which they claimed to bring freedom' (37).

Highlighting these three primary features of EN indicate why this document is considered a 'Magna Carta' for the rebirth of the understanding of mission. We now move ahead fifteen years to the next major Catholic teaching on mission.

Redemptoris Missio (1990)

Redemptoris Missio (RM) was issued on December 7, 1990, the eve of the twenty-fifth anniversary of AG and the fifteenth anniversary of EN. In keeping with the significance of this date, Marcello Zago – later to become Secretary of the Congregation for the Evangelization of Peoples – stated the following regarding this encyclical of John Paul II: 'From a missiological viewpoint it is certainly the most significant and authoritative document of his pontificate' (in Burrows 1993: 56). Furthermore, RM represents the best articulation of a systematic reflection on mission in official Catholic documents.

While affirming new developments in mission during the fifteen years after EN, John Paul II along with others became concerned that the significance of Christ and the church was not being sufficiently upheld by some theologians and missionaries. First of all, an over-emphasis on the holiness of the world, cultures and religions from the Trinitarian foundation of AG could lead to losing focus on Jesus as the unique savior and judge of cultures. Secondly, an over-emphasis on the holistic mission from the reign of God foundation of EN could lead to losing focus on the importance of the church in mission. A third issue is that an over-emphasis on the all-encompassing nature of mission for the church, universal and local, in every part of the world, and on the multiplicity of the forms of mission could lead to losing focus on mission *ad gentes* and proclamation. The pope returned to the term 'mission' with a multifaceted meaning, while 'evangelization' is used both in a broad and narrow sense. Since even a summary of this lengthy and comprehensive encyclical would be too much here, we shall highlight three major aspects for understanding mission from RM, as done above for EN.

Christocentric focus

In response to the three above-mentioned concerns, the pope presented a Christocentric theology as the foundation for mission, explicitly in Chapter I and throughout the document. While maintaining the teaching of Vatican II that people have the possibility of being saved outside of explicit faith in Christ (RM 10), all grace comes through Christ, and Christ alone. 'No one, therefore, can enter into communion with God except through Christ, by the working of the Holy Spirit ... Although participated forms of mediation of different kinds and degrees are not excluded, they acquire meaning and value *only* from Christ's own mediation, and they cannot be understood as parallel or complementary to his' (5). Furthermore, the church 'has been established as the universal sacrament of salvation' (9). All humanity has a right to the truth and life offered by the gospel, but this is done in a way that respects human freedom (7-8).

In chapter II, the pope affirms the centrality of the reign of God in Jesus' work and life. While the church is not an end unto itself (19), 'the Kingdom cannot be detached either from Christ or from the Church' (18). Chapter III builds upon the Trinitarian theology of AG in focusing on the Holy Spirit as the principal agent of evangelization. 'The Spirit's presence and activity affect not only individuals but also society and history, peoples, cultures and religions' (28). Furthermore, the encyclical insists that this is the same Spirit of Christ and 'the universal activity of the Spirit is not to be separated from ... the Church' (29). These three foundational chapters, while building upon AG and EN, highlight the specificity of Christ and the necessity of proclaiming Jesus' lordship. In response to the question 'Why mission?' the pope responds, 'Because to us, as to St. Paul, 'this grace was given, to preach to the Gentiles the unsearchable riches of Christ' (Eph. 3:8)...' (11).

Expanded idea of mission

The encyclical expands the idea of mission in terms of the 'horizons' (Chapter IV), and the 'paths' of mission (Chapter V). Regarding the former, the first of the three 'horizons' or 'situations' is mission *ad gentes*, that is, the witnessing and direct proclamation of the gospel where Christ is not known or where the church is not mature enough 'to incarnate the faith in their own environment and proclaim it to other groups' (RM 33). John Paul II says that this is mission in the proper sense. However, he then describes the second 'situation' of the pastoral care of the faithful, and the third 'situation' which was historically Christian but is no longer so. The mission response required in the latter 'horizon' is called 'new evangelization' or 're-evangelization' (33). While mission *ad gentes* is mission in its proper sense, the encyclical expands this idea to areas such as cities, youth, and communities of migrants and the poor (37b). Furthermore, in referring to the incident of Paul at the Areopagus in Athens, the pope insists on the need to respond creatively in mission to the modern Areopagi or equivalent cultural sectors, such as the world of communications. He includes a 'commitment to peace, development and the liberation of peoples; the rights of individuals and peoples, especially those of minorities; the advancement of women and children; safeguarding the created world' (37c). The encyclical highlights the importance of mission *ad gentes* and at the same time expanded its scope.

Secondly, RM describes the various 'paths' of the 'single but complex reality' (41) of mission. The first form of evangelization is witness, the witness of Christian individuals, families, communities and ecclesial bodies (42), and 'proclamation is the permanent priority of mission' (44). This can lead to conversion, baptism and forming local churches (46-49). The pope adds to the list of various paths with the inclusion of inculturation, inter-religious dialogue, promoting development and works of charity (52-60). In its treatment of the 'paths' and earlier the 'horizons' of mission, RM clarified and expanded the idea of mission for a post-Vatican II church that is 'missionary by nature'.

Inter-religious dialogue

The above-mentioned aspect of inter-religious dialogue is singled out as the third major contribution of RM, since this is relatively new in official church teachings. Paragraph 53 of EN had reaffirmed the positive assessment of other religions from the Second Vatican Council but didn't elaborate. The Secretariat for Non-Christians described inter-religious dialogue as integral to evangelization in its 1984 document on 'Dialogue and Mission' (DM 1984). However, RM was the first papal encyclical to include such dialogue as 'part of the church's evangelizing mission' (55).

The pope states that inter-religious dialogue is consistent with other aspects of mission. The church engages in respectful dialogue because of God's presence in all religions, but this does not detract from the facts that '*salvation comes from Christ and that dialogue does not dispense from evangelization*' (55). In interactions with believers of other religions,

Catholics maintain their faith conviction and hold that 'the Church is the ordinary means of salvation and that she alone possesses the fullness of the means of salvation' (55). John Paul II states that inter-religious dialogue, however, 'does not originate from tactical concerns or self-interests' but rather is founded on 'deep respect' for the movement of the Spirit in the other (56). Those engaged in such dialogue should approach others 'without pretence or close-mindedness, but with truth, humility and frankness, knowing that dialogue can enrich each side' (56). The encyclical adds that dialogue is not only for experts, but rather Christians can participate in their daily lives.

Much more could be written about the systematic treatment of mission in RM, but the three themes we have treated are perhaps the encyclical's most important ones.

Dialogue and Proclamation (1991)

The Pontifical Council for Inter-religious Dialogue, which had produced a document on dialogue and mission in 1984 (DM) under its earlier name of the Secretariat for Non-Christians, and the Congregation for the Evangelization of Peoples together published the very important document *Dialogue and Proclamation* (DP) just a few months after the publication of RM. John Paul II had pointed to the relationship between inter-religious dialogue and proclamation, but DP elaborated on their vital connection. The document is divided into three parts: the first on dialogue, the second on proclamation and the third on the relationship of the two aspects. Dialogue was treated first not out of sense of priority, but rather because the document originated with the Council for Dialogue. The two components of mission, which are in a dynamic and tensive relationship, are rooted in God's action. God has always offered salvation to humankind, but always in dialogue as an invitation (see DP 38).

First, the document presents a well-developed theology of religions and the four forms of dialogue that had been introduced in DM: dialogue of life, action, theological exchange, and religious experience (DP 42). On the part of Christians, such dialogue requires balance, religious conviction, and openness to truth and it promises rich rewards (47-50). Some of the obstacles to inter-religious dialogue include an insufficient knowledge of one's own religion and/or that of the other, cultural differences, sociopolitical factors, and a misunderstanding of conversion, baptism and dialogue (52). However, 'despite the difficulties, the Church's commitment to dialogue remains firm and irreversible' (54).

The second major section of DP begins with a treatment of the mandate, content, and urgency of proclamation. In terms of manner, the church should remember that the hearers 'may have already been touched by the Spirit and in some ways associated unknowingly to the paschal mystery of Jesus Christ (cf. *Gaudium et Spes* 22)' (DP 68). For this reason, the gospel must be communicated in a way that draws on their experience and invites them to respond to God's initiative. Proclamation should be confident and faithful, on the one hand, and humble and dialogical, on the other (70). Obstacles to authentic proclamation include the gap between the Christian message and how it is lived by Christians, lack of respect for other religions, and external factors like a historical prejudice against Christianity (see 73-74).

In the final part, DP summarizes the close connection between the two key aspects of mission. 'Inter-religious dialogue and proclamation, though not on the same level, are both authentic elements of the Church's evangelizing mission. Both are legitimate and necessary. They are intimately related, but not interchangeable; true inter-religious dialogue on the part of the Christian supposes the desire to make Jesus Christ better known, recognized and loved, proclaiming Jesus Christ is to be carried out in the Gospel spirit of dialogue' (77).

Conclusion: From DP to the Present

Since *Dialogue and Proclamation* in 1991, there have been no major official Roman documents on mission of the status of EN, RM and DP. The primary focus of the past twenty years has been on the theological questions of inter-religious dialogue and the uniqueness of Jesus Christ as universal savior underlying DP. The Congregation of the Doctrine of the Faith issued the declaration *Dominus Iesus* in 2000 (DI) and a document entitled 'Doctrinal Note on Some Aspects of Evangelization' in 2007 (CDF). Both strongly emphasized the centrality of Christ as Savior to the degree that the equally central belief in God's grace outside Christianity and in inter-religious dialogue, though acknowledged, was underrepresented. However, these two documents were not intended to offer a systematic theology of mission, but rather were responding to the particular issues of relativism, the uniqueness of Christ, and to some degree the role of the church. It appears that issues of Christology are fundamental not only in terms of inter-religious dialogue but also with current discussions of inculturation.

According to many, the document EN marked the beginning of the rebirth of a new understanding of mission in the official teaching of the Catholic Church. The Second Vatican Council marked the end of one period of mission and the beginning of the next. After ten years of transition, Paul VI built upon the Trinitarian (*missio Dei*) theology of AG and the deliberations and reflections of the 1974 Synod of Bishops on evangelization in writing and promulgating EN with its focus on the theology of the reign of God. Fifteen years later, John Paul II in the encyclical RM offered the best systematic theology of mission in official Catholic teachings by including the theologies of AG and EN, but more specifically, by presenting a Christocentric theology and expanding the idea of mission. In the following year, the document of *Dialogue and Proclamation* represented an excellent systematic and balanced treatment of the most challenging theological and missiological issue for the post-Vatican II Church. Later official documents continue to respond to this issue and related concerns.

Today, official Catholic teaching on mission is founded upon three theologies of mission: participation in the mission of the Triune God (*missio Dei*), liberating service of the reign of God, and proclamation of Jesus Christ as universal savior. On the one hand, one theology may be more relevant in a particular context, but on the other hand, each theology in its diversity and with its roots in Christian tradition makes an important contribution to the whole. From a good Catholic approach and perspective, they can form a healthy synthesis of an understanding of mission that provides the basis for responding in practice to the call of mission in today's world.

PART THREE

ROMAN CATHOLIC MISSIOLOGY

THE BIBLE IN CATHOLIC MISSION 1910-2010

James Chukwuma Okoye, CSSp

Introduction

'Mission' needs be defined before one may seek its biblical foundations. The Catholic Church has shifted from '*the* missions' to 'evangelization' or 'evangelizing mission' back to 'mission' (RM 1990). Before the 1950s I went to the 'Catholic Mission' in my homeland in Nigeria. By 1960 (the date of independence from Britain), I was going to the Catholic Church. In between was the successful nationalist movement. Missionary activity varies according to contexts. I shall discern for each document the meaning and configurations of 'mission' before considering the biblical hermeneutics that undergird it.

Papal and Curial Documents: The Era of the Distant Missions

Encyclical Letter, *Maximum Illud* (MI 1919). The missions had been devastated by the First World War (1914-18). Beyond the appeal for prayer, fostering missionary vocations and financial solidarity (in that order), this tract focused on two areas. First, the mandate for a native clergy to be trained to the highest standards so it can take up God's work as equals to the missionaries. A well-trained local clergy that takes up leadership of the church is a measure of success of mission (MI 16). The second was the promotion of mission consciousness and the formation of missionaries. Missionaries were to acquire proficiency in all branches of learning (23) and ready competence in the language of the people to whom they would administer (24). The pope mandated the teaching of missiology in the Urbanianum in Rome (23); Propaganda Fide was to found seminaries, diocesan and regional (17) and supervise their growth. Superiors of religious orders were to choose the very best for the missions (35).

Mission meant the distant 'missions' – 'distant' or 'foreign', of course, from the perspective of Europe and North America – and was addressed to non-Christians, called 'infidels'. It was run by religious orders often of the same nation as the colonial power in the mission territory. Missionaries were primarily clergy. Schools, hospitals, and orphanages were an appendage of mission. Missionary activity was a combat in which 'picked troops of Christ' wrested peoples 'from the clutches of the devil' (35). Traditional religion was Satanic worship. Much more than the Great

Commission (Mk. 16:15), which appeared at the very beginning, the
generative motive of mission was rescuing helpless 'infidels' in darkness
and the shadow of death (18 – Ps. 107:30, though not cited).

Encyclical, *Rerum Ecclesiae* (RE 1926). Pius XI organized a Missionary
Exhibition in the Vatican in the Holy Year of 1925 that had over 100,000
objects in twenty-four pavilions. He continued the military metaphor: 'all
the officers in the mission army' (4) had made 'conquests... up to the
present hour for the Kingdom of Christ' (32). Beyond expanding the faith,
the promotion of civilization and culture became integral to mission (1; 10):
hence the plea to found institutions of higher learning, particularly in the
arts, the sciences and the professions (31). Native clergy ought to have
scientific education both in the sacred and profane sciences (25). New was
the emphasis on catechists and their training, so also the plea to found
religious congregations of native men and women (27). The principal
image for mission was carrying 'the light of the gospel' to dark regions.
The gospel was 'a light of revelation for the gentiles' (Lk. 2:32; Is. 42:6,
49:6). For this pope, the darkness was primarily that of error. Missionary
activity derived from the universal salvific will of God (1 Tim. 2:4), in the
service of which Christ gave the Great Commission (Matt. 28:18-20; Mk.
16:15). Christ first healed the sick and then preached the kingdom, (Lk.
10:8-9). So must the missionary.

Encyclical, *Evangelii Praecones* (EP 1951). The Second World War
(1945-1949) and the Marxist Revolution had changed geopolitics. In the
colonized countries, the wind of 'freedom' was blowing furiously. Pius XII
called for greater indigenization and penned the words repeated ever since:
'whatever there is in the native customs that is not inseparably bound up
with superstition and error' (59) should be cleansed and taken up. In light
of the new demands, missionaries 'should be sufficiently instructed in the
sciences of medicine, agriculture, ethnography, history, geography, etc.'
(21). Mission must be attentive to the education of youth who would take
over as leaders (42). It must also see to social reforms demanded by justice
and charity (49). However, mission still focused upon the individual 'till
the last man in the most remote corner of the earth has been reached' (24).
The metaphor of light continued: mission brought 'the light of the Gospel
to new races and ... [formed] new Christians' (22). It was activity done in
the wake of Jesus 'who came to seek and to save what was lost' (Lk. 19:10;
71). It went in search of over 1,000,000,000 people who sit in darkness and
the shadow of death (see Ps. 107:10). The missionary was 'ambassador' for
Christ (2 Cor. 5:20) in a mortal contest between two opposing camps, 'for
Christ or against Christ.'

On April 21, 1957, Pius XII issued the Encyclical, *Fidei Donum* (FD
1957), exhorting the churches of the West to send priests and other
missionaries for temporary mission to dioceses in the missions, especially
Africa.

Papal and Curial Documents: Period of Transition

Encyclical, *Princeps Pastorum* (PP 1959). New nations were emerging, several mission countries were undergoing speedy and transforming changes. Not a few former mission areas were now led by native clergy and were sending out missionaries (10). John XXIII sought in this encyclical to mobilize all the energies of the church for mission, above all the laity. Ordinaries should select seminary professors and formators from suitable local clergy (15). The new social order in its birthpangs needed be built on Christian principles. For this, an informed and active Christian laity was crucial. Schools of the apostolate were to be established for training Catholic executives (47), the first time this appears. The laity was to be trained for responsibility in the fields of education, public welfare, trade unions, and public administration (50). All must take on the responsibility of proclaiming the faith (32) and supporting church and mission (39).

The church's participation in the transformation of the social order now became part of mission. The goal remained 'to establish the Church firmly in *other* [emphasis mine] countries, and subsequently to entrust it to a local hierarchy ...' (8), but the kingdom aspects were beginning to appear. Sure that 'I am with you all days, even unto the consummation of the world' (Matt. 28:20), all Christians must 'let your light shine before men, in order that they may see your good work ...' (Matt. 5:16). The 'good fight' (2 Tim 4:7) in the cause of the faith must now be waged also in public life in all its forms. Love, at the roots of Christian life, must be exercised in material help for works of mission (38) and express itself in the Christian transformation of culture and society.

Vatican II, *Decree on the Missionary Activity of the Church* (AG 1965). As 'the *universal* sacrament of salvation' (emphasis mine) and of the unity of the human race, the church is the light of the world, reflecting the light of Christ to whom the text refers. There is some tension in the two approaches to mission in this document. There was the regno-centric view. 'The pilgrim Church is missionary by her very nature' (2) for it flows from the 'fountain of love' within the Trinity. As result, 'missionary activity is nothing else and nothing less than a manifestation or epiphany of God's will, and the fulfillment of that will in the world and in world history' (9). However, the ecclesio-centric view was the one most developed: 'the specific purpose of this missionary activity is evangelization and the planting of the Church among those peoples and groups where she has not yet taken root' (6). Mission, distinguished from pastoral activity, was carried out in the 'missions' (a search for this plural form turned up twenty-two matches, even though the singular 'mission' was dominant), and is usually exercised in certain territories recognized by the Holy See. It reaches its climax in solid and native particular churches that prolong the process of healing and renewing culture and environment in Christ. The church's role in the unity of the human race was founded in Matthew 5:13-14, John 11:52 (gather into one the scattered people of God) and Ephesians

1:10 (restore all things in Christ as head). There was also the command of Jesus to preach the gospel to the ends of the earth (Mk. 16:15-16 and par, Jn. 20:21, Acts 1:8). The church was further impelled by the fact that there is no other name in which people can be saved (Acts 4:12). Mission is the process of growing completely into Christ, by whom the whole body is fitted and joined together, growing until it has built itself up in love (see Eph. 4:16; AG 5, 7).

Papal and Curial Documents: The Era of Evangelization

Apostolic Exhortation, *Evangelii Nuntiandi* (EN 1975). The 1974 Synod of Bishops entrusted to Paul VI the task of producing a final document. He produced EN, acclaimed in the whole church as an epoch-making statement. The term 'evangelization' (used for the whole and the parts, also 'proclaiming the gospel' and 'proclaiming Christ') is 'a complex process made up of varied elements: the renewal of humanity, witness, explicit proclamation, inner adherence, entry into the community, acceptance of signs, apostolic witness' (24). Essential to evangelization is 'a total interior renewal' (10), 'transforming humanity from within and making it new' (18). It is no question of greater numbers of people or of extending boundaries, rather of affecting and upsetting, through the power of the gospel, humankind's criteria of judgment, 'determining values, points of interest, lines of thought, sources of inspiration and models of life, which are in contrast with the Word of God and the plan of salvation' (19). 'The Church is an evangelizer, but she begins by being evangelized' (15). Evangelization repeats Christ's 'I must proclaim the Good News of the kingdom of God ... that is what I was sent to do' (Lk. 4:43, EN 6, repeated in. 12 and 14), joined to Paul's 'woe to me if I preach not the Gospel' (1 Cor 9:6; EN 14). The key words of evangelization are *kingdom* and *salvation.* It works to 'put on the new self' (Eph. 4:24; Col. 3:10; Gal. 3:27; EN 2 and *passim*) for a new creation (2 Cor. 5:17; Gal. 6:15; Rev. 21:5). It brings the charge, 'be reconciled to God' (2 Cor. 5:20). The mission commission (Mk. 16:1; EN 15, 49) plays a subsidiary role in this configuration.

Papal and Curial Documents: Back to Mission

Dialogue and Mission (DM 1984). The Secretariat for Non-Christians (now the Pontifical Council for Inter-religious Dialogue) issued this document on the twentieth anniversary of its foundation and of *Ecclesiam Suam* of Paul VI (ES 1964). It was the first document of the universal magisterium or the Curia to reflect on the reciprocal relationships between dialogue and mission. Picking up EN 24 it described mission as 'a single but complex and articulated reality' (13). By 'mission' it generally meant the total activity of the church (see, however, Dupuis 1993: 129). *Redemptor*

Hominis (RH 1979) of John Paul II was of particular import. The teaching was founded on texts on God's nature as love: God is love (1 Jn. 4:8, 16) and the church is and must be sign of that love (9). Everything in the life and ministry of Jesus was an expression of his love (Jn. 3:16; 13:1). God has a loving plan for every nation (Acts 17:26-27). The very life of the Trinity (22-24) is shown all across scripture as one of 'communion and interchange' (22). Both dialogue and mission flow from the same fountain of love as the very life of God and of the church.

Encyclical, *Redemptoris Missio* (RM 1991). In the wake of EN, there began the 'insertion of missiology into ecclesiology' (32), with the term 'missionary' referring to all forms of the church's activity. The risk was one of 'reducing, even eliminating, the Church's mission and missionaries *ad gentes*' (32). John Paul II wrote RM to urge greater stress on initial proclamation. He reverted to the term 'mission' for the whole activity of the church, reserving the terms 'evangelization', 'proclamation' (Latin, *nuntius*) and mission *ad gentes* for preaching Christ to peoples and cultures that did not yet believe in him. Mission, though one and undivided, faces three different tasks and activities (31): mission *ad gentes*, new evangelization, and pastoral activity. Of these mission *ad gentes*, and in particular proclamation of the gospel, 'is the permanent priority of mission' (44). For without the mission *ad gentes*, the church's very missionary dimension would be deprived of its essential meaning and of the very activity that exemplifies it (34).

Ad gentes, of course, came from Matthew 28:18-20, 'make disciples of all nations'. The urgency was founded on the apostle Paul: 'woe to me if do not preach the Gospel' (1Cor 9:16), also on the necessity of Christ for salvation (Jn. 14:6; Acts 4:10, 12). God's plan was to 'unite all things in Christ, things in heaven and things on earth' (Eph. 1:10). Preaching Christ to peoples and groups who did not yet believe in him was not an option for the church, but rather a foundational demand. Christ provided for this through his mandate (Matt. 28:18-20 par; Jn. 20:21-23; RM 22-23) and the promise to 'be with you' till the close of the age. Christ's principal agent is the Holy Spirit, the promised power for evangelization 'to the ends of the earth' (Acts 1:8). The *how* of mission was to be modeled on Christ's own praxis of the kingdom (Mk. 1:14-15; Luke 4:14-21, and see RM ch. 2, 12-20). Such a kingdom was no concept, doctrine or program, but a person with the face and name of Jesus, such that 'if the kingdom is separated from Jesus, it is no longer the kingdom of God which he revealed' (18). The only reference to creation appeared in the condemnation of 'kingdom-centered' views that 'put great stress on the mystery of creation ... but ... keep silent about the mystery of redemption' (17). Creation perspectives on mission would feature in the work of scholars.

Dialogue and Proclamation (DP 1991). This was the first church document to give a formal theological treatment of religious traditions (Dupuis 1993: 132). Completed before RM though published some months after it, its terminology was somehow closer to EN (see, e.g. DP 8 and 10). Two different dicasteries worked on the first drafts, each on the element under its charge. The resulting points of view vary somewhat, though an attempt at harmonization was made in 77-86. The part on dialogue stands out for the somewhat new and extensive biblical foundations in the Old Testament: see DP 19-20. From the very beginning God made a covenant with all peoples (Gen. 1-11), showing there was but one history of salvation for all humankind. Isaiah promised that all the ends of the earth should see the salvation of God (Is. 52:10), and that in the last days the nations would stream to the house of the Lord to learn his ways and walk in his paths. Jesus explicitly announced the entry of Gentiles into the kingdom (Matt. 8:10-11, Matt. 25:31-32) and proclaimed that the time would come when worship would not be restricted to a particular place, rather true worshippers would 'worship the Father in spirit and in truth' (Jn. 4:23). The biblical foundations for proclamation appear especially in nos. 55-57. In the first place, there was the mandate to proclaim the gospel (Matt. 28:18-20; Mk. 16:15-16). Luke and Acts speak of this in terms of 'witness' to the ends of the earth (Lk. 23:46-48; Acts 1:8). In John 20:21, Jesus breathed the Spirit upon the disciples as he handed onto them the very mission he received from the Father. In conclusion, 'true inter-religious dialogue on the part of the Christian supposes the desire to make Jesus Christ better known, recognized and loved, proclaiming Jesus Christ is to be carried out in the Gospel spirit of dialogue' (77).

Catholic Books on Bible and Mission

For a long time the biblical foundation for mission appeared self-evident: the Great Commission. No post-colonial criticism existed as yet to question the apparent 'imperial' dimension in this mandate. Book-length studies of the biblical foundations for mission are recent and few. I restrict myself to those that deal with mission in the whole Bible or in either Testament, leaving out those limited to a theme or a biblical author, with two exceptions (Okure 1988, and Lohfink and Zenger 2000).

The Johannine Approach to Mission. A Contextual Study of John 4:1-42 (Okure 1988). 'The Gospel of John is a missionary document, *precisely because* it is a community document' (294, emphasis original). In John, mission is identified with the entire life and activity of Jesus as 'the one sent by the Father'. The missionary field was the whole world, the audience believers and unbelievers. Even believers need to be kept in God's word spoken by Jesus and preserved from 'this world' in which they are strangers. Jesus alone is the missionary, he alone and the Father are the real laborers in the missionary enterprise (286); disciples only reap the harvest. They thus must remain (*menein*) in him and do mission his way of humble service (the footwashing) and total dependence on the Father (*kathōs... egō... kai humeis*, 'as... I... you', Jn. 20:21). What characterizes the community and its mode of mission was mutual love and support, especially in a crisis of faith, whether initial or ongoing.

The God of Israel and the Nations. Studies in Isaiah and the Psalms (Lohfink and Zenger 2000). The authors wrote for Christian-Jewish dialogue, examining the themes of covenant and torah in Isaiah and the Psalms. Covenant is a prerogative of Israel and denotes God's special relationship with it. It is used in varied contexts in a dynamic manner and so can be opened to the nations/church, though never as replacement of Israel. God has a single plan of salvation that embraces the two groups; the two are not parallel ways of salvation. Tanak is no covenant (for Christians, Testament) but torah. And torah, not covenant, signifies the unity of the canon. Torah is offered to the nations through the mediation of Israel in the final pilgrimage of the nations to the mount of the Lord.

Salvation of the Gentiles and the Prophets (Rétif and Lamarche 1966). The authors assembled and briefly commented upon texts of the Old Testament they deemed open to universalism, sometimes noting the tensions with particularity and narrow nationalism. They were convinced that 'universalism is there from the beginning, like a seed waiting for the chance to grow' (13). There was universalism of origin (the creation account, the Table of Nations in Gen. 10) and universalism of salvation (Gen. 3:15; 12:1-3; Isa. 56:1-8). Gentiles were admitted in the very first Passover (Ex. 12) and among the people at the entrance into Canaan (Rahab, Josh. 2 and 6; the Gibeonites, Josh. 9). Zephaniah 3:9-10 promised that 'then I shall purge the lips of the peoples, so that all may invoke the name of Yahweh and serve him shoulder to shoulder.' The servant (Israel) was given a mission of 'light to the nations' (Is. 42:6; 49:6). The psalms called upon all the earth to acclaim Yahweh and serve Yahweh with gladness (Ps. 100:1). The enthronement psalms (47; 93; 96-99) sang of the (coming) sovereignty of YHWH over all the earth. Narrow nationalism can be seen, for example, in Ethiopia, Egypt and Sabaea coming *in chains* and professing that 'with you alone is God and nowhere else' (Is. 45:14). The authors could have done more stringent analyses of actual contexts.

Théologie missionarie de l'Ancient Testament (Raguin 1947). Raguin focused on mission spirituality with two dominant images: incarnation and light – redemption and illumination. Emanating from the processions within the Trinity, the Word effected the redemption of humans from sin and brought them to share in the life of the Trinity. Divine light, through '*la pensée chrétienne*' (Christian thought), throws full light (bringing to term the various partial lights) on the paths of God in human history and experience. The first aim of mission is the rescue of the 'pagan' world, inclusive of one's own country (in the light of Godin and Daniel's famous work, Raguin could not but concede to the importance of mission work at home – see Raguin 1947: 41 and 62). The problem of sin began in the garden, but God responded with the promise of redemption in Genesis 3:15. The call of Abraham seemed to create two groups, with blessing for one and curse for the other (36). Abraham prefigured the people to come from him, and especially Jesus Christ. God encountered Moses/Israel so this people could make God known to the world. Unfortunately, the Jewish religion took a formalist turn. The promise of a new heart and new spirit (Ez. 36:26-27) installed the interior principle of love over observances. The promise to Judah foretold the obedience of all peoples to the Messiah (Gen. 49:8-19; see Ps. 2); in the Song of Simeon (Lk. 2:29-32) the triumph of light replaced that of war. Isaiah 60 presented the temple bathed in eternal light to which the peoples come; Revelation 21 presented the Lamb as the light of the Jerusalem of the future. Isaiah 66:18 foretold the salvation of the nations, with the 'survivors' being sent to proclaim God's glory to the nations. Then would come the new age when the whole earth, submitting to the Messiah, would experience universal abundance and peace (Is 55:17-18).

Dieu Universel et Peuple Élu: L'universalism religieux en Israël depuis les origins jusqu'à la veille des lutes maccabéennes (Dion 1975). Classifying the texts according to historical periods and literary strata, Dion pursued the tension between Israel's consciousness as chosen people and its gradual awareness of the universality of its God. 'Holy nation' (Ex 19:6) was only a slight adaptation of Deuteronomy's 'holy people' which stressed the apartness of Israel. 'A kingdom of priests' in no way implied a mediatory role for Israel, but that Israel as a nation was set apart for God as a priest was among the people. The Yahwist situated Israel within humanity as a whole; the blessing of Genesis 12:3 functioned very much like the Greek middle voice: in blessing Abraham, the families of the earth acquire blessing. The prophets of the Assyrian period proclaimed that the bond of Yahweh with Israel was not unbreakable. Because Yahweh was impartial judge of all peoples, the 'day of Yahweh' would be a terror for Israel herself (Am. 5:18-20). Isaiah 2:1-2 foresaw a time when, in the style of Delphi, nations would send delegates to Zion, there receive instruction (*torah* here is not 'law') from Yahweh and end all wars. No question here of political domination or even of gifts brought for Israel. The period of the exile naturally gave rise to texts in which the enemies of Yahweh (typified by Babylon and Edom) would be crushed mercilessly. Counter traditions arose of the assault of the nations against Zion beside that of the pilgrimage of the nations to Zion. The priestly tradition underlined the unity of the human race and the universal gift of the image of God. Deutero-Isaiah (see Is 45:18-25) was the first biblical author to witness to religious universalism by demanding the conversion of all peoples to the unique God, Yahweh. In relating Israel's function as witness to that of election, Isaiah 43:10 turned it into election for service, no longer election-privilege (78-79). 'Light to the nations' (Is. 49:6) suggested a role leading to the salvation of the nations. In the restoration period, the term '*nilwah*' (be joined to) indicated remnants of strangers who rallied to Israel and bound themselves to Yahweh. On behalf of these, the prophet of Isaiah 56:1-8 engaged in polemics with currents represented in Ezekiel 44 that wished to banish them from cult and temple. In summary, opposing currents coexisted, but there was ongoing development.

The Biblical Foundations for Mission (Senior and Stuhlmueller 1983). This comprehensive treatment is a classic in the subject. In respect to mission, the scriptures are sources of vision and strategy. They open up possibilities for the church by showing varying responses and strategies through time, place, and culture (343). Mission or redemption involves much more than 'saving souls' or 'making converts'; it is total reality and includes body, spirit, structures, world, and cosmos (329). Internal to mission is a dialectic between outreach and identity. Mission is 'the God-given call to appreciate and share one's religious experience and insights, first within one's own community and tradition, and then with people and communities of other cultural, social, and religious traditions' (3). It operates through the dialogal mode of free and respectful invitation. In the Old Testament, there was a process of humanization: assimilation, indigenization and prophetic challenge and purification. For example, the kingship and aspects of cult were assimilated from Canaan; the very nation 'Israel' emerged from mixed roots. The pattern of seventy elders to help Moses in administration was suggested by Moses' father-in-law (Ex. 18) and validated by command of God in Numbers 11. There was no consistent policy towards 'outsiders' and no centrally accepted theology of universal salvation. Opposing currents coexisted in varied periods, political and economic factors constantly forcing Israel to rethink its theology. Even after the exile there were two voices represented by Ezekiel, Ezra-Nehemiah (turning inward) and Second Isaiah ('light to the nations'). In its prayer, however, Israel enshrined intuitions of the universal sovereignty of Yahweh over all peoples, with these forming one chorus with Israel in proclaiming Yahweh.

Foundational to New Testament mission is that in the event of Jesus Christ 'all flesh shall see the salvation of our God.' The evangelists have each his face of mission, so did Paul and the other books of the New Testament. There is no one theology of mission in the Bible, only a series of traditions, which may emphasize proclamation, prophetic challenge in word and sign, witness, especially the bond of unity and love, personal and social transformation. One lesson, among many, is the value of religious experience: the poetry and prayer of Israel and the early church always soared above the held certainties. The church may borrow this leaf from scripture in approaching the place of Israel in God's plans and the salvific dimension of non-Christian religions.

Unity and Plurality: Mission in the Bible (Legrand 1990). Legrand's encounter with Hinduism in India destroyed for him the reigning model of 'conquest' for Christ; besides, 'like the Christian life itself, mission is *koinonia* ...' (7), hence unity in diversity. The Old Testament was marked by the poles of election and the nations, the categories being 'universalism centered on Zion' and 'de-centralized universalism'. Some texts implied that God's covenant with Israel would be extended to other nations. For example, in Isaiah 19:19-25 'Israel will be third with Egypt and Assyria, a blessing in the midst of the earth' and Egypt is 'my people.' Isaiah 56:6-7 welcomed 'to my holy mountain' eunuchs and foreigners who joined themselves to Yahweh, 'for my house will be called a house of prayer for all nations.' Isaiah 66:18-21 contemplated sending messengers to Tarshish and various places and 'they will proclaim my glory to the nations' (Is. 66:19). Jonah illustrated universal divine compassion in the face of universal human misery. In fact, universalism and election are incomprehensible in disjunction, for 'God's call is addressed to the world, but it begins with Israel and invites the nations to join with the people of the election' (27). The second part of the book (41-88) treats the gospel of Jesus Christ and the accounts of the risen Christ. Across the pluralism of viewpoints, one central image imposed itself, that of Jesus as the envoy of the Father who preached the gospel in words and deeds. His ministry centered on Israel and evoked the eschatological gathering of the peoples. The evangelists, in varying forms, portrayed the Risen Christ as mandating mission to all nations. The third part presents the church as missionary. Luke in Acts emphasized witness and itinerant mission, Paul the outreach of the gospel to the Gentiles. The Gospel of John was a missionary synthesis: 'word' was equivalent of Markan 'gospel' and Lukan 'witness'. Standing out in John was the great missionary prayer (Jn. 17) and the Johannine sending (Jn. 20:21), both using the important word *'as'* that both models and hangs the mission of the disciples on that of the Son.

Israel and the Nations: A Mission Theology of the Old Testament (Okoye 2006). The little contribution of this book was to rephrase the question of mission in the Old Testament so as to enable new perspectives to emerge. Direct evangelism is not the only form of mission. Through close analyses of texts and contexts, four faces of mission were discovered in the Old Testament (10-12). The first face was that of the universality of salvation and of righteousness before Yahweh. The second face I designated 'community-in mission' – Israel was meant as a divine pattern for individual and social life that would both reveal God and draw all humanity to Yahweh. The third face was what scholars call 'centripetal' mission, the pilgrimage of the nations to Zion. Finally, there was centrifugal mission, with its zeal to convert outsiders to the worship of Yahweh.

Conclusion

This survey has shown how missionary activity responds to diverse contexts and needs while remaining one – the Word continuing to incarnate in human cultures and endeavors.

CATHOLIC MISSIOLOGY 1910-2010:
ORIGINS AND PERSPECTIVES

Francis Anekwe Oborji

Introduction

The origins of contemporary Catholic missiology can be traced back to the early 1900s. This period initiated the debate on missionary adaptation and the concept of mission as movement from the 'Christian land' to 'Non-Christian lands.' Contemporary Catholic missiology developed and grew under this debate and period and was therefore influenced by the theology of missionary adaptation in vogue at that time. This period coincided with the heyday of colonial activities in the southern continents of Africa, Asia and Latin America. This was the period also during which the Edinburgh 1910 Missionary Conference was conceived and convoked. It was the period that inaugurated, above all, the formulation in theological terms of the concepts and goal of Christian mission. In the Catholic circle, Josef Schmidlin of the State University of Münster in Germany became the leading figure in the development of Catholic missiology. Schmidlin was himself inspired by a similar effort in the German Protestant world by Gustav Warneck of Halle University. This means that missiological reflection in both Catholic and Protestant circles started almost at the same time and both faced the same problems, and shared methods and tendencies.

Pierre Charles, a Jesuit priest, teaching at the Catholic University of Louvain in Belgium, later became another leading figure in the development of Catholic missiology. The further development of the thoughts and vision of the two pioneer authors (Schmidlin and Charles) of Catholic missiology were to be continued and pursued by their successors in Münster and Louvain respectively, and also in other places as well. Furthermore, the last one hundred years has seen an increased interest in the study and appreciation of cultures and religious traditions of the non-Western world. People who were judged formerly to be without culture were suddenly discovered to have admirable cultural system and religious traditions. Contemporary missiology developed under that understanding and encounter. Its main concern was the meeting of the gospel message with the cultures and religious traditions of the peoples of the southern continents.

This is the meeting point of the old missionary paradigm of the last century (represented by the Edinburgh 1910 conference) and the emerging missionary outlook of Christians from the southern continents. If the concern in mission field and studies at the beginning of 1900s were about the meeting of Western Christianity with the peoples of the southern continents, today the debate reverts to the consequences of that meeting, especially with the recent southward shift in the Christian landscape. This is the perspective under which one can begin to appreciate the significance of the Edinburgh 1910 conference and the missiology that has its origin in that epoch. In our own context, it may not be an overstatement to say that in the last century, Catholic missiology has been sensitive of the cultures and religious traditions of peoples from the southern continents. What this means in effect, is that Catholic theologians of mission in the last one hundred years are increasingly becoming aware of the importance of indigenous cultures in incarnating the Christian message among the local population. This awareness and appreciation of the other peoples' cultures and religious traditions in the writings of pioneer Catholic missiologists preceded the present-day debate on the theology of inculturation and inter-religious dialogue. In other words, it is this gradual appreciation of the other people's cultures that has eventually aided the theologians in arriving at the present-day enhanced appreciation, also, of the non-Christian religions in the work of evangelization. This is so since religion is also an element of culture and so one should be careful not to separate the two in discussing the indigenous cultures of the people being evangelized.

This is the perspective under which I would like to discuss in the present study. In this respect, the focus of our study is the two principal schools of thought (Münster and Louvain) that were at the origin of Catholic missiology. For most of those who have been accustomed to viewing the two pioneer schools of thought (Münster and Louvain) in opposing ways (as if they were two different camps), the approach we are adopting here is meant to harmonize the two schools through the common task that they both faced some one hundred years ago. Indeed, a careful study of the two schools of thought would reveal their harmonious nature and meeting point in context and purpose.

Therefore, in what follows, I shall discuss the development of Catholic missiology by looking at the two pioneer schools of missiology (Münster and Louvain). I shall conclude the study by relating both the dominant Catholic missiology and the Edinburgh 1910 missionary paradigm to the challenges coming from the new Christian communities of the southern continents, taking Africa as a case study.

The Catholic Theories of Mission

Apart from tackling the challenges of the establishment of missiology as a science of its own in theological education (the same problem faced by pioneers of Protestant missiology as well), the two pioneer Catholic schools of missiology (Münster and Louvain), were mostly concerned with the question of the concepts and goal of the Christian mission in the non-Western world. Prior to this era, there was practically no defined concept or goal of missionary activity. Each missionary institute or congregation had been being guided by whatever instruction their founders or superiors might have given them as they went on mission. It is precisely for this reason that, in the Catholic context, the basic issues were about the concepts and goal of the Christian mission, including the missionary approach to other cultures and religions. The latter is more sophisticated today as a result of developments in the theology of religions. However, pioneers in the debate emphasized the issue of the concept and goal of mission: where mission has been defined virtually in terms of saving of souls or of church implantation, and in a situation in where missiology could only be the science of and for the missionary, a practical (if not pragmatic) subject which responded to the question: 'How do we execute our task?' (Bosch 1991: 492). So it is a problem of how to bring missiology to what is at the very heart of the church's mission and therefore of theological education. The basic approaches and attempts at solutions even among Catholic scholars are varied, yet all are confronted with the same problem. The discussion has given rise to the birth of the two famous Catholic pioneer schools of missiology: Münster and Louvain.

The Münster School of Missiology

Beginning with the Münster School of missiology, the basic argument is that the primary goal of mission is the conversion of non-Christian individuals. The Christian mission aims first and foremost at the salvation of souls (*salus animarum*). Once more, the systematic working out of this theory is traced back to Josef Schmidlin, the founder of the Münster school. Thus, to understand the conversion model we shall examine here the thought of Josef Schmidlin.

The first preoccupation of Schmidlin was to give a biblical foundation of the mission (Müller 1987: 36). In his *Einführung in die Missionswissenschaft* (1917), he deduces the mission of the church from the biblical text: 'As the Father has sent me, even so I send you' (Jn. 20:21). From here, Schmidlin distinguishes a twofold task for the church: 1) to proclaim and spread the Christian faith and the Christian gospel and so, of necessity propagate itself; and 2) to preserve and strengthen this faith and this church (Schmidlin 1917: 46-47). His recourse to Holy Scripture and the Church Fathers was to furnish proof for missionary activity. Missionary activity is rooted in the certainty that God is the origin of mission (Matt. 28:18-20).

From scriptural evidence Schmidlin goes on to cite the Church Fathers, the theologians, and the Magisterium of the church and observes: 'Every ecclesiastical epoch, whether present or past, confirms the statement that the obligatory character of the pagan missions is established by the teaching of the Bible and Tradition – by the command of God and of His Church' (Schmidlin 1933: 78). He also emphasizes the 'natural basis for mission.' According to him, 'In the eyes of unbelievers and pagans the chief justification of the Christian missions lies in the fact that, as the representatives and preachers of a superior and absolute religion, they bring to the pagan religious blessings which he had not before enjoyed – the true God and a bliss-giving redemption'. Then he adds that mission also has certain 'cultural objects and tasks' which, although 'secondary missionary motives' are nevertheless grounded 'in the very nature of the missions, and make the latter a cultural factor and civilizing agent of the first rank' (Schmidlin 1933: 108ff).

Schmidlin was next confronted with the task of defining the term mission. He realizes that the term mission can have different meanings. So, he distinguishes between 'mission in the subjective sense – narrower sense (missionary activity) and 'mission in the objective sense – wider sense' (missionary works). The first he defines as 'that ecclesiastical activity whose aim it is to plant and spread the Christian religion and church, and then to preserve it.' The second is 'the totality of all ecclesiastical organizations which serve the spread of the faith' (Schmidlin 1917: 48). Schmidlin is thinking here of the house or group in which or from which mission proceeds, or again of a mission limited by place or specific personnel, such as the mission in Honduras or the Franciscan missions. Schmidlin feels also that there is a sense in regarding Catholics as the 'object' of mission, 'especially those who outwardly count as church members but who, because of lack of faith or sin, are dead or estranged members, who stand in need of conversion anew' (Schmidlin 1917: 51). Thus, he extends the missionary activity of the church to all men and women, 'to those who belong to her (the church's) communion and already share in her faith, so that they may preserve it (Christian faith) and live according to its dictates, and to all others who still stand in the darkness of error and outside the fold, that they may be converted and join her communion' (Schmidlin 1923:38).

Schmidlin acknowledges the use of the term 'mission' in the wider sense by the Roman Propaganda Fide, the *Codex Iuris Canonici*, and also by reputable Catholic authors, particularly as defined by Theodore Grentrup: '*Est illa pars ministerii ecclesiastici, quae plantationem et consolidationem fidei catholicae in acatholicis operatur*' ('that part of the church's ministry that works for the planting and consolidation of the Catholic faith among non-Catholics' – Grentrup 1913: 265). Nevertheless, he himself chooses to emphasize the narrower interpretation and writes: 'Missions in the narrower sense, also called foreign missions … are thus missions among non-Christians, that is among those who are outside the Christian faith and the Christian religion' (Schmidlin 1933: 36). Schmidlin emphasizes the pre-eminence of the religious character of mission as the extension of the kingdom of God. This does not exclude cultural, intellectual, moral, social, charitable, and even economic purposes. He describes mission as 'the commission which issued from God the Father, in the fullness of time, and was given to His Apostles and His church by Christ Himself, on the conclusion of His life on earth – a commission to go forth and preach the Gospel to all peoples' (Schmidlin 1933: 43-44).

It is from this perspective that Schmidlin took the step to distinguish different stages in missionary work: 1) the proclamation of the gospel, the Christian faith among the heathen; 2) the internal conversion, the incorporation into the church and reception of baptism; 3) the organization of the church from the simple formation of communities to the establishment of the full hierarchy. The mission church becomes an established church when the people as a whole have accepted the faith and the church has become self-sufficient regarding personnel and finances (Müller 1987: 37).

On the goal of mission, Schmidlin writes that for practical and historical reasons, mission aims at the conversion of the non-Christian individual, at 'the spreading of the faith among non-Christians'. Schmidlin considers the 'confession of Christian teaching' (with simultaneous reception of baptism) and the 'grafting into the church' to be two aspects of the one mission, a 'twofold function found inseparable in the aim of the Catholic mission' (Schmidlin 1917: 56).

Later, in his *Missionslehre*, he distinguishes more clearly between the individual and social aims of mission, but still holds firmly that 'for mission of the Catholic Church the question does not arise in this absolute form, and the solution can only be individual conversion and the Christianization of a people. Mission must strive for both and unite both, if not at the same time then in successive development; on the one hand, it should seek to convert the individual, or rather individuals, and on the other, to join these individuals together in community, that through it the whole people may be renewed in Christ' (Schmidlin 1933: 243-44). In fact, for Schmidlin, 'conversion' means the profession of Christian teaching on the one hand, and baptism in the name of the Trinity, on the other (Schmidlin 1917: 55).

Schmidlin's theory has received some criticisms, especially in recent times. His theory of the goal of mission as the conversion of souls is the most criticized. The theory is said to be based on a type of dualistic anthropology. It ran the risk of disregarding the concrete, historical dimension of the integral salvation brought by Christ. It is also argued that Schmidlin's theory led to utter rejection of the cultural and religious traditions of the non-Christian peoples. The critics argue that the work of redemption is not opposed to the work of creation. Moreover, grace does not destroy nature but perfects it.

Thomas Ohm (1892-1962) to whom the chair of missiology at the Münster faculty fell after the death of Schmidlin corrected some lacunae in

Schmidlin's theory of mission. Among several of Ohm's publications, of particular interest here is his major work, *Machet zu Jüngern alle Völker: Theorie der Mission* (1962), translated into different languages (Anderson 1998: 505). The first task Ohm took was to clarify the meaning of the term 'mission'. He noticed that in recent years, there has been a remarkable escalation in the use of the term (mission) among Christians. This went hand in hand with significant broadening of the concept, at least in certain circles. Indeed until the 1950s 'mission', even if not used in a univocal sense, had a fairly circumscribed set of meanings. Ohm took time to summarize them. Mission referred to: 1) the sending of missionaries to a designated territory, 2) the activities undertaken by such missionaries, 3) the geographical area where the missionaries were active, 4) the agency which dispatched the missionaries, 5) the non-Christian world or 'mission field', 6) the center from which the missionaries operated on the 'mission field' (Ohm 1962: 52ff). In a slightly different context it could also refer to: 7) a local congregation without a resident minister and still dependent on the support of an older, established church, or 8) a series of special services intended to deepen or spread the Christian faith, usually in a nominally Christian environment (Bosch 1991: 1). Karl Müller, in a more specifically theological synopsis, made a synthesis of Ohm's concept of mission as it has traditionally been used. According to him, mission has been paraphrased as: 1) propagation of the faith, 2) expansion of the reign of God, 3) conversion of the heathen, and 4) the founding of new churches (Müller 1987: 31-34).

Ohm, however, insists that all these connotations attached to the word 'mission', familiar as they may be, are of fairly recent origins. Until the sixteenth century the term was used exclusively with reference to the doctrine of the Trinity, that is, of the sending of the Son by the Father and of the Holy Spirit by the Father and the Son. According to Ohm, the Jesuits were the first to use it in terms of the spread of the Christian faith among the non-Christians and other people (including Protestants) who were not members of the Catholic Church (Ohm 1962: 37-39). In this new sense it was intimately associated with colonial expansion of the Western world into what has more recently become known as the third or majority world.

In this situation, the term 'mission' presupposes a sender, a person or persons sent by the sender, those to whom one is sent, and an assignment. The entire terminology thus presumes that the one who sends has the *authority* to do so. Often it was argued that the real sender was God who had indisputable authority to decree that people be sent to execute his will. In practice, however, the authority was understood to be vested in the church or in a mission society, or even in a Christian potentate (Rütti 1972: 228). It was part of Ohm's entire approach to view mission in terms of expansion, occupation of fields, the conquest of other religions, and the like (Bosch 1991: 2). However, Ohm's thesis is based on the traditional interpretation of mission, one that today is gradually being modified, at least in some circles.

Another contribution of Ohm could be seen in his attempt to apply the principle of the conversion model in his interpretation of the theory of *accommodation* and *adaptation*. The problem is how to overcome the heated debate that the Western church should not be transported to Asia or Africa. All peoples have a right to express their religious and Christian experience in their own way; they have a right to have their own leaders and to develop their potential. But this right should not be made absolute. Christianity in particular should be a sign that the universal human and Christian solidarity is stronger than any nationalism or individualism, and that Christianity is essentially a matter of give and take in which all must be prepared to participate. We must certainly have 'indigenous' local churches, but never in exclusive sense; we are always, called to 'self-transcendence' (Müller 1987: 152).

Considering all this, Ohm spoke of the threefold process of adaptation: accommodation, assimilation, transformation (see Ohm 1962: 700). His thesis is that *accommodation* and *adaptation* are more than helps for establishing contact. According to him, all three aspects are important: accommodation, which is possible because our common nature gives us a natural disposition for contact; assimilation, because the church is able to absorb the riches of others, in fact needs them for its eschatological fulfillment; transformation, because everything in the world which is good, true and beautiful 'somehow or other can be raised to a higher level and thus serve salvation' (Ohm 1962: 702).

Adaptation and accommodation are as old as the church itself. Since diversity is inherent in God's plan for creation, mission must take it into account. Since it is from God himself it must, in principle, harmonize with the Christianizing process. Nothing that is essentially good should be destroyed, it should rather be developed and cultivated. The reign of God does not mean a ban on earthly things rather that he may be 'all in all' (1 Cor. 15:28). Thus, Ohm warns that we should not think in pessimistic way. Adaptation is needed not only for tactical but also for theological reasons (see Ohm 1962: 696). Since mission is a process of communication, it is first and foremost necessary to take seriously *those to whom the message is addressed* – just as God does. God sent the Son as message and messenger but through the Holy Spirit he moves the heart of women and men, prepares and arouses them, awakens understanding and finally leads to the insight expressed in Luke 24:32: 'Did not our hearts burn within us as he talked to us on the road and explained the scriptures to us?' The missionary addresses his message to real people of good will and understanding in whom God has been active all their lives through their consciences and the religious traditions in which they grew up. Maybe they are not yet or sufficiently aware of the fulfillment in Christ but deep down in their hearts they are receptive. This is what Ohm meant when he said that Christianity is accommodation, assimilation, transformation – but not only that;

Christianity also means 'contradiction'. Thus, Ohm insists that Christianity also demands 'struggle against nature' (see Ohm 1962:711).

However, the shortcomings in Ohm's thesis have come under serious attacks in recent times, especially from the Third World theologians. Gustavo Gutiérrez, for instance, points out that such theory as the accommodation or adaptation, succumb to 'the temptation of *concordism*, which equates the social groups and forces within first-century Palestine with those of our time' (Gutiérrez 1973: xi). Yet even where the socio-cultural gap between today's communities and those of the first Christians is narrow, it is there, and it should be respected. The approach called for requires an interaction between the self-definition of early Christian authors and actors and the self-definition of today's believers who wish to be inspired and guided by those early witnesses (Bosch 1991: 23).

Karl Müller (1918-2001), a contemporary interpreter of the Münster school, has responded to the critics regarding the shortcomings in the theories of conversion and accommodation/adaptation models. In his book, *Mission Theology: An Introduction*, Müller introduces the concept of 'integral' salvation to the conversion theory debate (Müller 1987: 82). Aware of many criticisms that have been leveled against the Münster school because of its one-sided emphasis of salvation (*salus animarum*), Müller acknowledges that: 'The concepts "salvation of souls" and "care of souls" are no longer in favor because, for one thing, they can lead to dichotomy of the human person, and secondly do not incorporate other problems such as poverty, hunger, suppression, exploitation, the armaments race, war, manipulation etc. which weigh on humanity today, especially in the Third World' (Müller 1987: 82). Considering all these reasons, Müller asserts that: 'Today "integral salvation" is the preferred term, that is, salvation that embraces man in his full reality' (Müller 1987: 82). This is in line with new thinking in missionary circles today, but elsewhere as well, the mediating of 'comprehensive', 'integral', 'total,' or 'universal' salvation is increasingly identified as the purpose of mission, in this way overcoming the inherent dualism in the traditional and more recent models. In this sense, of course, it is tautological to add any adjective to the noun 'salvation'. Salvation is, in the nature of the case, comprehensive and integral – or it is not salvation (see Bosch 1993: 532). However, according to Müller, the concept of integral salvation or human development is a recent phenomenon. But it presented hardly any problem for the Catholics because the way was prepared through the Thomistic doctrine on the unfolding of the individual person towards the *'familia Dei'* and through important church documents such as *Gaudium et Spes* (GS 25, 41) and the encyclical *Populorum Progressio* (PP 1967) of Paul VI (Müller 1987: 83). Again, the strength of Müller's thesis lies in his emphasis on the integral character of salvation – which demands that the scope of the church's mission be more comprehensive than has traditionally been the case. Salvation is as coherent, broad, and deep as the needs and exigencies of human existence. In addition, those who know that God will one day wipe away all tears will not accept with resignation the tears of those who suffer and are oppressed *now*. Anyone who knows that one day there will be no more disease can and must actively anticipate the conquest of disease in individuals and society *now*. And anyone who believes that the enemy of God and humans will be vanquished will already oppose him *now* in his machinations in family and society. For all of this has to do with *salvation* (cf. Bosch 1991: 400).

In spite of everything, however, the one-sided approach of the concept of mission by the authors of the Münster school with its emphasis on the proclamation and salvation as the goal of mission, was to be augmented by the Louvain school (which developed during World War II, regarded planting the church to be the goal of mission). It suffices to say that only after Schmidlin's death was the controversial question (between the two different approaches) tackled and finally settled at the Vatican Council II.

The Louvain School

The other important theory of mission in the Catholic circles is the Louvain school. The basic thesis of the Louvain school is that the goal of mission is the 'planting' of the church and so it is also called the 'plantation theory' (*plantatio ecclesiae*). The chief exponent of this theory is the Belgian Jesuit Pierre Charles. Other spokespersons include Joseph Masson (Louvain) and André Seumois (Rome). Apart from many mission journals which Pierre Charles (1883-1954) launched and directed personally for the promotion of missionary work in Belgium and France, he wrote several articles on different aspects of missiology. He published the *Dossiers* on missionary activity beginning in 1916, and started the Xaveriana series in 1923. In his *Les Dossiers de l'Action Missionnaire*, a manual of missiology, he outlined his theology of mission. Charles maintained that the aim of missionary activity should be the planting or formation of a church (with its own hierarchy, indigenous clergy, and sacraments) in non-Christian countries. This concept and goal of mission is somewhat a break away from the German Münster school of missiology (as noted before), which viewed the aim of missions as the conversion of individuals. The theological foundation of Charles' thesis is God's desire for the salvation of everyone not individually but in the church. His influence was definitive in Catholic missiology up to and including Vatican II (AG 6) (Anderson 1998:127).

Charles began by defining the object of mission. According to him, the formal object of mission is 'the establishment of the visible church in those countries where it is not yet established' (Charles 1939: 59). Furthermore, mission is aimed not only at the heathen but at all groups among whom the visible church is not permanently set up. Mission is a developing church growing towards maturity. It is not obedience to the mandate of Christ or concern for the salvation of souls that justify mission but the nature of the church itself which only achieves its full identity when it geographically embraces the whole world. Thus the concern for the saving of souls is only an imperfect motivation for mission. The one and only *raison d'être* of mission is rather the establishment of the visible church (Charles 1938: 37).

Thus, like Schmidlin, Charles understood mission primarily as an activity outside the country of the missionary. A mission territory is a country where the church is not yet visibly established. However, unlike Schmidlin, Charles does not see mission as converting non-Christian individuals or saving of souls. The primary goal of mission is to plant the church where it is not yet visibly established, with all its necessary organs, like a local hierarchy and clergy, a continuity of means of salvation, sacraments, morally accessible to the entire region. Where such a visible church is absent, theologically speaking, that is mission land. Thus the aim of missionary activity is to establish an 'adult church', a tangible society with its own structures and solidly attached to the soil, complete with favorable socioeconomic and material conditions for the teaching of doctrine and the celebration of the sacraments (Charles 1954/56: 15-32). Charles insists on his position that the real criterion whether a country is a 'mission country' or not is the absence of the visible church with all its established vital structures. The purpose of mission is thus 'to plant the visible church wherever it is not yet planted, that is, to bring the means of salvation (faith and the sacraments) within the reach of all souls of good will. In many countries this task is completed. Here mission as such no longer exists. Nevertheless, there are many souls to be converted and all souls here must still be saved' (Charles 1938: 65). Charles took exception to reducing the church to a means of saving of souls; for him the church is more than that because it is 'the divine form of the world, the one point of contact where the whole work of the Creator returns to its Savior; it is less because belonging to the church is by no means sufficient for salvation'. Thus he asserts: 'The special task of mission is to extend the boundaries of the visible church, to complete this work of growth, to strew the whole world with prayers and adoration, to win back for the Savior his whole inheritance' (Charles 1938: 84-87).

Charles's theology of the goal of mission as planting of the church is linked with his theory of adaptation. He argues that for a successful planting of the Church in mission lands genuine adaptation is necessary. No mere conversion of individuals is sufficient. The people to be evangelized have cultures that have lasting influence on them. From childhood the individual goes through a process of 'individual', by which he adapts to the discipline of his social group; so that by the time the person attains adulthood the local culture will have become a second 'nature' to him. (The term 'inculturation' is used here by Charles, in an anthropological sense – see Charles 1954/56: 20.) Thus the isolation of neophytes in Christian villages or mission posts to protect them from unchristian influences of their native culture is counterproductive. Instead the Christian message should be made to penetrate that culture and transform it from within, like yeast in dough. Only in this way will the negative influences of the local culture be neutralized and resistance to Christian conversions be overcome or weakened (Charles 1954/56: 20-27).

In planting the church in a mission land, the missionary does not encounter a religious vacuum that is to be filled with Christian truths. On the contrary, he encounters a culture, an organized system of life, with beliefs, customs, social systems, juridical conceptions, artistic taste, and so on. He needs to adapt himself to this socio-cultural ambient, not merely as a tactical ploy to win the favor of the people, but in order to become an effective ambassador for the people before God, so that the people may be more pleasing to God (Charles 1938: 169-70).

For Charles, adaptation is not merely a way of being or acting of the missionary; it is the attitude of the Catholic mission towards indigenous institutions. It is an important theological issue. The incarnation is the ideal model for adaptation. To save mankind and restore to human nature its dignity and divine value, the Word of God became flesh in human history. And as the Church Fathers used to say, by assuming our nature Christ saved that which he had become with us. In a similar manner, the missionary seeks to identify himself with the people he sets out to evangelize and to become a mediator of grace for them, so as to introduce a Christian soul into the people and to enable them to participate in a new richness (Charles 1954/56: 120-21).

Besides the incarnation of the Word, Charles gives other theological reasons for adaptation. One of these is the continuity between creation and the work of redemption. The church was willed by God to be a divine form for the world and its coming was prepared for by divine providence. Thus, the work of the creator is not opposed to the work of the redeemer. Indeed whatever is good in creation, and especially in the cultures of the people, contributes in some ways to the work of redemption and consequently to the mission of the church (Charles 1938: 170). However, Charles also admits that the theory of adaptation has suffered distortions in practice. For instance, in the rites controversies in the Far East in the seventeenth century and under the preponderance of Europeanism and 'missionary romanticism' of the nineteenth century (Charles 1938: 171-72). The latter was characterized by a taste for exoticism and voyages, a sentimental interest in the civilization of 'savages', in the salvation of souls, in near and in distant countries. To win sympathy for their cause, romantic missionaries painted bizarre pictures of the pitiful moral state of the 'savages ... to demonstrate their urgent need of salvation' from eternal damnation (Charles 1938: 379-82). With such an image of the people, their cultural values were not given due consideration in evangelization. Nevertheless, Charles insists that adaptation was the general policy of the church in the past. He refers particularly to two church documents which, according to him, constitute the charter for missionary adaptation: the letter of Gregory the Great to Mellitus in 601 and the *Instructio de Propaganda Fide* in 1659 (Charles 1938:171-72).

After Charles, the mission theology of the goal of mission as planting of the church was continued by Joseph Masson and André Seumois (Oborji 2006: 86-96). As said already, apart from these authors of the pioneer schools of thought, there were other protagonists at this stage of development of Catholic missiology who could be regarded as classical advocates of the missionary adaptation theory. These are the authors who have written extensively on the role of cultures in evangelization (in relation to the new terminology – *inculturation*). Among them are Angelo Santos Hernández and Louis Luzbetak (Oborji 2006: 100-05). Lack of space does not allow us to discuss their views here.

Be that as it may, the two mission theories of Münster and Louvain as well as the theology of missionary adaptation in general have received serious attacks and criticisms in recent times, especially from the theologians of the southern continents. For these scholars, be it the Münster or Louvain schools, or missionary adaptation itself, these are processes which seek to 'adapt the practices of the Western church as much as possible to the socio-cultural life of the non-Western peoples' (Mushete 1994: 27). They are mission theories employed to transplant a Christianity developed in European culture into the rest of the world, as if the other people outside Europe have no cultures of their own on which the Christian faith could anchor (Bosch 1991: 228). The contention of these critics of missionary adaptation is that even when the importance of culture in evangelization was realized, the aim of mission became search for 'points-of-contact' and cultural values of the people served only as 'stepping-stones' in evangelization.

Thus, mission, according to this school of thought, was conceived in the adaptation theory, as means of searching for elements in the people's culture for comparison and contrast with those of the missionary. Adaptation draws parallels between aspects of the local people's traditional religion and similar aspects in Christian doctrine. The critics commended the adaptation model for its attention to the values in local traditions; however, they criticize its method of search for stepping-stones, on the ground that it does not recognize the whole culture as a coherent whole of rationally organized elements. Furthermore, the critics say that in the final analysis, the adaptation model aimed at translating a Christianity developed elsewhere into the so-called 'mission lands', as if the people of the 'mission land' were condemned to reception of finished products and had not the ability to produce something new or original for themselves (Oborji 1998: 89). However, adaptation in its classical meaning refers to the efforts to employ the cultural and religious worldview of the people in the work of evangelization. This is with a view of discovering elements in the traditional religion and culture that could serve as *preparatio evangelica* and therefore might be purified for the mission of the church in the area. This effort is as old as Christianity itself as we tried to show earlier on.

In any case, the two perspectives, conversion of souls and implanting of the church are two aspects of the church's mission. The latter persisted unto Vatican II. The former has been broadened with the modern emphasis on the integral dimension of salvation and the recognition of cultural diversity, together with the present practice of inter-religious dialogue. The two perspectives were broadened and used by the Vatican II Fathers in the clarification of the meaning and purpose of mission. And this flows from the background of council's teaching on the church as being missionary by nature. Hence, in the decree *Ad Gentes*, we read the following about the meaning and purpose of the mission:

> 'Missions' is the term usually given to those particular undertakings by which the heralds of the Gospel are sent by the church and go forth into the whole world to carry out the task of preaching and planting the Church among peoples or groups who do not yet believe in Christ ... The special purpose of this missionary activity is *evangelization and the planting of the Church* [my emphasis] among those peoples and groups where she has not yet taken root (AG 6).

Commenting on this, Jacques Dupuis says that Vatican II's stance on mission should not be confused with the narrowly Western outlook on mission. With regards to the latter, the old continent, and later North America, established 'foreign missions' throughout the world and transported there the church and theology developed in the West (Dupuis 1994: 276). However, the Vatican II theology of mission, according to Dupuis, is biblical, since it focuses directly on the gospel image of the sowing of the good news. For Dupuis, the gospel image of the sowing of the good news is reflected in the Council's theology of the local churches that are established in every place and in the theology of mission as reciprocal activity between sister churches. This new theology of mission applies universally to all the churches, even while not denying their differences. Hence, from AG we read:

> All over the world indigenous particular churches ought to grow from seed of the word of God, churches which would be adequately organized and would possess their own proper strength and maturity. With their own hierarchy and faithful, and sufficiently endowed with means adapted to the full Christian life, they should contribute to the good of the whole church (AG 6).

The bottom line in the Council's theology of mission is the emphasis on cultural diversity in the church and the role of local churches (in communion with the universal church), for the work of evangelization and the planting of the church in their various cultural contexts. Another side of it is the council's recovery of the theology of reciprocity. In addition to assuming all that the church has acquired in its earthly pilgrimage, each local church is challenged to contribute something from its cultural-setting to enrich the patrimony of the universal church (LG 13; AG 22).

Furthermore, in the definition of the goal of mission, Vatican II presents a broader meaning of evangelization thus:

> Evangelization is that activity through which, in obedience to Christ's command and moved by the grace and love of the Holy Spirit, the church makes itself fully present to all persons and peoples in order to lead them to the faith, freedom and peace of Christ by example of its life and teaching, and also by the sacraments and other means of grace (AG 5).

From this definition, the mission of the church is explained in simple terms of evangelization and is all embracing. Theologically, its foundation is of divine origin. It is rooted in the doctrine of the Trinity. The emphasis is always on the mandate from Christ. Pastorally, it includes both the paths of evangelization (in the strict sense of the word, that is, the kerygma or rather the initial proclamation to non-Christians or neophytes), and the implanting of the church as a sign of its visible presence among any people and place. It embraces also the issue of integral dimension of the mission of the church. Through her life and teaching the church brings freedom and peace of Christ to the people. And on the other hand, by the means of sacraments and other means of grace, the church makes available to the people those means established by Christ for the sanctification and the eschatological salvation of man. With that one could say that Vatican II provided the needed leadership as regards the foundation, meaning and the purpose of mission. But the various dimensions of mission and ecclesial activities that go with the former are given broader meaning in the post-conciliar documents, in particular in EN and RM. Thus, once the meaning and purpose of mission have been defined in terms of evangelization and the planting of the church, the word evangelization itself took on an increasingly inclusive meaning in post-conciliar mission theology. While fully maintaining the traditional concept of the preaching or proclamation of the gospel, the word evangelization assumes a broader meaning, in which even the activities for the church implantation and others such as human development and struggle for justice, inter-religious dialogue and so forth, are considered part and parcel of evangelization (Giglioni 1996: 147).

In addition, post-conciliar Catholic missiology is today witnessing an enhanced debate and understanding of the so-called new dimensions or rather forms of mission: 1) ecumenical dialogue, 2) inculturation, 3) dialogue with the religions, and 4) human promotion (known in some quarters as liberation). To these, one may add the emerging interest in the Third World theologies; that is, mission as dialogue with the local contexts (see DM 1984; Bevans and Schroeder 2004).

Emerging Challenges: An African Perspective

From our discussions so far, one central point has emerged. The missiology of the twenty-first century will, to a large extent, be determined by the meeting of the inherited missiology of the past century (which the

Edinburgh 1910 conference typifies) and the missionary outlook of the Christian communities in the southern continents. This will be so, largely, because of the recent southward shift in the Christian landscape. The Edinburgh 1910 conference and the Catholic missiology discussed above both represent the form of missionary paradigm of the West that is today being challenged by the emerging missionary outlook of Christians from the southern continents. Therefore, the nature of the emerging missiology in large part, will depend on how prepared the two zones (global north and south) of Christian landscapes are ready to engage in a real mutual theological dialogue. Thus, in this twenty-first century, dialogue with the contextual theologies of Christians from the southern continents will determine the pace that the emerging missiology will take. This effort cuts across the traditional denominational boundaries. Catholics and Protestants as well as the Orthodox are all affected by it. This will be so since one of the critical issues facing Christian mission has always been to respect and preserve the cultural identity of the people being evangelized, and to help them find and recover their cultural and religious heritage in Christ. Culture gives its identity to the people. This is why cultural crisis has recently been recognized as the most profound of problems a people may claim to be having. This is also why most Christian communities in the southern continents today who have been in this serious crisis of cultural identity and are being crushed in the mortar of a merciless chain of events, prayed for prophets to arise and speak in the name of God of hope for the creation of a new identity (EAf 48).

Christian mission is about the encounter of the gospel message of Jesus Christ with different peoples and their ever-newer religious-cultural and sociopolitical contexts. It is about the impregnation of these contexts by the gospel, the assimilation of the cultures of the peoples by the gospel and that of the gospel by their cultures, and the history of the consequent changes in the process of evangelization and of the cultures of the people. In concrete terms, it is about the retrieval and modernization of the people's cultural matrix pursued from the point of view of the gospel values and of the people's daily struggles for survival. Theology, as is often said is born of mission and of the concrete situation in which the evangelizing church finds itself. Even the global north theology has started to become conscious of its contextualized nature despite its traditional tendency of claim to universalism (Bevans 2002: 139).

It is within this scenario that we find the critical issue facing Christianity worldwide today, namely that Christians from different parts of the world and with contrasting histories now face the common challenge of forging a viable Christian identity for the new millennium. The vast majority of Christians throughout the world now find themselves living as minorities in societies that are pluralist or where other religions and ideologies dominate. It follows from this insight that Christianity in its historical expansion has always reflected the tremendous diversity and dynamism of the peoples of the world. This characteristic of Christianity must not be taken as something only of the past. In fact, in our own day, it can be said that the world character of Christianity has expanded and deepened that diversity that has always characterized the people of God. Seen from this perspective, the new southward shift in Christianity is not a matter of worries but the triumph of its universality as well as adaptability to all peoples of the world. The history of Christian expansion and adaptability enabled Christianity itself to break the cultural barriers of its former domestication in the global north to create missionary resurgence and renewal that transformed the religion into a world faith. Today, attitudes must shift to acknowledge this new situation. There is much to be gained by it.

It is therefore, important that we end this chapter with a short note on what type of challenge this scenario presents to missiology today. In doing this, I will limit myself to the contributions of African authors who speak of theological dialogue as a way out of the impasse, of bridging the gap between the missionary paradigm of the older churches and the emerging missionary outlook of the younger churches of the global south. Modern African Christianity itself provides us with an indispensable example of what is at stake. The African approach cuts across denominational boundaries, and so, I will employ the contributions of both Catholic and Protestant authors on the debate.

Once more, the southward shift in global Christianity's center of gravity is extraordinary by any reckoning. In part because of what has been loosely described as 'structures of academic dependency', the most widely published interpretive analysis of this 'shift' has been produced by scholars of the global north. But it must be said that the seminal works on this topic came from the writings of African scholars such as John Mbiti (Mbiti 1976: 6-18; see also Mbiti 1976), and Engelbert Mveng (Mveng 1987). Jehu Hanciles has argued in his monumental book on mission and migration that most of the global north authors who have discussed this issue present secularist perspective of the new 'shift' with a tendency that appears to tag 'Southern Christianity' as destructive force within the new world order (Hanciles 2008: 131).

By far the best known assessment of this shift within global Christianity from a global north perspective is the book of Philip Jenkins, *The Next Christendom: The Coming of Global Christianity*. Jenkins anticipates the possibility that the massive religious upsurge in the south will implode with bloody conflicts (engendered by population growth and attitudes to religious conversion) between Christians and Muslims. Though Jenkins's book is a pointer to what is at stake, the author did not treat the question of the significance of the southward shift in the Christian landscape as a viable resource for understanding the history of Christian missionary expansion (Jenkins 2002:133ff). His concern was centered on population growth and the problem associated with it. In a later book, *The New Faces of*

Christianity: Believing the Bible in the Global South (2006), Jenkins also presents the relationship between Christianity of the global north and that of the southern continents in the same way, with a rereading that seems to label the Christian communities in the global south and tag the Bible reading and scholarship there as something characterized by the fundamentalist and conservative tendencies.

However, the African interpretation of the southward shift in the Christian landscape is different. The African authors speak of the new southward shift as the transformation of Christianity from *the margins* and the role of migration in Christian expansion. At this juncture, we may ask: why are the new centers of Christian landscape localized within the marginalized zones of the southern continents? In this context, the argument, generally speaking, is that the significance of the new southward 'shift' must be located within the global transformation of the Christian landscape by these new centers of Christianity's universality. The growth of Christianity in the southern continents does not mean a displacement of the 'old centers' of the faith. It does not also mean a redefinition of our missionary concept or goal. Rather it is a confirmation of the history of Christian mission that faith travels through missionary movement of the believing community. Faith travels through migration. When the Christian faith, first travelled, from Jerusalem to Athens, North Africa and then to Rome none of the previous centers was displaced by the new ones. And none of the new centers was considered inferior to the 'old centers' of Christianity's universality. Each encounter was, rather, a manifestation of how the evangelizing church was fulfilling its mission in the world (Sanneh 2003: 36ff.). Indeed, each encounter was a demonstration of Christianity's universality. Moreover, none of the centers, 'old' or 'new' considers itself as the sole bearers of the Christian mission. Each center sees itself as a full participant in the evangelizing mission of the church.

African authors see this new southward 'shift' as a sign that Christianity is really becoming the world religion that it is meant to be. Again, John Mbiti is a seminal voice of this perspective. According to him, the southward shift signals the birth of new centers of Christianity's universality (Mbiti 1976: 6-18). But Mbiti was quick to add that the southward shift in Christian landscape has presented us with two realities that are in sharp contrast, almost contradiction. While on the one hand, the church has become universal in a literal, geographical sense, thanks to the great missionary movement of the last two hundred years, on the other, theological outreach has not matched this expansion.

For Mbiti, this is a serious dilemma, and if we do not resolve it, it will destroy our foundations as the church in the world. Thus, he suggests that as the church becomes worldwide, as it affirms the universality for which God's dispersal of history has destined it, theology must strain its neck to see beyond the horizon of our traditional structures, beyond the comforts of our ready-made methodologies of theologizing. For Mbiti, this means that our theology should be with the church where it is, rubbing shoulders with human beings whose conditions, outlook, concerns, and worldviews are not those with which we are familiar (Mbiti 1976: 8-9). He opines that the dichotomy between older and younger churches, between Western Christianity and the Christianity of the southern continents, is a real one, but it is also a false dichotomy. We can overcome this false dichotomy if we really want to. The background for overcoming it, according to Mbiti, lies on our preparedness to embark on theological pilgrimages. Theologians from the new (or younger churches) have made their pilgrimages to the theological learning of older churches. They had no alternative. But it has been in a sense, one-sided theology.

The new southward shift in Christianity, therefore, challenges us to embark on pilgrimage of true theological reciprocity and mutuality. Because, as it is now, it is only one side that knows the other side fairly well, while the other side either does not know or does not want to know the first side. Mbiti concludes that 'there cannot be theological conversation or dialogue between North and South, East and West, until we can embrace each other's concerns and stretch to each other's horizons. Theologians from the southern continents believe that they know about most of the constantly changing concerns of older Christendom. They would also like their counterparts from the older Christendom to come to know about their concerns of human survival' (Mbiti 1976: 17).

While Mbiti discusses theological pilgrimage as a viable step in confronting the dichotomy between the older and the younger churches, Kwame Bediako returns to the original concept of Christianity's universality in the new centers of the faith in southern continents. For Bediako: 'By becoming a non-Western religion ... Christianity has also become a true world faith' (Bediako 1995: 265). Wherever the faith has been transmitted and assimilated are equally 'centers of Christianity's universality.' This is not to deny that there have been (and the modern Western world is not the first of these) instances of Christian recession. Bediako argues further that the new shift does not mean that the old centers of Christianity are no longer functioning or that the church has become sterile there. No. Rather what is being emphasized is that it is important that a shift in the center of gravity of Christianity is precisely what it is supposed to. It is a pointer to the nature of the faith and much less to the significance of human agencies of its transmission. 'Any absolutisation of the pattern of Christianity's transmission should consequently be avoided and the nature of Christian history itself be re-examined ... Since it is on the basis of the experience of faith in the living Christ in the Christian communities of the South that we speak of the present shift, it also signifies that there is no one center from which Christianity radiates, and that it was never intended to be so' (Bediako 1995: 163-64).

The universal relevance of the church's missionary experience in the Christian communities of the southern communities comes, then, to consist in this – 'the great things that God has done'. This view is also the answer to those scholars who have doubted whether the cross-cultural learning that Christian communities of the southern continent projects, can assist in mission to the modern secularized societies.

Engelbert Mveng (a Camerounian theologian) sees the southward shift as a sign that Christianity is fulfilling one of its missions, namely that of allowing itself to be enriched by other peoples and cultures. According to Mveng, our confession of faith in Jesus Christ invites us to overcome the dichotomy and the crisis about which we spoke earlier. Here, he argues that the fact that Africa has met Christianity for centuries is a historical data. But the question today is to know if the history of Christianity in Africa is, as some authors believe, successful or a mortal conflict between two interlocutors (African reality and Christianity). However, Mveng opines that many scholars refuse to accept a gloomy vision for African Christianity. This is because, majority of African Christians believe, that by becoming Christian, Africa progresses in its own religious experience, bearing in mind its historical fulfillment and self-transcendence (Mveng 1987: 82). Moreover, Christianity, by becoming African, continues in its religious experience in the horizon of its missionary journey and self-transcendence. This implies that in the meeting of Christianity and Africa, each of the two is an important interlocutor in dialogue. Where any of the two entities is missing, the dialogue is elusive. If we do not collocate the true African identity in Christianity today, the whole continent is in danger of being excluded from a possible true dialogue. The cause of the poverty of our style of dialoguing is the absence of one of the interlocutors (Oborji 2007: 72ff.).

Lamin Sanneh presents an argument about limitations of the concept of Christendom advanced at the Edinburgh 1910 conference. He makes the case most forcefully in connection with African experience: 'African Christianity has not been a bitterly fought religion: there have been no ecclesiastical courts condemning unbelievers, heretics, and witches to death, no bloody battles of doctrine and polity, no territorial aggrandizement by churches; no jihads against infidels, no *fatwas* against women, no amputations, lynchings, ostracism, penalties, or public condemnation of doctrinal differences or dissent. The lines of Christian profession have not been etched in the blood of enemies. To that extent, at least African Christianity has diverged strikingly from sixteenth and seventeenth-century Christendom' (Sanneh 2003: 39).

In addition, Sanneh advances the basic argument of intercultural process in the history of Christian mission. In the first place, he acknowledges that the statistical weight has moved Africa firmly into the Christian orbit, and that happened only a few years ago, which is why the notion 'Africa a Christian continent' is so novel and dramatic. But we should bear in mind that Christianity from its origins was marked by serial retreat and advance as an intercultural process. Bethlehem and Jerusalem were superseded by

Antioch and Athens, while Egypt and Carthage soon gave place to Rome. Rival centers multiplied the chances of further contraction and expansion. Then it was the turn of the global north to inherit the mantle before the next momentous phase brought the religion to the southern hemisphere, with Africa representing the most recent continental shift. Sanneh writes that: 'These developments went beyond merely adding more names to the books; they had to do with cultural shifts, with changing the books themselves. This serial feature of the history of Christianity is largely hidden from people in the West now living in a post-Christian culture. Even in Africa itself the churches were caught unprepared, and are scarcely able to cope with the elementary issue of absorbing new members, let alone with the deeper issues of formation and training' (Sanneh 2003: 36-37).

The point here is that the concept of Christendom (mission as movement from the Christian land to the Non-Christian lands) imprisons the study of non-Western Christianity within a Western theological framework and thus impoverishes understanding of its nature and significance. It entrenches the notion of Christian missionary movement as one-way traffic, as a movement from the 'Old Christendom' to the so-called 'non-Christian land'. The missionary significance as well as the real Christian identity of Christians from the former 'non-Christian land' or ('mission land') is thus suppressed by the concept of 'Christendom'. Moreover, the experience of Christendom perhaps predisposes Westerners to think of religious phenomena in terms of permanent center and structures of unilateral control.

Arguing this point further, Jehu Hanciles brings into the debate the question of globalization and migration. According to him, the southward 'shift' in the Christian landscape is not so much about the critique of the missionary outlook developed at Edinburgh 1910. Rather it is a realization that queries the widespread notion that processes of globalization perpetuate structures of Western hegemony. The fact is that the recent 'shift' in Christian landscape with its southward movement has launched us into an age of 'globalization from below', a movement of non-Western cultures, both secular and religious, with a global reach that impact at the same time both the North Atlantic world and the southern continents, in a subtle but also in a very profound manner. Western initiatives and projects appear to dominate the contemporary world order, the processes of globalization incorporate powerful trends and religious phenomena that originate in the non-Western world and will potentially impact the West in significant ways. Again, this point is often ignored by most of modern commentators on the significance of the recent 'shift' in Christian landscape.

But neglecting this important perspective of the southern authors only succeeds in projecting a kind of polemic or rather north-south divide between Christians of the global north and those of the southern continents.

A polemic of this kind harms the purpose of Christian mission as well as the faith itself.

Consequently, among the African authors, there is a growing recognition of the role of migrations in Christian expansion and missionary activity. Missiologists from other zones are yet to engage in a serious reflection about the way in which recent transformation within global Christianity itself was aided by global migration. Between 1500s and 1900s, the global migration was from north to the south. That made the southern continents major centers of missionary engagement. But in recent times, the trend has shifted. The present migration from south to the north, points to the West as a major frontier of religious interactions and missionary engagement.

The dynamic of international migrations in missionary enterprise is not new to the history of Christian mission. The Bible bears witness to the inextricable connection between migration and mission and sees such linkage as a prominent factor in the history of Christian expansion. The fact that this connection is largely overlooked in mission studies has something to do with the unwarranted distinction between 'Christendom' and 'non-Christian world' (or rather between 'Christian land' and 'mission land') that inspired the missiology of the old and Edinburgh 1910 missionary outlook, and which in turn has marked our theological reflection for the last two hundred years. Since 1970s, the number of non-white migrants has risen dramatically as escalating conflicts, brutal regimes and economic collapse (related to globalization) have induced colossal displacement of peoples. The possibility that the phenomenal growth of Christianity in the southern continents is as well impacted by such tremendous transfers of population need not be ignored. As an aspect of cultural globalization, non-white migration represents a significant example of global processes which originate outside the Western world and impact Western societies. The religiosity of the new immigrants potentially transforms the religious movements into missionary engagement. At the very least it implicates secular (largely post-Christian) Western societies as sites of new religious interactions. In this regard, the new modes of immigrants' assimilation within Western societies will hardly leave the latter unchanged.

Conclusion

The missiology which Catholics have inherited from the pioneer authors of Münster and Louvain schools of thought, as well as other protagonists of missionary adaptation and the Edinburgh 1910 missionary paradigm, is today being challenged by the recent southward shift in Christian landscape. The old missiology was meant to serve missionaries from the West for their evangelizing activities in the southern continents. That missiology has served its purpose since it has helped in planting Christianity in virtually every corner of the southern continents. And this happened only in the last two hundred years. However, given the nature of the emerging global Christianity, the complex interaction and interdependence between the global north and the southern continents, a new missiology is already under way. This is not to lose the sight that the missionary outlook of the Münster and Louvain schools of thought as well as that of the Edinburgh 1910 conference will, for the foreseeable future, represent an important lens through which many people conceive mission and respond to mission. What is being argued, however, is that the reshaping of global Christianity by the young churches of the southern continents, has rendered the old missionary outlook or rather the idea of mission as one-way traffic (as movement from the north to the south), a defunct and meaningless conception.

Inasmuch, however, as one recognizes the challenge, the new southward shift in Christian landscape brings to missiology today, it would be a mistake to glorify the still-inchoate non-Western missionary movement, to suggest that its missionary outlook to the still far more celebrated Western missiology confers on it special grace of divine favor. No doubt, the southward shift in Christian landscape represents a major turning point in the history of Christianity. Yet much about the missionary movement of these new zones of Christianity remains uncertain, and the assessment provided in this study is intended to be a preliminary, even provisional. What is not in doubt, however, is that the future of global Christianity and missiology itself, will be decided mainly by the outcome of such initiatives in the meeting of Christianity of the global north and that of the communities in the southern continents. This leads Christians of both zones into a meeting point in uncharted waters.

CATHOLIC THEOLOGY OF MISSION

William P. Gregory

Despite a strong practical interest in mission on the part of the popes in the first half of the twentieth century, significant theological reflection on the topic from the Roman Magisterium or other central teaching offices of the church did not begin to appear until the Second Vatican Council (1962-65 – see James Kroeger's chapter in this volume). The decree *Ad Gentes*, promulgated in 1965 at the last session of the Council, stated that 'the pilgrim church is missionary by her very nature' (AG 2), and thus it is the duty of the whole people of God to advance the church's mission (see Stephen Bevans's chapter in this volume). This marked an important shift that placed mission squarely in the center of church life – a shift that in combination with a number of other historical factors resulted in a steady increase in authoritative church reflection on the topic in the decades following the Council. Landmark statements in this development were Paul VI's *Evangelii Nuntiandi* (1975), John Paul II's *Redemptoris Missio* (1990), the Pontifical Council for Inter-religious Dialogue and the Congregation for Evangelization of Peoples' joint document *Dialogue and Proclamation* (1991), the Congregation for the Doctrine of the Faith's *Dominus Iesus* (2000), and *Doctrinal Note on Some Aspects of Evangelization* (2007) (see Roger Schroeder's chapter in this volume).

This essay presents an overview of the theology of mission that has appeared in these documents in the last five decades. Though each of the documents speaks with distinctive emphases given their differing authorships and originating circumstances, their points of agreement and overall internal consistency are noteworthy. Permeating all of them is a common set of theological affirmations on topics of crucial importance that together amount to a single, integral theology of mission. Though attempting to distill the wealth of ideas found in these writings into a short essay presents a number of interpretive challenges, my hope in the pages that follow is to delineate at least the central themes of the documents' shared theology of mission. I will address three questions: What is the church's mission? Why is the church's mission necessary? How does the church's mission relate to the ongoing activity of God? Examining these three questions in turn will help surface the major elements of the church's theology of mission.

What is the Church's Mission?

Until Vatican II, this was a fairly simple question. Mission is preaching the gospel and planting the church among groups of people who do not yet know Christ (see AG 6; EN 14, 28; DI 18). In the decades following the Council, however, mission came to be recognized as a more 'complex reality' (RM 41) also involving such activities as witness, inculturation, respect for human freedom, inter-religious dialogue, ecumenical activity, social justice, earth-care, prayer, and liturgy. The variety of activities along with the intricacy of their interconnections made mission a difficult concept to define. Nevertheless, at the heart of this diverse set of activities it is possible to identify a single dynamic that sums up the essence of mission: mission is mediating God's gift of salvation to humankind.

Repeatedly, the documents stress that mission centers on bringing about the salvation of humankind (AG 7; see EN 18). Salvation is the reception of the divine life, humans coming to share in the Trinitarian communion (see AG 2; EN 27; RM 7, 11, 23), which entails the complete transformation of human lives in conformity to divine love. 'The ultimate purpose of mission is to enable people to share in the communion which exists between the Father and the Son' (RM 23). The church has received this gift of divine life and it is called to share it. Its mission is to live out the '*radical newness of life* brought by Christ' (RM 7; see RM 11) and make the beauty of that life manifest and understood in every possible way for the purpose of others also coming to share in it fully as mature members of the church dedicated to Christ. This gift makes the church the communion of life and love that it is. Christ has united himself to the church (RM 18) and given it his Spirit (RM 29). '[H]e himself is in the Church and the Church is in him' (DI 16). People thus receive the gift of divine life through incorporation into the church. Mission mediates the extension of salvation to all by inviting all to become members of Christ's body (see RM 9).

The nature of salvation as expressed in the documents has several notable characteristics. It is a transcendent gift that the followers of Christ already know (RM 7, 11, 13) – coming to share in the Trinitarian life in the present, not in the hereafter or at the end of time – and one that is closely associated with the nature of the church itself. The church believes this gift will reach full bloom when the kingdom arrives in completeness at Christ's return. But what the church shares in its mission now is its foretaste of the kingdom already present in history, the fulfillment of the kingdom's coming in Christ (RM 16, 18). This gift defines the essence of the church – 'She is his Bride' (RM 9), the 'living image' of the kingdom (RM 19; see CDF 2007: 9) – and so sharing the gift involves inviting others to join the church. Doing so is the primary way the church serves the full coming of the kingdom (RM 20), for the communication of divine life is the necessary premise for the rejuvenation of humanity that is the essence of the kingdom (EN 18, 35-36; RM 18; CDF 2007: 9). The kingdom is 'liberation from evil in all its forms' (RM 15) and the establishment of a perfect communion of love among all human beings and with God (RM 14-15); it is the gathering together of the scattered human race into one family and one people of God (AG 1, 2, 3, 7). God's self-gift works to transform every sphere of life to this end. The salvation the church seeks to mediate in mission, therefore, is an integral and comprehensive one, and the church itself is established to serve as the focal point of this transforming work. The church has not only the mission of announcing and inaugurating the kingdom among all people (RM 18), but also the mission of being itself the seed, sign, beginning, and instrument of the kingdom (LG 5; RM 18), the 'universal sacrament of salvation' (LG 1, 48; DP 33; cf. RM 20).

The integral and transcendent nature of salvation along with the multiplicity of ways there are for mediating any of its many facets help explain why the forms of missionary activity are so numerous. Expressing the divine love of the Trinitarian communion embraces every imaginable good, from works of mercy, social justice, and efforts at reconciliation to the promotion of religious liberty, environmental conservation, and common understanding among religious traditions. Wherever the dignity of human life and the sacredness of existence require promotion or defense; wherever human relationships require nurturing or healing; wherever evil and sin tear at the fabric of life, there the mission of the church lies. Similarly, mission involves every celebration and sign of the Trinitarian life in the lives of the faithful and every attempt to make its meaning and truth known to others, thus embracing the whole contemplative and liturgical life of the Christian community as well as every form of witness, proclamation, catechesis, and inculturation of the gospel among peoples. All of these activities and the whole of Christian existence play their part in reflecting the radiance and force of God's salvation.

Animating all these forms of mission is a governing objective, which must not be overlooked. Above all, the church seeks that others may also come to participate in the mystery of salvation as it has experienced this (AG 7; EN 18; RM 46, 48; CDF 2007: 1-3, 8-9, 12; see EN 14, DI 22). Receiving the transcendent gift of salvation, again, is the necessary premise of the kingdom's full arrival, and the church functions as the instrument, seed, sign, and beginning of the kingdom's coming insofar as it focuses on passing on this specifically religious gift. The church does not believe that it holds a complete monopoly on this gift, but rather affirms that the wideness of God's mercy is such that the possibility of salvation is extended to all people 'in a manner known only to God' (GS 22). For itself, though, it affirms that it has been divinely established as the 'ordinary means' of salvation (RM 55), and that the most certain and complete path to salvation is through the conversion of individuals to explicit faith in Christ, leading to their incorporation into the church and their development into mature Christians. Therefore, the church's most fundamental aim is the conversion of people to the faith and to the ongoing path of conversion that is the nature of Christian life itself. As the 2007 *Doctrinal Note on Some*

Aspects of Evangelization declares, 'to help all persons to meet Christ in faith ... is the primary objective of evangelization ...' (CDF 2007: 2), or in the succinct statement of Paul VI:

> For the Church, evangelizing means bringing the Good News into all the strata of humanity, and through its influence transforming humanity from within and making it new... But there is no new humanity if there are not first of all new persons renewed by Baptism and by lives lived according to the Gospel. The purpose of evangelization is therefore precisely this interior change ... the Church evangelizes when she seeks to convert... (EN 18).

Identifying conversion as the ultimate goal of mission, however, does not mean that mission is reducible to proclamation. The salvation that mission mediates is as broad as the kingdom, and so the whole variety of activities noted earlier as well as the building up and existence of the church's communion are equally genuine and necessary forms of mission. But it does mean that the church's hope for people never comes to rest fully in any vision of the good life except one that includes the transcendent good of shared communion in God as the church has come to know this. Conversion to Christ through the church is the integrating center of the church's hope in mission.

Why is the Church's Mission Necessary?

The answer the church has consistently given to the question of the necessity of mission is humankind's need for salvation. But the theological context in which it expressed this answer changed significantly as a result of Vatican II's generally positive evaluation of human culture and non-Christian religions. As noted earlier, the council taught that all people of good will are offered the possibility of salvation through the Holy Spirit (GS 22; see AG 7; EN 80; RM 9, 10, 55). It also discerned the Holy Spirit's presence in the world, spreading goodness, truth, and grace (AG 9), planting 'seeds of the Word' (AG 11, 15) and 'seeds of contemplation' (AG 18), shining 'rays of that Truth which enlightens all human beings' (NA 2), and 'animating, purifying and reinforcing the noble aspirations which drive the human family' (GS 38; see RM 28). The church thus came to acknowledge the 'inchoate reality' of the kingdom beyond the borders of Christianity (RM 20; DP 35). At the same time, it insisted that salvation outside the church is salvation in Christ (DI 12), and that entrance into the kingdom depends entirely on him. Christ is 'the one Savior of all, the only one able to reveal God and lead to God' (RM 5; see RM 5-7, 9, 11); he, in essence, is the kingdom (RM 18; see CDF 2007: 9). The work of the Spirit, furthermore, is understood to be intrinsically joined to him. Christ and the Spirit together share a 'joint' mission in the one divine economy of salvation (DI 12; see RM 6, 9). The seeds of the Word, finally, 'receive from the mystery of Christ the elements of goodness and grace which they contain' (DI 8); they function to prepare people for the definitive revelation of the gospel (AG 3; EN 53; RM 28-29; DI 12, 21). Nevertheless, if salvation is possible outside the church, the question arises: Why engage in mission, especially if non-Christians can be saved 'in the sincere practice of what is good in their own religious traditions and by following the dictates of their conscience' (DP 29)? Is it not enough simply to 'help people to become more human or more faithful to their own religion' (CDF 2007: 3)?

The reply most often given in response to these concerns is that the full benefits and means of salvation are available to humankind only through the church (RM 18, 55; see EN 15). Other religions may be nourished in part by the Spirit and graced by seeds of the Word, but they lack the full revelation of God given in Jesus Christ (DI 5-6); they are marked by 'gaps, insufficiencies and errors' (RM 55; see DI 8, 21; CDF 2007: 7) that 'reflect the limitations of the human spirit, sometimes inclined to choose evil' (DP 31); and any seeds of the Word existing within them need to be freed 'from all taint of evil' as well as 'healed, uplifted, and perfected' (AG 9) through contact with the gospel. All told, the assessment is that the followers of other religions are '*objectively speaking* ... in a gravely deficient situation in comparison with those ... in the Church' (DI 22). For those without a religion or some transcendent reference point, the conclusion would be even more precarious. By contrast, the church believes that it has received the full, complete, and definitive revelation of the divine truth (DI 5-6), and incorporation into it allows one to 'participate fully in communion with God, the Father, Son and Holy Spirit' (DI 22). '[T]he religion of Jesus ... objectively places man in relation with the plan of God, with His living presence and with His action'; it 'causes an encounter with the mystery of divine paternity that bends over towards humanity' and 'effectively establishes with God an authentic and living relationship which the other religions do not succeed in doing ...' (EN 53). 'The result is a unique and special relationship [between God and the church] which, while not excluding the action of Christ and the Spirit outside the Church's visible boundaries, confers upon her a specific and necessary role' (RM 18). In short, the church continues to uphold the necessity of conversion, faith, and baptism in relation to salvation (RM 9), but it does this more so now through a claim regarding the unique benefits and means of salvation available within the church rather than through an insistence that it possesses the only means in existence.

At the same time, the question of the necessity of mission is also addressed from another perspective, more intrinsic to the church. The divine life that the church receives through its participation in the Trinity is understood to inflame the church with God's own burning love for humankind and fill it with the desire that all people come to know life in the Trinitarian communion (AG 7; EN 79; RM 89; CDF 2007: 7, 8, 10, 11, 13; see AG 12; RM 49). This "fount-like love' or charity of God' (AG 2), which makes the church the 'unity in love' (RM 23) that it is and gives it its innermost nature, of itself 'wells up' missionary activity (AG 6). The church is thus missionary by its very nature (AG 2; see EN 15). The love of the Trinity, the gift of salvation itself, provides 'the primary motive' (CDF 2007: 8), 'the fundamental reason' (RM 5; see DI 5), and the ultimate origin of the church's mission. In the words of John Paul II, 'we are missionaries above all because of *what we are* as a Church ... even before we become missionaries *in word or deed*' (RM 23). '[T]he Church's mission derives not only from the Lord's mandate but also from the profound demands of God's life within us' (RM 11; see AG 5). To the extent that the church immerses itself in the divine life through walking the path of holiness, it enables itself both to sense and to fulfill its missionary identity (RM 90). It comes to feel gratitude (CDF 2007: 11) as well as its obligation in love as the recipient of the divine gift 'to pass on to others in freedom what [it] has freely been given' (CDF 2007: 7). Missionary activity, then, is born out of the very nature of God as communicated to the church. The church engages in mission because it is engaged itself by an inherently missionary God (see AG 2).

How Does the Church's Mission Relate to God's Ongoing Activity?

This brings us to the third question. God's larger saving plan to bring about the kingdom through the missions of the Son, Spirit, and church has been addressed already. A final issue to be considered, though, concerns the role of the Holy Spirit in relation to the concrete performance of mission. The fundamental point the documents make is that the church's task 'is not exercised in a complete void' (DP 68); motivating, directing, and supporting all authentic forms of mission is the action and power of the Holy Spirit, who is the 'principal agent of evangelization' (EN 75; see RM 21) and the one without whom mission would be impossible (EN 75). Mission is not merely a human undertaking exercised in obedience to Christ's mandate. It is a joint divine-human endeavor in which the faithful allow themselves to become docile instruments of the Spirit (EN 75; see RM 87) and 'God's co-workers' in the salvation of the world (AG 9, 15; RM 9, 21). The Spirit instills 'into the hearts of the faithful the same mission spirit which impelled Christ Himself' (AG 4), prompting and impelling them to their task (EN 75; see DP 64), and assisting them in their role as mediators of salvation from beginning to end. The 'gentle action of the Spirit' (EN 75) is necessary, for mission is 'based not on human abilities but on the power of the risen Lord' (RM 23).

In general, the Spirit works to '[actualize] the salvific efficacy of the Son made man in the lives of all people' (DI 12). It does this in two ways. First, in the universal scope of its activity noted earlier, it draws all people mysteriously toward the paschal mystery and the life of the kingdom (see DP 17, 68), and second, in partnership with the church in mission, it moves this work to fulfillment by facilitating the conversion of all to Christ through the church, the growth of individuals in holiness, and the salutary transformation of every area of human existence. Within mission, the Spirit thus facilitates all forms of missionary activity, partnering with the church to continue the kingdom-work of Jesus (EN 15). The Spirit is present when the compelling power of evangelizers' own lives is manifest, reflecting Christ's image (RM 87) and serving as 'a sign of God and of transcendent realities' (RM 42). The Spirit is present in the hearts of those being evangelized (RM 21; DP 68), predisposing them 'to be open and receptive to the good news' (EN 75; see AG 13, RM 46, CDF 2007: 4, 10), and stirring up the gift of faith (AG 15; DP 64). To restate a point made earlier in regard to the church's mission: wherever the dignity of human life and the sacredness of existence require promotion or defense; wherever human relationships require nurturing or healing; wherever evil and sin tear at the fabric of life, there the Holy Spirit is active. Through all forms of its missionary activity and encounter, the Holy Spirit leads both evangelizers and evangelized deeper into the mystery of salvation.

Conclusion

While there has been a consistent understanding of mission in the last century as the church's work for the salvation of the world, that understanding has changed significantly in the last fifty years, since the Second Vatican Council. Authoritative church statements over the last five decades have given expression to a core Catholic theology of mission. This theology conceives of mission not as peripheral to Christian self-understanding but as fundamental to it. It is a theology that is deeply embedded in several of the most central mysteries of faith – those of salvation, the Trinity, and the church's communal significance in God's saving plan. The church in mission mediates God's salvation to humankind. It does this out of its own inner necessity as the recipient of the divine life and in response to the world's need. Authentic mission cooperates with the Spirit at every stage to mediate a comprehensive salvation, rooted in the new life made available through Christ's life, death, and resurrection. The church bears this gift to the world with frail hands, aware of its own sinfulness, but also with the confidence that the Word of God, the gospel message, has an 'intrinsic and mysterious power' (RM 45), a 'wisdom that is not of this world', that is 'able to stir up by itself faith' (EN 5; see CDF 2007: 5, 8, 9, 12).

A CENTURY OF HOPE AND TRANSFORMATION: MISSION AND UNITY IN CATHOLIC PERSPECTIVE

Jeffrey Gros, FSC

The New Evangelization

The Pontifical Council for the New Evangelization was the first new office of the Roman Curia opened by Pope Benedict XVI in 2010. It will give form to a vision of mission frequently proposed, as in this 1996 address of Pope John Paul in Germany:

> The new evangelization is therefore the order of the day.... The task of evangelization involves moving toward each other and moving together as Christians, and it must begin from within; evangelization and unity, evangelization and ecumenism are indissolubly linked with each other.... Because the question of the new evangelization is very close to my heart as bishop of Rome I consider overcoming the divisions of Christianity 'one of the pastoral priorities.' (John Paul II, 1996: 3, 5)

This thorough integration of the ecumenical unity of Christians and the mission of the Catholic Church contrasts with Catholic and non-Catholic mission thinking before the Second Vatican Council, including participants in the 1910 Edinburgh World Mission Conference that this volume celebrates. How did the Catholic Church and its ecumenical partners move from mutual proselytism, competition and estrangement to a greater understanding and practice of mission, embodied in the vision of a new evangelization?

This short essay will recount 1) some salient points about the Edinburgh Conference, 2) the mission situation in the half century before the Council, 3) the shifts in missiology brought about by the Second Vatican Council and the modern ecumenical movement, and 4) the developments in relationships among Christians, ecumenical dialogues and the expanded interpretations of the magisterium in the half century since the Council.

The Edinburg Conference 1910

Many credit 1910 as beginning the modern ecumenical movement because of several decisions: 1) to be a church sponsored rather than a nondenominational gathering; 2) to refrain from targeting Latin America, Russia and several Middle Eastern countries as 'mission territories' because of Catholic and Orthodox churches there; 3) to promote relationships and ecumenical methodologies which became essential to the ecumenical movement, and 4) to propose institutional continuity (Stanley 2009; Rouse 1954: 353). High Church Anglican pressure insured the gathering's ecclesial nature and the first two elements that presaged the ecclesial character of the twentieth century ecumenical movement. In spite of this Anglican desire to avoid theology, the interest of participants, including Bishop Charles Brent, led to the founding of the Faith and Order movement. The only Catholic engagement was a letter from a progressive Italian bishop and there was no Orthodox participation (Stanley 2009: 11-12).

However, it is ironic that for this conference: 1) in the title of this third world conference the word 'ecumenical' was dropped because of its ambiguity, 2) the theological and church order discussion were excluded, so the Faith and Order movement began to emerge in another venue, but with many of the same actors, 3) almost immediately (1916) American Protestant missionaries dissented from the Edinburgh decision to exclude Catholic Latin America, and targeted missionary expansion there (Piedra 2002: 4) owing to the newness of the Pentecostal movement (1906) its participation was not considered, and 5) those Protestants uncomfortable with the ecclesial character and perceived liberalism of Edinburgh founded their alternative *Interdenominational Foreign Mission Association* in 1917 (Frizen 1992). The meeting occurred before the Fundamentalist-Modernist ruptures that so burden Protestant ecumenism. Both evangelical and ecumenical Protestant mission work in the twentieth century are rooted in Edinburgh (Walls 2002: 38).

Nevertheless, processes and relationships were set in motion that would lead to the founding of the Life and Work and Faith and Order movements which united in the World Council of Churches (1948), the entry of the Catholic Church into the modern ecumenical movement (1962-1965), and the integration of the International Missionary Council into the World Council of Churches (1961) (Fey 1986: 171).

Catholic Missions and Ecumenism: Before the Council

The mission thrust of the Catholic Church was disrupted by the French Revolution, the liberation of Rome from the papacy, and the First World War. Nevertheless, the nineteenth and twentieth centuries witnessed strong missionary initiative, revitalization of traditional orders like the Jesuits and Franciscans, and new focused missionary zeal in groups like the Oblates of Mary Immaculate, the Society of the Divine Word, Missionaries of Africa (White Fathers) and national foundations like Mill Hill, Missionaries of Paris, Maryknoll and the Paulists.

One of the ironies of early twentieth century was the influence on Catholic missiology of the successful Protestant missionary expansion of the previous century. Catholics believed their church to be the one true church, and therefore sought to bring not only non-Christians, but fellow Christians to the fullness of the truth. In doing so, a group like the Paulists, for example, adopted methods for American evangelism not only from their founder Isaac Hecker, but also from the culture so deeply rooted in American Protestant piety and zeal (Bosch 1993: 275, 290; Dries 1993: 252). In Germany in the nineteenth century, Catholics followed Protestant university initiatives in setting up chairs of missiology (Bosch 1991: 491; see Oborji's chapter in this volume). Both Catholic and Protestant scholars note the importance of John R. Mott's Student Volunteer Movement on the Catholic Student Mission Crusade (Dries 1998: 87; Latourette 1922: 442). The International Missionary Council followed Catholic missiological developments as closely as any of its Protestant member churches, with reports provided by Catholic missiologists as early as 1932 (Hublou 1932; Stransky 1966).

Latourette's early report indicates the positive ecumenical perspective that a thoroughly Christ-centered missionary outlook provided: 'One of the most interesting and possibly significant religious developments in the past few years is a marked awakening among Roman Catholics in the United States in foreign missions.' (Latourette 1922: 439). In this he is thinking clearly of the Christian influence for the whole missionary family, and not merely Catholic or Protestant.

Also during this period, the Catholic Church claimed to mediate Christian salvation exclusively, and missionary movements were often devoted to making converts of fellow Christians as well as non-Christians, even if official documents made more careful distinctions. From its beginnings in 1622 the Congregation for the Propagation of the Faith had the task of spreading the faith, protecting the faith among the Catholic diaspora, and dialogue to restore unity. The bull establishing the congregation acknowledged the church's culpability in the divisions that marred the church's mission: 'In consequence of our sins ... unity was lost and continues to be lost' (Metzler 1985: 165). This congregation carried the responsibility for dialogue with other Christians until 1960.

There were those aware of the inevitable pluralism even in so-called 'Catholic cultures', and the need to collaborate in common witness, as one writer suggests in speaking of Latin America in 1931:

> Whether it is desirable or not, these lands have ceased to protect officially any one faith and their citizens are determined to discuss all types of religion and philosophy. Under such conditions, I feel that Protestantism will appeal to some people who are no longer Catholic ... If there was ever a time when any religious organization had a monopoly on any part of the world, it seems to me that such time has passed ... But this does not mean that we are to act hostile toward each other, calling each other names, regarding each other as enemies. But rather, while maintaining our peculiar beliefs, to act brotherly, as far as our humanity will allow us, toward all who believe in God. (Dries 1989: 98).

It would take the second Vatican Council and its *Decree on Religious Freedom* (DH 1965) to make such sentiments central to the Catholic understanding of mission. (Schreiter 1994: 113-25)

Another factor that laid the groundwork for an opening to a shared ecumenical vision in mission was common experiences in the world at mid-century. Like Protestant and Catholic relationships built in the foxholes and prisons of Europe during the Second World War, those struggling, often suffering, in mission fields or as minorities in distant places, developed common experiences and mutual support in the internment camps of China and other parts of Asia, as well as difficult situations in Africa.

The phenomenon of decolonization, though affecting different sections of the world in different ways, had a common impact on expatriate missionaries, on the perception of the Christian missionary project around the globe, and on the debates about how best to proceed as new levels of inculturation became possible (Neil 1966). In fact, in an amazingly few decades following the Council, the issues facing all mission communities, Catholic, historic and evangelical Protestant, and Orthodox began to look very similar, even when solutions varied: focus on God's mission, partnership between younger churches and their churches of origin, justice, evangelical methods, inculturation, liberation, common witness, the mission of the whole people of God, inter-religious dialogue, and the theological basis of mission. (Scherer 1994: Bosch 1991: Thomas 1995; Dries 1989: 253).

The Ecumenical Mission Shift in the Council

The debates on *Ad Gentes* and its implementation and challenges are well documented in other essays in this volume (see also Bevans and Gros 2009). However, there were some decisions in the ecumenical realm needed to make common witness possible in the new evangelization.

First, a hard fought discussion on religious freedom was necessary to not only give credibility to the Catholic call for common Christian mission, but also to understand the very nature of gospel witness in a free society. Brazilian Cardinal Rossi articulated clearly the missionary and pedagogical transformation necessary in Latin America (Bevans and Gros 2009: 230). It is ironic to note that during the Council Cardinal Silva Henriquez was called in to the Holy Office to be reprimanded for considering Chile to be a missionary country (Bevans and Gros 2009: 169) in 1964. By 2007 the Conference of Latin American Bishops Conferences (CELAM) took as its theme 'Disciples and Missionaries of Christ: the Way, Truth, and Life'. It was necessary for the Catholic Church to be a supporter of religious freedom for common ecumenical witness and renewal of mission in traditionally Catholic lands to be possible.

Second, some theological clarifications were necessary before a move could be made from the program to convert all to the Catholic Church, even fellow Christians to a vision of unity through ecumenical dialogue, and to common missionary witness and to living in the real communion we confess, even if yet imperfect.

The church had to recognize the ecclesial reality of other churches and ecclesial communities, if yet lacking some of what Catholics claimed necessary for the full visible unity of the church. This necessitated recognizing that the one, true church of Jesus Christ *subsists in* the Catholic Church, but is not totally identified with its structures in any time or place. Furthermore, it was necessary to recognize that some elements that Christ willed for the church are realized in communities separated from the Catholic Church in ways that can renew all Christians. This allows for sharing of gifts, learning from one another, and beginning the pilgrimage of dialogue that will discern together the shape of that unity for which Christ prayed in service to his mission in the world.

Thirdly, as the church turned away from conversion and 'return' in its approach to other Christians, it was critical to move away from the approach to the Eastern churches that implicitly denied them status as churches in the proper sense. In the centuries before the Council, Catholic missionary strategy toward the Eastern Orthodox was to either unite with parts of churches separated from their Orthodox patriarchates or to form churches with the liturgies, spiritualities and customs of the Orthodox churches of the region, but in union with Rome. This method of 'uniatism' had to be reviewed, and dialogue was to become the normal route toward restoring communion. The Council did not repudiate the Eastern churches already in union with Rome, but the approach for the future was to be dialogue not proselytism. In several cases, in the Middle East for example, this enabled Catholic religious orders to work for and with Orthodox churches in their mission and service with no intent to proselytize. This principle of dialogue and recognition as sister churches became especially important in discussing the Orthodox Catholic dialogue after 1989 and the relations that developed in Eastern Europe.

Collaboration is possible in respect and good faith, long before full ecclesiological agreement is achieved. Missiologists had been learning from one another for years. Even before the Council, levels of collaboration had begun in the rebuilding of Western Europe, for example among Catholics and Protestants in Britain (Rouse 1954: 688), and were approved on a limited and controlled scale by the Holy See in 1949 (Rouse 1954: 692). Already, in 1964 Cardinal Richard Cushing of Boston collaborated with Rev. Billy Graham the evangelist in his Boston crusade.

Ecumenical Developments Following the Council

Mission structures in Western Protestantism tended to follow the lines of voluntary association and independent churches, rivaling the mission boards of the churches of Europe and the United States. This development has some similarities to Catholic missionary orders (Motte 1981; Jenkinson and O'Sullivan 1991), mission societies, and new lay movements in the years after the Council (Gold 1992). International initiatives have given rise to other local discussions of common witness, for example in the United States (Lingas 1995). Mission societies like the American Society of Missiology (1973) and its journal *Missiology* are important venues for mutual interaction.

Early on following the Council there were discussions of *Ad Gentes* in Protestant circles (Gensichen 1967; Glasser 1985) The Congregation for the Evangelization of Peoples (formerly Propagation of the Faith). (Metzler 1985) and the Pontifical Council for Promoting Christian Unity (formerly Secretariat) have their appropriate roles (Duprey 1985: 29-40; Delaney 2001: 26-28l), and their collaborative mission as outlined in *Ad Gentes* (15, 29).

The World Council of Churches

The World Council of Churches is a primary venue for formal Catholic relations with the wider Christian community in mission. Since 1984 there has been a staff person appointed to and funded by the Holy See to the Commission on World Mission and Evangelism. This has enabled coordination and dialogue from the inside (Delaney 2001: 27; Thomas 2010: 91-95). The Joint Working Group of the World Council and the Vatican has produced a series of important studies on proselytism, common witness and other themes that touch on the mission work of the churches together (Scherer and Bevans, ed. 1992: 18-26, Briggs 2004: 144-146).

There have been eleven mission conferences since Edinburgh, and since 1973 Catholics have been intimately involved (Motte 1995; Briggs 2004: 125-48). Catholic input and responses to these texts have been an important enrichment to the dialogue and to the quality of the final texts (Stransky 1980, 1981, 1990; Mutiso-Mbinda 1983; Fitzgerald 1991; Schreiter 2005; Cooney 1996). While these mission texts are important, one shrewd participant notes that 'one of the most significant developments that has emerged from these gatherings is that of modeling new ways of participation' (Motte 1987: 26).

Mission and the theological dialogue serving Christian unity (Faith and Order) are in different sections of the World Council. Therefore, internal dialogue is necessary from time to time. An example is the Faith and Order text, *The Nature and Mission of the Church*. Special Catholic mission perspectives have been offered in this process (Klein 2001; Sjada 2001) in addition to the general Catholic membership in Faith and Order.

Mission in the dialogues

One of the unexpected developments after the Council was a series of dialogues to develop with Western Christians absent from the ecumenical movement: conservative evangelical, Pentecostal, and even agencies of these evangelistic movements (Rusch, Gros and Meyer, eds. 2000: 373-85, 713-79). One of the important learnings from some of these dialogues, especially the *Evangelical Roman Catholic Dialogue on Mission* (Rusch Gros and Meyer, eds. 2000: 399-437) was that the focus on the goal of mission enabled discussion of sensitive theological issues from a whole new vantage point (Bevans 1995; Armstrong 2010).

Furthermore, when it came to discussing ecclesiology itself, evangelicals were able to understand Catholics and the biblical message of *koinonia* much more effectively from the eschatological perspective of common service to the kingdom (Best et al. 2007: 268-95). The Orthodox-Catholic 1993 text on uniatism and proselytism is an important reiteration of Catholic mission practice with the Orthodox, especially significant since the reopening of Eastern Europe to mission activity (Rusch Gros and Meyer, eds. 2000: 680-85). A number of other dialogues have also focused on mission (International Anglican-Roman Catholic Commission for Unity and Mission 2007). Cardinal Walter Kasper is promoting the harvesting of the nearly fifty years of theological dialogue as part of the reception process (Kasper 2009). Other harvesting efforts have included the agreements on mission as well (Mulhal and Gros 2006: 212-43), and more needs to be done to make these agreements effective resources for mission education.

Ecumenical policy in Catholic evangelization

A) MISSION IN THE ECUMENICAL INITIATIVES OF THE MAGISTERIUM

Catholic ecumenism focuses on the theological agreements necessary to restore full communion, and therefore gives pride of place to dialogue on sacraments, soteriology and ecclesiology (Kasper 2009). However, the Council and subsequent directives are also clear that collaboration in mission is essential to Catholic ecumenism. Three texts of the 1990s are particularly important: the 1993 *Directory for the Application of Principles and Norms on Ecumenism* (PCPCU), Pope John Paul's twelfth encyclical *Ut Unum Sint* (1995), and 'The Ecumenical Dimension in the Formation of Pastoral Workers' (PCPCU 1998).

The *Directory* synthesizes the thirty years of ecumenical directives, in the context of the 1983 Code of Canon Law. It devotes a whole chapter to cooperation and common witness, including a focus on mission, building on twenty-five years of official teaching:

> The common witness given by all forms of ecumenical cooperation is already missionary. The ecumenical movement has, in fact, gone hand in hand with a new discovery by many communities of the missionary nature of the Church.
>
> Ecumenical cooperation shows to the world that those who believe in Christ and live by his Spirit, being thus made children of God who is Father of all,

can set about overcoming human divisions, even about such sensitive matters as religious faith and practice, with courage and hope. (PCPCU 1993: 205-9)

The text then goes on to outline suggested structures for common witness, and the variety of areas where ecumenical collaboration is encouraged: Bible and liturgical translation, prayer and study together, catechetics, social service and witness, education, inter-religious dialogue, environment, medicine, and media. In many places the Catholic Church is a member of national, regional and local councils of churches.

The Formation text outlines important dimensions that should be part of all seminaries and pastoral worker's training: 1) interpretive principles, 2) the hierarchy of truths, and 3) the results of ecumenical dialogues to date, clarifying for prospective Catholic leaders the common faith we share, remaining differences and issues that need to be resolved. The document suggests that a course in ecumenism be provided early in training. This will be especially important for cross-cultural ministers as they move into a new ecumenical context with its unique history of relations among Christians. They will need to be helped to find opportunities for common witness and moving sensitively out of their isolation into ecumenical cooperation. The suggested curricula also are to include 'the search for unity and the task of mission'; and 'common witness' (PCPCU 1998: 25).

The best known of these texts is Pope John Paul's encyclical on the ecumenical commitment. It is remembered most for its call for reform of the papacy with input from ecumenical colleagues, to better serve the unity of Christians (UUS 95-96); and its call to make the results of, now, forty-five years of dialogue a 'common heritage' (UUS 80). However, it also has a strong concluding exhortation on mission:

> How indeed can we proclaim the Gospel of reconciliation without at the same time being committed to working for reconciliation between Christians? ... When non-believers meet missionaries who do not agree among themselves, even though they all appeal to Christ, will they be in a position to receive the true message? Will they not think that the Gospel is a cause of division, despite the fact that it is presented as the fundamental law of love? (98)

B) ECUMENISM IN THE MISSIONARY MAGISTERIUM

Shifts in Catholic understanding of mission have been monumental since *Ad Gentes* and its subsequent implementation (Bevans and Gros 2009: 56-120). Not least of these is the persistent call to common witness in evangelization. In addition to the Decree on Missionary Activity from the Council, it is also helpful to look at a variety of other documents to discern the developments in Catholic teaching. Since these documents are treated elsewhere in this volume this section will recall only the Apostolic Exhortation *Evangelii Nuntiandi* (EN; Scherer and Bevans, eds. 1992: 91-96). There are other missiological texts with important ecumenical implications, like the encyclical *Redemptoris Missio* (RM; Scherer and

Bevans, eds. 1992: 169-76) and the Congregation of the Doctrine of the Faith's *Dominius Iesus* (2000) (Gros 2009; see Roger Schroeder's essay in this volume).

The 1974 Roman Synod of Bishops took up the theme of evangelization in the early phase of the reception of Vatican II when there was still a great deal of debate about the interpretation of the Council and its missionary and ecumenical renewal. Pope Paul's text provides yet another stage in the reception of the ecumenical imperative in Catholic understandings of evangelization:

> Is this [division among Christians] not perhaps one of the great sicknesses of evangelization today? Indeed, if the Gospel that we proclaim is seen to be rent by doctrinal disputes, ideological polarizations or mutual condemnations among Christians, at the mercy of the latter's differing views on Christ and the Church and even because of their different concepts of society and human institutions, how can those to whom we address our preaching fail to be disturbed, disoriented, even scandalized?

> The Lord's spiritual testament tells us that unity among His followers is not only the proof that we are His but also the proof that He is sent by the Father. It is the test of the credibility of Christians and of Christ Himself. As evangelizers, we must offer Christ's faithful not the image of people divided and separated by unedifying quarrels, but the image of people who are mature in faith and capable of finding a meeting-point beyond the real tensions, thanks to a shared, sincere and disinterested search for truth. Yes, the destiny of evangelization is certainly bound up with the witness of unity given by the Church. This is a source of responsibility and also of comfort. (EN 77)

Unity among Christians is a missionary imperative, and the zeal for evangelization is a challenge to bring divided Christians together in service to the kingdom.

Challenges into the Twenty-First Century

Edinburgh in 1910 spoke of Christians finally coming to imagine a global, universal church articulated then by Bishop Charles Gore (Ross 2009: 37), and asserted by Karl Rahner in a historic 1979 address (Rahner 1979). Living into this evolutionary, inculturated, post-Eurocentric vision will be the mission challenge for all Christians in a post-colonial, pluralistic globalized world Bosch 1991: 456).

Ecumenical formation for common witness and common understanding, and harvesting the dialogue results in pastorally accessible forms will be a continuing opportunity and challenge. Attention is needed especially to cross cultural contexts, to understand the ecumenical situation and the heritage of relationships or tensions, even – or possibly especially – for those from Asia, Africa and Latin American ministering in North Atlantic contexts.

It will be important to reach out to the most difficult fellow Christians and ecumenical formation in the most difficult Catholic contexts. For

Catholics it will be especially important to develop leaders with an ecumenical and missionary spirituality, among the bishops and curial leadership. Continuing attention needs to be given to include mission, cross-cultural and ecumenical training for catechists, clergy and pastoral workers, even as inter-religious formation continues in importance.

There will be need for continued dialogue on mission, ecumenical discussion of issues that are disputed within the churches, like inter-religious dialogue, inculturation and the Eurocentric heritage in a global Christian family, focusing on the new Pentecostal, African Initiated Churches, and evangelical voices (Bosch 1991: 474–89). Indeed, the future cannot be charted, but it will provide ever new challenges as the vision of unity and Christian mission evolve:

> Adding the historical dimension helps us to recognize that responses of Christians to the call for unity in mission are never static and unchanging, but rather dynamic and in flux (Thomas 2010: 271).

PART FOUR

ELEMENTS OF
CATHOLIC MISSION

MISSION AS WITNESS AND PROCLAMATION

Jonathan Y. Tan

This chapter seeks to explore the relationship between witness and proclamation in contemporary Catholic missiology. It surveys the discussion of these two tasks at Vatican II, papal and curial pronouncements, as well as in the documents of the Federation of Asian Bishops' Conferences (FABC), discussing their implications for evangelization in today's pluralistic world in general, and Asia in particular.

Vatican II

Lumen Gentium

The theological foundation of Vatican II's theology of mission is rooted in the Dogmatic Constitution on the Church, *Lumen Gentium* (LG). The missiological dimensions of ecclesiology permeate the opening sentence of the document, which comprises the explicit proclamation that 'Christ is the light of all nations. Hence, this most sacred Synod, which has been gathered in the Holy Spirit, eagerly desires to shed on all men that radiance of His which brightens the countenance of the Church. This it will do by proclaiming the gospel to every creature' (LG 1).

On the one hand, LG insists on the necessity of the church for salvation (*Ecclesiam necessariam esse ad salutem*, LG 14), explaining that the church is 'the universal sacrament of salvation' (*universale salutis sacramentum*), because the risen Christ is leading all peoples to the church (*ut homines ad Ecclesiam perducat*) and 'through her joining them more closely to Himself' (LG 48). On the other hand, LG also presents the possibility of an extra-ecclesial way of salvation when it suggests that non-Christians 'also can attain to everlasting salvation who through no fault of their own do not know the gospel of Christ or His Church, yet sincerely seek God and, moved by grace, strive by their deeds to do His will as it is known to them through the dictates of conscience' (LG 16). However, three strict conditions are laid down: (i) through no fault of their own (*sine culpa*), non-Christians do not know the gospel of Christ or the church; (ii) they must, with a sincere and open heart, seek God, the Creator whose existence they may know by reason, but whom they do not yet know as the

God revealed in Christ; and (iii) they must try to do God's will as they know it through conscience, i.e., on the basis of natural law, striving to lead a good life and moved by grace (*sub gratiae influxu*). On that basis, 'divine providence' will not deny them the assistance necessary for salvation, although the mode by which this grace operates (*modus gratia*) is left open.

By being cautious and refusing to speculate on the mysterious workings of God's grace outside the church, the Council Fathers left room for future dogmatic development of this principle. Even as they accepted the possibility that salvation can be mediated extra-ecclesially, nonetheless they took pains to argue against any lessening of the urgency of mission when they held that by 'promot[ing] the glory of God and procure the salvation of all such men, and mindful of the command of the Lord, 'Preach the gospel to every creature' (Mk. 16:16), the Church painstakingly fosters her missionary work' (LG 16).

Nostra Aetate

The 'Declaration on the Relation of the Church to Non-Christian Religions', *Nostra aetate* marks a paradigm shift in the church's understanding of other religions. Eschewing the traditional terminology such as 'pagan' (*paganus*), 'idolatry' (*idolatria*) and 'false religion' (*religio falsa*), the Council fathers introduced a new atmosphere of recognition, respect and dialogue, recognizing the plurality and diversity of religions. The most radical aspect of this declaration is its presumption that other religions contain at least some elements of truth, although this presumption does not lessen the dominical mandate to proclaim the gospel to the ends of the earth:

> The Catholic Church rejects nothing of which is true and holy in these religions. She looks with sincere respect upon those ways of conduct and of life, those rules and teachings which, though differing in particulars from what she holds and sets forth, nevertheless often reflect a ray of that Truth which enlightens all men. Indeed, she proclaims and must ever proclaim Christ, 'the way, the truth, and the life'... (NA 2).

The Declaration also lays out the foundations for inter-religious dialogue as a form of Christian *witnessing* when it urges Catholics to 'prudently and lovingly, through dialogue and collaboration with the followers of other religions, and in witness of Christian faith and life, acknowledge, preserve, and promote the spiritual and moral goods found among [them], as well as the values in their society and culture' (NA 2).

Gaudium et Spes

In the 'Pastoral Constitution on the Church in the Modern World', *Gaudium et Spes*, Vatican II acknowledged the diversity of cultures and the fact that the Christian gospel is not a communication of timeless truths, but rather God's intervention in human history. The Council Fathers explained the relevance of cultural discoveries to witnessing and proclaiming the gospel as follows:

> Living in various circumstances during the course of time, the Church, too has used in her preaching the discoveries of different cultures to spread and explain the message of Christ to all nations, to probe it and more deeply understand it. (GS 58)

The Council Fathers also asserted there is no one culturally normative way to be Christian. They pointed out that the church, which is 'sent to all peoples of every time and space, is not bound exclusively and indissolubly to any race or nation, nor to any particular way of life, or to any customary pattern of living, ancient or recent', and therefore it 'can enter into communion with various cultural modes, to her own enrichment and theirs too', as it 'strengthens, perfects, and restores them to Christ' (GS 58).

Ad Gentes

The missionary decree, *Ad Gentes*, begins with a statement that the church, which 'has been divinely sent to all nations that she might be "the universal sacrament of salvation"', strives 'to proclaim the gospel to all' in response to the innermost requirements of her own catholicity and in obedience to her Founder's mandate' (AG 1). It initiated a profound change in its fundamental understanding of the church's task of mission when it grounded the necessity of mission within the Trinitarian *missiones* of the Son and the Spirit, and insists that the whole church is missionary by its very nature (AG 2). It asserted that 'the specific purpose of this missionary activity is evangelization and the planting of the church among those people and groups where she has not yet taken root' (AG 6). While it insists on the necessity of preaching the gospel, notwithstanding the possibility that salvation may be available by other channels (AG 7), it also gives an expanded role to the Holy Spirit – 'Doubtless, the Holy Spirit was already at work in the world before Christ was glorified' (AG 4). In an application of Justin Martyr's notion of *logoi spermatikoi*, the decree suggests that the Holy Spirit 'calls all men to Christ by the seeds of the word and by the preaching of the gospel' (AG 15). It explains that these 'seeds of the Word' (*semina Verbi*) lie hidden in the national and religious traditions of peoples (AG 11).

Papal and Curial Pronouncements

Evangelii Nuntiandi

In his 1975 apostolic exhortation EN, Pope Paul VI emphasizes that evangelization is the *raison d'être* for the church's existence:

The church exists in order to preach the Gospel, that is to preach and teach the word of God so that through her the gift of grace may be given to us, sinners may be reconciled to God, and the sacrifice of the Mass, the memorial of his glorious death and Resurrection, may be perpetuated. (EN 14)

The pontiff defines evangelization 'as consisting in the proclamation of Christ our Lord to those who do not know him, in preaching, catechesis, baptism and the administration of the other sacraments' (EN 17-18). He insists that 'there is no true evangelization if the name, the teaching, the life, the promises, the Kingdom and the mystery of Jesus of Nazareth, the Son of God are not proclaimed' (EN 22). Going one step further, he also spoke of the necessity to evangelize human cultures:

The rift between the gospel and culture is undoubtedly an unhappy circumstance of our times just as it has been in other eras. Accordingly we must devote all our resources and all our efforts to the sedulous evangelization of human culture, or rather of the various human cultures. They must be regenerated through contact with the gospel. (EN 20)

While recognizing that evangelization entails the proclamation of 'an explicit message, adapted to the various conditions of life and constantly updated' (EN 29), Paul VI also held that the church is obliged to:

proclaim the liberation of these hundreds of millions of people since very many of them are her children. She has the duty of helping this liberation, of bearing witness on its behalf and of assuring its full development. All this is in no way irrelevant to evangelization. (EN 30)

Redemptoris Missio

Pope John Paul II's 1990 encyclical RM, which was written to commemorate the twenty-fifth anniversary of Vatican II's missionary decree, AG, stands as the most important missiological pronouncement of his pontificate. In this encyclical, the pope insists that '[m]issionary activity must first of all bear witness to and proclaim salvation in Christ' (RM 83). He defines the task of mission as 'directed to people or groups who do not yet believe in Christ, who are far from Christ, in whom the Church has not yet taken root... and whose culture has not yet been influenced by the Gospel ... It can thus be characterized as the work of proclaiming Christ and his Gospel, building up the local Church and promoting the values of the Kingdom' (RM 34).

From the beginning, John Paul II emphasizes the centrality of the explicit verbal proclamation of Christ, arguing that 'the moment has come to commit all of the church's energies to a new evangelization and to the mission *ad gentes*. No believer in Christ, no institution of the Church can avoid this supreme duty: to proclaim Christ to all peoples' (RM 3). He argues that that there 'must be no lessening of the impetus to preach the Gospel and to establish new Churches among peoples or communities where they do not yet exist, for this is the first task of the Church' (RM 34).

On the one hand, John Paul II acknowledges unequivocally that 'the first form of evangelization is witness.' He notes that (alluding to EN 41) 'people today put more trust in witnesses than in teachers, in experience than in teaching, and in life and action than in theories' (RM 42). He acknowledges that:

> The first form of witness *is the very life of the missionary, of the Christian family* and *of the ecclesial community,* which reveal a new way of living. The missionary who, despite all his or her human limitations and defects, lives a simple life, taking Christ as the model, is a sign of God and of transcendent realities. But everyone in the Church, striving to imitate the Divine Master, can and must bear this kind of witness; *in many cases it is the only possible way of being a missionary.* (RM 42, *emphasis added*)

But on the other hand, the pope also insists that life witness *per se* is insufficient. There has to be a proclamation of Christ as necessary for salvation. For him, 'proclamation is the permanent priority of mission', and because it has a 'central and irreplaceable role,' therefore 'the Church cannot elude Christ's explicit mandate' (RM 44). By proclamation, he means *verbal proclamation* from the evangelizers to those who are evangelized, who 'have a right to *hear*' (RM 44). He points out that the 'subject of proclamation is Christ who was crucified, died and is risen: through him is accomplished our full and authentic liberation from evil, sin and death; through him God bestows "new life" that is divine and eternal' (RM 44).

In RM, John Paul II also accepts that 'inter-religious dialogue is a part of the Church's evangelizing mission', recognizing that 'dialogue not in opposition to the mission *ad gentes*', but 'has special links with that mission and is one of its expressions' (RM 55). Nonetheless, he also emphasizes that dialogue 'does not lessen her duty and resolve to proclaim without fail Jesus Christ who is "the way, and the truth and the life"' (RM 55). Indeed, he underscores the 'permanent priority' of proclamation – 'all forms of missionary activity are directed to this proclamation' (RM 44). At the same time, the pontiff also acknowledges that proclamation is sometimes not possible because of particular restrictions, and under these circumstances *inter-religious dialogue* may be 'the only way of bearing sincere witness to Christ and offering generous service to others' (RM 57).

Dialogue and proclamation

The 1991 curial document, *Dialogue and Proclamation: Reflections and Orientations on Inter-religious Dialogue and the Proclamation of the Gospel of Jesus Christ* (DP), which was jointly published by the Pontifical Council for Inter-religious Dialogue and the Congregation for the Evangelization of Peoples, insists that dialogue and proclamation are not incompatible, pointing out that 'true inter-religious dialogue on the part of the Christian supposes the desire to make Jesus Christ better known, recognized and loved; proclaiming Jesus Christ is to be carried out in the Gospel spirit of dialogue' (DP 77).

More significantly, DP has gone beyond whatever other papal and magisterial documents have enunciated regarding the soteriological efficacy of other religions:

> From this mystery of unity it follows that all men and women who are saved, share, though differently, in the same mystery of salvation in Jesus Christ through his Spirit. Christians know this through their faith, while others remain unaware that Jesus Christ is the source of their salvation. The mystery of salvation reaches out to them, in a way known to God, through the invisible action of the Spirit of Christ. Concretely, it will be in the sincere practice of what is good in their own religious tradition and by following the dictates of their conscience that the members of other religions respond positively to God's invitation and receive salvation in Jesus Christ, even while they do not recognize or acknowledge him as their Savior. (DP 29)

Commenting on this paragraph, Jacques Dupuis is of the opinion that 'a door seems to be timidly opened here, for the first time, for the recognition on the part of the Church authority of a 'participated mediation' of religious traditions in the salvation of their members'. (Dupuis 1997: 178).

Moreover, DP also makes the radical suggestion that Christians not only witness their faith to others, but rather they must also be prepared *to be witnessed to by others through dialogue*:

> In the last analysis truth is not a thing we possess, but a person by whom we must allow ourselves to be possessed. This is an unending process. While keeping their identity intact, Christians must be prepared to learn and to receive from and through others the positive values of their traditions. Through dialogue they may be moved to give up ingrained prejudices, to revise preconceived ideas, and even sometimes to allow the understanding of their faith to be purified. (DP 49)

The Asian Bishops on Witness and Proclamation

From its founding, the Federation of Asian Bishops' Conferences (FABC) has consistently sought to work within the diverse pluralism of the Asian milieu with its manifold peoples, cultures and religions. The Asian Bishops have always maintained that at the heart of the task of mission of the Asian local churches lies the *dialogical* encounter between the local churches and the Asian milieu with its threefold reality of Asian poverty, cultures and religions (FABC I 1997: 14). For the FABC, dialogue is 'an integral part of evangelization' (FABC I 1997: 100), 'intrinsic to the very life of the Church' (FABC I 1997: 111), an 'essential mode of all evangelization' (FABC I 1997: 131), and 'a true expression of the Church's evangelizing action' (FABC I 1997: 101). As for the relationship between dialogue, proclamation and conversion, the FABC has pointed out, rightfully, that 'dialogue and proclamation are complementary. Sincere and authentic dialogue does not have for its objective the conversion of the other. For conversion depends solely on God's internal call and the person's free decision' (FABC I 1997: 120).

At the same time, the FABC has also explained that dialogue *does not preclude* the need for the proclamation of the Christian gospel: in fact there could be a moment when 'we shall not be timid when God opens the door for us to *proclaim* explicitly the Lord Jesus Christ as the Savior and the answer to the fundamental questions of human existence' (FABC I 1997: 282, *italics in the original*). However, a distinctively Asian approach of proclamation which is sensitive to the culturally diverse and religiously pluralistic Asian milieu is needed:

> Mission may find its greatest urgency in Asia; it also finds in our continent a distinctive mode. We affirm, together with others, that 'the proclamation of Jesus Christ is the center and primary element of evangelization' ...But the proclamation of Jesus Christ in Asia means, first of all, the witness of Christians and of Christian communities to the values of the Kingdom of God, *a proclamation through Christlike deeds*. For Christians in Asia, to proclaim Christ means above all to live like him, in the midst of our neighbors of other faiths and persuasions, and to do his deeds by the power of his grace. Proclamation through dialogue and deeds – this is the first call to the Churches in Asia. (FABC I 1997: 281-282, *italics in the original*)

On the basis of the foregoing, the Fifth Plenary Assembly equates the triple dialogue with the Christian mission imperative and concludes thus:

> Mission includes: being with the people, responding to their needs, with sensitiveness to the presence of God in cultures and other religious traditions, and witnessing to the values of God's Kingdom through presence, solidarity, sharing and word. *Mission will mean a dialogue with Asian's poor, with its local cultures, and with other religious traditions.* (FABC I 1992: 280, *emphasis added*)

It is at the Seventh Plenary Assembly (Samphran, 2000) that the Asian Bishops emphasized their preference for the 'witness of life' as the Asian way of proclaiming the Christian gospel in Asia:

> The most effective means of evangelization and service in the name of Christ has always been and continues to be the witness of life. The embodiment of our faith in sharing and compassion (sacrament) supports the credibility of our obedience to the Word (proclamation). This witnessing has to become the way of the Gospel for persons, institutions and the whole Church community. Asian people will recognize the Gospel that we announce when they see in our life the transparency of the message of Jesus and the inspiring and healing figure of men and women immersed in God. (FABC III 2002: 12-13)

This identification of proclamation with life witness builds upon the earlier statement made by the Third Bishops' Institute for Missionary Apostolate meeting in Changhua in 1982:

> It is true that in many places [in Asia] Christ cannot yet be proclaimed openly by words. But He can, and should be, proclaimed through other ways, namely: through the witness of life of the Christian community and family, and their striving to know and live more fully the faith they possess; through

their desire to live in peace and harmony with those who do not share our faith; through the appreciation by Christians of the human and religious values possessed by their non-Christian neighbors, and through these same Christians' willingness to collaborate in those activities which promote the human community. (FABC I 1997: 105)

Moreover, the Seventh Plenary Assembly of the FABC coined a new term – 'active integral evangelization' to describe an approach to mission which integrates commitment and service to life, life witness, dialogue, and building up the kingdom of God. The Assembly explains the rationale for this term as follows:

For thirty years, as we have tried to reformulate our Christian identity in Asia, we have addressed different issues, one after another: evangelization, inculturation, dialogue, the Asian-ness of the Church, justice, the option for the poor, etc. Today, after three decades, we no longer speak of such distinct issues. We are addressing present needs that are massive and increasingly complex. These issues are not separate topics to be discussed, but aspects of an integrated approach to our Mission of Love and Service. We need to feel and act 'integrally'. As we face the needs of the 21st century, we do so with Asian hearts, in solidarity with the poor and the marginalized, in union with all our Christian brothers and sisters, and by joining hands with all men and women of Asia of many different faiths. Inculturation, dialogue, justice and the option for the poor are aspects of whatever we do. (FABC III 2002:8)

CONTEMPLATION AND SERVICE: CENTRAL DYNAMISM OF CHRISTIAN MISSION

Maria Clara Luchetti Bingemer

The concept of mission has been constitutive of the deepest identity of Christianity since its beginnings, and is a concept that has gone through many modifications and transformations through the two thousand years of history of the Christian churches. From 'the salvation of souls' at any price to dialogue; from Christian conversion as goal to the respect fostered by inter-religious dialogue; from the midst of the tension between intra-church affairs and social activism – mission is something which is always being rethought and reflected upon by theology. Our intention here is to try to offer again a contribution that looks at the essential core of mission, where contemplation and service intersect and mutually enrich each other.

To do that, we will first examine the meaning mission has for theology, turning our attention above all to the Trinitarian matrix of mission. Then we will see how, when speaking of Christian mission, service is constitutive of that same mission and configures it utterly to the incarnate and redeeming work of Jesus Christ. We will seek to highlight how that process of con-figuration is given within the contemplation of the person of Jesus. Finally, we will see how missionary service today gets its face and form in the ecclesial community and what might be some of its priorities given the questions posed by the world today. In a concluding part, we will give highlights of reflections made on this theme in Latin-American theology in the last few decades.

The Missionary, Trinitarian Sendings

In Christian theology, mission is understood as coming from great distance and great height. Its origin is divine and, more specifically, Trinitarian. According to Christian doctrine, mission is above all the sending of one of the divine persons outward, into time and into history (see Rahner 1979). Understood in this way in Christian doctrine, mission has the sense of a movement of sending which begins with God the Father who, from all eternity, sends the Son. With the Son, dead and risen, the Father sends through his mediation the Holy Spirit, who will henceforth craft mission. It is this Spirit who will then send the ecclesial community, which is called to effect and give continuity in the world to the same mission of the Son.

Consequently, the Trinitarian mission is a response of God's very self –
Father, Son and Holy Spirit – to the lack of meaning that humanity finds in
its life project and to the disorder of sin that causes suffering to human
creatures. The incarnation and mission of Christ is a response of the most
Holy Trinity to the disorientation and to the sins that afflict the world. Jesus
of Nazareth – recognized by the Christian community as the Word
Incarnate and Son of God – gradually comes to understand himself as such
(as the Gospels imply) as the One sent by the Father, coming to the world
so as to bring about and complete God's will.

This conception of a God who sends the only Son in mission to serve a
sinful humanity is not found exclusively in the New Testament. Already in
the First Testament, the idea of a God who sends appears above all in the
stories of prophetic call (Ex. 3:10; Jer. 1:7; Ez. 2:3-10; 3:4-11). And so,
with these prophets sent by God, a hope is born in Israel of a conversion of
the nations to faith in the one God. The post-exilic literature evokes the
case of proselytes who become Jews.

In the New Testament the evangelists and other writers see Jesus first of
all as the one sent by God in the midst of human beings. It is above all the
Fourth Gospel that bases the authority of Jesus on this sending (see Jn. 17).
However, the earliest texts of the New Testament see this sending of the
Son as directed primarily to the lost sheep of the house of Israel (Matt.
15:24). Gradually the Christian community comes to understand that the
mission of the crucified and risen Lord also has universal significance,
which will be shown in a nearness and attitude of solidarity and fraternity
of service with those who have been marginalized in all manner of ways:
women, children, the poor, those who suffer, sinners, pagans and gentiles –
those who, hearing him, show many times more faith in his person and
mission than do the Jews (see Matt. 15: 22-28; Lk. 17:12-18; Lk. 10:30-
37).

After the death and resurrection of Jesus, the disciples reconsider Jesus'
life, death, and resurrection, and come to understand his true identity as Son
of God. It is at that moment that the community comes to begin to acquire
the words that seem less inadequate to express the truth of a mystery so
enormous and so sublime as the incarnation of God, sent in mission amid
humanity to show them the way of service as the way of salvation (see
Kasper 1976 and 1984).

Jesus moved to the interior of Judea and of Galilee, even without having
left his cultural context, indicated by his radical exodus from his divine
privileges and by the attitude with which he approached persons, the form
of his divesting himself and of abandonment into the hands of God as a
radical process for those who wished to follow him. The meaning of the
way of Jesus, the first missionary, in truth began long before his public
ministry. It had its start in the moment in when he left the status belonging
to him as God and is made a person, enfleshed, in our midst. 'He did not
regard equality with God as something to be exploited, but emptied

himself, taking the form of a slave, being born in human likeness. And being found in human form, he humbled himself, and became obedient to the point of death – even death on a cross' (see Phil. 2:5-11). After these strong words that indicate the radicality of the *kenosis* of the Messiah, the text makes a sudden move: 'Therefore God also highly exalted him and gave him the name that is above every name, so that at the name of Jesus every knee should bend, in heaven and on earth and under the earth, and every tongue should confess that Jesus Christ is Lord to the glory of God the Father' (Phil. 2:8-11). In order to translate this 'name above every other name' the Christian community created and set in place various titles of glory and lordship to speak of Jesus (see Bingemer 1998).

Among the titles of glory that Jesus was to receive after the resurrection was that of 'Lord' (*Kyrios*), a Greek word which designates a lordship that enjoys legitimacy and represents recognized authority. The designation of Jesus as *Kyrios* corresponds to the form of address of which the same Jesus had become more aware of throughout his public life and which he passed on to his disciples. It is possible that this title refers to that of 'rabbi' ('master') which implies the recognition of his person as Lord – hence the disposition to obey him required of those who would follow him (see Matt. 7:21; 21:28-32; Lk. 6:46).

This has to do with Jesus' standing above human and religious institutions, such as the sabbath, and that with which the earthly Jesus has unquestioned authority for the community, even after his death and resurrection (Duquoc 1985). The invocation in faith of *Kyrios* – especially as originated within the pre-Pauline Hellenistic community – signified that the community of the New Testament submitted itself to its Lord, confessing at the same time that he is sovereign over the world (see Rom. 10:9a; 1 Cor. 12:3; Phil. 2:11 – see Bingemer 2009: 183).

As the exalted *Kyrios*, Jesus Christ is Lord over all humanity and the entire cosmos. Given this, all the beings in the cosmos must bend the knee, and in paying homage to him, they honor God the Father in his person, at whose right hand he sits (Eph. 1:20; 1 Pet. 3:22). Thus, Jesus Christ receives the same titles as God (see 1 Tim. 6:15; see Dan. 2:47). Nonetheless, the proclamation of Jesus Christ as Lord has a particularity that makes him different from all the other lords. The lordship of Jesus Christ is inseparable from his service. The Exalted Lord is inseparably the Servant of God, and it is because of his condition as servant that we can proclaim him Lord.

The concept of service and servant that appears in Mark 10:44 for example has, without a shadow of a doubt, the backdrop of Isaiah 53. That is to say that it carries within itself the *'ebed YHWH*, the center of interest of the Suffering Servant Songs, that is applied, according to an ancient tradition, to Jesus. This theme had passed by all the synoptic evangelists, even if had not been expressed many times by the word 'servant' (*doulos, pais*), but as *huios* (son). The same is true for John: the naming of Jesus as 'servant' (*doulos*, *pais*) is not expressed, but only as the 'son' (*huios* – see Mk. 1:11 compared with Mk. 9:7). That notwithstanding, according to the circumstances of the gospel, there is also the thematic motif of servant present (see Jn. 13:3-11: the washing of the feet, the humble service of a slave done by Jesus on the eve of his Passion). Further on in John, Jesus calls himself the Lamb of God (*amnos tou Theou*) with obvious references to the servant of Isaiah 53, 'like a lamb led to the slaughter, he did not open his mouth' (see Is 53:4-7). The Johannine community understood, for that matter, Jesus to be the true Lamb of God (see Jn. 1:29, 36; Acts 8:32; 1 Pet. 1:19).

Thus Jesus Christ the exalted Lord at the right hand of God the Father is inseparably the servant who divests himself of the prerogatives of glory of his divine condition in order to go down a path of obedience that will deliver him up to the sacrifice of the cross (see Phil. 2:5). This implies for all Christians that entering into the way of Jesus Christ, to participate in his mission, is also ineluctably and inseparably to enter into the mystery of his obedience, his humble service, his fidelity to Abba, the Father, up to death on the cross. It is also to enter into the mystery of his love for his brothers and sisters up to the point of giving one's life for them. Only in this way is it possible to participate in his glory, insofar as the infinite knowledge, wisdom and lordship of God determines. The understanding of mission within the primitive church will absorb this Jesuanic model.

The Church: A Community of Service in Mission

To be with him and to announce the good news, Jesus chose twelve disciples whom he sent and to whom he gave 'authority over all demons and the power to cure diseases' (Lk. 9:1) and the mission to preach repentance for the sake of conversion. He invested them with his authority: 'Whoever welcomes you, welcomes me, and who welcomes me welcomes Him who sent me' (Matt. 10:40). One of them, Peter (Matt. 16:19), and afterwards the Twelve (Matt. 18:18) receive the keys to the kingdom 'to bind and to loosen' in his name. It is of little importance here whether the mandate is temporary or not: what draws our attention is the move toward institution. For the Jewish *shalia*, it is a representation of a juridical clause; for the apostle, it becomes a vital reality: the master acts in him and for him, in his words and in his deeds ... The story of Pentecost wishes to point to this: Jesus, having revealed himself as 'Lord' of the universe, sends the Apostles into the whole world, with full powers: 'All power has been given to me ... Go therefore: make disciples of all nations. And I will be with you until the end of the ages' (Matt. 28:20).

The disciples receive that mission from the Spirit of Christ by means of a particular gift (1 Cor. 12; Rom. 12:6-8; Eph. 4:11). After this it happens that some who were not of the twelve also receive, although in a different way, the grace and mission of the apostles: Paul, Matthias, Barnabas. In this way they are also, although in a different key, their successors. There is however no essential difference between the Apostles, the twelve and Paul, and those who come after them. It is indeed about the faith of the Apostles on which the church is built: they are the corner stones, the pillars. Only they were 'inspired' to understand and diffuse the message of God in Christ. Revelation in a certain way is 'concluded' with their testimony (see DV 4).

For early theology, and up to the sixteenth century, the term 'mission' had a clear meaning: it recalled the sending of the Son by the Father and the sending of the Spirit by the Father (and by the Son, according to the Latin Church). These were distinguished, on the one hand, from the visible divine sendings or missions, such as the incarnation, in which the sonship is revealed. God does not change nor stop being God by sending the Son to the fallen world; but the Father, the Son, and the Spirit do that by being united to human nature with the Son and the event of Pentecost, the visible sending or mission of the Spirit. On the other hand, there are the invisible missions: there is, for example, the invisible mission of grace, which enables the human being to know and to love God as God is, or the mission given to the church to teach, sanctify, shepherd the flock of God.

In the sixteenth and seventeenth centuries, the term 'mission' took on a special meaning. It did not recover the connection with the Trinitarian and Christological missions defined above, but came to designate in a particular way a certain sector within them. The theology of mission did the same. This change of perspective had historical causes (for this and what follows, see the *Encyclopedia Universalis* on line).

Mission in the New World

In 1492, Christopher Columbus disembarked on an island of the archipelago known today as the Bahamas, believing that he had reached the lands of the Indies dreamt of so fervently by Europeans. The sailors discovered what an ungrateful humanity will call 'America': a new continent in a time when it was naively thought that the gospel had been brought and proclaimed to the whole world. It was a turning back to the time of the Apostles, and for the term 'mission' – reserved up to that time for the twelve and those who were connected to them – a new era was inaugurated. Now the term was applied to the heralds of the gospel to those new territories.

The differences, however, were noteworthy. The first apostles were regularly and cruelly persecuted by the emperors. The new ones were chosen and sent with the complete support of Their Most Christian Majesties, the kings of Spain and Portugal.

Protected and transported by royal power, companions of the armies that combated the 'Indios', the new apostles were also and equally sustained by a powerful church, strongly hierarchical, solidly organized in terms of doctrine and discipline. It was the epoch of the Counter Reformation, of baroque art, of a church 'triumphant over heresy'. The native people were given a word of God that had not emptied itself, had not taken on the condition of a slave, did not make itself similar to those being evangelized, as had the Word Incarnate. Some did contest this, and throughout this period defended the gospel, denouncing the abuses of power (e.g. Las Casa, Montesinos, Veira). Most of the preachers, however, lived peaceably with the enslavement they practiced, and forced the populations to accept baptism. For a long time the Indios were barred from the priesthood and the episcopate. The result is, even today, the absence of an 'autochthonous' church, even in certain parts of the Andean mountain – e.g. Bolivia and Peru – where the indigenous population constitutes at times 85% of all the inhabitants. In addition, African slaves, especially in Brazil and Colombia, were forced to accept the religion of the whites, or to pretend to do so, giving their divinities the names of Catholic saints.

The church extended through every region its Latin character: hierarchical, disciplining, doctrinal and focusing on the intellect. This extension is understood equally with respect to current doctrines: the new apostles were impregnated with the 'dogmas' and the mentality of the Counter Reformation, and they spread the new catechism issued by the Council of Trent with greater enthusiasm than the Sacred Scriptures. They insisted upon the 'powers' that were unique to the ordained: to bring and preach the Word of God and sacramental functions.

In the sixteenth and seventeenth centuries, the European monarchs reinforced their centralized and absolutist character. Obedience was made a key virtue, a mandate implying the authority of those who send and the availability of those sent. This did not have any special connotation at the time, mainly because one could be sent in the same way to some community of 'the faithful' anywhere in Christendom. Little by little, however, in the course of the seventeenth century, the word 'mission' became more specialized. Mission came to designate being sent to those most far away from Christendom. Missionaries were sent on mission amid the Turks in the East, as well as to the empire of Cuzco in Peru. Even more, in the context of the time, the word 'mission' took on a meaning that was more juridical than theological. 'Missions' became less the missions of God into the world than missions to a part of the earth and to the entire planet – from Western and European Christendom to other latitudes. It would be a long time before the earthly 'missions' came back together with the 'divine missions'. The visible mediation now occupies the stage in this process.

The semantic evolution ended in the first quarter of the seventeenth century. It is then that 'mission' comes to designate exclusively the Catholic apostolate to the pagans who are far away from Christendom. Why this new terminology? In fact, from its very beginnings the gospel had not ceased to be spread among the Gentiles, and other terms were used to express this reality. It was spoken of as the 'promulgation' of the gospel, or simply 'the Gospel', in the Pauline sense (Gal. 2:7; Rom. 15:19; Phil. 4:15). It would be spoken of as well as 'the announcement of the Good News', 'the ministry of the Word', 'preaching' or 'prophecy', 'enlightenment of the Gentiles', 'labor for the salvation of the nations', 'spreading or propagation of the faith' (see Martina 1971). The privileged (and specialized) use of this term 'mission' had, without a doubt, two reasons.

First, the faith is not spread any more as it was in the beginning – by word of mouth. To evangelize the pagans, it is not enough any more to spread it around oneself; it is precisely about leaving the place where one lives, to undertake an individual and social adventure, and to have the means to do this. For that adventure, it is not about leaving for wherever one wants to go, with some exceptions. It is precisely about being sent. And this kind of departure requires a special word. Now that word (this is the second reason) is already there to be used: it is the word 'mission', which will enjoy such great importance in the seventeenth century. It does not evoke primarily the gospel, but the mandate to go out. It puts into relief the authority of the one sending and the submission of the one sent. All of modern mission is shaped by this emphasis on the hierarchical sending. Mission comes from above, it 'goes in the direction of' and 'descends' upon the infidels; it acts with authority; it speaks, it teaches – it does not listen. It exports its own structures of Christendom, imposing them from the outside on conquered territories that are then colonized. Mission comes to mean the evangelization of distant peoples as it was conceived in the sixteenth century, in the climate of the Counter Reformation, of the new religious orders and the conquistadores. It is not the work of evangelizers, but of missionaries.

At the same time, the word 'preaching' – which translates the word *kerygma* of the New Testament, the announcing of the Good News – underwent a decline. In the thirteenth century the Order of Preachers still evoked, in great part, this original meaning. In the nineteenth century, the preacher is no more than a sacred leader of prayer of the Christian assemblies. The meaning has been reversed: preaching is not concerned any longer with infidels, but with the faithful.

Without a doubt, for these two reasons – the novelty of going out, and complacency in a spirituality of the mandate – the term 'mission' acquires in the seventeenth century a connotation that means 'a special sending of some persons to evangelize the non-Christian nations outside Europe.' Words have their destiny: for a curious turn, the term 'mission' (and 'missionary') is being more and more questioned and even abandoned in the twenty-first century, in places like Africa, Latin America, and Asia – places that, from the seventeenth century, were spoken of as 'the missions' The necessity of 'de-missionizing' is now being spoken of just like the so-called 'decolonizing'.

The matter was brought forward even more because of the theological renewal of the twentieth century as a consequence of the Second Vatican Council, with the rediscovery of the importance of the mark 'apostolic' of the church and the extension of 'mission' – the sending of the Father – to whom it is attributed: to announce the gospel, to teach, sanctify, education, and guide, in an evangelical life of justice and charity. The overriding concern was to broaden this dimension of the mission of the gospel – evangelizing the pagans – to the total nexus of its responsibilities, on the one hand, and the original sending of the Father and the Son or divine missions, on the other. Thus, one does not speak any more of Christendom sending out to those places called 'mission countries', but of the Father sending the entire church into every part of the world, even to Christian countries that show themselves in an increasingly alarming manner to be 'mission territory' (see LG, GS, EN and RM).

A new theology of mission is being established little by little, growing and deepening. Catholics and Protestants, with their very different histories, find themselves agreeing today on this definition: the mission of first evangelization is the fundamental activity of the church when, sent by the Father to the world to save it, it confronts itself with this fact. It is in this sense that we will speak of mission from this point forward.

A New Understanding: The Center of Mission – Service to God's Reign

From the point of view of the purposes of mission, the conception of missionaries has passed through different stages. In the sixteenth century then, it was moving from 'rescuing souls from hell' to all the pagans who were destined to go there. Thereafter, it went from 'saving souls' to instructing them in the gospel, in order to 'convert them' and bring them into the church. Missionary encyclicals in the first half of the twentieth century spoke the *plantatio Ecclesiae* as the goal of mission (see the chapter by James Kroeger in this volume).

As the twentieth century progressed, however, this individualist and ecclesiocentric vision began to be disavowed (see Bevans and Schroeder 2004: 239-80). Today it would be said to be dangerous to make evangelization the monopoly of specialists: the missionaries. Post-conciliar theology will affirm that the entire church is 'missionary by its very nature' (AG 2). Missionaries do not impose the gospel, but remind Christians of their mission and guide them in the direction of it.

Mission as proclamation from above to below, a form of imposition, began to be re-evaluated in depth. Jesus did not require books – or publishers – to make known his designs for the nations. It was the apostles whom he sent forth to be his witnesses. The word of God, for that matter, has to always be 'rediscovered' in the heart and spirit of those who spread it, to the extent that it must be sought in the encounter with the aspirations that God places in the heart of its heralds and interlocutors. The Word, which is never given apart from human beings, would be dead and inaudible if it is not equally revelatory of the life that its messengers are trying to bring. Preceding or accompanying the explicit proclamation of the gospel, the life of faith and prayer of the missionary remains fundamental. In spite of their ease of use and their widespread presence today, the means of mass communication cannot substitute for this (see RM 37).

To be a missionary today, therefore, consists first of all in contemplating Jesus and seeking to make one's own his criteria, his attitudes, his words. The central inspiration of life of a missionary must be derived fundamentally from the radical relationship with the living Jesus Christ in order to be configured to him and sent by him.

Secondly, it involves living like the people to whom gospel is being proclaimed. The missionary ought not speak from the outside like a professor. The missionary is called to be a witness and because of this must be immersed in the depths of the social fabric, going to the poor, suffering their bitterness and difficulties, in order to have a minimum of credibility in trying to show Jesus as the way. The missionary will be at the crossroads of life, there where social relations are built that model a society. The missionary ought finally to share not just the language of the people, but even their joys and collective trials.

Thirdly, mission has to do with dialogue. Modern mission is not unilateral instruction but an effort to have a mutual 'conversation' with Christians as well as with their interlocutors: each and all in search of a more comprehensive understanding of the truth. The missionary realizes as well that the truth to which one adheres with all one's might remains hidden until it is encountered face-to-face on the last day. Until then, one asks and is asked. And one allows oneself to be questioned by others.

Finally, mission is for that matter the effort to awaken the 'human' which is at the base of every person. This is the real problem of growing and becoming aware about mission. The 'growth' is the advance in the direction of optimizing 'being' by the mediation of all the 'you have's' – food, clothing, knowledge, education – necessary for every people and for every person, within a given time, to have in view of this advance. In a certain sense, mission is identified with this growth, since faith, for the believer, constitutes the ultimate qualification for being human (see PP 1967). But the problem is not simple: the accumulation of goods, as much as with poverty, can lead to the diminishment of being. The ideal proportion is always being defined and this investigation constitutes one of the key problems of evangelization today, for establishing this harmonious relationship as well as for denouncing the false schemes that impede the authentic growth of the human being. A 'single-crop culture' can enrich a country and alienate the masses; an educational system can multiply the number of graduates ... and the number of unemployed.

To summarize, the objective of mission is to promote love. In the New Testament, in effect, the Ten Commandments are summed up in two: love of God and love of neighbor, and the two are summed up in the second (see Konings 2004). All of this is recapitulated in this love of neighbor that does not exempt persons but tries to include even the 'enemy' in its redemptive plan. For this reason, the missionary must be at the same time a contemplative who 'receives' a practice of the other in order to make that practice happen in the world.

The Ear and the Language of the Disciple

Very early the people of Israel came to understand their vocation on the basis of having heard what God was saying to them. Listening to the Word of God and putting it into practice was what made Israel, intensely loved by God, able to proceed ahead in the dynamic of the covenant, growing as a people of God between fidelities and infidelities.

The prophets, spokespersons of God and of the people, understood this mystery and lived it in their lives, many times with sorrow and being torn to pieces internally. They understood their vocation as a discipleship in which they were constantly and patiently being instructed by God. Called to listen to God's word and possessed by God's spirit, they carried this Word which scorched their mouths and burned their insides, and spoke and transmitted it in turn to the people to turn them to the love of their God (see, e.g. Is. 6:1-13).

Second Isaiah prophesied in a situation of suffering and sorrow. In the exile of Babylon, the people felt unhappy and despairing. It seemed that all roads were closed to them. Similar to the situation of the people of Latin America who are immersed in poverty and oppression, the exiled Israelites suffered from the sorrow of exile, injustice, and a yearning for the land that once was theirs, asking themselves whether God had abandoned them. The prophet presents to them in his songs, in his efforts to console this desolate people, the figure of the servant who knows how to listen attentively to the plan of God, bearing the sufferings inherent to mission and trusting in the support and assistance of the Lord. His attitude of unquenchable trust contrasts with that of the people, who have reached the point of being submerged in sorrow and despair.

In the third Servant Song, Second Isaiah presents his style of discipleship, inseparable from his ministry of the Word. He introduces before our eyes what is and what is not implied in the identity, the vocation, and the mission of the servant, which is above every disciple that listens lovingly and allows himself to be shaped and sent by the Word of God. In that very beautiful and inspiring text we see the entire adventure and destiny of the disciple-missionary who has opted for a people who suffer. Such a disciple-missionary is someone who hears, who obeys, who is sent and who bears fruit (Is. 50:4, 6-8).

The disciple can pass on the word and console on behalf of God because the disciple listens every morning and has an open ear. Put another way, the disciple-missionary is always in communion with God who speaks to the disciple-missionary lovingly and sends him or her. To sustain those who are weary or are losing hope or who are downcast, the disciple-missionary has to be instructed by God. It is compulsory that such a person be a person of prayer and be docile to the Spirit of God. The sufferings that come their way for carrying out what they have heard will support them and not let them flee. The disciple-missionary will confront the conflicts and not be tempted to escape them. Because they trust fully in that which awakens their ear and tongue each morning that consoles them that they may be, in their turn, consolers of a people who are at the point of losing hope and trust.

In the New Testament, the ministry of Jesus of Nazareth will be seen and recognized by his disciples and by all those who believe in that obedient service: a service that listens to God and to the people without ceasing, that carries on its shoulders the sufferings and infirmities of all in order to bring them consolation and freedom.

Jesus is at once the Word and the perfect hearer. He is the Word of God turned toward the contemplation of the face of the Father from all eternity (see Jn. 1:1), and by his incarnation will be the face of the Father turned toward humanity (see Jn. 1:18). The Son of God lives from the love the Father transmits to him, which he communicates to him all that he is. And it is those things that make his disciples. He will teach everything that he has heard as the perfect disciple and beloved Son of the Father so that – sent by his Spirit after his *Pascha* – he may be his face in the world, his mouth and his body given as an oblation and service to all.

The distinctive elements of the identity of the Christian disciple are thus above all: listening to the call of Jesus, a believing and loving response, a connection to a community of faith and the mission which communion of the life and destiny of Jesus goes to carry out. The verification of the authenticity of discipleship will be able to be seen in the fruits that come forth from the mission to which the disciple has been sent by the Lord Jesus in the power of his Spirit.

That mission, learned and formed in the following of Jesus under the impulse of the Holy Spirit, ought to bring the disciple, in the face of the summons of reality, to assume the attitudes and to realize the gestures and actions that Jesus would make. This will necessarily have to bring the disciple of Jesus to the encounter with the poor and with the little ones, bringing the feelings of compassion and emotional proximity of Jesus to the place where most of humanity resides. Because of this the disciple 'contemplates Jesus Christ as well as transmits the Gospel in order to know what He is doing and in order to discern what we must do in the actual circumstances' (Aparecida 2007: 139).

Because this is the case, the method adopted at Aparecida, in faithful continuity with the previous assemblies of Medellín and Puebla – see, judge, act – will be a valuable help in the sense of true discipleship having to do and to hear by turning properly to the reality which, in turn, is illuminated by the contemplation of Jesus Christ and his gospel. Starting from this critical analysis of historical circumstances to be interpreted and from the contemplation of Jesus as a desire to build his reign, the disciple can be thus sent by the Spirit of the same Jesus to transform conflictual and unjust realities according to the heart of God.

Conclusion: Contemplation and Action as the Central Dynamism of Mission

The mission of the church is nothing more, therefore, than the loving obedience to a movement initiated within God's own being. It is, in fact, the prolongation and continuation that the church, community of faith, brings about from the divine action. Put another way, before it is the mission of the church, it is the mission of God's own self. Mission wishes to witness to God being in action in the world, to conserve and redeem creation, reconciling persons among themselves, serving the poor and the dispossessed with his mercy and his forgiveness, creating communities of fraternity and solidarity around Jesus, God's Son and glorious Messiah. It is for this reason that when we ask ourselves where the church is going, the answer that the Bible and the tradition give us is: toward the full realization of the reign of God. Mission has no meaning except for its bringing about its full realization (Boff 1985).

The reign is the eschatological reference point of mission. The church is the historical representation and expression in time and in space of this Reign. There one finds the proper theological articulation of the relation between church and the reign of God. The church in itself is not the reign of God, but its agent. It is able to advance or slow down the reign in a fragmented way, owing to its own ambiguities. The church is holy, but also sinful. The church does not encompass the reign, but rather is encompassed by it. The reign does not belong to the church, but the church to the reign. The plan that guides the reign of God is not in the hands of the church, but is solely in the hands of God (see Boff 1985). The deepest identity of the church is to be the church of Christ.

In this fertile tension, Jesus Christ – and not the church – is the true center of history, not solely through the results of a study of chronology, but in terms of a deep spiritual significance. The reign, the project of Jesus, is indeed latent in many regions and cultures. As a consequence, mission is the entire activity of the church to seek the transformation of this latent character into a clear and transparent manifestation of the reign of God.

This is not an attempt to say here that non-Christians are 'anonymous Christians' as Karl Rahner had put it, but affirms that God is at work in all cultures and among all peoples, by guiding them to the reception of his revelation – albeit not named – and the consummation of his reign. In other words, the universal revelation of God prepares the way for the *kairos*, the fullness of time, the time of God. As a consequence, the significance of the foundation of mission is not Christianizing or Christianity, because mission is not imposed upon cultural models. Mission is, on the contrary, a plan to unite different religions around the principles present in the gospels, such as justice, peace, solidarity, without requiring a specific religious belonging (see Küng 1986 and Dupuis 1997).

Mission is fundamentally transformation. It is a plan to create structures and strategies that seek to transform the latent condition of the reign and of the church – present in all world religions and all cultures – into a visible condition of the reign, into something new: the new reality in Jesus as the Christ. Such transformation is therefore the greatest significance of mission. This activity of the missionary is in process because God's own self calls, gathers, challenges, and qualifies the actual church. And the church shows already the fact of its cooperation in the work of the restoration of the world, of the preserving of creation and the transformation so that the manifestation of the ultimate eschatological objective of the reign might appear.

In general lines, it is this missionary understanding that has been growing a great deal after the Council. Mission is the mission of God's own self who hears the cries of his people and wishes to liberate them. It concerns those persons who by their achievements and efforts in evangelization, are witnessing through words and deeds. It is nourished by spirituality; it is expressed in community and turns toward the same community. It has its most visible and concrete sacramental manifestation in liturgical service. The church brings witness in service, in defending the lesser ones and those less favored, denouncing injustice, trying always to focus attention on the context in which it is situated. In line with this understanding, it can be understood that the church must proclaim the grace of God and the good news of the gospel of Jesus so that every person can become a new creature. It is called too to denounce social injustices, to look after justice and to safeguard creation in its integrity. It must also – today more than ever – care for the 'others': the other gender, the other race, the other ethnicity, the other social class, the other religion – the humble and available service of an attentive and loving, contemplative listening.

(Translated from Portuguese by Robert J. Schreiter)

THE CONSTITUTIVE NATURE OF JUSTICE, PEACE AND LIBERATION FOR MISSION

Paulo Suess

I

Whoever might ask about the constitutive nature or the essence of a person or thing is concerned about a moral foundational principle and a universal claim for appropriate action based thereon. The constitutive nature can be given already beforehand in the 'nature of the thing.' But it is also possible, through application to a new setting or on the basis of new options or social givens, to acquire a second nature. We speak in that case in an analogical sense of nature and essence. Analogical discourse is the normal situation of our religious language, indeed of our talk about God in any fashion, because the particular that is to be spoken about God cannot be captured in words. The same holds also for when we speak of the constitutive nature of justice, peace, and liberation for the missionary nature of church, which, in this analogical manner of speaking, 'derives its origin from the mission of the Son and the Holy Spirit' (AG 2).

Mission 'by nature' is both given beforehand and is acquired. It is presented as vocation and sending. Justice, peace, and liberation belong to the complex reality that we describe as mission, but they must be continually acquired anew historically, and tested in an unending process contextually. Thus when we claim that the triad 'justice', 'peace', and 'liberation' belong to the essence and nature of mission, we are proceeding from presuppositional and acquired structural principles that reach beyond historical and cultural contextualizations and adhere to something elementarily enduring and universally binding.

'Justice', 'peace', and 'liberation' can be derived as constitutive principles of mission from scripture and the tradition of the church. Because of their internal relation with one another, no single part of this triad can be eliminated without substitution. 'Liberation', in the double meaning of salvation and healing in which redemption and emancipation merge into a whole, is the mediating activity that attempts to achieve 'peace' on the basis of 'justice'. They are not only principles, but also tasks, goals, and horizons.

The missionary task and horizon come to expression in a concentrated way in the Lord's Prayer (Matt. 6:7-15) in asking God to forgive us our debts and deliver us from evil. 'Forgiveness of debts' and 'deliverance from evil' are articulated in the two ideal situations imagined in the Jubilee Year and in the reign of God. In the synagogue at Nazareth, Jesus concerns himself with the unrealized ideal of the Jubilee Year and declares it as programmatic for his life project (Lk. 4:16-18), as a year of grace for the poor, the liberation of captives, and healing of the blind. The project of the Year of Jubilee receives in the preaching of the reign of God a universal, historical-eschatological dimension. The coming of the reign of God means conversion as a rupture with evil in its social-structural forms and in its guilt deriving from personal responsibility. Jesus of Nazareth proclaims it as the sustaining vision of the possibility of a successful life. In its missionary praxis, Christianity makes the claim to proclaim both 'ideals' – Jubilee Year and the reign of God – within the horizon of the liberation from evil through the definitive action of Jesus Christ.

Salvation history is the history of a liberation. Israel experienced the liberative action of its God in its being chosen out of anonymous meaninglessness and its deliverance from slavery, in the making of the covenant and taking possession of the land, in exile and then finally in its being brought home from captivity. And it also understood this liberative action cosmically as God's creative intervention that banished a chaos without purpose.

The way of liberation manifests itself in a concentrated fashion in the incarnation of the Son. Despite the New Creation in Christ (2 Cor. 5:17), the eschatological work of separating out good from evil proceeds in a history itself undecided. In the parable of the weeds and the wheat the wisdom of a meaningful life is hidden in an undecided world in which the weeds (see Matt. 13:24-30) are conceded that merciful hope in which the bent reed is not broken nor the little spark is not extinguished. The parable characterizes the 'true religion' of the suffering servant of God as 'righteous verdict' (see Is. 42:3; Matt. 12:20). Justice is also grace, but grace is not a sponge that wipes away injustice: 'In the final analysis, wrongdoers will not sit with victims as equals at the table of the wedding banquet as though nothing had happened' (SS 44). Missionary proclamation recalls that human beings' being made in God's image is never entirely lost; it recalls the process of universal new creation through Christ, and his coming again. In faith we trust in judgment and conversion: the wrongdoing of history will not be the final word, and wrongdoing is given the opportunity of conversion until the very end.

II

Justice, peace, and liberation as constitutive of the nature of mission can have its meaning clarified not only on the basis of the sources of revelation and tradition. Mission can actually first be indicated in the context of historical challenges, that it stands for God's justice, i.e., for God's historically efficacious action through God's crucified and risen servant,

Jesus Christ. The life and mission of the Messiah Jesus we understand as a giving 'for the life of the world' (see Jn. 6:51) and as a gathering in of the New Israel. In following him, we understand the constitutive nature of mission to be a public dedication to and 'obligation' to the life of the world under the concrete 'social and cultural conditions of human beings' (see AG 10).

We live in a world in which being made in God's image and being considered a child of God, thus the dignity and equality of human beings, are the motivational bonds for engagement for universal justice, and are relevant in both a missionary and a counter-cultural sense. The goods provided by nature and produced by human beings are unequally distributed and are produced under humiliating conditions. More and more people of different nations and cultures are heading into densely populated metropolitan areas to seek work or a meager measure of quality of life. In the context of transnational migration and urbanization they encounter difficulties in forming a somewhat noticeable identity, in holding their families together, and ensuring a highly precarious place of employment in highly competitive situations. The concluding document of the fifth General Assembly of the Episcopal Conferences of Latin America and the Caribbean describes this reality with striking words: 'A new dramatic phenomenon in Latin America and the Caribbean is that of the emigrants, those driven out and as refugees are on the move for economic and political reasons or because of violence' (Aparecida 2007: 411).

The central crises of our planet earth present transversal economic, social, political, cultural and ecological challenges. Low-wage countries and ever more precarious working conditions contribute to a worldwide increase in a situation of economic competition in which whoever wants to survive has to be more successful than their neighbor. Growth, expansion and acceleration are magic words that accompany a technology that requires ever fewer workers and ever more consumption.

Workers' movements, trade unions, and social movements have in the most recent time, after the seizure of power by transnational corporations, adjusted themselves to this new reality, and have surrendered their own contesting perspectives. The global economic system is incapable of guaranteeing economic well-being to the world's citizens. Growth, based on consumption and quick attrition of products, is the flip side of hunger and exploitation. Consumer society heightens social distinctions.

The irrational exploitation is aimed not only at workers and migrants, but also at the entirety of nature itself, which as the work of creation and the basis for human life has to be taken into account in a comprehensive pattern of missionary activity. For the process of destruction of the forests, the pollution of the rivers, and the destruction of biodiversity, 'the contemporary economic model has to take decisive responsibility for giving preference to the unbridled striving for profit above the lives of individuals and whole peoples and above a more reasonable interaction with nature'

(Aparecida 2007: 473). And the lives of the coming generations and of the whole universe are at risk (see Aparecida 2007: 125).

Political action is supposed to have the task of leading us out of this economic, social and ecological crisis. But politics itself is deeply implicated in all these crises. The state is only able to intervene in the spheres of interest in a highly unsatisfactory way, because it is itself the product of those interests. That is evident in elections that are very costly, and so provide the economic sector huge advantages from the get-go. The market society devours not only natural resources, but also the competitive structures that constitute the moral resources of democracy upon which the right to solidarity depends.

The utter impossibility of guaranteeing a minimum of human rights, of freedom and equality and political participation above all for the poor is mirrored also in the law. Justice has become expensive and through its bureaucracy and formalities largely unattainable for the poor. The poorly paid police forces, frequently undermined by bribery and criminality, are themselves often a factor in the unevenness of the law. Prisons are as a rule not places of resocialization, but are rather schools of crime.

All these phenomena of crisis are intertwined in the questioning of the meaning of life, either through premodern dogmatism – that in a fundamentalist style considers the question of meaning already resolved – or through nihilistic-postmodern streams – that declare the question of meaning as *a priori* meaningless. But even modernity is not necessarily interested in the question of meaning. The dissolution of the meaning of history and reality into a purely natural history or the claim of an *a priori* possession of a monological truth bound up with one's own religious community or community of interest leads to a negation of the recognition of the other and represents a continuing cause of violence. The recognition of the other extends beyond mere tolerance. It is the basis for the unity of the human race in the diversity of worldviews and cultures.

Tasks that are difficult to solve are not unsolvable ones. The vision of a transnational society of citizens who do not capitulate to the laws of the market nor to the imperatives of cutthroat competition is possible. Critique of the current economic systems has to call into question the contemporary model of development. When it is only about the distribution of goods, the production of those goods is already presumed and consigned to a 'relentless work ethic'. Who could say that the consideration of such horizons is not a task of mission theology? The tools of purely economic and technical reason are always skewed when it is about a good life for all.

III

In the midst of these dauntingly complex knots into which the threads of unjust structures and personal guilt are tangled, mission has the task of remembering that it was not thus at the beginning and will not be so at the end. Even in this intervening period another kind of life is possible. In that time the messianic future has become present in Jesus Christ, because 'God who is our justice' (Jer. 23:6; 33:16) has been revealed. The proclamation of this new life guaranteed by God's word and its realization in signs is a fundamental missionary task. Missionary presence lays down traces of meaning in the world that point to the possibility and the lure of a entirely concrete different kind of life.

From an historical point of view, there have existed in the church two very different perspectives – one of tolerating a presumed lesser evil and one of a radical questioning of systemic complicity. For example, mission had connected up with colonial powers in order to overcome the greater evil of paganism. In doing so, it conceded an amelioration of the conditions of those colonial forces. While arguing it was avoiding the greater evil, mission tried to avoid 'excesses', alleviate suffering, and dissuade the poor and the 'others' (the indigenous people!) from the ethical rigor of resistance.

But mission can also be critical of the system and proclaim prophetically the maxims of the good and just life. In a society of conformist accommodation to competition and consumerism, prophecy, asceticism and gratuitousness have eminently political and practical roots. This prophetic horizon unfolds not only through focused denunciation, but also in asceticism as the counter-cultural dimension of refusal to consume, as an emergency brake on development projects that are pushed through with blinding speed, and as gratuitousness. The struggle for a good life for all as missionary task is a struggle not only for the distribution of goods, but also their reconfiguration in new, human-friendly relations of production that correspond to the project of creation, and for their proper use and for mutual recognition.

'Mission' has a prophetic character also within the church: the church must itself undergo continuing conversion. The royal entrance of the cathedral in Bamberg, Germany, which depicts the twelve apostles standing on the shoulders of the twelve prophets, points to the fact that church authorities must always understand that their work will be short sighted without that prophetic underpinning. Mission declares to the world that lives under the dictatorship of cost-benefit accounting that redemption comes from grace, i.e., through the gift that transforms our non-symmetrical relation to God into that New Covenant of peace through which we take responsibility for the world. We struggle in the form of a servant so that the 'others' and the poor, with heads raised high, can refuse this form of servitude. The guarantor of this covenant is the messianic Prince of Peace (see Is. 9:5; Zech. 9:9; Lk. 2:14).

Hope for peace draws us into the horizon of creation as prefiguring paradise, into the horizon of history as historic task and promise and into the perspective of the messianic reign of God as eschatological gift. This hope is realized continually concretely on the basis of the special presence of the Spirit in the life of the poor. Peace is a fruit of the Spirit, who is especially alive in the poor who for that very reason feel themselves drawn to the most diverse Pentecostal movements (see Gal. 5:22). The transformation of the ever-obligatory gift of peace into the positive-asymmetrical love of enemy: that is the core of the mission of Christianity, on the basis of which its incarnational solidarity becomes relevant as a critique of society. This relevance finds its social deployment in the proclamation of the reign of God as 'liberation from the servitude of corruption' (See LG 9) and in the praxis of the 'greater love' (Jn. 5:13) and the 'greater justice' (Matt. 5:20), that are enjoined upon us in the ethical constitutions of the Beatitudes and in the testament of Jesus' Farewell Discourse.

IV

The first two of the sixteen documents of the 'Resolutions of the Second General Assembly of the Latin American Bishops' Conferences' (Medellín 1968), which had as it theme 'The Church in the Presence Transformation of Latin America in Light of the Council', were devoted to 'justice' and 'peace'. Since Medellín the local churches of Latin America have continually deepened 'justice' and 'peace' in their constitutive nature for their historical and eschatological mission. With 'justice and peace will embrace' (Ps. 85:11) the psalmist summarizes the prophetic proclamation of the messianic kingdom (see 32:17) and points to the great missionary ideal of the reign of God as a reign of (justice, peace, and joy) (Rom. 14:17). Mission is the place of transmission and memory where the dream of the peace that comes out of the struggle for justice is not forgotten, and where the 'situation of injustice', that represents a 'condition of sin' (Medellín 1968: 1) and a form of 'institutionalized violence' (Medellín 1968: 16), will not be accepted either silently or without action.

What we are always able to do in the large conflicts that confront us in missiological reflection and missionary praxis is the possibility of being a 'sign of contradiction' (see Lk. 2:34) by being a 'sign of justice'. To speak of a sign of justice might imply that we have long given up the hope of real justice. Just what do we mean when we speak of real justice? In professional circles it is not yet clear what has to count as a justice-relevant context, whether it for example is about nation-state or internal state relations, or about transnational relations in world society. In each of these contexts one can argue on three different levels: on the level of social justice regarding goods, on the level of political structures and questions of power, or finally on the level of formal legal action.

Social justice regarding goods promises to each his or her own. Here one thinks of the distribution of goods; but this leaves the political roots of inequality untouched. A purely statistical poverty reduction, which waylays the immediate threat of death of the poor by starvation through the distribution of basic foodstuffs, but leaves social injustice untouched, is a false development goal.

We encounter another modality of justice in the sphere of legal action. Here it is about an application of law and the taking into account of law for people whose rights are violated or who are denied their rights through the slow pace of judicial processes or through excessive cost. Despite formal rights, this too is a structural injustice that is designated for the poor from the get-go.

Finally one has to take a look at the level of political justice, where it concerns questions of the relations of production. How do we ever come to the added value that permits the distribution of the 'gentle gifts' of social welfare? Is there here not a logic that says human beings first have to be exploited, that jobs have to be eliminated in the name of efficiency, and working conditions have to be made more precarious, in order then to distribute to the poor a miniscule percentage of profit that is gained by those moves? The assurance of subsistence for those in need that is not mediated through work brings neither self-determination nor social recognition. Social welfare is what work creates under social conditions (see Walzer 1983 and Forst 2003).

Even today, more than forty years since Medellín, we can still say: 'The reality described represents a negation of peace as the Christian tradition understands it' (Medellín 1968: 'Peace,' 14). How can justice as a constitutive principle of mission be understood under these sociopolitical presuppositions, as a unity of evangelical consistency and social relevance?

V

How can we translate the articles of the Creed, the signs of justice, the images of hope, and the symbolic praxis of solidarity for our conversation partner 'world' and 'humanity'? Justice and peace are the Easter proclamation. On Good Friday the disciples of Jesus complained of the loss of hope. The messianic path of justice (see Matt. 21:32) seemed to show itself on the cross to be a mistaken one. But then an upheaval in their way of thinking occurred that presented new historical facts. The disciples of Jesus experienced the resurrection of the Messiah as God's greater and definitive justice, which quashed the death sentence given on the cross. The resurrection of the just one opened the way for a definitive justice: the justice of the resurrection. The engagement for the crucified of history is the attempt to rescind their death sentence not only in the final instance of the 'greater justice' of God, but also to nullify it even historically. The missionary Easter proclamation in the cry of the survivors and through an outstretched hand that touches the wounds of a violated humanity! Life is strengthened by the solidarity of that touch, and is exhausted when we focus on our own needs and anxious protection of self.

The justice of the resurrection gestures toward disinterest in self as presupposition for just distribution – toward asceticism, toward 'education in a lifestyle of simplicity and frugality' (Aparecida 2007: 474a) – toward inclusion and participation as the core of Christian identity; and finally to gratuitousness because the dignity of the human being and the human being's redemption is not for sale. The justice of the resurrection is not earned but is given as a gift, yet in spite of that we struggle for it in daily life under the signs of sympathy, commitment and disinterest in self, in which we again and again 'experience the power of the resurrection' (Aparecida 2007: 256).

'Men and women of today ... listen more to witnesses than to teachers, and when they listen to teachers, it is because they are witnesses' (EN 41). And Aparecida clarifies yet again the connection of holistic mission when it demands 'that the missionary charge of evangelization may not be separated from solidarity with the poor and their integral promotion' (Aparecida 2007: 545). The authors of the new grammar of justice and peace have placed political justice ahead of the social justice of distribution of goods. They align themselves with a structurally different socialization of land and law, with a democracy of self-determining subjects in which the voice of the poor is granted a special hearing, and with a model of development that is tune with an 'ecology that is humane and open to transcendence' (Aparecida 2007: 126). These are the confessors and martyrs too numerous to be counted, that 'have come through the great tribulation' (Rev 7:14). They stand for the credibility of an ultimate justice that is promised to us as resurrection.

VI

The justice of God as the peace-building moment of mission wears no blindfold. The statue of 'blind' Justice does not look people (and above all, those who have no esteem) in the face. She symbolizes a mere formal equality before the law, which the politico-economically well esteemed setup before courts of law. Blind Justice does not guarantee a world for all, but rather a world for the few, for the stronger ones. Universal human rights do not eventuate without the principle of an option for the poor. Human rights are the rights of the poor! 'Behold the human one!' The *ecce homo* stands for the exploited humanity of every century! The justice of God is justice for victims. It takes responsibility for a one-sided turn toward the weak and injured subjects. The historical shift of this one-sided turn we call the option for and with the poor or struggle for justice.

The poor and the 'others' belong to God whose name is justice (Jer. 23:6), especially loved and esteemed (Ps. 146:7f-8; Matt. 25:31-46). Yes, God is so deeply struck by the victims of injustice that God declares them as mediators of his presence until the moment of the Lord's second coming. Whoever stands on the side of the poor, will find him or herself *a fortiori* on the right side. The ruthlessness of the stronger one and the blind happenstance of destiny do not have the final word.

The Latin American 'option for the poor', first thought of as a program for structuring a colonial church, can be dated from the Second General Assembly of the Latin American Bishops' Conferences in Medellín. Medellín declared itself responsible for the defense 'of the rights of the poor and oppressed' (Medellín 1968: 22). The denouncing of structural and arbitrary violence, the suing for the right to self-determination, and the appeal to the victims of the world to become organized are still relevant today (Medellín 1968: 18-19, 27). Right up to the Fifth General Assembly of the Bishops' Conferences of Latin America and the Caribbean, in 2007 in Aparecida, which designated the church as the 'house of the poor' (Aparecida 2008: 8) and 'advocate of just and of the poor' (Aparecida 2007: 395), 'the pre-eminent option for the poor belongs to the characteristic traits of our Church in Latin America and the Caribbean' (Aparecida 2007: 391). And 'pre-eminent means, that it is to permeate all our pastoral priorities and structures' (Aparecida 2007: 396).

The partisanship of this option thus has nothing to do with group-egoism. In the option for the poor a global consciousness of responsibility comes to expression, that considers the dignity, equality, and recognition of all human beings as a good worthy of protection. Because there is no provincial liberation and privileged redemption, one is enjoined to hold on to the principle of the universality of the love of God for all human beings and simultaneously the preference for the least and the 'others'. Redemption happens for all, but through the mediation of the poor. The rich young man and the teachers of the Law who asked about eternal life are made aware by Jesus that there is no special way of the Law that leads to eternal life, but only a 'detour' through gratuitousness with the poor and care for those who fall among robbers. In the strategic discourse in the synagogue at Nazareth (Lk. 4), the Beatitudes (Matt. 5) and the Parable of the Judgment (Matt. 25), Jesus proposes new addressees and actors for the proclamation of the reign of God. The transmitters of his project are the poor, the imprisoned, the blind, the hungry, the strangers, and the sick. They are not only the ones who transmit his project, they are also the representatives of God in the world.

The option for the poor is therefore first of all the option of God. God's preference for the poor is not merited, but rather makes the gratuitousness of God's love evident. They do not have to exhibit any compensating virtues. The option for the poor is valid 'irrespective of their moral and personal situation' (Puebla 1979: 1142). Although many poor may dream of it, their 'good life' does not lead to integration into the surplus-society. Whoever in a Brazilian slum dreams of waking up in Disney World has no horizon of hope. The dreams of conforming to the rich that the poor may have is also the object of liberating evangelization, as much as the dreams of isolation of the rich that keep out the poor.

VII

Mission is the attempt to ever mend the hole-riddled net of human life's projects and relationships. The becoming-flesh movement of self-giving of the Word in the incarnation and the pouring out and sending out of the Spirit at Pentecost shape the missionary identity of all the baptized. Missionary activity will always bring to expression its constitutive nature of justice, peace, and liberation in its incarnating commitment and Pentecostal mission. Mission is directed toward the gathering in of humanity as the people of God, who are called to eschatological completion in which God 'will be all in all' (1 Cor. 15:28).

Regression into non-freedom and a fall into meaninglessness are always possible. But it is also possible to create new facts through images of hope and signs of justice. God commanded a despairing Moses, whose people wanted to go back into the prison of slavery out of fear of persecution by Pharaoh and out of anxiety about freedom: 'Say to the people that they must dare a step forward!' (see Ex. 14:15).

Golden cages are sites of non-peace, of anxiety, of immaturity and hopelessness. The Risen One – sign of the justice of God and primal image of hope – says simply: 'Put your hand into my wounds!' 'Be not afraid!' 'Peace be with you!' He has promised all people rescue from want and from the humiliation of a damaged life. The excluded and the imprisoned, the poor and the 'others' are guaranteed their irreplaceable individuality and dignity. In a universal alliance he encourages us – because redemption is drawing near – to solidarity and struggle for the straight path, the head held high, and the fullness of life for all.

(Translated from German by Robert J. Schreiter)

ECOLOGY AT THE HEART OF MISSION: REFLECTIONS ON RECENT CATHOLIC TEACHING

Denis Edwards

Led by the Spirit, the community of faith proclaims salvation in Christ and God's kingdom of mercy, peace and justice in ever new contexts. Mission is of the essence of being church: 'Mission is the church preaching Christ for the first time; it is the act of Christians struggling against injustice and oppression; it is the binding of wounds in reconciliation; it is the church learning from other religious ways and being challenged by the world's cultures' (Bevans and Schroeder 2004: 9). In this chapter I will propose that mission is also the church witnessing to the integrity of creation and to its place in God's creating and redeeming act.

The church is in mission today in a world threatened by global climate change, loss of biodiversity, deforestation, degraded land, damaged rivers and depleted fisheries. It was always true, I believe, that mission involved the whole creation. But in our day there is a new urgency to locate the ecological at the very heart of Christian mission. There are countless instances where ecological practice is already central to mission, as when missionaries work with others in programs for access to clean water or for land restoration, or when bishops of a bioregion write and act in defense of local ecosystems such as rainforests or coral reefs. In our time we are also witnessing the emergence of the important field of ecological theology. My focus will not be directly on missionary ecological practice, nor on recent expressions of ecological theology, but simply on recent church teaching on ecology and its implications for a Catholic approach to mission.

Already in 1971, Paul VI had recognized the environmental problem as an urgent wide-ranging social problem that concerns the whole human family, and had called Christians to take up responsibility with others for our shared future (OA 21). But the more recent contributions of John Paul II and Benedict XVI are far more detailed. I will begin with John Paul II's 1990 Message for the World Day of Peace, and then consider his social encyclicals, and his advocacy of ecological conversion. Then I will turn to Pope Benedict, focusing on his encyclical *Caritas in Veritate* and on his *2010 Message for the World Day of Peace*. I will conclude by gathering some thoughts from John Paul II on the way central mysteries of faith might be proclaimed in ecological terms.

John Paul II's Message for the 1990 World Day of Peace

The foundational document in Catholic teaching on ecological issues is Pope John Paul II's text for the World Day of Peace, January 1, 1990, entitled *Peace with God the Creator; Peace with All of Creation*. Now more than twenty years old, this short text was released on December 8, 1989. In it, the pope recognizes that world peace is threatened by a lack of proper respect for nature and by the plundering of natural resources. At the same time he celebrates the emergence of a new global movement of people concerned about the future of our planet: 'Moreover, a new *ecological awareness* is beginning to emerge which, rather than being downplayed, ought to be encouraged to develop into concrete programmes and initiatives' (John Paul II 1990, 3). The encouragement of the emergence of this new global, ecological awareness is a constant in John Paul II's teaching, which he describes elsewhere as ecological conversion. In this text his focus is on the ecological crisis as a moral issue, shifting ethical thinking beyond the inter-human to include the natural world:

Certain elements of today's ecological crisis reveal its moral character. First among these is the indiscriminate application of advances in science and technology. Many recent discoveries have brought undeniable benefits to humanity. Indeed they demonstrate the nobility of the human vocation to participate *responsibly* in God's creative action in the world. Unfortunately it is now clear that the application of these discoveries in the fields of industry and agriculture have produced harmful long-term effects. This has led to the painful realization that *we cannot interfere in one area of the ecosystem without paying due attention both to the consequences of such interference in other areas and to the well-being of future generations* (John Paul II 1990: 6 – here and elsewhere, italics in the original).

The pope goes on to speak of the depletion of the ozone layer and the 'greenhouse effect', pointing to the harm done to the atmosphere through industrial waste, the burning of fossil fuels and deforestation, and 'the resulting meteorological and atmospheric changes' that range from 'damage to health to possible future submersion of low-lying lands'. He points to two moral aspects of the ecological crisis. There is lack of respect for life, a reductionist vision of the human that involves contempt for the human person. And there is the destruction of animal and plant life and the reckless exploitation of natural resources. This leads the pope to formulate (7) a two-fold fundamental principle for a peaceful society: '*No peaceful society can afford to neglect either respect for life or the fact that there is an integrity to creation.*' He develops the idea of the integrity of creation along with that of common heritage:

Theology, philosophy and science all speak of a harmonious universe, of a 'cosmos' endowed with its own integrity, its own internal, dynamic balance. *This order must be respected.* The human race is called to explore this order, to examine it with due care and to make use of it while safeguarding its integrity.

On the other hand, the earth is ultimately a common heritage, the fruits of which are for the benefit of all.... Today, the dramatic threat of ecological breakdown is teaching us the extent to which greed and selfishness – both individual and collective – are contrary to the order of creation, an order which is characterized by mutual independence. (8)

The concepts of the integrity of creation and common heritage lead John Paul to call for international and national agreements on caring for the good of the planetary community. Essential to this is addressing the large issues of structural poverty, and the ecological and human damage caused by war. At a more personal level, he teaches (13), it means a change in life-style: 'Simplicity, moderation, and discipline, as well as a spirit of sacrifice, must become part of everyday life.' Education in ecological responsibility is urgent: 'a true education in responsibility entails a genuine conversion in ways of thought and behavior.' Churches and the whole of society have a role to play, but the first educator is the family 'where the child learns to respect his [or her] neighbour and to love nature.' An important aspect of this education is aesthetic and contemplative education into the beauty of creation (14).

Again, the pope insists (15) on the order in creation that needs to be respected by everyone, on our inter-generational responsibilities to our children and grandchildren, and states that '*the ecological crisis is a moral issue*'. He then turns to the Catholic Church community reminding them of their serious obligation to care for the whole creation, based on the theology of creation and of redemption in Christ. In the last paragraph of this text (16) John Paul II explicitly extends respect for life to non-human creation: 'Respect for life and for the dignity of the human person extends also to the rest of creation, which is called to join [the human] in praising God (see Ps. 148:96).'

The Social Encyclicals

In his social encyclicals, John Paul II begins to integrate ecology into the tradition of Catholic social teaching. In *Sollicitudo Rei Socialis* (SRS 34) he offers three considerations that ground respect for the order and interconnectedness of the whole creation:

The first consideration is the appropriateness of acquiring a growing awareness of the fact that one cannot use with impunity the different categories of beings, whether living or inanimate – animals, plants, the natural elements – simply as one wishes, according to one's own economic needs. On the contrary, one must take into account the nature of each being and of its mutual connection in an ordered system, which is precisely the cosmos.

The second consideration is based on the realization – which is perhaps more urgent – that natural resources are limited; some are not, as it is said, renewable. Using them as if they were inexhaustible, with absolute dominion, seriously endangers their availability not only for the present generation but above all for generations to come.

The third consideration refers directly to the consequences of a certain type of development on the quality of life in the industrialized zones. We all know that the direct or indirect result of industrialization is, ever more frequently, the pollution of the environment, with serious consequences for the health of the population.

In the light of all this, the pope insists that in our engagement with the natural world, 'we are subject not only to biological laws but also to moral ones, which cannot be violated with impunity' (SRS 34). On May 1, 1991, John Paul II issued *Centesimus Annus* (CA), on the hundredth anniversary of Pope Leo XIII's *Rerum Novarum*. In this text, the pope presents the ecological crisis as due to an error about the nature of the human in relation to the natural world:

At the root of the senseless destruction of the natural environment lies an anthropological error, which unfortunately is widespread in our day. [Humanity], who discovers [its] capacity to transform and in a certain sense create the world through [its] own work, forgets that this is always based on God's prior and original gift of the things that are. [Humanity] thinks that [it] can make arbitrary use of the earth, subjecting it without restraint to [its] will, as though it did not have its own requisites and a prior God-given purpose, which [humanity] can indeed develop but must not betray. (CA 37)

Again, the pope points to aesthetic attitude of wonder at the beauty of creation that enables us to see in creatures around us the message of God who creates them. He insists on humanity's responsibility to preserve this beauty for future generations and goes on to present his own characteristic view of 'human ecology':

Although people are rightly worried – though much less than they should be – about preserving the natural habitats of the various animal species threatened with extinction, because they realize that each of these species makes its particular contribution to the balance of nature in general, too little effort is made to *safeguard the moral conditions for an authentic 'human ecology'* ... In this context, mention should be made of the serious problems of modern urbanization, of the need for urban planning which is concerned with how people are to live, and of the attention which should be given to a 'social ecology' of work. (CA 38)

The most fundamental structure for human ecology is the family, based on mutual self-giving of husband and wife. John Paul II makes it clear that he sees the family as at the heart of the culture of life, as a sanctuary of life. In his encyclical on life issues, *Evangelium Vitae* (EV 42), John Paul II strongly affirms the unique dignity of the human person, and points to humanity's responsibility for the rest of creation:

As one called to till and look after the garden of the world (cf. Gen. 2:15), [humanity] has a specific responsibility towards the environment in which [it] lives, towards the creation which God has put at the service of [its] personal dignity, of [its] life, not only for the present but also for future generations. It is the ecological question – ranging from the preservation of the natural habitats of the different species of animals and of other forms of life to 'human ecology' properly speaking – which finds in the Bible clear and strong ethical direction, leading to a solution which respects the great good of life, of every life.

The dominion given to humanity is not an absolute power, but something to be exercised only as sharing in the divine Wisdom and divine love for creation. Again John Paul II teaches that in our interaction with the natural world, 'we are subject not only to biological laws but also to moral ones, which cannot be violated with impunity' (EV 42).

John Paul II's Concepts of Ecological Conversion and Ecological Vocation

John Paul II's encouragement of ecological conversion is stated most explicitly in his General Audience Address (John Paul II 2001: 3-4) where he writes:

> Unfortunately, if we scan the regions of our planet, we immediately see that humanity has disappointed God's expectations. [Humanity], especially in our time, has without hesitation devastated wooded plains and valleys, polluted waters, disfigured the earth's habitat, made the air unbreatheable, disturbed the hydrogeological and atmospheric systems, turned luxuriant areas into deserts and undertaken forms of unrestrained industrialization, degrading that 'flowerbed' – to use an image from Dante Alighieri (*Paradiso*, XXII, 151) – which is the earth, our dwelling-place. We must therefore encourage and support the 'ecological conversion' which in recent decades has made humanity more sensitive to the catastrophe to which it has been heading.

It is clear that the whole human race is called to this conversion, but the Christian community is committed to it for deeply theological reasons. This call to repentance and to a new ecological awareness and action is further developed in the 'Joint Statement' (John Paul II and Bartholomew I 2004), signed by the pope and the ecologically minded Ecumenical Patriarch of Constantinople on June 10, 2004.

In his 'Angelus Address' given at Castel Gandolfo on August 25 that year (John Paul II 2002: 1) John Paul II introduced the idea of an ecological *vocation*: 'Human beings are appointed by God as stewards of the earth to cultivate and protect it. From this fact there comes what we might call their 'ecological vocation', which in our time has become more urgent than ever.' These themes of ecological conversion and ecological vocation have been important in the education of the Christian community to begin to see ecology as central to Christian witness and mission in the world.

Benedict XVI's *Caritas in Veritate*

Like his predecessor, Pope Benedict has spoken often about ecology in a variety of speeches and documents. He has also taken public action by, in

2008, installing an array of solar panels on the large Vatican audience hall and working to off set the Vatican's carbon emissions by involvement in a reforestation project in Hungary. Some have gone so far as to describe Benedict as 'the green pope' (Pepinster 2010). I will focus on his comments in his 2009 social encyclical *Caritas in Veritate* (CV) and his 2010 World Day of Peace Message.

Caritas in Veritate takes up the theme of integral human development from Pope Paul VI's *Populorum Progressio*, issued more than forty years earlier. A substantial section is devoted to ecology. The pope teaches that the natural world is God's gift to everyone, and that it is the expression of divine love:

> *Nature expresses a design of love and truth.* It is prior to us, and it has been given to us by God as the setting for our life. Nature speaks to us of the Creator (cf. Rom. 1:20) and his love for humanity. It is destined to be 'recapitulated' in Christ at the end of time (cf. Eph. 1:9-10; Col. 1:19-20). Thus it too is a 'vocation'. (Benedict XVI 2009: 48)

Because it is an expression of divine love and truth, because it is God's gift to us, because it speaks of the Creator and because its 'vocation' is to share with human beings in their transformation in Christ, the natural world has its own integrity. Benedict rejects two positions: new forms of paganism and pantheism that elevate nature above the human and the opposite idea that humans have total dominion over nature as raw material for their manipulation. He sees the natural world as a wondrous work of the Creator that has its own 'grammar' which humans are called respect, not recklessly exploit. He points out as well that in using resources such as non-renewable sources of energy, we are called to solidarity, which involves ensuring access for poorer counties, and inter-generational justice:

> This responsibility is a global one, for it is concerned not just with energy but with the whole of creation, which must not be bequeathed to future generations depleted of its resources. Human beings legitimately exercise a *responsible stewardship over nature*, in order to protect it, to enjoy its fruits and to cultivate it in new ways, with the assistance of advanced technologies, so that it can worthily accommodate and feed the world's population ... At the same time we must recognize our grave duty to hand the earth on to future generations in such a condition that they too can worthily inhabit it and continue to cultivate it. This means being committed to making joint decisions 'after pondering responsibly the road to be taken, decisions aimed at strengthening that *covenant between human beings and the environment*, which should mirror the creative love of God, from whom we come and towards whom we are journeying'. (Benedict XVI 2009: 50)

Benedict reinforces the idea of a covenant bond of love with the rest of creation that mirrors the creative love of God for all God's creatures, which he had introduced in the 2008 World Day of Peace. He goes on to insist that the way we treat other creatures is deeply connected to the way we treat each other as human beings:

The way humanity treats the environment influences the way it treats itself, and vice versa. This invites contemporary society to a serious review of its life-style, which, in many parts of the world, is prone to hedonism and consumerism, regardless of their harmful consequences.' What is needed is an effective shift in mentality that can lead to the adoption of *new life-styles.* (Benedict XVI 2009: 51)

The shift in mentality and in life-styles echoes the ecological conversion advocated by John Paul II. Benedict goes on to spell out what this means for the church. It is called not just to ecological education but also to advocacy on behalf of the natural world as well as for 'human ecology':

The Church has a responsibility towards creation and she must assert this responsibility in the public sphere. In so doing, she must defend not only earth, water and air as gifts of creation that belong to everyone. She must above all protect [humankind] from self-destruction. There is need for what might be called a human ecology, correctly understood. The deterioration of nature is in fact closely connected to the culture that shapes human coexistence: *when 'human ecology' is respected within society, environmental ecology also benefits.* (Benedict XVI 2009: 51)

Our responsibilities to the rest of creation cannot be separated from our responsibilities towards human beings: 'The book of nature is one and indivisible.' For Benedict as for John Paul II, environmental ecology and human ecology belong together, interrelated in the prior gift of the Creator, the God who is 'Truth and Love'. (Benedict XVI 2009: 52)

2010 World Day of Peace Message

Twenty years after John Paul 11's 1990 message, Benedict issued the 2010 World Day of Peace Message with the theme: *If You Want to Cultivate Peace, Protect Creation.* He calls the human community to respect for creation as the beginning of all God's works, and again speaks of the covenant between humans and the natural world that should mirror the creative love of God. He points to the beauty of creation, and the words of Dante: 'Contemplating the beauty of creation inspires us to recognize the love of the Creator, that Love which "moves the sun and the other stars"' (Benedict XVI 2010: 2). He asks:

Can we remain indifferent before the problems associated with such realities as climate change, desertification, the deterioration and loss of productivity in vast agricultural areas, the pollution of rivers and aquifers, the loss of biodiversity, the increase of natural catastrophes and the deforestation of equatorial and tropical regions? Can we disregard the growing phenomenon of 'environmental refugees', people who are forced by the degradation of their natural habitat to forsake it – and often their possessions as well – in order to face the dangers and uncertainties of forced displacement? Can we remain impassive in the face of actual and potential conflicts involving access to natural resources? (Benedict XVI 2010: 4).

All of this is the context for Christian mission in today's world. These issues invite us to 'rethink the path which we are travelling together.' For Benedict, 'dominion' (Gen. 1:28) is not a permission for domination, but a call to be stewards of God, a summons to responsibility. This means that 'when making use of natural resources, we should be concerned for their protection and consider the cost entailed – environmentally and socially – as an essential part of the overall expenses incurred'. Benedict (2010: 5) encourages research and action on solar energy and the water cycle, 'whose stability could be seriously jeopardized by climate change.' Again, he calls for a new life style: 'It is becoming more and more evident that the issue of environmental degradation challenges us to examine our life-style and the prevailing models of consumption and production, which are often unsustainable from a social, environmental and even economic point of view. We can no longer do without a real change of outlook which will result in *new life styles*.' This involves far-reaching decisions on the part of individuals, families, communities and states and, of course the Church – and, of course, its mission:

> *The Church has a responsibility towards creation*, and she considers it her duty to exercise that responsibility in public life, in order to protect earth, water and air as gifts of God the Creator meant for everyone, and above all to save [humankind] from the danger of self-destruction. The degradation of nature is closely linked to the cultural models shaping human coexistence: consequently, 'when "human ecology" is respected within society, environmental ecology also benefits.... The book of nature is one and indivisible; it includes not only the environment but also individual, family and social ethics. (Benedict XVI 2010: 12)

For Benedict, the natural world is where humans can experience beauty, peace, and reinvigoration. Again, he rejects absolutizing of nature over the human, expressing misgivings about 'ecocentrism' and 'biocentrism', and seeks to uphold the distinctiveness of the human. In my view, his position is not so much anthropocentric, as theocentric. What he seeks to emphasize (Benedict XVI 2010: 14) is 'the indivisible relationship between God, human beings and the whole of creation.'

Francis on the Vocation to Protect Creation

On 19th March 2013, Pope Francis began his petrine ministry as bishop of Rome with a Eucharist in St. Peter's Square in which he received the pallium and the fisherman's ring. In his homily Francis gives central place to the theme of the protection of the creation along with the protection of all human beings. Celebrating the feast of St. Joseph, he sees Joseph as protector of Mary and Jesus, and of the whole Body of Christ. He says of Joseph: "In him, dear friends, we learn how to respond to God's call, readily and willingly, but we also see the core of the Christian vocation, which is Christ! Let us protect Christ in our lives, so that we can protect others, so that we can protect creation!" (Francis 2013). This protection is a vocation to which all humans are called:

> The vocation of being a "protector", however, is not just something involving us Christians alone; it also has a prior dimension which is simply human, involving everyone. It means protecting all creation, the beauty of the created world, as the Book of Genesis tells us and as Saint Francis of Assisi showed us. It means respecting each of God's creatures and respecting the environment in which we live. It means protecting people, showing loving concern for each and every person, especially children, the elderly, those in need, who are often the last we think about. It means caring for one another in our families: husbands and wives first protect one another, and then, as parents, they care for their children, and children themselves, in time, protect their parents. It means building sincere friendships in which we protect one another in trust, respect, and goodness. In the end, everything has been entrusted to our protection, and all of us are responsible for it. Be protectors of God's gifts! (Francis 2013)

The failure to respond to this vocation ends in tragedy: "Whenever human beings fail to live up to this responsibility, whenever we fail to care for creation and for our brothers and sisters, the way is opened to destruction and hearts are hardened." (Francis 2013) There are always "Herods" who arise in different ages to bring death. Francis invites leaders of peoples to join him in the work of protection of creation and of our human brothers and sisters: "Please, I would like to ask all those who have positions of responsibility in economic, political and social life, and all men and women of goodwill: let us be "protectors" of creation, protectors of God's plan inscribed in nature, protectors of one another and of the environment" (Francis 2013).

Francis sees protection of creation and of human beings as involving not only compassion, but love and tenderness: "To protect creation, to protect every man and every woman, to look upon them with tenderness and love, is to open up a horizon of hope; it is to let a shaft of light break through the heavy clouds; it is to bring the warmth of hope!"(Francis 2013) Towards the end of his homily, Francis speaks of this protection as central to his own ministry as bishop of Rome, and also as the vocation of each person: "To protect Jesus with Mary, to protect the whole of creation, to protect each person, especially the poorest, to protect ourselves: this is a service that the Bishop of Rome is called to carry out, yet one to which all of us are called, so that the star of hope will shine brightly. Let us protect with love all that God has given us!" (Francis 2013).

What John Paul II called our ecological vocation is summed up by Francis with his view of the vocation to protect creation and each and every human being, above all those who are poorest. Commitment to the good of the natural world and commitment to social justice are united in the one following of Jesus. Protection of the natural world and protection of our brothers and sisters is part of protecting Christ.

Ecology at the Heart of Christian Mission

As Benedict says, Christians view nature as grounded in the deepest mysteries of faith, creation and redemption in Christ: 'They contemplate the cosmos and its marvels in light of the creative work of the Father and the redemptive work of Christ, who by his death and resurrection has reconciled with God "all things, whether on earth or in heaven" (Col. 1:20)' (Benedict XVI 2010: 14). Ecology is at the heart of mission because the natural world is intrinsic to the deepest mysteries of faith. What the doctrine of creation means, John Paul II tells us (John Paul II 1995: 15), is that the triune God is present as the mystery of love in the whole universe: 'There is nothing created that is not filled with the ceaseless exchange of love that marks the innermost life of the Trinity, filled that is with the Holy Spirit: "the Spirit of the Lord has filled the world" (Wis. 1:7).' In another text, he points out what the doctrine of the incarnation means for non-human creation:

> The Incarnation of God the Son signifies the taking up into unity with God not only of human nature, but in *this human nature, in a sense, of everything that is 'flesh'*: the whole of humanity, the entire visible and material world. The Incarnation, then, also has a cosmic significance, a cosmic dimension. The 'first-born of all creation', becoming incarnate in the individual humanity of Christ, unites himself in some way with the entire reality of [humanity], which is also 'flesh' – and in this reality with all 'flesh', with the whole of creation. (DV 1986: 50)

In the Word made flesh, God is united with all flesh, with the whole interconnected, biological world of fleshly reality, and with all the entities and processes that make up the matter of our universe. All this is to be recapitulated in Christ (Eph. 1:10) and transformed in Christ to share in freedom and the glory of the children of God (Rom. 8:21). This is the truth we celebrate in the Eucharist, so that John Paul (John Paul II 2003: 8) says that every Eucharist in some way has 'a cosmic character' and is 'celebrated *on the altar of the world*.' Christian mission has an ecological character because it proclaims a God who gives God's self to us, first in creation and then in the Word made flesh, who, in and through the death and resurrection of Jesus, promises to transform all things, all the creatures of Earth and of the universe, in Christ.

MISSION AS INTER-RELIGIOUS DIALOGUE

Edmund Chia

It was my first visit to the Hindu kingdom of Nepal. I was on an exposure program to explore Christian mission and ministries in Asia. Upon my arrival in the capital city Kathmandu I was whisked away by taxi to the mission headquarters, a huge colonial mansion within a gated compound adjacent to a Christian hospital, which also shelters a social services' center and a kindergarten. I felt as if I had come from another world and landed in two different worlds all at once.

The teeming masses of the local residents outside the gate were radically different in feature and lifestyle from the few who resided within the compound. Those outside were Nepalese, basically very poor, while those within were foreigners, generally affluent. Those outside went about their Hindu ritual practices passionately while those inside professed faith in the Lordship of Jesus Christ the savior of the world. Some members of the former were also within but primarily as ancillary workers and servants of the latter whom they address by the titles 'Sir' or 'Ma'am.'

The mission had been in Nepal for several decades and by all standards a tremendous success. The missionaries minister to hundreds of sick and wounded each day, attend to the material and emotional needs of the residents, and provide education and formation to young Nepalese. While these are the success stories often told in mission brochures, the true measure of success seems to be the number of conversions and the increase in membership amongst the local Nepalese Christian community.

From '*Missio ad Gentes*' to '*Missio inter Gentes*'

The above scenario represents the commonly held understanding of Christian mission. It is mission undertaken in the spirit of Matthew 28:19 ('Go therefore and make disciples of all nations, baptizing them in the name of the Father and of the Son and of the Holy Spirit'), where missionaries literally leave home to preach the gospel in order to make disciples. This sending forth and discipling mandate is regarded as Jesus' final commandment and the church's universal mission is none other than the proclamation of the mystery of God and especially the mystery of God's incarnation in Jesus Christ to peoples of all nations. This is the *missio ad gentes* (mission to the nations), aimed specifically at the heathens or those who have not heard the gospel, the ultimate objective of which is the saving of their souls and the planting of new churches. The *kerygma* and *koinonia* aspects are the primary emphases for this understanding of mission.

But it is also observed that these missions of bringing non-believers to the Christian faith are almost always accompanied by 'good works,' which could take a variety of forms including healing, education, or social ministries. Matthew 25:35 ('for I was hungry and you gave me food, I was thirsty and you gave me something to drink, I was a stranger and you welcomed me') serves as inspiration for this *diakonia* aspect of mission. Convinced that Jesus has come to bring 'life in all its fullness' (Jn. 10:10) the missionary is tasked with not only sharing the gospel of eternal life but also the mending of the broken bodies of the earthly life. This, in part, accounts for the fact that even as Asia is no more than 2 or 3 per cent Christian the church runs more than 25 per cent of its schools, hospitals and social services.

This, on the other hand, can also be where the problem lies. The objects and targets of Christian mission charge that *diakonia* is used as a proselytizing tool to facilitate the acceptance of the *kerygma* and the establishment of the *koinonia*. This charge is not without its validity. The term 'rice Christians' gained currency already in the last century, suggesting that the phenomenon of people embracing Christianity for material gain is not uncommon. There are churches in Thailand and Cambodia where attendance at Sunday services qualifies one's family for literally a bag of rice! Missionaries in Malaysia and Bangladesh testify to the fact that people have come up to them asking 'What will I get if I become a Christian?' Eternal life and salvation are probably further away from the questioner's mind than food, money, or clothing!

On the other side of the coin, there is a school of thought that views mission as consisting primarily and even solely of *diakonia*. Mission, as the Lord's Prayer teaches, is enabling God's Kingdom to come and doing God's will 'on earth' as in heaven. The missioner's task therefore is not so much the institutional conversion of the beneficiaries but their holistic and spiritual conversion as evidenced in their being able to live whole and holy lives before death. This perspective of mission focuses on the teaching and practice of Jesus on the coming of the reign of God and especially his preferential option for the poor and commitments to justice, peace and the integrity of creation.

Taking seriously Matthew 6:33 to 'seek first the Kingdom of God,' it shifts the focus from a church-centered or ecclesiocentric understanding of mission to a kingdom-centered or regnocentric perspective of mission (Dupuis 1997: 193; Knitter 1996: 108). Mission is seen as essentially the building up of the reign of God and not that of the church. The aim of mission is not so much the conversion of the *gentes* but the alleviation of the suffering, oppression and inhuman conditions that keep people from living in dignity and integrity. No longer is emphasis given to portraying

Christ as Lord of Lords and King of Kings and the triumphant church as bestowed with power and glory and having dominion over all darkness. Instead, Christology now highlights a Jesus who, 'though he was in the form of God, did not regard equality with God as something to be exploited, but emptied himself, taking the form of a slave' (Phil. 2:6-7). In other words, there is conscious awareness that the church is but a servant of the kingdom and therefore sent not so much for its own mission but for that of the *missio Dei*.

In this respect it is acknowledged that Christians are not the only ones engaged in these *diakonia* activities or serving the *missio Dei*. Peoples of other religions are as much involved and some with even greater zeal and effectiveness than Christian missionaries. Mission, therefore, can no longer be conceived of as Christians bringing Christ to peoples who are not Christians but as peoples of all religious traditions bringing life and hope to those who have none and working together to help build a better tomorrow. While the Nepalese mission portrayed in the opening paragraphs above would still be necessary, it is now looked upon more as missioners serving the Nepalese community not because they are not Christians but because they are poor or in need of healing. And since Christians are engaged in this alongside missionaries of other religions, we now have what Jonathan Tan (Tan 2003: 65) and William Burrows (Burrows 2008: 5) call *missio inter gentes* (mission *among* the nations).

Here, instead of viewing peoples of other religions as objects of conversion or competitors of mission, they will be looked upon more as associates and partners and even 'agents of the Kingdom' (Knitter 1996: 118). Likewise, instead of Christian mission culminating with the annihilation or replacement of these religions, the entire mission process becomes an occasion for building bridges across religions as well as opportunity for both parties to be learning about each other's religion. The partnership becomes not only a collaborative venture but a transformative encounter as well.

Towards a Church of Dialogue

The partnership model of mission is relatively new, evolving within Christianity and especially the Roman Catholic Church only within the last half century. The Second Vatican Council is often regarded as the watershed for this. It was a momentous and transformative event in that, unlike a reform council called to address heresies (as was Vatican I to address the challenge of Modernity or Trent the Reformation), Vatican II was a renewal council. Pope John XXIII called it an *aggiornamento* and meant for it as an occasion for the church to update itself and to catch up with the developments of society. Inherent in this updating is the activity of dialogue, which the church must engage in if it wishes to relate to and integrate with other entities of the social community.

Pope Paul VI's first encyclical, *Ecclesiam Suam* (ES), put into words the appropriate attitude for such a dialogue. The document's intent was to examine 'how vital it is for the world, and how greatly desired by the Catholic Church, that the two should meet together, and get to know and love one another' (ES 3). The pope then exhorts the members of the church to enter into fraternal dialogue with one another, with their fellow Christians of other denominations in ecumenical dialogue, with believers of other religious traditions in inter-religious dialogue, and with the world in general. The motif of dialogue was so central to the encyclical that it has often been regarded as a dialogue document. Incidentally, this was also the first time the word dialogue is used explicitly in a church document, indicating a significant milestone. ES was emphatic that the Church's missionary activity be conducted in a dialogical way rather than through overt force or subtle pressure. By emphasizing dialogue the document reminds Christians that respect must govern the relationships they have with those whom they encounter and that the missionary task has to be understood as a two-way process of both sides talking and listening, as well as sharing and learning. These attitudes provide the foundations for a missiology where Christians must reach out to others in dialogue, much the same way 'God Himself took the initiative in the dialogue of salvation' (ES 72).

If John XXIII paved the way for the church's renewal and Paul VI set the stage for a dialogical church, it was the Council Fathers of Vatican II who really spelled out the church's position with regard to mission, dialogue, and the other religions. The first of such documents was *Lumen Gentium* (LG), the Dogmatic Constitution on the Church, issued towards the end of 1964. It opened up the church's teachings about peoples of other religions. If the Council of Florence insisted that 'those who are outside the catholic church, not only pagans but also Jews or heretics and schismatics, cannot share in eternal life and will go into the everlasting fire which was prepared for the devil and his angels, unless they are joined to the catholic church before the end of their lives' (ND: 1005; DS: 1351) and the Council of Trent admitted to the possibility of a 'baptism of desire' in place of baptism by water (ND 1928; DS 1524), LG solemnly stated that '[t]hose also can attain to salvation who through no fault of their own do not know the Gospel of Christ or His Church' (LG 16). Though meant to be pastoral in nature (to help in cultivating the church's relationship with the rest of the world), this assertion is at the same time doctrinally loaded and the pronouncement has had significant implications for the church's mission.

An even more radical assertion (at least by the ecclesial standards of the time) was the Vatican II document *Nostra Aetate* (NA), which is the Declaration on the Relation of the Church to Non-Christian Religions. Hitherto the church had only pronounced on the possibility of salvation of peoples of other religions; it had said nothing about the authenticity or value of the religions themselves. In that sense NA was taking a great leap forward when it pronounced that '[t]he Catholic Church rejects nothing that is true and holy in these religions' (NA 2). It also points to the positive elements in these religions, identifying Hinduism, Buddhism, Islam, and Judaism by name. The declaration then asserts that the church 'regards with sincere reverence those ways of conduct and of life, those precepts and teachings which, though differing in many aspects from the ones she holds and sets forth, nonetheless often reflect a ray of that Truth which enlightens all men' (NA 2). Going beyond merely heaping praise at these religions NA had this to say: 'The Church, therefore, exhorts its sons and daughters, that through dialogue and collaboration with the followers of other religions, carried out with prudence and love and in witness to the Christian faith and life, they recognize, preserve and promote the good things, spiritual and moral, as well as the socio-cultural values found among these women and men' (NA 2). Notice that the declaration is exhorting Christians to not only recognize but to also 'preserve' and 'promote' the good things found in the other religions. Such unambiguous pronouncements make very clear that the Church no longer sees mission through only the replacement or conquest model but also through partnership, dialogue and collaboration with believers of other religious traditions.

This thrust was given further practical elaboration in the Decree on the Mission Activity of the Church, *Ad Gentes* (AG), where it was recommended that in priestly formation care should be given to ensuring that future priests are 'educated in the ecumenical spirit, and duly prepared for fraternal dialogue with non-Christians' (AG 16). Likewise, the decree recommends the same for the laity, especially those engaged in teaching and research ministries, exhorting them to 'cooperate in a brotherly spirit with other Christians, with non-Christians, and with members of international organizations' (AG 41).

Dialogue and/or Mission?

While Vatican II exhorts the church to be in dialogue with other religions, it does not mean the traditional understandings of *missio ad gentes* became obsolete. If anything, dialogue and mission continue to be proffered and promoted even as they may seem contradictory to one another. In fact, when Paul VI established the Secretariat for Non-Christians in 1964 to help actualize the new thrust of dialogue it was met with apprehensions, especially vis-à-vis its impact on the church's missionary activities. The Secretariat had to issue a pamphlet to the Council Fathers explaining its role and especially the distinction between the task of dialogue and the task of mission. Both are essential though, according to the pamphlet, dialogue 'prepares the way for missionary work in areas where overt evangelization is impossible' (Sheard 1987: 37). Ten years after the end of Vatican II Paul VI issued *Evangelii Nuntiandi* (EN), an apostolic exhortation devoted to evangelization, where he made it explicit that dialogue is by no way a replacement for mission: 'We wish to point out, above all today, that neither respect and esteem for these religions nor the complexity of the questions raised is an invitation to the Church to withhold from these non-Christians the proclamation of Jesus Christ' (EN 53).

With another decade the church further developed in its understanding of dialogue and in 1984 on the twentieth anniversary of the establishment of the Secretariat for Non-Christians (which in 1988 was renamed the Pontifical Council for Inter-religious Dialogue [PCID]) it issued a document on The Attitude of the Church toward Followers of Other Religions: Reflections and Orientations on Dialogue and Mission (DM). Here, for the first time, dialogue is not only regarded as 'both the norm and ideal' (DM 3) but also listed as a 'principal element' of the 'single and complex and articulated reality' of the Church's mission (DM 13). In other words, inter-religious dialogue has now become integral to '[t]he totality of Christian mission' (DM 13), without which, we can conjecture, one would not call it Christian mission.

Pope John Paul II elaborated on this in his 1990 encyclical R*edemptoris Missio* (RM) which is On the Permanent Validity of the Church's Missionary Mandate. 'Inter-religious dialogue,' the pope proclaims, 'is a part of the church's evangelizing mission. Understood as a method and means of mutual knowledge and enrichment, dialogue is not in opposition to the mission *ad gentes*; indeed, it has special links with that mission and is one of its expressions' (RM 55). This dialogue is not only for the purpose of working together towards a better world but also for discerning what it means to be Christian as '[o]ther religions constitute a positive challenge for the Church: they stimulate her both to discover and acknowledge the signs of Christ's presence and of the working of the Spirit, as well as to examine more deeply her own identity and to bear witness to the fullness of Revelation which she has received for the good of all' (RM 56). That accounts for why the pope insists that '[e]ach member of the faithful and all Christian communities are called to practice dialogue' as '[d]ialogue is a path toward the kingdom' (RM 57).

That this did not put the dialogue-mission dichotomy and debate to rest was evidenced by the need for the PCID to come together with the Congregation for the Evangelization of Peoples (the new name for the Sacred Congregation for the Propagation of the Faith) in 1991 to issue a joint statement entitled *Dialogue and Proclamation* (DP). The document was aimed at addressing these concerns:

> The practice of dialogue raises problems in the minds of many. There are those who would seem to think, erroneously, that in the Church's mission today dialogue should simply replace proclamation. At the other extreme, some fail to see the value of inter-religious dialogue. Yet others are perplexed and ask: if inter-religious dialogue has become so important, has the proclamation of the Gospel message lost its urgency?' (DP 4).

Its response is that '[i]nterreligious dialogue and proclamation, though not on the same level, are both authentic elements of the Church's evangelizing mission. Both are legitimate and necessary. They are intimately related, but not interchangeable … The two activities remain distinct but, as experience shows, one and the same local Church, one and the same person, can be diversely engaged in both' (DP 77). But, at the end of the day, it has to be acknowledged that 'dialogue, as has already been said, does not constitute the whole mission of the Church, that it cannot simply replace proclamation, but remains *oriented* towards proclamation in so far as the dynamic process of the Church's evangelizing mission reaches in it its climax and its fullness' (DP 82 – emphasis added).

In 2000 the Congregation for the Doctrine of the Faith finally weighed in and issued the Declaration *Dominus Iesus* (DI): On the University and Salvific Universality of Jesus Christ and the Church. Paraphrasing and reiterating RM and DP the declaration clearly instrumentalizes dialogue with this assertion: 'Continuing in this line of thought, the Church's proclamation of Jesus Christ, 'the way, the truth, and the life' (Jn. 14:6), today also makes use of the practice of inter-religious dialogue' (DI 2). Instead of dialogue being at the service of the more holistic understanding of evangelization it now puts it in the service of the more limited view of mission: 'Inter-religious dialogue, therefore, as part of her evangelizing mission, is just one of the actions of the Church in her mission *ad gentes*' (DI 22). It is no wonder that the the declaration was met with vociferous reactions, both from the Catholic community as well as from persons of other religions. This, together with a note expressing similar concerns issued by the Congregation for the Doctrine of the Faith in in 2007 (CDF 2007), represent the latest and most recent statements on the matter from the Roman Magisterium.

Mission through Dialogue

Perhaps as a way out of the dialogue-mission conundrum, and in conclusion, I would look towards the positions taken by the Asian Church's magisterium. Having grown up alongside the other religions the Asian Church is best poised to offer some leads regarding the relationship between mission and dialogue. This can be discerned through the official documents issued by the Federation of Asian Bishops' Conferences (FABC), the highest authority of the churches in Asia, most of which exist as small minorities in contexts that are religiously plural.

As early as 1974, in their first plenary assembly on the theme of Evangelization in Modern Day Asia, the Asian bishops affirmed the following: 'The preaching of Jesus Christ and His Gospel to our peoples in Asia becomes a task which today assumes an urgency' (FABC I 1997: 13). They then went on to state almost immediately that 'to preach the Gospel in Asia today we must make the message and life of Christ truly incarnate in the minds and lives of our peoples' (FABC I 1997: 14). In this regard, 'the building up of a truly local church' (FABC I 1997: 14) is of prime importance and, for this to happen, the church must be 'in continuous, humble and loving dialogue with the living traditions, the cultures, the religions' (FABC I 1997: 14). The bishops insist on this because they believe that the other religions are indeed 'significant and positive elements in the economy of God's design of salvation' (FABC I 1997: 14). They are also conscious that these religions of Asia have been the source and inspiration for generations of peoples and have helped in the spiritual development and growth of an entire continent for millennia. In light of this they asked, albeit rhetorically: 'How then can we not give them [the other religions] reverence and honor? And how can we not acknowledge that God has drawn our peoples to Himself through them?' (FABC I 1997: 14).

It is in this context that they insist at their fifth assembly in 1990 that 'mission includes: being with the people, responding to their needs, with sensitiveness to the presence of God in cultures and other religious traditions, and witnessing to the values of God's Kingdom through presence, solidarity, sharing and word' (FABC I 1997: 279). Hence, '[f]or Christians in Asia, to proclaim Christ means above all to live like him, in the midst of our neighbors of other faiths and persuasions, and to do his deeds by the power of his grace. Proclamation through dialogue and deeds – this is the first call to the Churches in Asia' (FABC I 1997: 282).

The bishops therefore do not see dialogue and mission as contradictory or from the perspective that one element serves the other. Instead, they truly believe, as they should given their years of helping the Asian Church negotiate the realities of religious pluralism, that the whole process of evangelization should be integrated so that it is at once sensitive and respectful of the Asian cultures and religions and at the same time authentic to the Christian tradition. The most critical aspect of this integration is that we see peoples of other religions as partners in our evangelization and we witness to our faith through our lives and deeds. Likewise, we invite them to do the same to us as they witness to their faith. This is the dialogical method which the Asian Church espouses and this, ultimately, is its mission of evangelization. In other words, our mission is engaged in through dialogue and dialogue becomes our mission.

MISSION AND INCULTURATION

José M. de Mesa

Inculturation is the in-depth re-appropriation and re-expression, as well as the fresh rethinking and reformulation of the gospel in each human culture in a manner that is dialogically affirming and prophetic. It affects persons in a fundamental way because people are inextricably cultural. As a participation in the very action of God as the life-giving Word 'becoming flesh', inculturation makes the *missio Dei* visible and palpable in cultural terms and is, therefore, a constitutive dimension of mission.

In the history of the church, however, it is struggle that has characterized the practice of the church. The twentieth century is a singularly clear example of the church's earnest striving to be faithful to the vision of inculturation, the results of which represent a mixture of success and failure. The first half of the century manifests a general neglect, or even denial of inculturation, but not without instances of realizing it. The second half is witness to the church's realization as to how vitally important culture is in its life and mission and to a vigorous effort to retrieve the tradition of inculturation, albeit with undeniable occasions demonstrating opposition to it. In its holding of the Second Vatican Council (1962-1965) the Roman Catholic Church recalled its tradition of inculturation, clarified and broadened its understanding of it, and renewed its resolve to seriously realize it in the context of the plurality of cultures.

Vision and Struggle

The church's conviction regarding inculturation was already attested to in the event of Pentecost and in the early adoption of the principle of cultural catholicity in the so-called Council of Jerusalem (Acts 15:1-20). The former describes its vision about inculturation by narrating how those listening to the Apostles heard them speak of the mighty acts of God in their own native language (see Acts 2:8, 11); the latter not only tells of a church decision that implied the gospel of salvation could be thought and lived in a plurality of cultural ways, but also how the church has to struggle through 'fierce dissension and controversy' (Acts 15:2). The church of the second century was able to relativize and disengage itself from its Jewish cultural rootedness as it engaged the surrounding Hellenistic culture in the West and Persian culture in the East, but it did not fully learn the lesson that it ought to have been gained from it. In particular, the church's success at inculturation within what was to become the Western civilization also proved to be the very obstacle to inculturate itself in another culture.

The Western European church failed to see the validity and legitimacy of a Chinese expression of the faith in the seventeenth century when it dealt with the latter's rites of ancestor veneration. Such inability was also generally true, though not without notable exceptions (de Nobili in India, de Rhodes in Vietnam, the Testarian manuscripts in Mexico), in its efforts to evangelize the peoples of Africa, Asia, Latin and Caribbean America and the Pacific in the context of colonization from the sixteenth up till mid twentieth century. It was not inclined to give up its culturally conditioned dominance on the newly established mission churches. Given the way culture and Western Christianity were understood at the time, *accommodation* to the customs of these peoples was the only concession it could make to these churches. It was an approach to evangelization that assumed that Western theology and Christian practice was universally and perennially valid. Especially after the Council of Trent (1545-1563) the general rule was that every mission church should conform as closely as possible to the Roman way. As a form of adaptation, accommodation only applied to non-essential matters regarding the faith and to cultural elements uncomtaminated by paganism (Bosch 1991: 448-49). The consideration of human experience, which would play an indispensable role in the renewal that was Vatican II, was remarkably absent in this accomodative way of thinking within the church.

Retrieval and Renewal in the Twentieth Century

The retrieval and renewal of the vision of inculturation in the church represents a historically forged and evolving understanding of the interconnection between gospel and culture. Notwithstanding the widespread and unquestioned practical identification of Western Christianity to Christianity itself, there were also important instances of cultural sensitivity within the church. These were developments not consciously aimed at recovering the vision of inculturation. But they helped prepare a climate for thinking about the church differently: that it ought to be born anew in each new culture instead of the Western church just being expanded.

Such were mission encyclicals like Benedict XV's 1919 encyclical *Maximum Illud* that recommended the establishment of local churches (*plantatio ecclesiae*) together with the formation of indigenous clergy and the ordination of indigenous bishops (see James Kroeger's chapter in this volume). The call of the Belgian Vincentian missionary to China, Vincent Lebbe, to de-Westernize Christianity and the suggestion of the American Bishop, Francis X. Ford for a self-governing and self-reliant indigenous local church were significant in this regard. Charles de Foucauld's actual practice of mission as presence and the development of Catholic social teachings made the church conscious of conditions in which people lived. And Wilhelm Schimdt's thought highlighted the importance of culture and the social sciences in missionary endeavors (see Bevans and Schroeder 2004: 244-49).

Factors Leading to the Renewal of the
Vision of Inculturation in Vatican II

A transformation that singularly impacted Catholic thought on inculturation was the shift regarding the way culture is understood. Prior to this change, it was widely assumed by both society and church that there was only one culture for all human groups in the world. As the Western civilization it represented, the peak of the development of this one universal culture was, therefore, normative. Consequently, the Western European local church also considered evangelization as a way of civilizing the uncivilized and developing the undeveloped.

This *classical* perspective on culture was abandoned, thanks particularly to the efforts of social scientists who brought to the attention of contemporary society the fact of plurality of cultures. Instead an *empirical* mode of understanding culture, which asserted that there is a plurality of cultures with a diversity of norms, began to be adopted in society (see Lonergan 1972: 124, 301, 326-330, 362-63). Through the influence of this shift on Vatican II, consciousness regarding culture and cultures became an important reality in the church once more. Vatican II not only spoke of 'culture' to refer in general to a dynamic human and humanizing way of life that becomes second-nature to a group of people, but also of 'cultures' to specify the specific traditions which different human groups have developed in order to live and to flourish (see GS 53). It also reminded the church of its tradition of cultural pluralism which goes all the way back to its beginnings.

The anthropological shift regarding culture influenced Catholic thought on inculturation from the outside. But the retrieval of the importance of culture in the life and mission of the church, specifically in theology, was made possible by theological shifts in Vatican II itself. These are reflected in its four pivotal documents: *Dei Verbum* (DV), the Dogmatic Constitution on Divine Revelation; *Lumen Gentium* (LG), the Dogmatic Constitution on the Church, *Gaudium et Spes* (GS), the Pastoral Constitution on the Church in the Modern World; and *Sacrosanctum Concilium* (SC), the Constitution on the Sacred Liturgy. The changes embodied in these documents, when seen in the light of the previous theological views they have transcended, paved the way for considering culture not merely as a theological consideration, but also as a theological *locus*. Together with the gospel, culture became an essential and constitutive element for understanding the faith.

Vatican II's document on revelation, *Dei Verbum* (DV), moved away from the context-less neo-scholastic understanding of revelation as God making known immutable and absolute truths and of faith as the assent of the mind to these unchanging divinely revealed truths. DV opted for a more biblically oriented interpretation of revelation as God's self-communication in history; that is, in and through the experiences of people (DV 2, 14). The importance of this recovery of experience in theological thought cannnot be exaggerated. For if revelation occurs in and through human experiences in the world, then the fact that people are inextricably cultural must be taken into account in understanding their relationship with God. Consequently those who study the Bible as a witness to revelation must be attentive to the 'literary forms in accordance with the situation of [the sacred writer's] own time and culture' (DV 12). This turn to experience in DV would lead the church to acknowledge in another document the role that culture plays in the broader process of evangelization.

Change was also made possible by the new understanding of church in LG. The Tridentine image of the church was a divinely willed (Western) institution that must be transplanted as it was in different places. In Vatican II this has been replaced by the more ancient and more scriptural understanding of the church as 'the People of God' (LG 9). The imagery of the church as a community of people called attention to the particularities inherent in being a human group such as culture. The document insists that the church as the people of God takes nothing away from the temporary welfare of any people. Just the opposite is supposed to happen: that the church fosters and takes to herself, insofar as they are good, the ability, resources, and customs of each people. These the people of God 'heal, ennoble and perfect' (see LG 13, 17).

Following this line of thinking, the Constitution on the Sacred Liturgy, *Sacrosanctum Concilium* (SC), asserts that the church 'respects and fosters the spiritual adornments and gifts of various races and peoples.' Hence, 'even in liturgy, the Church has no wish to impose a rigid uniformity in matters which do not involve the faith or the good of the whole community.' Its commendation to use the vernacular in the celebration of the Eucharist is noteworthy (SC 54). Provided cultural elements are 'not indissolubly bound up with superstition and error,' these are to be studied with sympathy and, if possible, preserved intact. In fact, these elements may even be admitted into official liturgy 'as long as they harmonize with its true and authentic spirit' (SC 37).

The shift in theological method from one which started from doctrine to another which began with human experience also contributed greatly to the focusing on culture within church life. The neo-scholastic procedure starts with the presentation of official church teaching identified as the divinely revealed truths, followed by a justification from scripture and tradition and ended with a speculative elaboration. In this methodology experience and, therefore, culture are incidental, serving as mere occasions to apply in a practical way the doctrine presented in the very beginning. Human experience, which ought to be a constitutive element of every theological reflection, is in effect neglected. But GS, for its part, insists that the number of particularly urgent needs characterizing the present age needs to be considered 'in the light of the gospel and of human experience' (GS 46). Moreover, it suggests that theologizing should start with the 'joys and hopes, the griefs and anxieties of the people of this age', for these are the self-same joys, hopes, griefs and anxieties of the followers of Christ (GS 1). Such contemporary human experiences are better understood when the specifically cultural dimension of these experiences is earnestly taken into account. It is for this reason that the church as 'living in various circumstances during the course of time' has consistently used the resources of different cultures to evangelize, to theologize, to worship and to structure church life (GS 58). It 'has learned to express the message of Christ with the help of the ideas and terminologies of various peoples' for 'each nation develops the ability to express Christ's message in its own way' (GS 44).

Consequences of the Renewal in Vatican II

Official elaboration

This regaining of cultural sensitivity has had an increasing impact on the consciousness of the church's leadership beyond the time of the council. Pope Paul VI in his 1976 Apostolic Exhortation, *Evangelii Nuntiandi* (EN), declares that 'what matters is to evangelize human culture and cultures' (EN 20) as evidence that indeed culture has become a theological category of high import in our times. For him the effectiveness of evangelization is largely dependent of attention to culture (EN 63). Pope John Paul II introduced the term 'inculturation' as he understands it into official church language and utilized it in his 1979 apostolic exhortation, *Catechesi Tradendae* (CT) and in his 1990 encyclical, *Redemptoris Missio* (RM). The official *Catechism of the Catholic Church* acknowledges too that the 'foundation of local churches ... must involve a process of inculturation if the Gospel is to take flesh in each people's culture' (CCC 1994: art. 854).

A respectful and appreciative approach to culture

Another important consequence of the above theological shifts, particularly the one on theological method, is connected to, and yet is more than the anthropological shift which influenced the Council itself. It concerns the conciliar view that because of 'the many links between the message of salvation and human culture' and that revelation happens in and through culture (see GS 58), a respectful and appreciative approach to culture which we find in the Decree on the Church's Missionary Activity is most appropriate (see AG 11). This hermeneutics of appreciation (see de Mesa 2003: 112-71) regarding culture clearly differs from the earlier colonialist attitude exhibited by the majority of the Western missionaries evangelizing the peoples of the Third World which belittled local customs and traditions as irrelevant or worse as something to be done away with. Rather than harp on about the anthropological poverty of peoples or suspiciously judge culture as basically flawed, AG speaks of culture as 'treasures which a bountiful God has distributed among the nations of the earth.' It highlights the positive aspects of a given culture and exhorts everyone to 'learn' from them by 'sincere and patient dialogue'. And without letting go of its apppreciative stance, it is careful to point out that even these treasures, presumably not perfect, have need of the illumination that the gospel can bring.

Attention to the soteriological

Attention to the soteriological in culture also resulted from the theological shifts connected to inculturation in Vatican II. Overall inculturation can be seen as a process of experiencing within culture the salvific Word of God that both affirms and challenges it. As a particular endeavor, it is a vital way of making concrete John's declaration of what has been heard, seen, looked upon and touched with one's own hands as being proclaimed in order to foster intimate communion with God and with one another (see 1 Jn. 1:1-3). Inculturation sensitizes us to God's saving presence in and through our specific cultures which, ultimately, is us in particularity.

GS also hints at this soteriological aspect in the endeavor and process of inculturation. Salvation, as we have come to realize in theology and spirituality, is wholeness that includes both the historical and the transhistorical dimensions of well-being. The historical aspect of salvation is the minimum content of a Christian understanding of this divine gift. Yet even this dimension of salvation is complex. To elucidate this one can consider a scheme of seven anthropological constants suggested by the Dominican theologian, Edward Schillebeeckx (1983: 734-43). These are areas of our humanity within which salvation is to be experienced as truly human. Of the seven identified constants one is the conditioning of persons and people by culture. Vatican II asserts that 'it is a fact bearing on the very person of [human beings] that [they] can come to an authentic and full humanity only through culture ...' (GS 53). To be whole, people need cultural identity and integrity. If Christianity proclaims a message of salvation, and undeniably it does, then the promotion of the gospel must necessarily include the furtherance of a people's culture. Without meaning to equate it with the totality of salvation, we can still rightfully say that cultural identity and integrity constitute a soteriological issue.

The doing of theology in an inculturated manner

Because of the renewal wrought by the council, different terms like 'radical adaptation' to the culture, 'indigenization', 'localization', and 'inculturation' have been proposed to indicate the meaning and the process involved in integrating gospel and culture in a particular setting. Today the term 'contextualization' is at times regarded as synonymous to a broad interpretation of inculturation and at other times proposed as the more suitable term. It may be that only actual work on inculturation, which is undeniably the more important concern, that will show what sort of terminology will be most helpful.

An indicative summary of what has been done so far and how, is spelled out and illustrated in a most helpful manner by Stephen Bevans in *Models of Contextual Theology* (2002). Six models of inculturating the faith – the translation model, the anthropological model, the synthetic model, the praxis model, the transcendental model and the counter-cultural model – are pinpointed, described, critically analyzed and illustrated with the work of different theologians. Each model takes into account both the gospel and the culture as well as other contextual elements in its own special way. Actual use and benefit of a particular model really depends on what the context requires.

The above models demonstrate how a local church can tentatively re-appropriate the gospel culturally by ensuring the mutual interaction between the gospel and human experience. These focus on the dynamic and continuous construction of local theologies. Building on such methodological developments, the notion of 'prophetic dialogue' has been proposed to emphasize the dialogical nature of the inculturation process: a respectful listening to the culture, but also an alert prophetic stand whenever needed (Bevans and Schroeder 2004: 348-95; see Bevans and Schroeder 2011). But in a world that is increasingly becoming globalized, calls for attentiveness to interconnection, mutual affirmation and challenge are being made. As a result inculturation is already being spoken of as 'inter-culturation' (Bosch 1991: 455-57). In a world of cultural plurality interculturality is inevitable. In order to avoid the perception that what is intended is merely a cross-cultural interaction between local churches, it may be beneficial to suggest a term like 'inter-traditionality' that denotes a dialogue between local theological traditions. Such concept will have to build on inculturation as the specific utilization by a local church of its cultural resources to interpret, embody and express the faith, while taking into account the inter-cultural dynamics that is happening today. Its focus, however, will be the ongoing dialogue and the mutual learning of local churches regarding how each one has used and is using its cultural resources for inculturation. In this sense, a local theological tradition is created and developed vis-à-vis other local theological traditions.

The Future of Inculturation

The twentieth century has been most significant for the Roman Catholic church in terms of inculturation. Not only had there been a change in the fundamental understanding of culture and cultures in the church, inculturation has begun to be perceived as a challenge of utmost importance for mission in the coming decades (Bevans and Schroeder 2004: 387). The theological impact of such consciousness may perhaps be gleaned in the following assertions the Second Vatican Council had made on the subject: inculturation anthropologically presupposes the necessity of culture in the process of humanization (GS 53), theologically assumes that culture is potentially revelatory (GS 58), ecclesiologically takes for granted that inculturation is normal church practice, and missiologically believes that the church would be enriched when it enters into 'communion with various cultural modes' (GS 58).

There is also a practical component to the challenge of inculturation today, particularly for the Western European local church. It has to wrestle with the very same question that Jewish Christians had earlier faced: can the church be truly church without being Western European in its theology and practice? While the theoretical answer in the declarations of Vatican II is straightforward in the affirmative, the practical one appears to be ambiguous and reluctant. The Roman rite is to be kept intact as the main reference to inculturating the liturgy (Congregation for Divine Worship 1994). The *Catechism of the Catholic Church* speaking about the liturgy in relation to culture uses the term 'cultural adaptation' rather than 'inculturation' (CCC 1994: 1205-1206). The celebration of the Latin Mass is officially approved and encouraged. Pope John Paul II, believing that culture is something thoroughly ambiguous, taught that inculturation is a matter of 'how largely pre-set tradition and institution can have the greatest possible impact on any particular cultural situation while preserving what is good in that culture' (Doyle 1991 cited in Bevans 2002: 50). These instances would seem to indicate, as in earlier times, that the realization of inculturation will remain a struggle.

RECONCILIATION AS A MODEL OF MISSION

Robert J. Schreiter, CPPS

It has become commonplace in missiological circles to organize thought about mission through the use of paradigms or models. David Bosch's ground-breaking work on the history of mission (1991) first set the standard for thinking in this way by the use of the language of 'paradigms'. Such thinking continues to shape our description, analysis and critique of mission. In their magisterial work, *Constants in Context: A Theology of Mission for Today*, Stephen Bevans and Roger Schroeder (2004) speak of 'models' – both to describe historical forms of mission as well as reflect upon contemporary ones. If we use the idea of models as a heuristic device, Clifford Geertz's distinction (1973) of 'models of' (as descriptive) and 'models for' (as normative) is useful. By making this distinction as we think about approaches to mission, it allows us to see how models of mission arise out of the praxis of missionaries as a response to the world around them, as well as they might serve as normative theological models for appraising and guiding any future praxis.

I would like in this chapter to use the framework of models to examine one important development in mission that has occurred in the past quarter century; namely, the emergence of reconciliation as a model of and a model for mission. By so doing I hope to sketch something of how this model has been developed, and then turn to how it can help us see the *missio Dei* at work in the world today.

The Emergence of Reconciliation as a Model of Mission

The second half of the twentieth century ushered in both crisis and opportunity to the understanding of Christian mission. The struggle for independence from colonialism in many parts of the global south led to a profound questioning of the very nature of mission itself. Was it simply part of the imperial schemes of domination and exploitation of Europe? Should the presence of foreign missionaries in newly independent lands be tolerated at all? Such searching questions seared the very heart of mission as it had been understood among the churches of the global north, both churches in the newly founded World Council of Churches as well as the missionary religious orders in the Roman Catholic Church. For the latter, the breakthrough that refocused the crisis of the 'why' of mission into a renewed sense of the 'how' of mission came in the 1981 SEDOS Seminar on the Future of Mission (Lang and Motte 1982). There a hundred missionaries, mission scholars, and leaders of those missionary orders pondered together these questions of 'why' and 'how.' What resulted was a fourfold way of seeing the 'how' of mission: mission as (1) proclamation, (2) dialogue, (3) inculturation, and (4) liberation of the poor. The significance of this outcome was twofold. First of all, it focused more directly on the interaction of missionaries and those to whom they had been sent, rather than giving attention only to the task or charge to the missionary; this created a greater sense of mutuality in mission. Second, it made the concrete contexts of mission the starting point for reflection rather than *a priori* concept of mission. Or put another way, an effort to discern the *missio Dei* as it was unfolding in specific places provided the prompting toward renewed missionary praxis.

The fall of the Berlin Wall in 1989 and the dissolution of the Soviet Union were the first of a series of events that reshaped the context for mission. This demise of a bipolar world order had two immediate impacts that were to reverberate through mission. The freeing up of the nations once part of the Soviet bloc in Central and Eastern Europe opened the opportunity for a revitalization of the Christian churches there. But in the rush to rebuild and evangelize it became apparent that deep divisions ran through churches and society. Churches and church leaders had been severely compromised by being part of the surveillance network of government informers. This would have to be confronted and healed.

The second impact of this demise of a world order was to be seen in the upsurge in the number of armed conflicts taking place in countries of the global south and parts of the global north (especially the Balkan Peninsula), as well as the Rwandan genocide. The conflicts happened within countries rather than between countries. What this meant is that the rebuilding after the conflict was even more difficult since combatants were often neighbors. The genocide in Rwanda brought that point home even more. Missionaries often found themselves in the midst of violence and churches were often being called upon – as one of the few remaining credible actors in civil society – to lead peace processes and efforts at rebuilding society. These were tasks for which the churches were unprepared. The end of apartheid in South Africa put a spotlight on this role of the churches there in a special way.

Other events in the decade pushed missionaries and churches into roles as agents of reconciliation. The commemoration of the arrival of Christopher Columbus in the Americas prompted the United Nations to declare 1992 the Year of Indigenous Peoples. Indigenous peoples in the Americas, in Australia and New Zealand, and elsewhere used this opportunity to testify to their suffering (and in some places, near extinction) under domination by European colonial powers. This prompted nations and churches to consider how to heal these grievous wounds. The year 1994 saw the UN Conference on Women in Beijing, an event that underscored the worldwide pattern of violence against women.

The end of the bipolar political order and the consolidation of neoliberal capitalism as the sole worldwide economic system became more evident with the advance of globalization. The effects of globalization included an increase in migration (the majority of migrants are women and are Christian), more multicultural societies, greater polarization in societies (due to growing economic inequality around the world and social hyper-differentiation [enclaves of like-minded people who tend not to communicate with others who think differently] in wealthy cultures), and a compression of time and space through information technology and the media. These effects produce new fissures, divisions, and wounds in society, often at a quicker pace than such effects did in the past. Within the Roman Catholic Church in the United States and in countries in Europe, the revelation of the sexual abuse of minors by the clergy has added an additional layer of challenge for reconciliation and healing.

In the midst of all of these challenges arising from human interaction, yet another challenge began to loom ever more largely: climate change and the consequences this would have within the coming decades.

It is out of this miasma of violence and division that the theme of reconciliation began to surface as a compelling response to all that was happening in terms of mission (Schreiter 1992, 2001, 2005; De Gruchy 2002). By the turn of the twenty-first century, it had been a theme for the British and Irish Association of Mission Studies (2002), the WCC's Commission on World Mission and Evangelism (2005) and the International Association of Mission Studies (2008), as well as a perspective explored in the Lausanne Movement.

It had become evident that the world was in need of reconciliation in some many places and in so many different ways. Reconciliation – with its implications for healing and for service – was something people expected to find in the churches. The churches and missionaries found themselves drawn into work for reconciliation at many different levels. Why did the events of the 1990s spawn such an interest? Some suggest that the utopian visions that had played such a role beginning in the optimistic 1960s (in the theology of hope and the theologies of liberation) had crumbled in the face of the challenges that the end of the Cold War era now portended. Reconciliation was a more modest way of building the future by attending especially to healing past wounds that could compromise future well-being – be it the wounds of war, of social injustice, of exploitation of the earth. We are probably still too close to all these events to have a clearer picture. What is clear, however, is that reconciliation provided a model of twenty-first century mission. We now turn to how reconciliation is a model *for* mission, based on scripture and a theology of reconciliation arising out of missionary praxis today.

Reconciliation as a Model for Mission

The theme of reconciliation is prominent in the scriptures although it is spoken of directly very little. The word 'reconciliation' does not appear in the Hebrew scriptures, although there are powerful stories of reconciliation, such as that of Esau and Jacob, and of Joseph and his brothers. Even in the New Testament, the language of reconciliation is largely to be found in the Pauline writings. Indeed, Paul's message has been called a 'gospel of reconciliation' inasmuch as he had experienced being reconciled to God and the followers of Jesus by a gracious act on the part of God, not due to anything he himself had done.

Most of the earlier theological literature on reconciliation focused on what has been called the 'vertical' dimension of reconciliation; that is, God's reconciling humanity to God's own self. Indeed, this vertical dimension constitutes the central Christian narrative of what God has done for humanity. It is presented concisely in Romans 5:1-11: while we were still sinners, Christ died for us so that we might be reconciled to God. It is this vertical dimension that the sacraments – baptism, Eucharist, and reconciliation especially – draw upon as their source and place in Christian life.

The interest in reconciliation as a model for mission that began in the 1990s continues to draw its life from this vertical dimension. What is new is the deeper exploration of the 'horizontal' dimension of reconciliation; that is, reconciliation between humans, as individuals and as groups. This too is rooted in Pauline teaching, especially 2 Corinthians 5:17-20, Ephesians 2:12-20, and its cosmic consummation in Christ in Ephesians 1:10 and Colossians 1:20. Christians believe that such horizontal reconciliation is possible precisely because it is rooted in God's action of reconciliation of all creation to God's own self.

What might be seen as the characteristics of this horizontal reconciliation as understood by Christians? I would note five basic points.

First of all, reconciliation is first and foremost the work of God, who makes it a gift to us in which we in turn are called to cooperate. From a theological point of view, only God can bring about reconciliation. It is based in the very *missio Dei* of God in the world. And the ministry of reconciliation is entrusted to us, as ambassadors for Christ's sake. Our work for reconciliation, then, is in cooperation with God's grace.

Second, God begins the reconciling process with the healing of the victim. Christians believe that God looks out in a special way for the victims and the marginalized generally; this is encapsulated in Catholic Social Teaching's option for the poor. This does not ignore or exonerate the wrongdoer. Rather, it recognizes that the wrongdoer sometimes does not repent. The healing of the victim is thus not totally dependent upon the wrongdoers' remorse and apology. The healing of the victim can even create the social space in which the wrongdoer can come to repent.

Third, reconciliation makes of both victim and wrongdoer a 'new creation' (2 Cor. 5:17). That is to say, the healing that takes place is not a return to the *status quo ante*, but takes all the parties involved to a new place, often a place that they could not have imagined.

Fourth, the release from suffering is patterned on the passion, death and resurrection of Christ. Christians believe that suffering in and of itself is destructive. It can only become redemptive for individuals and for societies if it is patterned onto a narrative larger than itself. This narrative is that of the suffering, death and resurrection of Christ, the central part of the larger narrative of God's reconciliation of the world to God's own self. Only by being patterned onto the narrative of Christ's suffering and death can we hope to come to know the power of the resurrection (see Phil. 3:10-11).

Fifth and finally, reconciliation will only be complete when God has reconciled the whole universe in Christ (Eph. 1:10), when God will be 'all in all' (1 Cor. 15:28). This accounts for why we typically experience every effort at reconciliation we undertake as ultimately incomplete. We are reminded that reconciliation is not only a goal or end; it is also a process in which we are called to cooperate.

If this provides the theological framework for reconciliation as a model for mission – based as it is on the *missio Dei* itself – what are its concrete manifestations, and what are the practices that move the reconciliation process along?

The concrete manifestations that reconciliation is taking place are often talked about as *healing*. For individuals, reconciliation might be seen as the restoration of their humanity; that is, their refulgence as having been created in the image and likeness of God. This healing affects their agency or capacity to act. It restores their dignity. It rebuilds broken relationships with self, with others, and with God. For societies, reconciliation means coming to terms with a destructive past that often remains toxic for the present and unduly delimits the future. It means assuring that the wrongful deeds in the past cannot be repeated in the future. Put another way, reconciliation is about healing wounds, rebuilding trust, and restoring right relationships.

What then are the practices of a ministry of reconciliation that make up reconciliation as a model for mission? I would like to note four of them here.

The first is *healing*. Healing is extended into three dimensions: the healing of memories, the healing of victims and the healing of wrongdoers. The healing of memories involves coming to terms with the traumatic memories of the past in such a way that they are no longer toxic to the present and the future. This requires reconstituting the narratives we have about the past. Memories are powerful vehicles of both individual and collective identity. How we narrate the past shapes how we relate to the past. To attempt simply to repress the memories of a traumatic past does not erase the past; rather, it sets the stage for what Freudians have called 'the return of the repressed'. It can portend a return of violence through revenge, retaliation or victims themselves turning into perpetrators.

The healing of victims, as already noted, is about restoring their humanity, theologically understood; that is, their dignity, their relationships and their violated rights. Their own narratives about the past will need to be reconstructed. This entails acknowledging loss, lamenting what has been lost, and finding new sources of meaning and hope.

The healing of perpetrators is best mapped out by the Western Christian tradition of penitential practices as set forth in the early church, however they might today be enacted. Acknowledging wrongdoing, seeking forgiveness, promising amendment of life, and accepting punishment are all part of those practices. The ancient tradition of separation of the penitent from the community may need to be practiced, because perpetrators – by their deeds – have separated themselves from the community and have to go through a process of gestation and rebirth before they can be readmitted to the human family.

The second practice is *truth-telling*. Situations that call for reconciliation often become saturated with lies and are muffled under palls of silence. Breaking through a culture of lies and a culture of silence that sustains those lies is a key part of reconciliation. Truth-telling involves testimony to what really happened in the past, and a common effort to reconstruct a public truth. The Truth and Reconciliation Commission in South Africa has helped us see the four dimensions of that public truth: objective truth (the who, what, when and where of events), narrative truth (the why or possible meaning and causality of events), dialogical truth (a narrative where conflicting sides can discover their own and others' truth), and moral truth (what lesson can be drawn from the past for the future). Such practices of truth-telling help establish a culture of truthfulness for the future, as envisioned in the Hebrew concept of *'emet*: trustworthiness, dependability, and reliability.

The third practice of reconciliation as mission is the *pursuit of justice*. Truth-telling must in some measure precede the pursuit of justice, lest efforts at justice turn into revenge or 'victors' justice'. Specifically three forms of justice come into view here. The first is punitive justice: the punishment of wrongdoers to impress upon them their wrongdoing and to say publicly that such wrongdoing will not be tolerated in the future. This is justice for the wrongdoer and the state. The second form of justice is restorative justice, which is directed toward the healing of victims. It may involve restitution and reparation, as well as opportunities to explore how to rebuild a just and meaningful society. The third form is structural justice, which involves changing social structures through deliberative and political processes in order to reduce economic, social and political structures in society becoming sites that promote and sustain injustice.

Within the discourse of human rights that is so central to the liberal model of peace building, there can be a tendency to reduce reconciliation to the pursuit of justice, or to say that there can be no reconciliation unless there is full justice. From the theological view this is an inadequate view of both justice and of reconciliation. As noted above, we do not experience full reconciliation – and therefore full justice – until all things have been brought together in Christ. Thus to demand the fulfillment of complete justice is can paralyze or obviate other practices going into the process of reconciliation.

The fourth practice of reconciliation is *forgiveness*. Forgiveness is itself a process, both for individuals and for societies. The process can be a long and difficult one. After social trauma, it is not uncommon that the work on forgiveness can take more than a generation. Difficult as it is, Christians believe that, with the grace of God once again, it is possible. It is God who forgives, and we participate in that forgiveness. It is not accidental that forgiveness is placed as the last of the four practices being considered here (although processes of reconciliation are rarely linear). There is a constant danger of cheap forgiveness or forgiveness being forced upon victims. There are fears that forgiveness means foregoing justice or punishment (it does not mean that). There are fears that forgiving requires forgetting (it does not; when we forgive we do not forget – we remember in a different way that is not toxic to the present and the future). Forgiveness entails coming to see that the wrongdoer is a child of God as is the victim. It does not condone the deed but seeks the rehabilitation of the wrongdoer. Without forgiveness, the past continues to determine the present and the future. Indeed, in the words of Archbishop Desmond Tutu, there is no future without forgiveness (1999).

Conclusion

Reconciliation as a model of and for mission will likely continue to gain relevance in the twenty-first century. A remarkable recent development is the way it is being introduced into international relations as an ethic, based upon the Abrahamic faith traditions, to bring about genuine peace (Philpott 2012). In a world where the presence of religion is being recognized as an important social force, both positive and negative (Shah et al. 2012), Christian mission as reconciliation may be able to contribute something significant both to the realization of the *missio Dei* and a better, more peaceful, and sustainable world.

MISSION AND CATHOLIC EDUCATION

Jim and Therese D'Orsa

This chapter seeks to address the often problematic nexus between missiology and Catholic education. Neither at the level of official Catholic documentation, nor at the level of practice, is this nexus as secure as it should be given that education is a major ministry of the Catholic Church.

The authors' social and cultural location is Australia where approximately 20% of all Australian school students attend Catholic schools. In 2009 over 54,000 teachers were engaged in this enterprise in nearly 1,700 schools. While there are 700,000 students attending these schools, nearly one third of these are from backgrounds other than Catholic (National Catholic Education Commission 2009: 2-29). The Catholic school systems are agencies of a church in which just 14% (approximately) of its self-declared membership regularly join the community in worship on a Sunday (Dixon, Kunciunas and Reid 2008: 3).

Nexus between Missiology and Education

These facts indicate some of the missional challenges faced by Catholic educators working in the schools. For them mission has a number of facets, some placing the focus inwards on what the school is attempting to achieve for students and teachers, and others placing it outwards on what is being attempted for parents and the wider community. While the school continues to educate students *in* faith, in many instances its best hope is to educate them *towards* faith.

There is a further consideration that needs to be acknowledged at the outset. Most of the missional work of the church is carried on by lay people in homes, workplaces, schools, and the public square. If the mission of the church is to be effected, the education of Catholics is a vital consideration. Here both the home and the school play a crucial role.

Obviously then, school leaders and teachers need a sound mission theology to guide the day-to-day life of the school so that it may be an effective vehicle for the mission of the local church. However, like other areas of ministry, education is a victim of the lack of impact of mission theology on the total life of the church. In general, missiologists tend to speak to missiologists and other theologians, and educators speak to educators. The focus of our work has been to open up lines of communication so that, through dialogue, educators can benefit from sound mission theology. In this process missiologists also gain new insight into the demands of mission as they work with educators helping them understand and address their major mission challenges. The benefit of a dialogue between missiologists and educators lies in its potential to refocus the work of schools by sharpening the mission theology of school leaders who, in our experience, are prone to confuse mission thinking with strategic planning.

Mission as Purpose

When educators speak of mission they use the term with its commonly accepted meaning. In this usage 'mission' means purpose – the considered reason we do what we do. By extension, 'mission' has come to incorporate what an organization or group *actually does* to achieve its purpose. This usage is evident in school mission statements that spell out the mission directions which focus strategic planning in important ways. When educators discuss the church's mission, they think of it largely within this understanding.

In many dioceses there is a developing practice of the local church attempting to make its mission directions concrete through the development of pastoral plans. In Australia it is becoming common for the mission directions of Catholic school systems to reflect a high degree of alignment with the pastoral plan of the local diocese. There are many benefits to having the diocesan planning cycle and the school system's planning cycle moving together when this is possible. However, the purpose of education in a modern democracy is not established exclusively to enhance or complement diocesan goals, important as this is. The mission of the school is also set in response to the need to prepare young people to live and flourish in a world characterized by the growing phenomena of globalization, pluralization of societies, and the new manifestations of secularization, which are impacting in various ways on all societies. It is a world in which competing worldviews clamor for space on the educational agenda of a public curriculum mandated for all schools.

The ambiguities inherent in our present context mean that, for many young people, life is experienced as fragmented and lived mainly in the 'now' because they see the future as uncertain. Young people create their worldview from fragments of the traditions they encounter in the course of their education. None of these traditions, including the Christian tradition, is taken as authoritative. The consequence is that young people are often quite uncertain about their personal beliefs, even when they are the beneficiaries of a solid religious education (Hughes 2007: 143).

Today in many Western countries society operates on the basis of an ephemeral consensus that often serves as the basis for moral decisions, and people's attitudes and lives are increasingly shaped by the dictates of political correctness. There is a progressive tendency to politicize values and to secularize morality. This is the context in which Catholic educators seek to help young people construct a worldview, develop their talents, and put them at the service of others. This is no small mission challenge!

Mission Theology and the Epistemological Challenge

In our modern/post-modern world a serious dialogue between missiology and education seems long overdue. One of the positive contributions missiologists bring to this dialogue is an understanding of *culture* and *worldview* and the important role these play in the life of an individual, of society, and hence in mission theology. Another allied understanding is the way in which the *spirit of an age* shapes culture by changing human aspiration (D'Orsa and D'Orsa 2010: 175-93). Missiologists have been particularly active in exploring the mission challenges posed by the shift from modernity to what is often called post-modernity (e.g. Bosch 1991: 349-62, Hiebert 2008: 141-240). Much of the thinking about culture, worldview and the modern to post-modern shift, has yet to filter through to Catholic educators.

Catholic education, like most school education, operates largely out of a modern worldview with its roots in the Enlightenment, the assumptions of which are so much a part of the culture of school education that they remain substantially unexamined and unacknowledged. This worldview is conveyed to students more or less by default. The Catholic Church has a long history of wariness with respect to the modern worldview, particularly its designation of 'public knowledge' and the relegation of faith to the status of 'personal opinion'. The post-modern critique of modernity also challenges the modern construction of knowledge and raises important issues about how individuals construct their worldview and how trustworthy these processes are. One consequence of this critique, noted in a number of major studies into the worldview of young people, is that the latter are quite uncertain about their personal beliefs (see Hughes 2007 and Smith 2005). This affects their attitude to religion in particular. Since a central aim of Catholic education is to promote a worldview that is Christian in its orientation and Catholic in its character, addressing these *epistemological concerns* is important if the Catholic school is to be effective in its mission. They are therefore, *prima facie*, missiological concerns.

The epistemological dimension of Catholic missiology seems underdeveloped by comparison with the work undertaken by contemporary Protestant missiologists (e.g. Hiebert 2008 and Kirk 2007). Few Catholic missiologists have made a significant contribution in helping Catholic educators deal with one of their major challenges – addressing the issues posed by the pervasive pluralism that young people, wishing to be seen as tolerant, often equate with relativism. It is insufficient to decry relativism; what is required is foundational work that addresses in a meaningful way how young people construct knowledge, so that they and their teachers have greater confidence in their pursuit of truth.

Mission Returns to the Heart of the Church

The historical separation of mission and ecclesiology, its recent reversal in response to the extraordinary challenges of a new missional environment, and the enshrining of that reversal in official church documentation, are significant aspects of the contemporary narrative of Catholicism. Up until quite recent times, the Catholic community worldwide has operated from a seriously deficient theology of mission, echoes of which are to be found in the church's documents on education. It is both noteworthy and extraordinary that, in the entire corpus of recent Vatican documents relating to Catholic education, there are only three substantive references to the major church documents on mission and evangelization. The deficiency in mission theology can be substantiated quite readily by tracing the significant developments in the church's official teaching on mission and evangelization across the past half century (D'Orsa and D'Orsa 2010: 134-52). In its official documentation, the church has reclaimed the original understanding of mission as we have it in the New Testament, *locating mission at the heart of the church.*

It is important to understand how this perspective was lost if we are to appreciate the significance of reclaiming it. The New Testament communities were confronted with different mission challenges from those faced by Jesus and members of the apostolic generation who lived and ministered in a Jewish cultural context. In the post-resurrection period, and in dramatically changed circumstances, the leaders of these communities recognized that a new missional environment required them to understand the call to discipleship in new ways. The worldview they inherited from the apostolic generation needed to expand as its premises were simply too restrictive to encompass new mission challenges. While they found this situation challenging and disconcerting, in time they came to see the Spirit at work in the life of community, an insight especially dear to the writer of Luke and Acts (see Brown 1984: 31-60 and Bevans and Schroeder 2004: 10-31).

The shift that occurred as history moved forward saw later church leaders lose sight of this founding inspiration. The development of mission theology, which had been spurred on by the demands of a changing missional environment, came to a substantial halt once Christianity became the religion of empire. The mission impetus became submerged as theological interest turned inwards. It resurfaced from time to time across future centuries, but its concerns and questions were never again to have the level of impact on the development of either ecclesiology or theology that they had in the early centuries of Christianity. A church that had once interpreted mission primarily in terms of the action of the Spirit at work in the world had became self-sufficient. For many of its members, the church became the kingdom of God on earth.

Reworking the Christian Worldview: The Mission Challenge

In contrast to the present, the church throughout most of its history lacked the means of communication and the structures to allow insights from the missional frontier to impact sufficiently on its theology and life. In addition, historical developments focused the church's attention in a range of other ways. Even during the eras when Christianity expanded into the new world of the Americas, and subsequently into Africa and Asia, it did so under the impetus of an inadequate mission theology.

In the late twentieth century this situation has changed. *The missional context has become the global context.* New structures within the church, and new means of communication, expedited a change of outlook. The Christian worldview is again expanding to encompass the demands of the new missional environment generated by globalization. Mission is being reformulated in response to such factors as new configurations of privilege and poverty; regional conflicts with accompanying human cries for reconciliation; recognition of the presence of indigenous inhabitants and the implications for justice and reconciliation; the growing acceptance of the equality of women in many societies and the new aspirations of women in others; mass migration of peoples including refugees created by famine, conflict and persecution; and the presence of peoples of all the major faiths in most cities and regions of the world, with the consequent need for inter-religious dialogue. These are just some of the major contextual challenges that mission now embraces.

Education in Mission

We have been reminded by the Second Vatican Council that not only is the church community, *in its entirety*, missional by nature, but also why this is so (AG 2). The origin of the church's mission is Trinitarian. It lies in God's life of overflowing love, God's loving purpose in entering into human history in the person of Jesus, and the subsequent sending of the Holy Spirit. This perspective is now foundational to education in mission.

In the period since the Second Vatican Council Christian communities, often from an embattled position, and again conscious of the need to discern the Spirit at work in the world, are allowing the concerns and challenges of mission to shape theology. There is now wide recognition that the mission of the church can take a number of *forms* that have different levels of relevance in different parts of the world and different social contexts. There is also recognition that each form must *proclaim* the message of Jesus in both word and witness, and that this proclamation needs to be accompanied by a process of *dialogue* (D'Orsa and D'Orsa

2010: 151-52). Effective witness prompts people to ask why Christians do what they do. 'Always be ready to give an explanation to anyone who asks you for a reason for your hope' (1 Pet. 3:15). Proclamation (by word and witness) and dialogue are the *essential modalities* of mission. Education in mission needs to address this distinction as far too many church leaders, when talking of evangelization, consistently *confuse its modalities with its forms*. The clarity now emerging in this matter should prompt educators to consider the huge potential education has to further the church's evangelizing mission in its fundamental modalities and the various forms that these take in different contexts. This is unlikely to happen without appropriate *education in mission*.

There is now also wider recognition within the church that mission is primarily *God's mission*, and that the church's mission is situated within the broader reality of God's purpose in the universe and in our world. As a consequence, greater attention is paid to culture, understood as a people's way of life, and both the milieu and a powerful means by which God's mission is effected. There are significant differences between how culture is understood and treated in mission theology and how it is addressed in Vatican documentation on Catholic education. These differences need to be addressed as part of teachers' education in mission.

The concept of *communio* developed by Pope John Paul II (NMI 43), is a new theme in missiology, one capable of much further development. As used by the pope, it implies something deeper than structures; it has the nature and status of a fundamental spiritual orientation (Norris 2008: 5). The sense of the church as a *communio-in-mission* is now increasingly understood as a manifestation of the identity of the Catholic Church, and the value of its extension to the entire Christian church is obvious. *Communio-in-mission* creates an expectation that local churches will support each other in mission as a consequence of being part of a communion. A theology and spirituality of communion has an important place in the development of an understanding among Catholics in Western countries as to why their parish priest may be newly arrived from Nigeria, India, the Philippines etc.; or why it is appropriate to ensure students form relationships with young Christians in other parts of the world.

If the local churches form a *communio-in-mission*, then *communio* can, and must, also exist *within* these churches. This has consequences for how agencies in mission think of themselves and how they see themselves in relationship to each other. This understanding is clearly relevant to the nexus between missiologists and educators.

We began this paper by considering the 'mission of education' and have subsequently highlighted some important themes in 'education for mission'. It is impossible in our view to sustain the one without the other, yet efforts in this vital area of education within the Catholic community seem minimal. The reconnection of mission and theology is an important first step. While this reconnection has implications for *all ministries* and for the style of theological reflection used within them, it has special relevance for Catholic education given the mission challenges that exist in this field at the present time.

There seems to be a developing sense among Catholic educators that they form a *communio-in-mission*. Despite the different circumstances in which they operate, they face common challenges and have the capacity to inspire new hope in each other, assuming that there are means for the various narratives of Catholic schooling to be communicated. Catholic schools in England and Wales, for example, are doing great work in exploring the mission of the Catholic school in the context of a multi-faith and multicultural society. In the United States, despite great financial pressures, there is exemplary practice in placing Catholic education at the service of the marginalized in major urban centers. In our own country, Australia, Catholic schools are at the service of people wanting a faith-based education including those living in rural and regional areas as well as cities. Delivering such education has required a generous pooling of resources. The exchange and exposure programs, sponsored by religious orders and dioceses for Australian teachers and students, involving counterparts in Asia, Africa, South America and Oceania, have opened up the exemplary missional practices in these countries.

A most significant initiative, one that has the potential to promote both awareness and global communion for mission, is the initiative of the Centre for Research and Development in Catholic Education based within the University of London. In publishing a journal, *International Studies in Catholic Education*, as a vehicle for bringing important research-based initiatives in Catholic education to the attention of Catholic educators worldwide, the centre provides a previously unavailable opportunity for Catholic educators to benefit from each other's initiatives in a spirit of mutual support and enrichment. It is a vital example of *communio-in-mission*.

One of the major challenges for leaders in Catholic education systems is to help teachers understand the mission of the Catholic school and the significance of their work *in a global context*. Too often the imaginal horizon of educators, with respect to mission, lies inside the school gate. Education in mission needs to address this form of myopia and, for those teaching in schools, recapture the missiological imagination that drove developments in the early church. Catholic education needs to reclaim a heritage that has been lost. Again, education in mission is essential if this is to occur.

The Mission and Education Project: A Particular Response

In the Australian context the *Mission and Education Project* is a concerted effort by Catholic school systems to deal with the challenges of re-connection discussed above, *recognizing mission at the heart of Catholic education*. The project is supported by twenty Catholic education systems across the country, opening up a dialogue between Catholic education and missiology, focused on meeting the missional demands faced by schools in contemporary Australia. The Catholic education systems face similar, but also some quite different, missional challenges, scattered as they are across a vast continent including rural, regional and urban dioceses.

The *Mission and Education Project* takes the form of a book series with two titles to be published each year reflecting the mission concerns and priorities of the participating school systems. The genesis of particular titles in the series lies in research carried out, or commissioned, by the systems themselves and the common concerns such projects address. This work, and the people driving it, are brought into dialogue with contemporary missiology primarily, but not exclusively, through the staff of the Mission and Culture faculty of the Broken Bay Institute in Sydney.

In 2010 we published the first title in the series, *Explorers Guides and Meaning-makers: Mission Theology for Catholic Educators* (D'Orsa and D'Orsa 2010) as a foundational document to underpin the series. Its goals are to help educators develop a mission theology by gaining skills in theological reflection on the challenges faced in their day-to-day work. In 2012 the book *Catholic Curriculum: A Mission to the Heart of Young People* was published which explores how the Catholic worldview can be presented to young people in a way that is meaningful to them. This is to be followed by *Leading for Mission: Integrating Life, Culture and Faith in Catholic Education* (forthcoming), which deals with the nexus between mission thinking, strategic thinking and operational thinking in school settings. Beyond 2011 it is expected that the series will deal with topics such as *Mission and Identity, Catholic Pedagogy, School Improvement for Mission*, and *Parish-School Connection: Models and Prospects*. While the *Mission and Education Project* is developed out of the Australian context, the aim of the series is to be at the service of mission on behalf of the kingdom of God, contributing to a wider conversation within the communion of communities that comprises Catholic education globally.

Conclusion

In conclusion, we return to a key issue: that the mission of the church is carried out in the world, predominantly by lay people. Education plays a crucial role in preparing the next generation of people to carry forward Jesus' mission in their homes, workplaces and the broader society. However, the majority of those involved in delivering such education, that is missiologists, are clergy and religious. There is a pressing need to develop *lay missiologists* if education in mission, and hence mission itself, is to be sustained, and the challenges facing laity in mission are to be adequately addressed. This is an issue that church leaders now need to address as a matter of some urgency. It provides a sharp edge at the nexus between missiology and education.

MISSION AND MIGRATION

Gioacchino Campese, CS

Introduction

The Mission Comes to Us: this is the title of a collection of essays published in Italian on the most recent instruction by the Pontifical Council for the Pastoral Care of Migrants and Itinerant People, *Erga Migrantes Caritas Christi* (The Love of Christ towards Migrants), which was issued in 2004 (Battistella, ed. 2005; EMCC 2004). Certainly the delegates who participated to the Edinburgh World Missionary Conference in 1910 would not normally have thought of mission in this way. They were cast in the framework of Christendom and they saw the world as more or less clearly divided into two sides: the already evangelized, the Christian Western world, and the still to be evangelized, parts of what today would be called the global south (see Stanley 2006). The task of the former was to leave their countries and go as missionaries to evangelize the non-Christians.

Interestingly, Edinburgh 1910 happens during the period of what has been named the Great European Migration (1800-1914) toward the Americas, Oceania and East and South Africa which involved up to 60 million people (see Hanciles 2008: 378 and Castles and Miller 2009: 87), but this massive phenomenon does not appear to have been of much concern to the participants of this momentous missionary conference. This was precisely because it was mostly a movement of people within what was considered Christendom.

A century later the phrase 'mission comes to us', even if not the most suitable formula for mission today, pushes Christian believers from the Western world to begin thinking differently about mission – starting from the reality of migration. Christian mission, as we have just seen, had been in the past understood and practiced as *missio ad gentes*, that is, the mission to evangelize the 'pagan' nations often mired in poverty and, from a colonial viewpoint, not even 'civilized'. This was a task reserved to a few people, trained 'professional' missionaries mostly belonging to religious orders and missionary societies, and it entailed crossing national, and consequently cultural, linguistic and religious, boundaries.

Migration has been changing these conditions because today millions of people from the global south have arrived and settled in the Western world. Christian believers who normally supported the ministry of 'their' missionaries and came to know about Africans, Asians and Latin

Americans through talks, pictures, documentaries and even some short trips
to these foreign and exotic lands, find themselves in a wholly different
situation. Today, people seen previously only in photos and documentary
films are now walking in our streets and living in our neighborhoods,
worshipping in our churches. It was easier to deal with them when they
were in the 'mission territories'. Their presence on 'our' turf, which is not
normally considered as a 'mission land', often provokes strange reactions
within Christian communities often still influenced by the Christendom
pattern.

The questions posed to missiology by the transformations brought about
by human mobility (i.e. migration) are many and far-reaching. For
example: if mission does not necessarily mean to go to 'them' because it
comes to 'us', what is then Christian mission today? And from a Christian
perspective and in a world in which migration facilitates the
encounter/clash of people from different nationalities, cultures, and
religions is it correct to continue to speak in terms of 'us' and 'them'? Who
are 'us' and who are 'them' in a Christian community and in a world in
which hyphenated existence (e.g. Mexican-Americans or Italo-Nigerians) is
no longer the exception, but is becoming the norm? The phenomenon of
human mobility brings these and many other important issues to the
attention of missiological thinking, and it is the objective of this article to
explore some of them.

This essay will be divided into four main sections. The first will
overview the rediscovery of the theme of migration by the theology of
mission in the last decade. In the second, human mobility will be
considered as a main context of Christian missiology today. The third
section will reflect on migration as a *locus missiologicus*, that is as a
fundamental theological source for missiological thinking (see Campese
2010: 1019-24 and Bevans forthcoming). In the fourth and final section
cross-cultural friendship will be highlighted as an essential dimension of
mission in the context of migration.

Theology of Mission Rediscovers Migration

The rediscovery of migration by missiology has occurred at the beginning
of the twenty-first century in a global landscape that is in many ways very
different from that in which Edinburgh 1910 occurred. Here we will
enunciate just four elements of this new landscape.

First, the main migration flows are mostly from global south to global
north or the Western world. There are also movements of people from
south to south, especially refugees and migrants who do not have the
minimal resources to go north, and from north to north, particularly highly
skilled workers and managers who go wherever their skills are better paid.
But what has really captured the attention of public opinion, politics, and
media are the massive flows of migrants from the so-called 'Third World'

to the so-called 'First World'. This phenomenon, often depicted negatively in terms of 'invasion', is transforming in many ways the Western world.

Second, the make-up of world Christianity has changed drastically. The delegates who participated to Edinburgh 1910, most of whom were men from Great Britain and the USA (see Robert 2011), shape a picture that portrays quite well the composition of Christianity at that time. In 1900 only 18% of the world's Christian population lived outside Europe and the USA. Today more than 60% of the Christian population resides outside the West and by 2025 this figure is expected to rise to 70%. Moreover by 2025 half of the Christians in the world will come from Africa and Latin America (see Jenkins 2002: 2-3 and Hanciles 2008: 121-23). Already in 1974 Swiss Roman Catholic missiologist Walbert Bühlmann, in a groundbreaking book entitled *The Coming of the Third Church*, was anticipating this dramatic shift in world Christianity by reflecting on the profound implications of the estimate that by the year 2000 58% of the world Christian population would come from the southern hemisphere (Bühlmann).

Third, one of the key consequences of the transformation of the make-up of global Christianity is represented by a new and fundamental development in Christian mission. The missionaries who participated in Edinburgh 1910 left with a glimpse of what the Christian worldwide church should be, a truly Catholic church, in which all peoples and cultures contribute to express and communicate the good news of Jesus Christ. They had a glimpse of what it meant to reflect and pray together regardless of denominations and so it is legitimate to consider this also as a pioneer event of the modern ecumenical movement (Robert 2011: 57). Yet Edinburgh 1910 remains substantially a portrait of how Christians understood mission during that time. According to the Christian missiology and demographics of the beginning of the twentieth century, mission was an enterprise performed by a few specialized people 'from the West to the rest.' The powerful shift of Christianity toward the global south and vast migration flows have made possible also important and numerous missionary movements 'from the rest to the West' (see Vethanayagamony 2010 and Walls 1996).

Fourth, mission theology has gone through some significant transformations since Edinburgh 1910 (see Phan 2003: 32-44). Among others, three groundbreaking events stand out in this process of theological transformation of mission: the International Missionary Council conference of Willingen in 1952 where the concept of *missio Dei* was initially conceived (see Bosch 1991: 389-93 and Bevans and Schroeder 2004: 286-304); the World Council of Churches conference in Mexico City in 1963 whose final message described mission as 'the common witness of the whole church, bringing the whole Gospel to the whole world' (see Robert 2011: 61); and finally the Second Vatican Council (1962-1965), in the Decree on the Missionary Activity of the Church (AG 2), which affirmed that 'The pilgrim Church is missionary by her very nature, since it is from the mission of the Son and the mission of the Holy Spirit that she draws her origin, in accordance with the decree of God the Father' (see Bevans and Gros 2009: 3-148). Karl Rahner correctly interpreted this Council as the first major event in which the Roman Catholic church was actualized as a 'world church' (Rahner 1979).

To these three events correspond three essential tenets of contemporary missiology. First, the main protagonist of mission is God, not the Christian churches. Christian believers in fact participate in a mission that has been initiated, is brought forward and is entrusted to them by God, who is Holy Mystery, in Jesus Christ and through the Holy Spirit. The Trinitarian Christian God is a missionary God, a God who does not just have a mission, but a God who is mission, infinite love that reaches out to the whole creation. Second, the church does not have a mission, but God who is mission has a church of followers who are invited to continue to proclaim, witness to and serve the good news of the reign of God. The 'whole church', and not just some of its members, is missionary by its very nature, and it is the Trinitarian mission that shapes it and not vice versa. Third, mission does not start in some particular place and is not directed to some other particular location. Its location is the 'whole world' (Bevans and Schroeder 2011: 9-18). There are not 'mission territories' and 'territories that do not need mission'. Mission is from 'anywhere to anywhere' or 'from everywhere to everywhere' (Walls 2008: 202-4; George 2011; Nazir-Ali 2009) and its content is the 'whole gospel'.

The concept of the 'whole gospel' leads our reflection to a key issue in missiology, that is, the multi-faceted character of mission that has been enunciated by John Paul II in the Encyclical *Redemptoris Missio* (RM 1990): 'mission is a single but complex reality, and it develops in a variety of ways' (RM 41). Different missiologists have attempted to elucidate this complexity (e.g. Bosch 1991 and Kirk 1999) but here we will just mention one of the most recent and insightful syntheses of this fundamental debate that has been proposed by Stephen Bevans and Roger Schroeder. According to these two scholars the essential elements of mission, that they list under the definition of mission as 'prophetic dialogue', are six: 1) witness and proclamation; 2) liturgy, prayer and contemplation; 3) justice, peace and the integrity of creation; 4) inter-religious dialogue; 5) inculturation; 6) reconciliation (see Bevans 2003; Bevans and Schroeder 2004: 348-95; Bevans and Schroeder 2011).

It is within this new landscape that migration has started to become a missiological issue. Going back to John Paul II's words: 'Mission is a single but complex reality, and it develops in a variety of ways. Among these ways, some have particular importance in the present situation of the Church and the world' (RM 41). This sentence leaves no doubt as to the relevance of a specific situation in the way mission is understood and develops. It is also important to add that a particular situation tends to underscore some aspects of mission that have not been previously taken into due consideration or have been ignored. So it should not be a surprise that, in the present situation of the world and the church, characterized as never before in human history by the movements of peoples, a structural aspect of Christian mission such as migration has started to acquire a particular importance in theological thinking for social, ecclesial, pastoral and theological or, in this case, missiological, reasons (see Campese 2012 and 2012b).

Actually, however, it is surprising that the first more specific and systematic essays on the relation between migration and mission have started to appear only at the beginning of the 2000s (see Barrena Sánchez 2001). Before that we had some stimulating reflections on the model of missionary as stranger as central to Christian mission and on a spirituality for missionaries ministering with migrants, but no well-organized attempt to approach the subject of mission and human mobility (see Gittins 1989: 111-38; Bevans 1991: 50-53; Gittins 2002:121-60; Campese 1997).

Andrew Walls, one of the leading scholars of global Christianity and mission, writes an article on the importance of the 'diaspora factor' in the expansion of World Christianity, which was to be followed by other essays (Walls 2002b; 2005; 2008). In 2003 *Missiology*, the journal of the American Society of Missiology, published the proceedings of its annual conference the previous June and included articles on mission and migration by Christine D. Pohl, Samuel Escobar, Jan A. B. Jongeneel, Enoch Wan, and Jean Stromberg (see *Missiology* 2003 31.1). In the same year was published the first article on this theme by Jehu Hanciles, a mission historian from Sierra Leone, then teaching at Fuller Theological Seminary in California (now at Emory University, Atlanta). Hanciles has now arguably become the outstanding and most influential scholar of the inherent connection between mission and migration in world Christianity (Hanciles 2008b; 2003; 2004; 2011).

In the following years other missionaries and scholars have considered the implications of human mobility for the development of Christian mission particularly in the European and Asian continent, underlining the fact that this issue had received little theological and missiological attention (see Palomino 2004; Rigoni 2004; Colzani 2005; Ross 2005; Lussi 2005; LaRousse 2008; Rogers 2008; Kroeger 2008; Phan 2010). Stephen Bevans in 2008 published an important essay on mission and migration in which he distinguished between the mission of the church to and among migrants and the migrants as subjects of the mission of the church (Bevans 2008; Bevans and Gros 2009: 117-18). Noteworthy are also some articles on the multi-faceted role of migrants in the *missio Dei* from a biblical perspective (Ocaña 2007; van Engen 2010).

In 2010 and 2011 other important pieces have been added to the growing body of literature on mission and migration, each underscoring different dimensions of the intimate and unescapable relation between these two realities (Cruz 2010; Moreno 2010; Barreda 2010; Jackson 2011; Kim 2011; George 2011). Among the most recent writings on the theme stand out those of Italian missionary and scholar Gaetano Parolin who insists particularly on migration as a paradigm of mission today, that is, as a phenomenon that in its multidimensional nature helps define the very meaning of mission in our globalized world (Parolin 2010; 2010b; 2011). Intriguingly, Dietrich Werner, discussing the agenda of theological education today, starts from the insights of Edinburgh 1910 that affirmed the importance of theological education as an indispensable element of Christian mission, and lists migration as one of the six major specific challenges to theological formation for the twenty-first century. He rightly observes that 'the fundamental implications of global migration and increasingly diverse constituencies for programs of theological education have not yet been fully spelled out' (Werner 2011: 96).

Werner's observation clearly implies that the multiple implications of the connection between mission and migration will surely need more attention and reflection in the years to come since human mobility will remain one of the key issues of the twenty-first century. Yet, the now quite consistent body of literature that has been briefly surveyed shows that missiology is already understanding the centrality of this multidimensional phenomenon for Christian mission today. Most of the insights that have inspired the next two sections of this essay will be taken from these writings. For a much more thorough survey of the literature, see Campese 2012.

Migration as a Context of Mission Today

Robert Schreiter, in an article in which he discusses the transformations that occurred in the context of mission forty years after Vatican II, includes mass migration as one of the main demographic changes that define today's world and, consequently, today's church (Schreiter 2005b: 80-81). Certainly Schreiter does not mean to say here that migration has never before been part of the scenery of Christian mission. Since the very beginning the gospel has been handed on thanks to the migration networks of the Roman Empire and later of other empires and nations. In other words, through the centuries thanks to the mobility of believers and 'professional' missionaries the Christian gospel has reached the further ends of the earth. Hanciles remarks that it is not a coincidence that the greatest Christian missionary movements have been concomitant with the Great European Migration (1800-1914) (Hanciles 2008: 378). What Schreiter indicates here is rather that today, for multiple reasons such as the easier access to and rapidity of means of long-distance transportation, human mobility has reached unprecedented proportions: this is what has been called the globalization of migration in the sense that more and more countries are affected by migration flows and the acceleration of migration, which means that these flows are growing in the major regions of the world (Castles and Miller 2009: 10-11).

What does it mean for missiology to consider migration as a central element of the context in which Christian mission is occurring today? It means, in our opinion, at least to take seriously and reflect on the missionary implications of the main characteristics of and issues that emerge from contemporary human mobility. Here we will consider just a few of them with the help of some prominent migration scholars (Castles and Miller 2009; Portes and Rumbaut 2006; Massey, Durand and Malone 2002; Ambrosini 2011).

First, a missiology that wants to take seriously the complexity and centrality of migration today must be necessarily interdisciplinary. The church is certainly in touch with the lives of millions of migrants worldwide and theology of mission must dedicate attention and learn from their experiences, but this is not enough. Missiology has to enter into a permanent and constructive dialogue with other disciplines that study of human mobility, such as history, sociology, anthropology, psychology, demographics, and economics in order to have a more adequate picture of such a multi-faceted phenomenon.

Second, the globalization and acceleration of migration means not only that the number of migrants in the world is progressively growing and there is hardly a country in the world that is not affected by human mobility, it means also that movement of peoples create more cultural and religious plurality even in countries that have been considered, often erroneously, quite homegeneous in cultural and religious terms. Missiology is challenged by this growing pluralism and the transformations that it causes in societies and Christian communities, and so it must concretely equip itself and Christian believers to deal with it by acquiring and providing the tools that facilitate inter-cultural and inter-religious dialogue.

Third, migration has become one of the most controversial political issues at national and international levels. The 'politicization' of migration requires a sustained national and international conversation in which all the parties involved, and especially the migrants themselves, are invited to the table to find ways to pursue the national and universal common good. The political debate about migration must be built on real facts, on an honest analysis of the causes and consequences of human mobility. Migration policies cannot be based on selfish economic interests, on racial and xenophobic motives, or even less on exclusivistic religious reasons. The human dignity of migrants must be protected against political campaigns and policies that scapegoat and 'alienize' them, that is, transforms them 'illegal aliens', which concretely means to treat people as less than human beings. Policies that endanger the lives of migrants (e.g. those resulting in the deaths of thousands of migrants on the U.S.-Mexican border and in the Mediterranean Sea) must be denounced and serious and global problems such as human trafficking and the exploitation of migrant labor must be dealt with effectively. The whole issue of irregular (undocumented) migration, a migration that is needed and wanted on economic terms, but then denied on legal and human terms, calls for more humane and just migration reforms. Theology of mission analyzes these issues, which are at the same time local and global, from the perspective of a Christian understanding of justice and with the collaboration of disciplines such as ethics and human rights studies (see Heyer 2012; Battistella 2008; Kierwin 2008), and promotes the option for the most vulnerable among migrants.

Fourth, a crucial trait of migration today is its 'feminization' that refers both to the major role that women play in all types of migration flows and the growing awareness of the significance of this phenomenon. It is not only the fact that today women represent 50% of the migrants worldwide, but also the knowledge that their experience and perspective on human mobility is different and makes essential contributions to the understanding of its complex dynamics. In the field of migration studies this growing awareness has given birth to numerous works on gender and migration, a research field that is characterized by a plurality of approaches that show the faults of a still existing male-dominated perspective on migration (Hondagneu-Sotelo 2011). It would be certainly interesting and fruitful for missiology to facilitate a sustained encounter and dialogue between this stream of migration research and the approach to world Christianity as a women's movement (Robert 2006). One of the most fascinating dimensions of this dialogue would be to discover not only that more often than not a typical Christian would be a woman from the global south, but also what is the probability that this woman could be an immigrant in the Western world.

Fifth, the many questions related to the second or 1.5 generations (i.e. children born in the country of origin but growing up in the new country of residence). How are they faring or integrating in the country and church in which they grow up and live? What is, for instance, the relation that they have with the religion of their parents? Will they be 'contaminated' by secularization processes that characterize many Western countries or will they be caught up in the dynamics of 'immigrant Christianity'? (see Schreiter 2011: 32-33). This is surely another interesting field of study for mission theology (see Jackson 2011: 21-23).

Sixth, and finally, there is the issue of the religion of the migrants and its role in their journeys and lives. Some interesting essays have been recently written by migration scholars on this issue since they have realized that faith, especially popular Catholicism, is a significant element of the whole process of migration (see Durand and Massey 1995; Hagan 2008; Hondagneu-Sotelo 2008; Gálvez 2010). One of the aspects that stands out in the study of migrant religion is that human mobility does not only engender religion pluralism in societies that, especially in the Western world, have been traditionally Christian, but has introduced plurality within Christianity itself. In fact, some statistics suggest that, despite a lot of political propaganda to the contrary, propaganda that likes to wave the spectre of the 'invasion of Islam', most of the migrants living in the Western world, Europe included, are Christians. Indeed, argues Philip Jenkins, the forecast of an 'Islamicized Europe' is 'wildly unlikely.' (Jenkins 2007: 284).

Kirsteen Kim has called it 'Christian migration', and this phenomenon is to be considered as a substantial dimension of the rise of southern Christianity in the world. In other words, Southern Christianity is to be found not only in the global south, but is moving steadily toward the Western world and is visible in the numerous ethnic groups present within the Roman Catholic Church and in the Protestant churches, but particularly in the flourishing of numerous independent Evangelical and Pentecostal churches (Kim 2011). So what migration is precipitating in the Western world is not only religious diversity, but also and especially diversity within Christianity itself. Sociologist Stephen Warner observes that immigration in the United States is causing the 'de-europeization' of U.S. Christianity (Warner 2004), and in many ways the same evaluation can be applied to what is happening today in Europe. In Europe, unfortunately, few Christian ministers and theologians discuss whether the churches in this continent are really journeying toward an authentic multiculturalism that gives equal opportunity to Christian immigrants and helps to construct together a common vision of what it means to be Christians in a world characterized by cultural and religious difference (Noort 2011; Fredericks and Pruiksma 2010).

Migration as *Locus Missiologicus*

Migration becomes a *locus theologicus*, or better, a *locus missiologicus*, when the Christian community, inspired by the Spirit of the God of Jesus Christ, starts listening attentively to this phenomenon, to the human voices that emerge from its complexity, and in the midst of its ambiguities 'labors' to discern or 'decipher authentic signs of God's presence and purpose' (GS 11). It is now with this intention that we approach human mobility to see some of the different ways in which it prods our 'missiological imagination' (Bevans 2009: 56-57) and so becomes a precious and rich source of missiological thinking.

To begin doing missiology from the perspective of the phenomenon of migration adds a different perspective to the depiction of the Trinitarian God of Christianity. As we have seen earlier, missiologists have provided stimulating readings of the God of the Judaeo-Christian tradition as a missionary God. What migration supplements to this picture is the image of a God on the move with deep biblical roots, which are already visible in God's original call to Abraham at the very beginning of the journey of what will become Israel, the people of God (Gen. 12). Starting from this narrative, Brother John of Taize reaches the following conclusion: 'one thing makes this god different from the divinities found just about everywhere in those days. All those deities were linked to particular places – mountains, rivers, cities, regions – whereas the God that speaks to Abraham is a god who is not tied down to one spot. This god is a sojourner god, a pilgrim god' (Brother John of Taize 1985: 13). A crucial symbol of the 'mobile presence' of this God that cuts across the whole biblical narrative is the twin image of tent/tabernacle found especially in the Pentateuch (for instance Num. 2:2), but also later on in different New Testament texts. This is how a biblical scholar communicates the significance of this symbol: 'To have such a portable sanctuary is also more accurately to reflect *the God who dwells there* .... This is a God on the move, who cannot be localized, who cannot be pinned down to one time and place .... This God takes up residence with the people, tabernacles with them. This God dwells, not at the edges of Israel's life, but right at the center of things. This God is committed to the journey .... It is no wonder that the New Testament utilizes this tabernacling language to speak of the Word becoming flesh in Jesus (Jn. 1:14) and of God in eschatological vision (Rev. 21:3)' (Fretheim 1991: 275). This is to say that the missionary God is a pilgrim, a migrant God, and in fact it is missionary precisely because it is a God who in Jesus Christ and the Spirit moves freely and lovingly toward the whole creation and establishes Godself in the midst of humanity. The missionary God is the one who pitches a tent in the midst of this world in order to be with and guide humankind in its journey.

Migration enriches our understanding of mission, a multidimensional concept that has to do with the mystery of God, the *missio Dei*, and for this reason it can never be exhaustively explored (see Parolin 2010: 424-81). One of the most important aspects of the traditional understanding of Christian mission has been the notion of 'crossing boundaries'. When mission was construed in terms of going to the pagans in order to convert them, the boundaries to be crossed were geographic: the true and only missionary was, therefore, the person who had the courage and made the sacrifice to go overseas. In this sense human mobility has always been an indispensable element of mission. Now that migration is making national borders more relative and the separation between 'us' (the citizens) and 'them' (the migrants) much more blurred, mission remains still a matter of crossing boundaries, but especially other types of boundaries: cultural borders, religious borders, the borders of our established ways of thinking about God, church, and human beings, of our prejudices about who belongs and who does not, borders between center and margins. Many of the people who work in the field of migration rightly observe that the hardest boundaries to cross are those within our minds and hearts. In this context mission can be still defined as a conversion, but in terms of a movement, a migration of our imagination so that it becomes less 'parochial' and more 'catholic', able and ready to listen to the choir of voices that emerge from human mobility and learn from them all (Campese 2007: 186-88). It is a movement toward and with humanity in the direction of that fullness and abundance that God has prepared for the whole creation.

Migration enhances our vision of world Christianity in a globalized world. From this particular viewpoint we comprehend much better the two principles of Christianity suggested by Andrew Walls: the indigenizing principle, which affirms that Christian faith must take root and feel at home in any particular context; and the pilgrim principle, which at the same time tells Christians to go beyond their particular contexts, to be on the journey because 'God's home', the reign to which we are invited is always 'beyond' (Walls 1996: 7-9). These seemingly 'opposing tendencies', as Walls defines them, seen from the perspective of migration come together to explain both the human and Christian adventures that happen between the desire, the dream of having a home, of belonging somewhere, of having an identity and the awareness that to have all this we must be on the road, on a journey, on a pilgrimage. Human and Christian identities are not something static, something acquired at the moment of birth. They represent, rather, a dynamic journey in which we grow as human beings in the encounter with the others and the Other that means ongoing mutual enrichment. Christianity is, therefore, home and journey, roots and wings, faith in pilgrimage. And with Hanciles we can conclude saying: 'What is certain is that the future of the Christian faith, as it was in the past, is bound up with that most basic of traits of the human condition: migration' (Hanciles 2011: 241).

Migration gives us a better grasp of who we are as human beings and as Christian believers. According to French scholar Jacques Attali, settled life is just a short parenthesis of human history which has been characterized by nomadism and it is returning to it. Human beings are people in movement and it is precisely the travelers, the nomads who have laid the foundations of what we now call civilizations (Attali 2006). This peculiar perspective on history besides highlighting migration as structural dimension of the journey of humankind on this earth, is attuned to what the Bible says about the nature of human being and of the believer in the presence of God. The Italian writer Erri de Luca puts it beautifully: 'The human species is stranger on the face of the earth: 'for the land is mine; with me you are but aliens and tenants' (Lev. 25:23). This, the acceptance of being a stranger and a transient, is not a goal of perfection to be reached through contemplation: it is our point of departure, our premise' (de Luca 2011: 84). It is also from this fundamental premise that Christian mission must begin.

Migration, finally, revitalizes our understanding of the church, the community of the believers. Missiologists, particularly within the Roman Catholic tradition, have underscored the missionary nature of the whole church, a concept that, as seen earlier, has been officially stated by the Vatican II in AG 2: 'The pilgrim Church is missionary by its very nature.' While it is true that normally ecclesiologists have not given the

A Century of Catholic Mission

consideration that is due to this fundamental dimension of the church in their works (e.g. it is missing in Gaillardetz and Clifford 2012), it is undeniable that the 'pilgrim' dimension of the church has been accorded even less attention (see, however, Orobator 2005: 143-79; Mazzolini 2010: 145-50; Lakeland 2009: 149-54). Different images and models have been used to explain and reflect on the mystery of the church, but rarely has the pilgrim metaphor being employed to describe it. Yet in the globalized world characterized by human mobility the pilgrim image would be one of the most relevant ways to speak about the missionary church that finds its origin and source in a missionary and pilgrim God (see Jackson 2011: 15; CWME 2010: 116-21).

It is important also to note that the migrants are not just on the receiving end of the church's missionary activity. They, as the pilgrims par excellence, do not just represent a symbolic reminder of the pilgrim dimension of the church. The migrants are becoming the protagonists of the missionary Christian community, the unlikely Christian witnesses who, with their tenacious faith in the midst of countless difficulties, evangelize the world and re-evangelize the church itself. They are not only the main characters of the 'Great Reverse Migration' (Walls 2008: 194), but also, and most importantly, of the reverse missionary movement that from the global South has reached the Western world (see especially Hanciles 2008). Looking at the differences between the nineteenth and twentieth century European migration and contemporary and mostly southern-based migration, between the ecclesial and missiological contexts in which these phenomena have happened, perhaps we can conclude that while in the case of the Great European Migration we had the missionary elites as strangers and migrants, today in the era of the Great Reverse Migration we have the multitudes of Christian migrants, who make up a significant part of the church, as missionaries and so we are closer to the ideal of a migrant and pilgrim church as a missionary church.

Conclusion

In this chapter we have tried to lay out the main aspects of the intimate and structural relationship between Christian mission and migration. In the first part we have shown the relatively abundant literature that has been generated by the encounter at the beginning of the twenty-first century between missiology and migration. In the second part we have analyzed different features of contemporary migration as a context of and challenge to the theology of mission. In the third part we have seen how migration can, and has, become in many ways a rich source for missiological thinking, that is, paraphrasing the traditional theological language, a *locus missiologicus*. In this fourth and final part of the article we would like to somehow conclude our reflection on mission and migration by highlighting cross-cultural friendship as a vital dimension of mission in an age of human mobility.

This reflection is the result of the meeting of some of the multiple threads that connect mission and migration. The first is the idea of cross-cultural, and cross-religious, friendship as a main channel of Christian mission today suggested by Dana Robert who goes back to the memorable and prophetic speech given by V.S. Azariah, a young Indian Anglican clergyman, at Edinburgh 1910. This is the most famous passage of Azariah's speech: 'Through all the ages to come the Indian Church will rise up in gratitude to attest the heroism and self-denying labours of the missionary body. You have given your goods to feed the poor. You have given your bodies to be burned. We also ask for love. Give us friends!' (Robert 2011: 57-58 and 2011b; see Stanley 2009: 125). Azariah's words express the deep longing for a relationship on equal terms that must stand as one of the foundations of any missionary activity and that was almost impossible in an era in which Christian mission was theologically and financially controlled by the Western colonial powers. While this is still the case for some southern churches in relation to the politically, intellectually and financially powerful Western churches, we are inexorably going in the direction of a world Christianity in which these lines of discrimination will gradually, and hopefully, fall in the background.

The second thread is revealed by Jesus's words on friendship to his disciples in John 15:15: 'I do not call you servants any longer, because the servant does not know what the master is doing; but I have called you friends, because I have made known to you everything that I have heard from my Father.' The Christian community based on mutual love and friendship, a community where the master calls and treats his followers as friends and not as servants, is appointed to become a missionary community by going and bearing fruit (Jn. 15:16), by being sent into the world by Jesus as Jesus himself has been sent by the Father (Jn. 17:18, 20:21) (see Nissen 2002: 75-97).

The third thread is represented by the voices of the migrants themselves who very often ask for the material things that they lack, such as a house, a job, documents. Yet one of the things that too often is ignored, and that they always express, is their fundamental need of belonging, a community, a family, some healthy human relations or, in other words, friendship. Some migrant women interviewed for research on domestic helpers in the Los Angeles area have affirmed that they are not just after a decent pay and working conditions, but what is as important or more important for them is to be treated as human beings, as equals and in a friendly manner (Hondagneu-Sotelo 2001: 201). This longing for friendship is confirmed in the fourth thread by pastoral agents who work in the field of migration. They observe that often the services offered to migrants are wrapped in a paternalistic and victimized perspective that puts them in a position of inferiority especially in the context of hospitality. What the migrants really need are not just helpers, people who serve them food, but companions (*cum panis*), that is, people who seat at table with them and share bread and life. This is why Ed Loring, from the Open Door Community in Atlanta says: 'justice is important, but supper is essential', which means that without table companionship even something so fundamental as justice loses some of its meaning and strength (cited in Pohl 1999: 74).

These four threads together send a key message: cross-cultural and cross-religious friendship is an essential component of mission in a world in which human mobility plays a central role. This kind of friendship finds its source in the most intimate Trinitarian friendship among God, Jesus Christ and the Holy Spirit, and builds bridges across cultural and religious divides and prejudices. This friendship builds up *convivencia* and harmony in a world in which too frequently differences become an easy excuse for conflicts and violence against human dignity. In this way cross-cultural friendship becomes a privileged channel to continue today the mission entrusted to the church by God: to continue to preach, serve and witness to the good news of the reign initiated by Jesus Christ.

PART FIVE

CATHOLIC MISSION SPIRITUALITY

A SPIRITUALITY OF MISSION

Madge Karecki, OFM-TOR

Introduction

The opening decade of the twenty-first century has witnessed a burgeoning of interest in spirituality. There is an array of books, articles and other resources available under the heading of 'spirituality' in any bookstore. Michael Downey (1997: 6-29) likens this selection to a 'buffet table' of spirituality dealing with everything from dream work to apparitions of Our Lady to New Age crystals and Tai Chi. Authors like Thomas Merton and Henri Nouwen can be found next to Deepak Chopra and Erich von Däniken. With such an assortment of resources it is important to approach them with a measure of discernment. In the midst of a plethora of opinions about what is or is not spirituality, we need to begin by exploring definitions of spirituality so that we can establish some common ground for focusing on mission spirituality. But first a disclaimer is in order.

A study of mission spirituality can take many approaches. Traditionally, it has been studied in the historical contexts in which missionaries worked. Theological studies of mission spirituality have often dealt with spirituality in relationship to the specific charism of religious orders or in terms of particular theological concepts and frameworks usually taken from ecclesiology or systematic theology. The social sciences, especially anthropology, have looked at the effects of spirituality on mission praxis.

In the context of my own research I have found few sources in English devoted exclusively to the spirituality of mission. In the latest edition of the *Bibliographia Missionaria* (2010: 258-66), in which missiological articles from around the world are listed, a mere fifteen articles in English out of 106 are listed under the topic of Missionary Spirituality. Of the fifteen only two have spirituality as a central focus. I concentrated on the English language articles because of the perceived audience of this volume. That said, we need to attend to the topic at hand.

Defining Spirituality

Sandra Schneiders (2003: 165), well-known proponent of spirituality as an academic discipline, has defined spirituality as 'the capacity of persons to transcend themselves through knowledge and love, that is, to reach beyond themselves in relationship to others, and thus become more than self-enclosed material monads'. *The Westminster Dictionary of Christian Spirituality* Schneiders (2005:1-2) named four characteristics of contemporary spirituality. First, spirituality today is understood as an ongoing life project in contrast to isolated spiritual practices. Second, the ultimate purpose of spirituality is to assist a person in the process of life integration. Its scope is holistic and brings into play a matrix of varied relationships and experiences. Third, spirituality is a process in which people grow in their capacity for self-transcendence. Fourth, authentic spirituality is oriented toward the transcendent or some ultimate value.

Philip Sheldrake (1998: 35) has formulated a definition of spirituality that centers on a relationship with the persons of the Trinity in a community of faith. He wrote: 'Spirituality is the whole of human life viewed in terms of a conscious relationship with God, in Jesus Christ, through the indwelling of the Spirit, and within the community of believers.'

Finally, Michael Downey, like Sheldrake, looked specifically at Christian spirituality and defined it as:

> the whole of the Christian's life as this is oriented to self-transcending knowledge, freedom, and love in light of the ultimate values and highest ideals perceived and pursued in the mystery of Jesus Christ through the Holy Spirit in the church, the community of disciples. That is to say, spirituality is concerned with everything that constitutes Christian experience, specifically the perception and pursuit of the highest ideal or goal of Christian life, e.g., an ever more intense union with God disclosed in Christ through life in the Spirit (Downey 1997: 271-72).

What these definitions indicate about Christian spirituality, at its best, is that it is Trinitarian, leads to self-transcendence, is enriched by relationships in a community of faith through which a person is sustained in his/her ever-deepening relationship with the Trinity and with others so that the individual becomes the person God intended her/him to be.

It is the mutual relationality that exists among the persons of the Trinity through which the capacity of the human person to reach out to others is nurtured. The pulsating Trinitarian life within a person enables him/her to cultivate relationships and engage with society and the world at the level of faith and meaning. It is this gift of Trinitarian dynamism that prepares one to share in the *missio Dei*.

Spirituality of Mission

By 1910 the Catholic Church's missionary spirituality had undergone many permutations, beginning with the spirituality of Jesus. The spirituality he embodied is expressed in the Gospel of Luke 4:18-19. The verses are from the prophet Isaiah and might be called his mission statement. We are familiar with the text: 'The Spirit of the Lord is upon me, because he has anointed me to bring glad tidings to the poor. He has sent me to proclaim liberty to captives and recovery of sight to the blind, to let the oppressed go free, and to proclaim a year acceptable to the Lord.' These verses express Jesus' self-understanding of his mission. Jesus confirmed this in the comment made about the text being fulfilled in their hearing (Lk. 4:21). He made it clear to the whole assembly gathered in the synagogue that day that he was the embodiment of the prophetic text from Isaiah. In no uncertain terms he declared himself the One sent by the Father. He was anointed by the Spirit to fulfill the mission given to him by the Father. It was the raison d'être for his coming among humankind.

The Lukan passage tells us something about how mission happens within the context of the relationships that exist among the persons of the Trinity: God bestows the Spirit on the Son and the Son is sent to carry out the mission of the Father. Jesus is the fulfillment of that mission. The text also holds significant meaning for an understanding of mission spirituality as rooted in baptism.

We have been baptized with the same Spirit to share in God's mission in the world and so we are sent to be bearers of this good news that Jesus proclaimed in Nazareth that day. It is vitally important that we understand the profound dynamic at work through baptism in bringing each of us into relationship with the Trinity so that we grasp the fact that all of us are called to be on mission (Bühlmann 1979: 115). It is a grace that holds a potential that we can only unlock if we are serious about reaching our full stature in Christ (Eph. 4:13).

Through baptism we become members of the sending community of the Trinity. By our participation in the life of the Father, Son and Holy Spirit we learn what it means to be missionary disciples. The *Aparecida Document* (Aparecida 2007) says this more eloquently:

> An authentic proposal of an encounter with Jesus Christ must be established upon a solid foundation of Trinity-Love. The experience of a triune God who is inseparable unity and community enables us to overcome selfishness and fully find ourselves in service to the other. The baptismal experience is the starting point of all Christian spirituality, which is based on the Trinity. (Aparecida 2007: 240).

The community of the Trinity is not a closed community, quite the contrary. Consciously claiming what is ours by reason of baptism does not happen all at once. If we are to be on mission we must first learn to be disciples in this community of love. Discipleship grows out of communion. The communion we share with the Trinity presupposes that we are serious about living up to the dignity conferred on us at our birth: we are made unto God's image and likeness. 'The nature of God, therefore, fundamentally determines the character of Christian life' (Volf 2006: 4). We are made to be like God; hence, the process of becoming God's likeness and the call to conversion.

Missionary Conversion

Sharing life with the persons of the Trinity always leads to mission, but we have to acknowledge their presence dwelling deep within our being, wanting us, loving us and sending us forth on mission and conversion (Strynkowski 2006:190). It must be this way because the first challenge of following Jesus is change our lives so that we can experience in some measure the fullness of the kingdom of God, who is the Christ (Mk. 1:15).

We need to be willing to face our limitations and be serious about our ongoing conversion. Unfortunately, mission history holds vivid reminders of zealous missionaries whose entire focus was the conversion of others while not confronting their own need for conversion. Missionaries were often caught in webs of division based on competing national powers. The ruling powers had the resources that enabled them to conquer indigenous peoples. Their actions were fueled by a theological vision that allowed for forced conversions and disregard for cultural uniqueness. Now we realize that the gift of baptism is only fully realized when we wholeheartedly open our minds and hearts to God's call to conversion as we experience it in our lives.

If we allow the Holy Spirit to work within us we will soon find that the obstacles to our own growth in Christ gradually become apparent. Once this happens we can engage in the lifelong task of conversion. We are led on this journey so that we can in turn be compassionate to others because 'the meaning that brings greatest satisfaction is personal relationships and one's ability to do something for others....' (Strynkowski 2006: 14-15).

The Cistercian monk, Michael Casey, commenting on the need to rely on the work of the Holy Spirit in the conversion process, wrote: 'By the action of the Holy Spirit what is worst in us can give rise to what is best. This is an alchemy we do not comprehend and can never anticipate, no matter how often it happens. God transforms human limitation into something beautiful, taking what is of least value and ennobling it from within' (Casey 1996:7). Casey's words remind us that ultimately, conversion happens when we open ourselves to the work of the Spirit so that God's transforming grace can save us, free us and send us on mission.

Responding to the grace of conversion is fundamental to mission spirituality if we are to remain true to the evangelical mission of Jesus. We need to allow the Spirit to have free reign within us. We are helped in this life project when we are serious about fostering communion with Christ through prayer and especially contemplation.

Authentic, Christ-centered contemplation always leads to our transformation: affective, intellectual, moral, sociopolitical and religious conversion (Gelpi 1998: 42). As we begin to see the dark side of ourselves and situations in the world and draw near to Christ we see ourselves, others, and the world in a new light. Conversion then happens gradually. As we respond to the grace of conversion we become convinced that we are called to work for the transformation of the world so that it more clearly reflects the presence of God.

Shaping Mission Spirituality

Growing in holiness

The Second Vatican Council caused a revolution in Catholic thinking about identity, mission, the nature of the church, attitudes to people of other faiths, society and the created world. One of the most significant teachings of Vatican II that has implications for mission is found in chapter five of the *Dogmatic Constitution on the Church* (LG) which says:

> [I]t is evident to everyone, that all the faithful of Christ of whatever rank or status, are called to the fullness of the Christian life and to the perfection of charity; by this holiness as such a more human manner of living is promoted in this earthly society. In order that the faithful may reach this perfection, they must use their strength accordingly as they have received it, as a gift from Christ. They must follow in His footsteps and conform themselves to His image seeking the will of the Father in all things. They must devote themselves with all their being to the glory of God and the service of their neighbor. In this way, the holiness of the People of God will grow into an abundant harvest of good, as is admirably shown by the life of so many saints in Church history. (LG 40)

Holiness is then one of the essentials of missionary spirituality. It means that prayer, especially contemplation, is the seedbed where a missionary spirit takes root.

As we grow in intimacy with Christ we do whatever is necessary to make this relationship the primary one of our lives. Slowly, we find that we are able to make choices that better reflect God's love for the world. Contemplation is not an escape from reality. In the contemplative experience of union with Christ one is called out of one's self in progressive stages of growth in love. In the Lord's embrace we become empowered for love, a love that we are taught by the one who is love. True contemplation does not lead us away from people. On the contrary, it leads us to be more loving and generous toward all people, but especially those who are in most need of the liberating love and mercy of Christ (Karecki 2010: 3).

Contemplation leads to the most radical self-giving possible because union with the Lord as a gift of the Spirit ultimately leads to *kenosis* (Downey 2006: 26), a sharing in the paschal mystery of Jesus. With Christ we learn to walk in his footsteps along the way that leads to self-emptying, a way that we take in obedience to the will of the Father. It is the self-emptying of Jesus that becomes the source of hope for all those who are weighed down by pain and grief, injustice and oppression, suffering and sin because in radical self-oblation new hope is born from the gift of self.

In the post-resurrection appearances Christ reveals himself to the women and to the apostles as one transformed by the resurrection, but still bearing the wounds of his crucifixion. It is there in the midst of the wounds that wisdom and hope are revealed. They become an epiphany of the new life that self-emptying brings to the to the world (Downey 1997: 39). The one who has experienced intimacy with Christ is not estranged or somehow exempted from the pain of human suffering; on the contrary genuine mystical union plunges one into the very depths of the world and opens one's heart to the mystery of the other, all others (Karecki 2010: 3).

Unlike some missionaries in past centuries who used the conquest-settlement-evangelize approach (Bevans and Schroeder 2004: 175) missionaries today need a profound sense of humility born out of their union with the poor, humble kenotic Christ. We are sent on mission to accompany others on their faith journeys. Like Paul we have nothing to boast about except the cross of our Lord Jesus Christ (see Gal. 6:14).

Missio Dei

Mission as presented in *Ad Gentes* (AG) is not connected to a work, but to the very identity of who we are as church. We cannot not be missionary because our Catholic identity as church is rooted in the very life of the Trinity. Mission is the way the persons of the Trinity manifest themselves in the world. Our part is to be in union with the persons of the Trinity as privileged participants in the *missio Dei, the mission of God.* There are not multiple missions, there is only one, God's mission; to claim another is to betray our very identity.

This Trinitarian view informed the earlier discussion about the spirituality of mission. I have based my approach to missionary spirituality on the Trinitarian theology of the late Catherine Mowry LaCugna who beautifully articulated a profound reflection on our life in the *economy* of God:

> God's economy is not the austere distribution of meager resources but lavish grace, a glorious inheritance, bestowed in prodigal good pleasure … God's economy, *oikonomia tou theou*, is the well-spring of trinitarian faith. The economy is not an abstract idea, not a theological principle, but the life of God and creature existing together as one. (LaCugna 1991: 377)

It is out of the lavishness of God's life that the Spirit anoints the Son and is sent to anoint us so that sharing in God's life we become sharers in the mission of God. It is on this foundation that the church's missionary nature rests (AG 2).

Witness

We are sent on mission by the Spirit through Christ to give witness by our lives and through a myriad of ministries, but always it is God's mission for which we spend ourselves. John Paul II highlighted the importance of witness as the most fundamental way to be on mission when he wrote: 'The witness of a Christian life is the first and irreplaceable form of mission: Christ, whose mission we continue, is the 'witness' *par excellence* and the model of all Christian witness'. (RM 42)

A witness does not bear testimony to him/herself, but always points to another. For the Christian this means a living union with Christ, nourished by the scriptures and the sacraments. When this is a reality then mission is 'sharing the experience of the event of the encounter with Christ, witnessing it and announcing it from person to person, from community, and from the Church to the ends of the earth (cf. Acts 1:8)' (Aparecida 2007: 145). Witness to and proclamation of Christ as *the* good news, are essential to mission, though in various contexts they may need to take the form of presence among the people to whom we are sent.

Ecumenical, inter-religious and cultural contexts

John Paul II entitled the fourth chapter of RM 'The Vast Horizons of Mission Ad Gentes' and subtitled the section on the permanent nature of mission *ad gentes* as 'A Complex and Ever Changing Religious Picture,' giving us some indication that mission is always contextual. This has been made clear in the publications of Bevans, Schreiter, Gutiérrez, Nasimiyu-Wasike, and Uzukwu to name just a few Catholic authors. Nevertheless, there is a need to highlight the fact that even though *mission ad gentes* remains primary in the Catholic understanding of mission, the context of that mission has changed drastically in the last century and those changes are significant for how we develop a spirituality of mission.

The need for a serious commitment to ecumenism is beyond question. The unity of the Body of Christ is at stake. The dictum 'no salvation outside the church' (*extra ecclesiam nulla salus*), the phrase of the third century bishop Cyprian of Carthage taken somewhat out of context, was one of the primary theological teachings motivating mission from patristic times until the Second Vatican Council (Bosch 1991: 218). The very first line of the *Decree on Ecumenism* (UR) signaled a change in the church's teaching and gave voice to one of its primary concerns: 'restoration of the unity among all Christians' (UR 1). In the same paragraph the Council Fathers clearly stated their motivation for their concern about ecumenical relationships: 'Such division openly contradicts the will of Christ, scandalizes the world, and damages the holy cause of preaching the Gospel to every creature' (UR 1). The implications for mission are evident: we must give concrete proof of the church's desire for Christian unity through our willingness to work together with other Christians, to engage in the kind of theological dialogue that makes the reconciliation of differences possible.

The fruits of such dialogue have been seen in the Joint Declaration on the Doctrine of Justification that was made between the Lutheran World Federation and the Catholic Church in 1999 (Joint Declaration 1999). In

2010, the United States Conference of Catholic Bishops voted unanimously
to accept the Agreement on Mutual Recognition of the Baptism that was
made with the Christian Reformed Church in North America, the
Presbyterian Church-USA, the Reformed Church in America, the United
Church of Christ ('These Living Waters' 2010). These agreements are
implemented by local parish churches where Christians gather. In order for
this to happen these decisions need to be motivated by the deep desire
Christ had that there be 'one flock and one shepherd' (Jn. 16:10).

   *The Declaration on the Relationship of the Church with Non-Christian
Religions* (NA) from the Second Vatican Council was promulgated on
October 28, 1965. Today its summons to the church to engage in inter-
religious dialogue is as relevant as when it was voted on by the bishops
gathered for Vatican II. This document was especially significant for
people of the Jewish faith because it addressed the difficult issue of anti-
semitism (NA 4).

   In general, it evidenced a clear respect for all people of good will and
recognized all that is 'true and holy' in other religions (NA 2). This led to
another significant document published jointly in 1991 by the Congregation
for the Evangelization of Peoples and the Pontifical Council for Inter-
religious Dialogue, entitled, *Dialogue and Proclamation* (DP). The point is
that missionary proclamation of Christ is not incompatible with dialogue
with people of other religions.

   In paragraph 42 the document outlines four forms of dialogue. Each one
requires that we have a firm knowledge of our faith and respect for the faith
of the other. The dialogue of life and dialogue of social action are lived out
in the context in which we live and serve. When we get to know people of
other faiths we meet them as persons committed to their faith, but more
fundamentally as our sisters and brothers, images of the God in whom 'we
live and move and have our being' (Acts 17:28).

   The dialogue of theological exchange usually unfolds in situations where
people share a common commitment to the theological foundations of their
faith and are willing to listen and learn from one another. The dialogue of
religious experience is most often initiated by people whose lives have been
shaped by their experience of God in prayer and contemplation. The
significance of such an experience cannot be underestimated. John Paul II
knew this and organized the Assisi Experiences to foster solidarity among
the world religions and give a prayerful witness for peace and the grace of
self-transcendence. John Paul II was convinced that the Holy Spirit is
mysteriously present within every human person drawing them to God
through prayer:

> In every authentic religious experience, the most characteristic expression is
> prayer. Because of the human spirit's constitutive openness to God's action
> urging it to self-transcendence, we can hold that every authentic prayer is
> called forth by the Holy Spirit, who is mysteriously present in the heart of
> every person (in Johnston 2000: 224-25).

The pontiff's teaching is clear: the Holy Spirit is the initiator of every true religious experience. The Spirit works imperceptibly to draw people to Christ so that even when they do not consciously acknowledge it they are being invited to experience salvation in Christ Jesus.

It would be naïve to think that today mission *ad gentes* takes place in mono-religious settings. Our world is a global village and if we are going to make Christ known then we will have to take cognizance of people of other faiths if we are to live in harmony and peace with them while giving the reason for the hope we have in our hearts (1 Pet. 3:15).

Catholic missionary spirituality calls us to have the same attitude of respect for the cultural uniqueness of others. Inculturation is one of the challenges every local church throughout the world is facing today. The dialogue between faith and life is enormously important if the church is going to have a place in societies throughout the world. This requires deep and profound religious formation at every stage of faith development. Culture has the capacity to mediate faith and help create a 'home' for the gospel for people in diverse contexts (Gallagher 1997: 78).

We might say that faith is at home everywhere, but never fully at home anywhere. This is an acknowledgment of the need for the gospel to be incarnated in people's lives just as Christ became incarnated into a specific culture. The gospel is not tied to any culture, but the reign of God which it makes known is lived within the cultural realties of people's lives. As women and men of every culture respond to God in faith the gospel gradually and mysteriously transforms people and acting in faith they, in turn, transform their cultures (Karecki 2000: 26).

The missiological challenge is to appreciate our own culture with all its strengths and weaknesses, while being open to learning other cultures and delighting in the diversity of the cultural riches God has implanted in the people of God. This is no easy task and many missionaries have failed in this enterprise. Nevertheless, we need to foster holistic cultural development in ourselves and engender it in others. Once again, respect is a principal attitude that needs to characterize our behavior so that our witness is clear and trustworthy.

Concern for the environment

Today people talk of others as having a sense of entitlement. This kind of attitude is the antithesis of a missionary perspective on the created world. Mission spirituality rooted as it is in the experience of being sent teaches that we are on pilgrimage here on earth and we have received the resources of the earth as gift. The psalmist sings out in praise to God for the gifts of creation. Francis of Assisi calls on all creation to join him in praise of God, the creator of earth and all its gifts. Francis saw himself in relationship to the created world. All the elements were his brothers and sisters. He received them from the Lord as gifts. Francis not only admired creation, he also used it sparingly and in this regard he has a lot to teach us.

Mission spirituality always has practical implications for our life; it yearns as it were to be expressed in concrete lifestyles. If it is to be authentic then it will always lead us to some concrete ways to express it in our mission praxis. In our concern for justice in the world we need to evaluate our witness in terms of the impact we make on the environment by the way we live.

In order to do this we need to have a profound sense of solidarity with all the people of the earth as well as with the generations yet to come. This calls for an appropriation of the kind of communion with the Trinity that flows out from us and is seen as a communion with humanity and the whole created world. Our ecological footprint enables us to measure the impact our way of life is having on the environment.

Having a concern for creation is not just a matter of science. It is related to the worldview that we have inherited and imbibed from our faith, but also what we have learned from our society. We need to let ourselves be challenged by the gospel and by the social teaching of the church to look for ways to help us distinguish needs from wants, live more abstemiously, share our resources with others and praise God for the gifts of Mother Earth. If we are all to experience 'the new heavens and the new earth' (Rev. 21:1) when the Lord comes again in glory then we, like Saint Francis, have to live differently in society. We need to cut down on our use of the earth's resources so that we can shrink our ecological footprint and be good stewards of creation (Delio, Warner, and Wood 2008: 33-34).

This is not an exhaustive list of the elements of a spirituality of mission. I have chosen these because they can each be related to a spirituality of mission that is related to the life of the Trinity. Mission is the result of the communion we share with the Trinity (AG 2). It cannot be otherwise if it is the *missio Dei* that we are privileged in which to share. Mission is indeed a soul-size enterprise.

Conclusion

In his book, *The Future Church: How Ten Trends are Revolutionizing the Catholic Church, National Catholic Reporter* columnist John L. Allen, he concluded the book with a postscript in which he indicated that it would take more than making a contribution for the annual celebration of World Mission Sunday to bring Catholics to a point where they are willing to forge their global identity and take their place in a world church. He says that to do this it would take a large measure of courage to think and act beyond the boundaries Catholics have set for themselves (Allen 2009: 453). It would mean making a conscious response to the God who always calls us beyond ourselves to think and act as people who share the loving communion of the Trinity and willingly live that communion in communion with people of every tribe and tongue and nation (Rev. 5:9).

Only then will we have the grace and energy to live out of a spirituality of mission worthy of the One who sends us on mission.

MISSION AS ACCOMPANIMENT

Claude Marie Barbour and Eleanor Doidge, LoB

While the use of the term 'accompaniment' as a model of missionary practice is relatively new, it would not be too difficult to point to some well known historical figures who might serve as examples as we explore the importance of 'mission as accompaniment' for today. When understood within his historical context perhaps the best representative would be Bartolomé de Las Casas (Bevans and Schroeder 2004: 176). Las Casas' own conversion of mind and heart through his work with and for the indigenous of the Americas serves as an example of how the spirituality and practice of accompaniment, 'walking with' (Goizueta 1995: 203), can affect a transformation that reaches much further than the hoped-for conversion or transformation of the intended recipient(s) of mission. With images and examples from the Chicago based Shalom Ministries and Community, this article will show how the lived spirituality of accompaniment is grounded in the very life of Jesus, the perfect model of a life lived in mission for the wholeness and well-being of the other. Even as he lived his mission close to the outcast, the poor, the alienated, Jesus was changed himself and came to a greater understanding of his father's love for all creation and the role of humans in it.

Shalom Ministries and Community

The authors have spent more than thirty years each ministering and training others as part of our community. The ministry and lives of Shalom members will be used to illustrate and contextualize mission as accompaniment. The Rev. Dr. Claude Marie Barbour founded Shalom in 1975 as an ecumenical, Christ-centered, covenant community of women and men. Members live and work in a variety of countries and mission contexts, often among the poor and most marginalized. Their covenant, the Shalom Mission Statement reads: 'Seeking to live as followers of Christ, We, the workers of Shalom will strive to be signs of unity, reconciliation and healing in a broken world, and to work for justice and peace. When there is division, we seek to be bridges, to carry the burdens of others, sharing concretely in their suffering, to take risks, never standing still, to be signs of joy and love, to be present and open, ready to receive as well as to give, freeing us all to become who we are meant to be.' Shalom members promise to live by five central theological principles:

Mission-in-reverse: We believe that as ministers and missionaries, we can and should learn from the people we serve – especially from the poor and marginalized. When ministry is grounded in mutuality and solidarity, ministers become persons immersed in the world of others, like Jesus was in the world of His time. A minister's mission emerges in dialogue with others and is given definite direction as the result of this mutuality.

Community building: We recognize that the locus of ministry is the grassroots, the base community. We strive to discover and help build community with our teachers – the poor and marginalized. When we meet as a community, we discover a new synthesis of life and faith in Christ.

Contextualization: We recognize that fundamental to the proclamation of God's revelation to humanity is the discernment of how God is already present and active in the cultures of the world. We believe in the incarnation of Christ and his redeeming presence in our lives. We recognize that this message must be interpreted, made relevant, by God's people for their own life context.

Bridge-building: We believe in our call to a radical life of reconciliation, which includes engaging with people of diverse cultural, religious, and political backgrounds in building bridges of justice, mutuality, and solidarity.

Reconciliation: We believe that God's grace begins in us the process of healing and reconciliation. We believe that Christ calls us to live and work in contexts where misunderstanding, injustice, and violence continue to prevent people from living fully human existences in peace and with the basic necessities. We believe in our call to overcome, with others, narratives of pain and violence, to make peace with former enemies, and to develop a spirituality of reconciliation.

These ideas were borne during Barbour's missionary assignments in Lesotho and later in Soweto, South Africa. Like thousands of others, she experienced human rights abuses due to her commitment to justice, solidarity and racial equality. Living among the people of Lesotho and Soweto solidified these commitments and led later to them being articulated for the members of Shalom.

Accompaniment as Spirituality and Practice

Using similar ideas as those found in the discipline of practical theology in which there is an integration of theological concepts with lived experience, (Graham 2006: 300) accompaniment is a 'practical spirituality' that requires an integration of faith and spirituality with lived experience. The following paragraphs provide working definitions of the terms spirituality, experience, mission and accompaniment. This will provide a foundation for the idea that mission as accompaniment can and does lead to a transformation that includes the 'missioner' as well as those who are the intended receivers. As we were often taught by a grassroots leader in an impoverished neighborhood on Chicago's south side, 'You are the reachers, we are the teachers.' She wanted to make sure that we understood that doing any form of ministry in her community would require us to be open to learning from the people.

Spirituality

Since we are most clearly committed to working from a Christian perspective the fundamentals of the definition of spirituality will be rooted in Trinitarian theology and the emphasis on community, rather than the individual.

> The goal of the spiritual life entails perfection of one's relationships with others .... From this perspective, spirituality naturally connects with the ethical demands of the Christian life, which flourishes in the increase of communion among persons.... Spiritual disciplines such as almsgiving, abstinence, and fasting are aimed at purifying one's relationships and establishing rightly ordered relationships based on mutuality, equality, and reciprocity rather than on domination and submission of one race to another, one class to another, one sex to another, and so on (Downey 1997: 45).

This is a spirituality grounded in the very community that is God: Father, Son and Spirit (Bevans and Schroeder 2004: 287). Mutuality, equality and reciprocity are central to the call to wholeness as humans respond to and participate in extending the relationship we have received in the community that the Trinity both models and provides us with.

Experience

Experience will be described here using a 'thick description,' (Geertz, 1973: ch.1) taking into account all aspects of individual and communal experience, including the sociocultural context within which it is found. Practical spirituality will of necessity be in constant dialogue with the multiplicity of experiences that impact the individual's or community's spirituality. Experience is more than an event, a relationship, an emotion or a memory held by an individual or community. It is rather a whole complex of interpretations that derive from what one has lived through, the socio-cultural and political influences, the religious and ethical convictions one holds, and even the influences of the interpretations of others. Thus experience of any two individuals united by time and circumstances can be vastly different depending on their personal histories, religious convictions and commitment to peace and justice.

It is proposed that a 'thick description' experience should be in a mutually critical correlation with spirituality 'in which each can challenge the other and contribute both descriptive and normative statements, coming to a deeper understanding through their essentially equal dialogue' (Poling and Miller 1985: 31). In other words, in order to have a 'practical spirituality' it must be in constant dialogue with experience. Each will be changed through this dialogue. Spirituality will become grounded in the realities of the human community, challenged by the concerns for all of God's creation, both human and all elements of the natural environment. And experience will be changed in a renewed depth of interpretation in the light of faith, theology and prayer.

Mission

The Vatican II decree on the missionary activity of the church, AG, refers to the '"fount-like love" or charity of God the Father' (AG 2). David Bosch expands on this phrase to ground our understanding of mission in God's mission, the *missio Dei*. Mission and love have their beginning 'in the heart of God'. God's love for creation is the center, origin, energy and goal of all human love. God's love for creation gives meaning and purpose to human existence and establishes how we are to relate to each other and to the rest of creation. God's love for creation defines what it means to be truly human. 'God is the fountain of sending love' (Bosch 1991: 392), God's mission is our mission.

This is a call to mission with an emphasis on the transformation of all humanity and creation by our participation in the *missio Dei*. The community that is God: Father, Son and Spirit, invites us to become co-creators. The earth and all that is in it depend on our participation in God's mission.

Accompaniment

The term accompaniment can be understood in several different contexts. One might accompany a friend on a shopping trip. An ill or injured person might need to be accompanied to the doctor. In the field of psychology and mental health a professional might accompany a person as they explore their memories, emotions, traumas and relationships with the world around them. However, when considering mission as accompaniment the term takes on yet another depth of meaning. This is not to minimize the importance of the previous uses of the term, but to point to the role accompaniment can play in an inclusive transformation, one that transforms the 'reachers' and the 'teachers' in the words of our grass-roots leader in Chicago:

> By definition, the act of accompaniment 'suggests going with another on an equal basis' and, thus, implies the transgression of discriminatory barriers. Only in and through the concrete *act* of accompaniment do we love others as 'others,' as equals, and are we, in turn, loved by them. As action, or praxis, accompaniment includes not only 'being' with another or feeling with another, but also 'doing' with another. (Goizueta 1995: 206)

Robert Schreiter writes that the Christian response to the challenges in today's globalized world should build on the missiological developments after Vatican Council II. '[W]ords that capture the theology and spirituality of Catholic missionaries since the Second Vatican Council … [are] incarnation, accompaniment and solidarity' (Schreiter 2001:136). To these we can add the biblical and theological concepts of love, mercy, and compassion as elements of mission as accompaniment (Doidge 2000: 165).

Accompaniment borne out of solidarity, love and compassion challenges us to enter deeply into the lives of the one suffering (Aquino 1993: 105), whether in poverty, oppression, illness, trauma or in immediate danger. While we cannot always alleviate the cause of the suffering, by taking away the cross, we are challenged to do what we can to make the cross lighter. Just as Simon Peter had to face his own humanity when he denied knowing Jesus three times (Jn. 18:1-27), solidarity, compassion and accompaniment ask us to surrender our security when it endangers another. Mission as accompaniment opens the horizon for the transformation of both parties in the relationship to a fully human existence. Jesus is our ultimate example. This is expressed poignantly and beautifully in a poem by Jon Sobrino and Juan Hernandez Pico:

In the pain, misfortune, oppression,
and death
of the people,
God is silent.
God is silent on the cross,
in the crucified.
And this silence is God's word,
God's cry.

In solidarity God speaks the language of love,
God makes a statement,
utters a self-revelation,
and takes up a presence
in solidarity.

God is love,
God stands in solidarity,
God is solidarity,
Where there is solidarity,
There is God.
(Sobrino and Pico 1985: vii)

Shalom and *Mitakuye Oyas'in*

A Convergence

The authors have each spent more than a quarter century in dialogue with Lakota (Sioux) on the Pine Ridge and Rosebud Reservations in South Dakota. Central to the spirituality and way of life of the Lakota is the prayer, '*mitakuye oyas'in*' or 'all my relatives'. '*Mitakuye oyas'in*' expresses the relationship of all that is; the two-legged, four-legged, creeping, crawling, swimming, flying, plants, trees, rocks, water, air, earth. In plain words, we are related to all that is, be it a small mosquito or magnificent ocean. The spirituality this prayer expresses entails the belief that our relationship is a responsibility, and that this relationship is at its core mutual and reciprocal, that the well-being of one aspect of creation is dependent on the well-being of all the others. Although not a new idea for those conscious of the delicate balance played out in the ecosystem, it is neither a fact nor a spirituality for most of the world's human inhabitants.

The Covenant and theological principles that the members of Shalom Ministries and Community affirm and commit to live by find their roots in the biblical notion of shalom, the Hebrew word for peace:

> Shalom has many dimensions of meaning: wholeness, completeness, well-being, peace, justice, salvation and even prosperity. Shalom also designates innocence from moral wrongdoing (Gen. 44:17; 1 Kgs. 5:19). Shalom is indeed a gift, but its maintenance in human life depends upon human response to God's order that values and acts in accord with the divine moral order. (Swartley 2006: 29)

Daniel J. Harrington sums up the OT meaning of shalom 'as the fullness of God's gifts' (Harrington 2007: 79). In the prayer and deeply imbedded spirituality conveyed in the meaning of '*mitakuye oyas'in*' our Lakota teachers have given us a new hermeneutical key to the meaning of Shalom. Understood with this new insight, the 'fullness of God's gifts' can be obtained when our actions are understood to effect all of creation, the two-legged, four-legged, creeping, crawling, flying, etc. Acting 'in accord with the divine moral order' embraces the belief in mutuality and reciprocity as we strive to live God's mission in the world.

The Accompanied and the Accompanier

The question might really be, who is being accompanied and who is the accompanier. In trying to live according to the biblical notion of shalom, those of us who have had sustained relationship with members of various marginalized individuals and communities have discovered that mutuality, compassion, solidarity, accompaniment are more than mere words. The conversion of hearts and minds through this process can be radical, leading to an entirely new way of perceiving and living reality.

Many of Jesus' encounters in the gospels invite us to understand the meaning of this kind of transformation as he lived it, and our own call to be transformed. There are multiple examples of Jesus living what we might call a mission of accompaniment as he encountered others along his way. The story of the Syrophoenician woman (Matt. 15:1-28) comes immediately to mind as a central example. This familiar story is often referred to as a turning point in Jesus' understanding of his mission. We have seen that he directs his disciples to confine their mission to the lost sheep of Israel (Matt. 10:5-6). And the woman's request for help for her daughter received this reply, 'I have been sent only to the lost sheep of the house of Israel' (v.24). The subsequent discussion about bread for the children and food for the dogs ends with Jesus healing the daughter. The border was breached. The Gentile woman's encounter and appeal was a wedge and Jesus responded by acting with mercy and compassion and healed her daughter. Jesus proclaimed her daughter healed, thereby extending himself, and his mission beyond the house of Israel. His solidarity with and compassion for others was a call for them to go beyond the externals of healing and forgiveness. How often we read that after an encounter with Jesus, the healed and forgiven individual is instructed, 'Go and sin no more.' On the one hand Jesus is saying, 'Change your actions'. On the other hand, we know he is saying, 'Change who you are', be transformed, become who you are called to be.

There are many examples of how the mission of accompaniment has extended far and wide beyond the initial contact made. One of these is when Barbour was invited to speak to a group of missionaries on the Rosebud Reservation about 'mission in reverse' and the Shalom Ministries approach to mission. During her visit to the reservation she had the opportunity to meet Moses Big Crow. This encounter between a wise, blind Native American spiritual leader and a French woman who had been a missionary in Lesotho and South Africa grew into a friendship that endured until Moses' death. During Barbour's visits to Rosebud the two shared about many different and wide ranging topics, including the similarities of the Lakota living conditions on the reservation with what she had seen in South Africa under the system of apartheid. The South African experience reaffirmed and strengthened her commitment to the marginalized and oppressed.

Subsequent to Barbour's initial encounter the authors have traveled more than one hundred times with a total of some 1,500 theology students and others to meet with Lakota leaders and teachers. The traveling seminars are conducted with the purpose of training for inter-cultural mission and ministry. Several other members of Shalom have joined the traveling seminars multiple times. With a growing sense of trust, respect and friendship these occasions are like visits to family for many of us. Accompaniment according to the Shalom theological principles has both enabled and challenged us to enter into relationships of mutuality and trust. We have become partners with our Lakota friends in a 'ministry' of training others how to minister in inter-cultural contexts.

The Accompanied Becomes Accompanier

Entering honestly into dialogue with a people who have every reason for rejection requires an open heart and mind. It requires letting go of one's excuses and temptations to defensiveness. It requires listening, listening, listening. Accompaniment, 'walking with', in these circumstances asks of us to listen in such a way as to provide the other a sense of safety (Herman 1997: 155) to tell their story. Our Lakota friends, like many who have suffered the trauma of oppression and loss of their culture, still find it necessary in the twenty-first century to tell their story, be heard and believed as to what has happened to them as individuals and a people. Accompaniment means allowing the story to be told, as many times over again as needed. But listening is not enough. As we heard the story(ies) revealing the destruction of a culture, loss of land, language and the forbidden rituals and spirituality, we could not help but be changed. Recognizing injustice requires a changed mind and heart; it also requires a commitment to work to overcome injustice.

The story of Francis White Lance, Oglala Lakota, Christian practioner of traditional Lakota spirituality, sundance leader, spiritual leader and follower of the ways of the Sacred Pipe (White Lance 2000:24) epitomizes how accompanying one individual can become transformative for countless others. In the article cited, and in presentations made to mission and ministry students, Francis tells how he met Barbour during his theology studies in the Chicago area. Her invitation to him to speak about his culture and spirituality to her students became a catalyst in his search to learn more about a spiritual tradition that he had learned virtually nothing about as the son of an Episcopal priest on the reservation. This was a result of the imposition of 'Western', i.e., white people's cultural values, norms and Christianity that was supported by the government and Christian churches to 'destroy the Indian and save the man (sic).' Acceptance of Christianity meant denying the traditional spiritual beliefs and practices so closely entwined with their cultural ways.

Francis had an undergraduate degree in philosophy and was well on his way toward obtaining a Masters of Divinity degree and ordination as an Episcopal priest. He added to this a new, almost insatiable thirst for knowledge and understanding of the traditional spirituality of his own people. Each new time Francis would speak to students it became evident that he was not only learning more, but in fact was being transformed by what he was learning. His words and actions reflected a new sense of his identity as a Lakota. One crucial step in this journey was when he joined the authors on one of the traveling seminars to the reservation that bordered his own. There he met two significant Lakota leaders who could provide him with the spiritual guidance needed as he embraced his traditional Lakota identity while remaining a Christian.

More than twenty years have passed since Barbour first asked Francis to speak to a group of seminarians about his culture and spirituality. He in turn attributes this as a turning point in his own identity and with other words says that she and Shalom have been his accompaniers in this process. We, however, know the story has not ended with Francis. He is a spiritual leader to many on his reservation and teacher of the traditions to adults and children, helping them to understand their history, culture and traditions, to embrace their identity.

This is one of the most effective challenges received by students of mission and ministry when we visit Francis and his family in South Dakota: 'Know your own culture, understand your people's history. Before you go out to work as missionaries among people of different cultures you need to know who you are as a member of your own "tribe".' This refrain is often repeated in the final interviews and papers by our students, be they Chinese, Polish, Vietnamese, Kenyan, Mexican, Nigerian, and North American. The transformed becomes an instrument and challenge to a new generation to be transformed. The accompanied becomes accompanier.

Conclusion

The experience of mission as accompaniment among the Lakota has challenged and nurtured the spirituality of many members of Shalom Ministries and countless graduate theology students. They in turn have gone on to become accompaniers of others in various parts of the world. Accompaniment is an important model for mission and has become more and more important in the last several decades in both the theology of and practice of Catholic mission today.

BIBLIOGRAPHY

AAS 1939. *Acta Apostolicae Sedis*. S. C. de Propaganda Fide. 'Instructio circa prudentiorem de rebus missionalibus tractandi rationem.' 9 June, 1939: 269.

AAS 1930. *Acta Apostolicae Sedis*. S. C. de Propaganda Fide, 'Instructio ad vicarios prefectosque et ad superiors institutorum, quibus a S. Sede missionibus sunt. 8 December, 1929: 111-15.

AG 1965. Vatican Council II. Decree on the Missionary Activity of the Church (*Ad Gentes*). http://www.vatican.va/archive/hist_councils/ii_vatican_council/documents/vat-ii_decree_19651207_ad-gentes_en.html.

Alberigo, Giuseppe and Komonchak, Joseph, Eds. 1995. *History of Vatican II, Volume 1: Announcing and Preparing Vatican Council II, Toward a New Era in Catholicism*. Maryknoll, NY: Orbis Books / Leuven, Belgium: Peeters.

_____ 1997. *History of Vatican II, Volume 2: Formation of the Council's Identity, First Period and Intersession, October 1962-September 1963*. Maryknoll, NY: Orbis Books / Leuven, Belgium: Peeters.

_____ 2000. *History of Vatican II, Volume 3: The Mature Council, Second Period and Intersession, October 1963 – September 1964*. Maryknoll, NY: Orbis Books / Leuven, Belgium: Peeters.

Allen, John L., Jr. 2009 *The Future Church: How Ten Trends Are Revolutionizing the Catholic Church*. New York: Doubleday.

AM 2011. Benedict XVI. Post-synodal Exhortation *Africae Munus*. http://www.vatican.va/holy_father/benedict_xvi/apost_exhortations/documents/hf_ben-xvi_exh_20111119_africae-munus_en.html.

Ambrosini, Maurizio 2011. *Sociologia delle Migrazioni*. Seconda Editizione. Bologna: Mulino.

American Society of Missiology 1973. http://www.asmweb.org/index.htm.

Anderson, Gerald H. 1998. *Biographical Dictionary of Christian Missions*. New York: Macmillan.

Anderson, Gerald H., Robert T. Coote, Norman A. Horner and James M. Philips, Eds. 1994. *Mission Legacies: Biographical Studies of Leaders of the Modern Missionary Movement*. Maryknoll, NY: Orbis Books.

Aparecida 2007. Final Document of the Fifth General Assembly of the Bishops' Conferences of Latin America and the Carribean. http://www.slideshare.net/cscctt/aparecida-document.

Aquino, Maria Pilar 1993. *Our Cry For Life*. Maryknoll, NY: Orbis Books.

Armstrong, John H. 2010. *Your Church is Too Small: Why Unity in Christ's Mission Is Vital to the Future of the Church*. Grand Rapids: Zondervan.

AS 1977. *Acta Synodalia S. Concilii Oecumenici Vaticani II*. IV. III. Vatican City: Vatican Polyglot Press.

Athyal, Saphir, Ed. 1996. *Church in Asia Today*. Singapore: The Asia Lausanne Committee for World Evangelization.

Attali, Jacques 2006. *L'Uomo Nomade*. Firenze: Spirali. French original published 2003.

Baggio, Fabio and Agnes Brazal, Eds. 2008. *Faith on the Move: Toward a Theology of Migration in Asia*. Manila: Ateneo de Manila University Press.

Barreda, Jesús-Angel 2010. 'Missione.' In Battistella, Ed. 666-76.

Barrena Sánchez, Félix 2010. 'La inmigración come Desafío a la Misión.'
http://www.sedosmission.org/site/index.php?option=com_docman&task=cat_v
uew&gid=38&Utewnud=59&kabg=it.

Battistella, Graziano 2010, Ed. *Migrazioni: Dizionario Socio-Pastorale.* Cinisello
Balsamo: San Paolo.

_____ 2008. 'Migration and Human Dignity: From Policies of Exclusion to
Policies Based on Human Rights.' In Groody and Campese, Ed., 177-91.

_____ 2005. *La Missione Viene a Noi. In Margine all'Istruzione Erga
Migrantes Caritas Christi.* Vatican City: Urbaniana University Press, 2005.

Baur, J. 1994. *2000 Years of Christianity in Africa: An African History 62-1992.*
Nairobi: Paulines Publications – Africa.

Bechtold, Paul 1993. *Catholic Theological Union at Chicago: The Founding Years.
History and Memoir.* Chicago, IL: Catholic Theological Union.

Bediako, Kwame 1995. *Christianity in Africa: The Renewal of a Non-Western
Religion.* Maryknoll, NY: Orbis Books.

Bellagamba, Anthony 1994. *Mission and Ministry in the Global Church.*
Maryknoll, NY: Orbis Books.

'Before Vatican II' 1978. 'Missionary Encyclicals before Vatican II.' *Omnis Terra*
(English) 12, 297-300. (Identical presentation in *Fundamental Correspondence
Course for Mission Animators.* Rome: Pontifical Missionary Union
International Secretariat, 115-18).

Benedict XV 1919. Encyclical Letter *Maximum Illud* , ('Spreading the Catholic
Faith') [MI]. http://www.vatican.va/holy_father/benedict_xv/apost_letters/
documents/hf_ben-xv_apl_19191130_maximum-illud_it.html. (Italian
version).

Benedict XVI 2010. 'Message for the World Day of Peace, 1 January 2010: If You
Want to Cultivate Peace, Protect Creation.' http://www.vatican.va/holy_
father/benedict_xvi/messages/peace/documents/hf_ben-
xvi_mes_20091208_xliii-woeld-day-peace_en.html.

_____ 2008. 'Address to Bishops and Representatives of Ecclesial Movements
and New Communities. http://www.catholicculture.org/culture/library/
view.cfm?recnum=8285.

Best, Thomas, Lorelei Fuchs, and Jeffrey Gros, Eds. 2007. *Growth in Agreement
III.* Geneva / Grand Rapids, MI: World Council of Churches / William B.
Eerdmans Publishing Company.

Bettscheider, Heribert 2001. 'Mission for the Twenty-First Century in Europe.' In
Bevans and Schroeder, Ed. 110-28.

Bevans, Stephen B. forthcoming. 'Migration and Mission: Pastoral Challenges,
Theological Insights.' In projected three-volume work edited by Peter C. Phan
and Elaine Padilla. New York: Palgrave Macmillan.

_____ 2009. *An Introduction to Theology in Global Perspective.* Maryknoll,
NY: Orbis Books.

_____ 2008. 'Mission *among* Migrants, Mission *of* Migrants: Mission of the
Church.' In Groody and Campese, Ed. 89-106.

_____ 2003. 'Unraveling a 'Complex Reality': Six Elements of Mission.'
International Bulletin of Missionary Research 27:2, 50-53.

_____ 2002. *Models of Contextual Theology.* Revised and Expanded Edition.
Maryknoll, NY: Orbis Books.

_____ 1995. 'What Catholics Can Learn from Evangelical Mission Theology.'
Missiology: An International Review 23:2, 155-64.

_____ 1991. 'Seeing Mission through Images.' *Missiology: An International Review* 19:1, 45-57.

Bevans, Stephen and Jeffrey Gros 2009. *Evangelization and Religious Freedom: Ad Gentes, Dignitatis Humanae*. New York: Paulist Press.

Bevans, Stephen B. and Roger P. Schroeder 2011. *Prophetic Dialogue: Reflections on Christian Mission Today*. Maryknoll, NY: Orbis Books.

_____ 2004. *Constants in Context: A Theology of Mission for Today*. Maryknoll, NY: Orbis Books.

Bevans, Stephen B. and Roger P. Schroeder, Eds. 2001. *Mission for the Twenty-First Century*. Chicago, IL: CCGM Publications.

Bingemer, Maria Clara 2009. *Jesus Cristo: Serve de Deus e Messias glorioso*. Sao Paulo: Paulinas.

_____ 1998. 'Jesus Christ' in *The International Bible Commentary*, Ed. W. Farmer, Collegeville, MN: The Liturgical Press, 182-86.

Bingemer, Maria Clara and Vitor Galdino Feller 2000, *Deus Trinidade: A Vida No Coracao Do Mundo*. Valencia/Sao Paulo: Siquem/Paulinas.

Boff, Leonardo 1985. *Church: Charism and Power*. Maryknoll, NY: Orbis Books.

Bosch, David J. 1993. 'Hermeneutical Principles in the Biblical Foundation for Mission.' *Evangelical Review of Theology* 19, 437-51.

_____ 1991. *Transforming Mission: Paradigm Shifts in Theology and Mission*. Maryknoll, NY: Orbis Books.

Bouchaud, J. 1967. 'Africa.' In *The New Catholic Encyclopedia*. Volume 5. Washington, DC: Catholic University of America Press, 172-86.

Brechter, Suso 1969. 'Decree on Missionary Activity.' In *Commentary on the Documents of Vatican II*, ed. Herbert Vorgrimler. Volume 4. Freiburg: Herder / Montreal: Palm Publishers, 87-181.

Brett, M. 1978 'The Arab Conquest and the Rise of Islam in North Africa.' In *The Cambridge History of Africa, volume 2, c.500 BC – 1050 AD*, J. D. Fage Ed.. Cambridge: University Press, 490-555.

Briggs, John, Mercy Amba Oduyoye and George Tsetsis 2004. *A History of the Ecumenical Movement 1968-2000*. Volume 3. Geneva: World Council of Churches.

Broadbent, John 2003. 'New Zealand, The Catholic Church in: The Modern Church. *New Catholic Encyclopedia – Second Edition*. Volume 10, 326-28. New York: Thomson-Gale.

Brother John of Taize 1985. *The Pilgrim God: A Biblical Journey*. Washington, DC: Pastoral Press.

Brown, Raymond E. 1984. *The Churches the Apostles Left Behind*. Mahwah, NJ: Paulist Press.

Bühlmann, Walbert 1984. *Weltkriche*. Graz, Austria: Styria.

_____ 1983. *God's Chosen Peoples*. Maryknoll, NY: Orbis Books.

_____ 1979. "Missionary Spirituality." In ed. Padraig Flanagan. *A New Missionary Era*. 113-18. Maryknoll, NY: Orbis Books.

_____ 1978. *The Missions on Trial*. Slough, UK: St Paul Publications.

_____ 1976. *The Coming of the Third Church: An Analysis of the Present and Future of the Church*. Slough, UK: St Paul Publications.

Bünker, Arnd 2004. *Missionarish Kirche sein?* Münster: LIT Verlag.

Burke, Thomas J., Ed. 1957. *Catholic Missions: Four Great Encyclicals*. New York: Fordham University Press.

Burrows, William R., Ed. 1993. *Redemption and Dialogue: Reading Redemptoris Missio and Dialogue and Proclamation*. Maryknoll, NY: Orbis Books.
_____ 2007. "Intercultural Formation for Mission: Ad et Inter Gentes." *Australian eJournal of Theology*. 11, 1-22.
_____ 1986. 'Decree on the Church's Missionary Activity, *Ad Gentes Divinitus*, 7 December, 1965.' In *Vatican II and its Documents: An American Reappraisal*, ed. Timothy E. O'Connell. Wilmington, DE: Michael Glazier, Inc, 180-96.
CA 1991. John Paul II. Encyclical Letter *Centesimus Annus*. http://www.vatican.va/holy_father/john_paul_ii/encyclicals/documents/hf_jp-ii_enc_01051991_centesimus-annus_en.html.
Campese, Gioacchino 2012. 'The Irruption of Migrants: Theology of Migration in the 21st Century.' *Theological Studies* 73:1, 3-32.
_____ 2012b. 'La Théologie et les Migrations: La Redécouverte d'Une Dimension Structurelle de la Foi Chrétienne.' *Migration Société* 24:139, 135-55.
_____ 2010. 'Teologia delle Migrazioni.' In Battistella, Ed. 1019-24.
_____ 2007. 'Beyond Ethnic and National Imagination: Toward a Catholic Theology of U. S. Immigration.' In *Religion and Social Justice for Immigrants*, Ed. Pierrette Hondagneu-Sotelo. New Bruswick, NJ: Rutgers University Press, 175-90.
_____ 1997. 'Walk Humbly with Your God! Notes on a Spirituality of Missionaries with Migrants.' *Missiology: An International Review* 25:2, 131-40.
Carlen, Claudia 1990. *The Papal Encyclicals*. Five Volumes. Ypsilanti, MI: The Pieran Press.
Castles, Stephen and Mark J. Miller 2009. *The Age of Migration: International Populations Movements in the Modern World*. 4th ed. New York: Palgrave Macmillan.
Colzani, Gianni 2005. 'Missione e Missione con I Migranti: Linee per un Possibile Sviuppo.' In Battistella, Ed. 77-88.
CCC 1994. *Catechism of the Catholic Church*. New York: Doubleday Image Books, 1995. Original Latin edition 1994.
CCEE 1991. *The Bishops of Europe and New Evangelization*. Casale Monferrato, Italy: Piemme.
CDF 2007. Congregation for the Doctrine of the Faith. *Doctrinal Notes on Some Aspects of Evangelization*. http://www.vatican.va/roman_curia/congregations/cfaith/documents/rc_con_cfaith_doc_20071203_nota-evangelizzazione_en.html.
Charles, Pierre 1954/56. *Études Missiologiques*. Louvain: Desclée de Brouwer.
_____ 1947. *La Prière Missionaire*. Louvain: Editions de L'Aucam.
_____ 1939. *Missiologie*. Vol. I. Louvain: Editions de l'Aucam.
_____ 1938. *Les Dossiers de l'action missonnaire*. Volume I (2nd ed). Louvain: Editions de l'Aucam.
_____ 1932. *Principes et methods de l'Activité Missionnaire en Dehors du Catholicisme*. Louvain: Editions de l'Aucam.
Chiromba, F. 1996. 'The Life of the Church.' In *African Synod: Documents, Reflections, Perspectives*. Ed. African Faith and Justice Network. Maryknoll, NY: Orbis Books, 9-13.

CIC 1983. *Code of Canon Law*. http://www.vatican.va/archive/ENG1104/_
INDEX.HTM.

CIMI 2011. *Relatório Violéncia Contra Os Povos Indigenas No Brasil. Dados de
2010*. Brasilia: CIMI.

CIMI 2001. Conselho Indigenista Missionário. *Outros 500. Consruindo uma Nova
História*. Sao Paulo: Salesiana.

Clark, Francis X. 1948. *The Purpose of Missions: A Study of the Mission
Documents of the Holy See 1909-1946*. New York: The Missionary Union of
the Clergy.

CNBB 2010. Conferencia Nacional dos Bispos do Brazil, *Igreja e Quesao Agrarian
no Inicio do Século XXI*. Estudos da CNBB, 99. Brasilia: CNBB.

Coleman, William J. 1967. 'Missions, Papal Letters on.' *New Catholic
Encyclopedia* IX. Washington, DC: The Catholic University of America, 936-
37.

Collet, Giancarlo 2004. '...*Fino agli Estremi Confini della Terra*': Questioni
fondamentali di teologia della missione. Brescia: Queriniana.

Congregation for Divine Worship 1994. 'The Roman Liturgy and Inculturation:
IVth Instruction for the Right Application of the Conciliar Constitution on the
Liturgy (nn. 37-40).' http://www.ewtn.com/library/curia/cdwinclt.htm.

Considine, John J. 1952. 'Evangelii Praecones.' *The Homiletic and Pastoral Review*
5,: 420-23.

_____ 1925. *The Vatican Mission Expositions*. New York: The Macmillan
Company.

Coonan, John L. 1957. 'The Future of Africa: A Commentary on the Encyclical
'*Donum Fidei*'.' *The Tablet* 209, 534-36.

Cooney, Monica 1996. 'Toward Common Witness.' *International Review of
Mission* 86:343, 283-89.

Corboy, Thomas 1968. 'A Commentary on the Mission Decree.' In *Missions and
Religions*. Ed. Austin Flannery. Dublin: Scepter Publications, 9-20.

Cruz, Gemma Talud 2010. 'Expanding Boundaries, Turning Borders into Spaces.'
In Kalu, Vethanayagamony and Chia, Eds. 71-83.

Culhane, Robert 1950. 'The Primary Purpose of the Foreign Missions.' *The Irish
Ecclesiastical Record* 73, 385-92.

CV 2009. Benedict XVI. Encyclical Letter *Caritas in Veritate*.
http://www.vatican.va/holy_father/benedict_xvi/encyclicals/documents/hf_ben
-xvi_enc_20090629_caritas-in-veritate_en.html.

CWME 2010. Commission on World Mission and Evangelism. 'Mission
Spirituality and Discipleship: Beyond and through Contemporary Boundaries.'
International Review of Mission 99.1: 106-24.

Davis, Cyprian 1990. *The History of Black Catholics in the United States*. New
York: Crossroad.

Declaration of Barbados 1980. 'The Declaration of Barbados.' In *Em Defesa dos
Povas Indigenas*. Ed. Paulo Suess Sao Paulo: Loyola.

De Gruchy, John 2002. *Reconciliation: Restoring Justice*. Minneapolis, MN:
Fortress Press.

Delaney, Joan 2001. 'My Pilgrimage in Mission.' *International Bulletin of
Missionary Research* 25:1, 26-28.

_____ 2000. 'From Cremona to Edinburgh: Bishop Bonomelli and the World
Missionary Conference of 1910.' *The Ecumenical Review* 52.3: 418-31.

Delbrêl, Madeleine 2000. *We, the Ordinary People of the Streets*. Grand Rapids,
    MI: William B. Eerdmans Publishing Company.
de Letter, Prudent 1961. 'A Pontifical Vista of Forty Years.' *Worldmission* (USA)
    12: 22-32.
Delio, Ilia 2010. 'Godhead or God Ahead?' In *God, Grace, and Creation*ed. Philip
    J. Rossi, 3-22. Maryknoll, NY: Orbis Books, 3-22.
Delio, Ilia, Keith Douglass Warner and Pamela Wood 2008. *Care for Creation: A
    Franciscan Spirituality of Earth*. Cincinnati: St. Anthony Messenger Press.
DH 1965. Vatican Council II. Vatican Council II. Declaration on Religious
    Freedom (*Dignitatis Humanae*). http://www.vatican.va/archive/hist_councils/
    ii_vatican_council/documents/vat-ii_decl_19651207_dignitatis-
    humanae_en.html.
DI 2000. Congregation for the Doctrine of the Faith. Declaration 'Dominus Iesus'
    on the Unicity and Salvific Universality of Jesus Christ and the Church.
    http://www.vatican.va/roman_curia/congregations/cfaith/documents/rc_con_cf
    aith_doc_20000806_dominus-iesus_en.html.
Die Deutchen Bischöfe 2000. *Zeit zur Aussaat*. Bonn: Deutsche Bishofskonferenz.
Dion, Paul-Eugene 1975. *Dieu Universel et Peuple Élu*. Paris: Éditions du Cerf.
Dixon, Robert, Audra Kunciunas and Stephen Reid 2008. *Mass Attendance in
    Australia*. Canberra: Australian Catholic Bishops' Conference Pastoral
    Projects Office.
DM 1984. Secretariat for Non-Christians. 'The Attitude of the Church toward the
    Follows of Other Religions: Reflections and Orientations on Dialogue and
    Mission.' *Bulletin. Secretariatus Pro Non-Christianis* 56:13, 126-41.
Doidge, Eleanor. 2000. 'Accompaniment: Mission in the Heart of God,' In *The
    Healing Circle: Essays in Cross-Cultural Mission*. Eds. Stephen Bevans,
    Eleanor Doidge and Robert J. Schreiter. Chicago, IL: CCGM Publications,
    162-75
Dolan, Jay and Gilberto M. Hinojosa, Eds. 1994. *Mexican Americans and the
    Catholic Church, 1900-1965*. Notre Dame, IN: University of Notre Dame
    Press.
Downey, Michael 2006. "Consenting to Kenosis: Mission to Secularity." In ed. Ronald
    Rohlheiser. *Secularity and the Gospel: Being Missionaries to Our Children*. 116-
    34. New York: Crossroad.
_____ 1997. *Understanding Christian Spirituality*. New York: Paulist Press.
Doyle, Dennis 1991. 'Inculturation and the Interpretation of Vatican II in Recent
    Papal Documents.' Talk given at the College Theology Society in Chicago.
DP 1991. Pontifical Council for Dialogue and Congregation for the Evangelization
    of Peoples. *Dialogue and Proclamation*. http://www.vatican.va/roman_curia/
    pontifical_councils/interelg/documents/rc_pc_interelg_doc_19051991_dialogu
    e-and-proclamatio_en.html.
Dries, Angelyn 2001 / 1998. *The Missionary Movement in American Catholic
    History*. Maryknoll, NY: Orbis Books.
_____ 1989. ''The Whole Way into the Wilderness': The Foreign Mission
    Impulse of the American Catholic Church, 1893-1925.' Ph.D. Diss. Graduate
    Theological Union, Berkeley, CA.
DS 1976. Heinrich Denzinger and Adolf Schönmetzer, ed. *Enchiridion
    Symbolorum, Definitionum et Delcarationum de Rebus Fidei et Morum*. 34th
    Edition. Freiburg im Breisgau: Herder. NB: References are to paragraph
    numbers, not to page numbers.

DuBose, Francis M., Ed. 1979. *Classics of Christian Missions*. Nashville, TN: Broadman Press.

Duprey, Pierre 1985. 'Ecumenismo e Missione.' In *Portare Cristo all'uomo: Il Testimonianza*. Rome: Urbaniana University Press.

Dupuis, Jacques 1997. *Toward a Christian Theology of Religious Pluralism*. Maryknoll, NY: Orbis Books.

_____ 1994. 'Evangelization and Mission.' In *Dictionary of Fundamental Theology*. Eds. René Latourelle and R. Fischiella. New York: Crossroads Publishing Company, 275-82.

_____ 1993. 'A Theological Commentary: Dialogue and Proclamation.' In Burrows, Ed. 119-58.

Duquoc, Christian 1985. *Jésus, Homme Libre*. Paris: Editions du Cerf.

Durand, Jorje and Douglas S. Massey 1995. *Miracles on the Border: Retablos of Mexican Migrants to the United States*. Tucson, AZ: University of Arizona Press.

DV 1986. John Paul II. Encyclical Letter *Dominum et Vivificantem*. http://www.vatican.va/holy_father/john_paul_ii/encyclicals/documents/hf_jp-ii_enc_18051986_dominum-et-vivificantem_en.html.

DV 1965. Vatican Council II. Constitution on Divine Revelation. *Dei Verbum*. http://www.vatican.va/archive/hist_councils/ii_vatican_council/documents/vat-ii_const_19651118_dei-verbum_en.html.

EAf 1995. John Paul II. Apostolic Exhortation *Ecclesia in Africa*. http://www.vatican.va/holy_father/john_paul_ii/apost_exhortations/documents /hf_jp-ii_exh_14091995_ecclesia-in-africa_en.html.

EAs 1999. John Paul II. Apostolic Exhortation *Ecclesia in Asia*. http://www.vatican.va/holy_father/john_paul_ii/apost_exhortations/documents /hf_jp-ii_exh_06111999_ecclesia-in-asia_en.html.

EdE 2003. John Paul II. Encyclical Letter *Ecclesia de Eucharistia*. http://www.vatican.va/holy_father/john_paul_ii/encyclicals/documents/hf_jp-ii_enc_20030417_eccl-de-euch_en.html.

EE 2003. John Paul II. Apostolic Exhortation *Ecclesia in Europa*. http://www.vatican.va/holy_father/john_paul_ii/apost_exhortations/documents /hf_jp-ii_exh_20030628_ecclesia-in-europa_en.html.

Edwards, Denis 2010. *How God Acts: Creation, Redemption, and Special Divine Actions*. Minneapolis, MN: Fortress Press.

_____ 2009. 'Ecological Commitment and the Following of Christ. *Sedos Bulletin* 41:7/8, 159-95.

_____ 2008. *Ecology at the Heart of Faith: The Change of Heart that Leads to a New Way of Living on Earth*. Maryknoll, NY: Orbis Books.

Ela, Marc 1986. *African Cry*. Maryknoll, NY: Orbis Books.

EMCC 2004. Pontifical Council for the Pastoral Care of Migrants and Intinerant People. *Erga Migrantes Caritas Christi*. http://www.vatican.va/roman_curia/pontifical_councils/migrants/documents/rc _pc_migrants_doc_20040514_erga-migrantes-caritas-christi_en.html.

EN 1975. Paul VI. Apostolic Exhortation *Evangelii Nuntiandi*. http://www.vatican.va/holy_father/paul_vi/apost_exhortations/documents/hf_p -vi_exh_19751208_evangelii-nuntiandi_en.html.

Encyclopedia Universalis. http://www.universalis.fr/.

Endres, David 2010. *American Crusade: Catholic Youth in the World Mission Movement from World War I through Vatican II*. Eugene, Or: Pickwick Publications.
EO 2001. John Paul II. Apostolic Exhortation *Ecclesia in Oceania*.
http://www.vatican.va/holy_father/john_paul_ii/apost_exhortations/documents/hf_jp-ii_exh_20011122_ecclesia-in-oceania_en.html.
EP 1951. Pius XII. Encyclical Letter *Evangelii Praecones*.
http://www.vatican.va/holy_father/pius_xii/encyclicals/documents/hf_p-xii_enc_02061951_evangelii-praecones_en.html.
ES 1964. Paul VI. Encyclical Letter *Ecclesiam Suam*.
http://www.vatican.va/holy_father/paul_vi/encyclicals/documents/hf_p-vi_enc_06081964_ecclesiam_en.html.
EV 1995. John Paul II. Encyclical Letter *Evangelium Vitae*.
http://www.vatican.va/holy_father/john_paul_ii/encyclicals/documents/hf_jp-ii_enc_25031995_evangelium-vitae_en.html.
FABC I 1997. Gaudencio Rosales and Catalino G. Arévalo, Eds. *For All the People of Asia: Federation of Asian Bishops' Conferences, Documents from 1970 to 1991*. Quezon City, Philippines: Claretian Publicatons.
FABC II 1997. Fraz-Josef Eilers, Ed. *For All the Peoples of Asia, Volume 2: Federation of Asian Bishops' Conferences Documents from 1992 to 1996*. Quezon City, Philippines: Claretian Publications.
FABC III 2002. Franz-Josef Eilers, Ed. *For All the Peoples of Asia, Volume 3, Federation of Asian Bishops' Conferences Documents from 1997 to 2001*. Quezon City, Philippines: Claretian Publications.
FABC IV 2007. Franz-Josef Eilers, Ed. *For All the Peoples of Asia, Volume 4, Federation of Asian Bishops' Conferences Documents from 2002 to 2006*. Quezon City, Philippines: Claretian Publications.
Fassholé-Luke et al. Eds. 1978. *Christianity in Independent Africa*. Ibadan, Nigeria: University Press.
Fay, Terence J. 2003. *A History of Canadian Catholics*. Montreal & Kingston: McGill / Queen's University Press.
FD 1957. Pius XII. Encyclical Letter *Fidei Donum*.
http://www.vatican.va/holy_father/pius_xii/encyclicals/documents/hf_p-xii_enc_21041957_fidei-donum_en.html.
Fernandez, Francis 1996. *In Ways Known to God: A Theological Investigation of the Ways of Salvation Spoken of in Vatican II*. Shillong, India: Vendrame Institute Publications.
Fey, Harold, Ed. 1986. *The Ecumenical Advance: A History of the Ecumenical Movement 1948-1968*. Geneva: World Council of Churches.
Fitzgerald, Michael 1991. 'Mission at Canberra.' *International Review of Mission* 80:317, 315-472.
Foreman, Charles 1982. *The Island Churches of the South Pacific: Emergence in the Twentieth Century*. Maryknoll, NY: Orbis Books.
Forst, Rainer 2003. *Contexts of Justice: Political Philosophy beyond Liberalism and Communitarianism*. Berkeley, CA: University of California Press.
Francis 2013. Mass, Imposition of the Pallium and Bestowal of the Fisherman's Ring for the Beginning of the Petrine Ministry of the Bishop of Rome. Homily of Pope Francis, Saint Peter's Square, Tuesday 19th March 2013.
http://www.vatican.va/holy_father/francesco/homilies/2013/documents/papa-francesco_20130319_omelia-inizio-pontificato_en.html.

Fredericks, Martha Th. and Nienke Pruiksma. 'Journeying towards Multiculturalism? The Relationship between Immigrant Christians and Dutch Indigenous Churches.' *Journal of Religion in Europe* 3, 125-54.

Fretheim, Terrence E. 1991. *Exodus*. Louisville, KY: John Knox Press.

Frizen, Edwin 1992. *75 Years of the Interdenominational Foreign Mission Association of North America: 1917-1992*. Pasadena: William Carey Library.

'Future' 1957. 'The Future of Africa.' *The Tablet* 209:6102, 427-28.

Gaillardetz, Richard R. and Catherine Clifford 2012. *Keys to the Council: Unlocking the Teaching of Vatican II*. Collegeville, MN: The Liturgical Press.

Gálvez, Alisha 2010. *Guadalupe in New York: Devotion and Struggle for Citizenship Rights Among Mexican Immigrants*. New York: New York University Press.

Gateley, Edwina 2013. "Spirit and Lifestyle." http://www.vmmusa.org/spiritandlifestyle.html.

Geertz, Clifford 1973. *The Interpretation of Cultures*. New York: Harper Torchbooks.

Gelpi, Donald L. 1998. *The Conversion Experience*. Mahwah, NJ: Paulist Press.

Gensichen, Hans Werner 1967. 'The Second Vatican Council's Challenge to Protestant Mission.' *International Review of Mission* 56:223, 291-309.

Gentrup, Theodore 1913. 'Die Definition des Missionsgriffes.' *Zeitschrift für Missionswissenschaft* 3, 265-74.

George, Sam 2011. 'Diaspora: A Hidden Link to 'from Everywhere to Everywhere.'' *Missiology: An International Review* 39:1, 45-56.

Gibbs, Philip, Ed. 2006. *Alive in Chirst: The Synod for Oceania and the Catholic Church in Papua New Guinea 1998-2005*. Point 30. Goroka, Papua New Guinea: The Melanesian Institute.

Giglioni, Paolo 1996. *Teologia Pastorale Missionaria*. Cittá del Vaticano: Libreria Editrice.

Gittins, Anthony J. 2002. *Ministry at Margins: Strategy and Spirituality for Mission*. Maryknoll, NY: Orbis Books.

_____ 1989. *Gifts and Strangers: Meeting the Challenge of Inculturation*. Mahwah, NJ: Paulist Press.

Glasser, Arthur 1985. 'Vatican II and Mission 1965-1985: An Evangelical Appraisal.' *Missiology: An International Review* 13:4, 487-99.

Glazik, Josef 1971. 'Mission Encyclicals of the Popes.' In *Concise Dictionary of the Christian World Mission*, Ed. Stephen Neill et al. New York: Abingdon Press, 406-07.

_____ 1970. *Kommentar*. In *Instruktionen der Kongregation für die Evangelisation der Völker*. Trier: Paulinus Verlag

Godin, Henri 1950. *Zwischen Abfall und Bekehrung*. Offenburg. Dokumente Verlag

Godin, Henry and Yves Daniel 1943. *La France: Pays de Mission?* Paris. Editions du Cerf

Gioia, Francesco, Ed. 1997. *Inter-religious Dialogue: The Official Teaching of the Catholic Church: 1963-1995*. Boston: Pauline.

Goizueta, Roberto S. 1995. *Caminemos Con Jesús: Toward a Hispanic/Latino Theology of Accompaniment*. Maryknoll, NY: Orbis Books.

Gold, Lorna, and Dimitrij Bregant 1992. 'Case Study: The Focolare Movement – Evangelization and Contemporary Culture.' *International Review of Mission* 92:364, 22-28.

Graham, Elaine 2006. 'The Professional Doctorate in Practical Theology.'
    International Journal of Practical Theology. (October), 298-311.
Groody, Daniel G. and Gioacchino Campese, EdS. 2008. *A Promised Land, A
    Perilous Journey: Theological Perspectives on Migration.* Notre Dame, IN:
    University of Notre Dame Press.
Grootaers, Jan 1997. 'The Drama Continues between the Acts: The 'Second
    Preparation' and Its Opponents.' In Alberigo and Komonchak, EdS. 516-64.
Gros, Jeffrey 2009. 'The Healing of Memories: Finding One Another Again in
    Christ.' In *The Unity of the Church*, Ed. E. van der Borght, 189-210. Studies in
    Reformed Theology 19. Leiden /Boston: Brill.
Gutiérrez, Gustavo 1973. *A Theology of Liberation: Politics, History, and
    Salvation.* Maryknoll, NY: Orbis Books.
GS 1965. Vatican Council II. Pastoral Constitution on the Church in the Modern
    World (*Gaudium et Spes*). http://www.vatican.va/archive/hist_councils/
    ii_vatican_council/documents/vat-ii_cons_19651207_gaudium-et-
    spes_en.html.
Hagan, Jacqueline M. 2008. *Migration Miracle: Faith, Hope, and Meaning on the
    Undocumented Journey.* Cambridge, MA: Harvard University Press.
Hanciles, Jehu J. 2011. ''Migration and the Globalization of Christianity.' In
    Understanding World Christianity: The Vision and Work of Andrew F. Walls,
    Ed. William R. Burrows, Mark R. Gornik and Janice A. McLean. Maryknoll,
    NY: Orbis Books, 227-41.
_____ 2008. *Beyond Christendom: Globalization, African Migration, and the
    Transformation of the West.* Maryknoll, NY: Orbis Books.
_____ 2008b. 'Migration and Mission: The Religious Significance of the North-
    South Divide.' In ed. Andrew F. Walls and Cathy Ross, *Mission in the 21ˢᵗ
    Century: Exploring the Five Marks of Global Mission.* 18-29. London: Darton,
    Longman and Todd.
_____ 2004. 'Beyond Christendom: African Migration and the Transformations
    of Global Christianity.' *Studies in World Christianity* 10:1, 93-113.
_____ 2003. 'Migration and Mission: Some Implications for the Twenty-first
    Century.' *International Bulletin of Missionary Research* 27:4, 146-53.
Harrington, Daniel J. 2007. *The Gospel of Matthew.* Collegeville, MN: Liturgical
    Press.
Harris, John 1990. *One Blood: 200 Years of Aboriginal Encounter with
    Christianity: A Story of Hope.* Sutherland, Australia: An Albatross Book.
Haught, John F. 2010. *Making Sense of Evolution: Darwin, God, and the Drama of
    Life.* Louisville, KY: Westminster John Knox.
_____ 2007. *Christianity and Science: Towards a Theology of Nature.*
    Maryknoll, NY: Orbis Books.
Heisig, James 2002. 'O diálogo interreligioso e o desannemento teológico,' *MAGIS*
    42. Cadernos da Fé e Cultura, Rio de Janeiro.
Herman, Judith 1997. *Trauma and Recovery.* New York, NY: Basic Books.
Hernández, Angel Santos 1991. *Teología Systemática de la Misión.* Estella, Spain:
    Editorial Verbo Divino.
_____ 1958. *Adaptación Misionera.* Bilbao: El Siglo de la Misione.
Heyer, Kristin E 2012. 'Reframing Displacement and Membership: Ethics of
    Migration.' *Theological Studies* 73:1, 188-206.
Hickey, R. 1982. *Modern Missionary Documents and Africa.* Dublin: Dominican
    Publications.

Hiebert, Paul 2008. *Transforming Worldviews: An Anthropological Understanding of How People Change*. Grand Rapids, MI: Baker Academic.

Hondagneu-Sotelo, Pierette 2011. 'Gender and Migration Scholarship: An Overview from a 21st Century Perspective.' *Migraciones Internacionales* 6:1, 219-33.

_____ 2008. *God's Heart Has No Borders: How Religious Activists Are Working for Immigrant Rights*. Berkeley: University of California Press.

_____ 2001. *Domestica: Immigrant Workers Cleaning and Caring in the Shadows of Affluence*. Berkeley: University of California Press.

Hublou, Albert 1932. '10 Years of Roman Catholic Missions.' *International Review of Missions* 23, 516-20.

Hughes, Philip 2007. *Putting Life Together: Findings from Australian Youth Spirituality Research*. Fairfield: Fairfield Press.

Ilundain, José Antonio 2005. 'Fifty Years of the *'Fidei Donum'.' Omnis Terra* (English) 39, 342-47.

International Anglican-Roman Catholic Commission for Unity and Mission 2007. *Growing Together in Unity and Mission: Building on 40 Years of Anglican-Catholic Dialogue*. http://www.vatican.va/roman_curia/pontifical_councils/chrstuni/angl-commun-docs/re_pc_chrstuni_doc_20070914_growing-together_en.html.

Jackson, Darrell 2011. 'Europe and the Migrant Experience: Transforming Integration.' *Transformation* 28:1, 14-28.

Janssen, Hermann 1994. 'Vision & Foundation of the Melanesian Institute.' Point 19. Silver Jubilee of Melanesian Institution. Goroka, Papua New Guinea: The Melanesian Institute. 28-39.

Jenkins, Philip 2007. *God's Continent: Christianity, Islam and Europe's Religious Crisis*. New York: Oxford University Press.

_____ 2006. *The New Faces of Christianity: Believing the Bible in the Global South*. New York / Oxford: Oxford University Press.

_____ 2002. *The Next Christendom: The Coming of Global Christianity*. New York / Oxford: Oxford University Press.

Jenkinson, William and Helene O'Sullivan, Eds. 1991. *Trends in Mission: Towards the Third Millennium*. Maryknoll, NY: Orbis Books.

John XXIII 1961. Apostolic Constitution *Humanae Salutis*. In *The Documents of Vatican II*. Ed. Walter M. Abbot. New York: Guild Press / America Press / Association Press, 1966, 703-09.

John XXIII 1959. *Princeps Pastorum* ('Prince of the Shepherds' [PP]). http://www.vatican.va/holy_father/john_xxiii/encyclicals/documents/hf_j-xxiii_enc_28111959_princeps_en.html.

John Paul II 2002. Angelus, Castel Gandolfo. Sunday 25 August. http://www.vatican.va/holy_father_/john_paul_ii/angelus/2002/documents/hf_jp-ii_ang_20020825_en.html.

_____ 2001. General Audience, Wednesday 17 January. http://www.vatican.va/holy_father/john_paul_ii/audiences/2001/documents/hf_jp-ii_aud_20010117_en.html.

_____ 1998. 'Meeting with Ecclesial Movments and New Communities.' http://www.vatican.va/holy_father/john_paul_ii/speeches/1998/may/documents/hf_jp-ii_spe_19980530_riflessioni_en.html.

_____ 1990. 'Message for the World Day of Peace, 1 January 1990: 'Peace with God the Creator: Peace with All of Creation.'

http://www.vatican.va/holy_father/john_paul_ii/messages/peace/documents/hf
_jp-ii_mes_19891208_xxiii-world-day-for-peace_en.html.

_____ 1996. 'Ecumenical Celebration of the Word in the Cathedral of
Paderborn.' 22 June.
http://www.vatican.va/holy_father/john_paul_ii/speeches/1996/june/document
s/hf_jp-ii_spe_1996-622_cathedral-paderborn_ge.html.

_____ 1984. 'Ai Membri del Movimento dei Focolari.' August 19.
http://www.vatican.va/holy_father/john_paul_ii/speeches/1984/august/docume
nts/hf_jp-ii_spe_19840819_movimento-focolari_it.html.

John Paul II and Bartholomew I 2004. 'Common Declaration of Pope John Paul II
and the Ecumenical Patriarch Bartholomew I of Constantinople.'
http://www.vatican.va/holy_father/john_paul_ii/speeches/2004/july/documents
/hf_jp-ii_spe_20040701_jp-ii-bartholomew-i_en.html.

Johnson, Todd M. and Kenneth Ross, Eds. 2009. *Atlas of Global Christianity 1910-
2010*. Edinburgh: Edinburgh Centre for the Study of Global Christianity.

Johnston, William 2000. *"Arise My Love ... ": Mysticism for a New Era*. Maryknoll,
NY: Orbis Books.

Kalilombe, Patrick A. 1981. 'The Salvific Value of African Religion.' In *Mission
Trends No. 5: Faith Meets Faith*. Eds. Gerald H. Anderson and Thomas F.
Stransky, 50-68. New York: Paulist Press / Grand Rapids, MI: William B.
Eerdmans Publishing Company, 50-68.

Kalu, Ogbu, Peter Vethanayagamony and Edmund Kee-Fook Chia, Ed. *Mission
After Christendom: Emergent Themes in Contemporary Mission*. Louisville,
KY: Westminster John Knox Press.

Karecki, Madge 2010. "Contemplation and Mission: Exploring the Relationship."
Periodic Paper. *Mission Update – United States Catholic Mission Association*. 19.
2: 1-6.

_____ 2000. *Intercultural Communication of the Gospel*. Pretoria, South Africa:
University of South Africa.

Karotremprel, Sebastian 1998. *Heralds of the Gospel: A Study on Missionary
Institutions in Asia*. Shillong, India: FABC Office of Evangelization.

Karotemprel, Sebastian, Ed. 1995. *Following Christ in Misson: A Foundational
Course in Missiology*. Nairobi: Paulines Publications-Africa.

Kasper, Walter 2009. *Harvesting the Fruits: Basic Aspects of Christian Faith in
Ecumenical Dialogue*. New York: Continuum.

_____ 1984. *The God of Jesus Christ*. New York: Crossroad.

_____ 1976. *Jesus The Christ*. London: Burns & Oates.

Kelley, Francis Clement 1922. *The Story of Extension*. Chicago: Extension Press.

Kelley, Francis Clement, Ed. 1909 / 1913. *The Two Great American Catholic
Missionary Cogresses*. Chicago and Boston: J. S. Hyland.

Kerwin, Donald 2008. 'Natural Rights of Migrants and Newcomers: A Challenge to
U. S. Law and Policy.' In Groody and Campese, Ed., 192-209.

Kim, Hun 2010. 'Receiving Mission: Reflection on Reversed Phenomena in
Mission by Migrant Workers from Global Churches to Western Society.'
Transformation 28:1, 62-67.

Kim, Kirsteen 2011. 'Mission's Changing Landscape: Global Flows and Christian
Movements.' *International Review of Mission* 100:2, 254-59.

Kirk, J. Andrew 2007. *The Future of Reason, Science and Faith: Following
Modernity and Post-Modernity*. Aldershot: Ashgate Publishing.

_____ 1999. *What is Mission? Theological Explorations*. London: Darton, Longman, and Todd.

Klein, Aloys 2001. 'Ecclesiology and Mission: A Roman Catholic Perspective.' *International Review of Mission* 90:358, 260-63.

Knitter, Paul N. 1996. *Jesus and the Other Names: Christian Mission and Global Responsibility*. Maryknoll, NY: Orbis Books.

Komonchak, Joseph A. 1995. 'The Struggle for the Council during the Preparation of Vatican II (1960-1962). In Alberigo and Komonchak, Ed. 167-356.

Konings, Johann 2004. *Ser Cristao*. Sao Paulo: Loyola, 2004.

Kroeger, James H. 2010. *Dialogue: Interpretive Key for the Life of the Church in Asia*. FABC Papers, 130.

_____ 2008. 'Living in a Strange Land: Migration and Inter-religious Dialogue.' In Baggio and Brazal, Eds. 219-51.

Küng, Hans 1986. *Christianity and the World Religions*. Garden City, NY: Doubleday.

Lakeland, Paul. 2009. *The Church: Living Communion*. Collegeville, MN: The Liturgical Press.

Lang, Joseph and Mary Motte, Eds. 1982. *Mission in Dialogue: The Sedos Research Seminar on the Future of Mission*. Maryknoll, NY: Orbis Books.

Langdale, Eugene, Ed. 1955. *Challenges to Action: Addresses of Joseph Cardijn*. Chicago: Fides.

LaRousse, William 2008. ''Go Make Disciples of All Nations': Migration and Mission.' In Baggio and Brazal, Eds. 155-76.

Latourette, Kenneth S. 1975. *A History of Christianity Volume II: Reformation to the Present*. New York: Harper and Row.

_____ 1922. 'Awakening among Roman Catholics in the United States.' *International Review of Missions* 11, 439-44.

Legrand, Lucien 1990. *Unity and Plurality: Mission in the Bible*. Maryknoll, NY: Orbis Books.

Lévi-Straus, Claude, 1992. *Tristes Tropiques*. Harmondsworth: Penguin.

Les Evêques de France 1996. *Proposer la Foi dans la Société Actuelle: Lettre aux Catholiques de France*. Paris: Cerf.

LG 1964. Vatican Council II. Dogmatic Constitution on the Church (*Lumen Gentium*). http://www.vatican.va/archive/hist_councils/ii_vatican_council/documents/vat-ii_const_19641121_lumen-gentium_en.html.

Lingas, Catherine et al. 1995. 'Common Witness in a Changing World Order.' *Ecumenical Trends* 24:3, 33-41.

Lohfink, Norbert and Erich Zenger 2000. *The God of Israel and the Nations: Studies in Isaiah and the Psalms*. Collegeville, MN: The Liturgical Press.

Lonergan, Bernard J. F. 1972. *Method in Theology*. New York: Herder and Herder.

López-Gay, Jesús 1979. Missiologia Contemporanea. 2nd ed. Rome: Urbaniana University Press.

de Luca, Erri 2011. 'Ma Siamo Tutti Stranieri.' *Famiglia Cristiana* 52, 81-84.

Lussi, Carmem 2005. *La Missione della Chiesa nel Contexto della Mobilità Umana*. Città del Vaticano: Urbaniana University Press.

Lustosa, Oscar F. 1991. *A Igreja Católica no Brasil-Republica. Cem Anos de Compromisso (1889-1989)*. Sao Paulo: Paulinas.

Luzbetak, Louis J. 1988. *The Church and Cultures: New Perspectives in Missiological Anthropology*. Maryknoll, NY: Orbis Books.

_____ 1963. *The Church and Cultures: An Applied Anthropology for the Religious Worker*. Techny, IL: Divine Word Publications.

MA 1928. Pius XI, Encyclical Letter *Mortalium Animos*. http://www.vatican.va/holy_father/pius_xi/encyclicals/documents/hf_p-xi_enc_19280106_mortalium-animos_en.html.

Martina, M 1971. *La Chiesa, da Lutero ai Nostri Giorni*. Milano: Paoline.

Massey, Douglas S, Jorge Durand and Nolan J. Malone 2002. *Beyond Smoke and Mirrors: Mexican Immigration in an Era of Economic Integration*. New York: Russell Sage Foundation.

Masson, Joseph 1975. *La Missione Continua: Inizia un'epoca nuova nell'evangelizazione del mondo*. Bologna: EMI.

_____ 1966. *Vers l'Église Indigene: Catholicism ou Nationalism?* Bruxelle: Editions Universitaires Les Press de Belgique.

_____ 1966b. *L'Attività Missionaria della Chiesa. Testo e commento dell'Ad gentes*. Rome: Editrice Università Gregoriania.

_____ 1962. 'L'Église ouverte sur le Monde.' *Nouvelle Revue Thèologique* 84, 1032-43.

Mattam, Joseph, et al., eds. 2005. *Emerging Indian Missiology: Context and Concepts*. Delhi: FOIM/ISPCK.

Mazzolini, Sandra 2010. 'Chiesa Pellegrina.' In Battistella, Ed. 145-50.

Mbiti, John S. 1990. *African Religions and Philosophy*. Oxford: Heinemann.

_____ 1976. 'Theological Impotence and Universality in the Church.' In *Mission Trends No. 3: Third World Theologies*. Ed. Gerald H. Anderson and Thomas T. Stransky. New York / Grand Rapids, MI: Paulist Press / William B. Eerdmans Publishing Company, 6-18.

MC 1943. Pius XII. Encyclical Letter *Mystici Corporis*. http://www.vatican.va/holy_father/pius_xii/encyclicals/documents/hf_p-xii_enc_29061943_mystici-corporis-christi_en.html.

MD 1988. John Paul II. Apostolic Letter *Mulieris Dignitatem*. http://www.vatican.va/holy_father/john_paul_ii/apost_letters/documents/hf_jp-ii_apl_15081988_mulieris-dignitatem_en.html.

McBrien, Richard P. 1980. *Catholicism*. Two Volumes. Minneapolis, MN: Winston Press.

McFague, Sallie 2008. *A New Climate for Theology: God, the World, and Global Warming*. Minneapolis, MN: Fortress Press.

McGlone, Mary, for the NCCB Committee on the Church in Latin America 1997. *Sharing Faith Across the Hemisphere*. Maryknoll, NY: Orbis Books.

Medellin 1968. Second General Assembly of the Bishops' Conferences of Latin America. In *The Church in the Present-Day Transformation of Latin America in the Light of the Council*. Two Volumes. Washington, DC: U. S. Catholic Conference 1970.

de Mesa, José 2003. *Why Theology Is Never Far from Home*. Manila: De La Salle University Press.

Metzler, Josef 1993. 'Encicliche Missionarie.' In *Dizionari di Missiologia*, Eds. Paolo Giglioni, et al. Rome Pontificia Universitá Urbaniana and Bologna: Centro Editoriale Dehoniano, 219-26.

_____ 1985. 'Ecumenical Responsibilities of the Sacred Congregation for the Evangelization of Peoples.' *Portare*: 29-42.

MI 1919. Benedict XV. Encyclical Letter *Maximum Illud*.
http://www.vatican.va/holy_father/benedict_xv/apost_letters/documents/hf_be
n-xv_apl_19191130_maximum-illud_it.html (Italian version).

Missiology: An International Review 2003. 31:1. Issue dedicated to 'Mission and Migration.'

Moreno, Miguel Ángel Aragón 2010. 'La Misión entre Inmigrantes y Refugiados en Japón: Contribución de los Inmigrantes a la Evangelización.' *Misiones Extranjeras* 234, 65-85.

Mosman, G. 1961. L'Eglise à Heure de l'Afrique. Tournai: Casterman.

Motte, Mary 1995. 'World Mission Conferences in the 20th Century.' *International Review of Mission* 84:334, 211-222.

_____ 1987. 'Participating in Common Witness.' *Missiology: An International Review* 15:1, 25-29.

Motte, Mary and Joseph Lang, Eds. 1981. *Mission in Dialogue: SEDOS*. Maryknoll, NY: Orbis Books.

Mulcahy, M. 2003. 'New Zealand, The Catholic Church In,' *New Catholic Encyclopedia*. 2nd ed. Volume X. New York: Thomson-Gale, 324-25.

Mulhall, Daniel and Jeffrey Gros, Eds. 2006. *The Ecumenical Christian Dialogues and the Catechism of the Catholic Church*. New York: Paulist Press.

Müller, Karl 1989. *Josef Schmidlin (1876-1944): Papsthistoriter und Begründer der Katholischen Missionswissenschaft*. Nettetal, Germany: Steyler Verlag.

_____ 1987. *Mission Theology: An Introduction*. St. Augustin, Germany: Steyler Verlag.

_____ 1978. ''Holistic Mission' oder das 'Umfassende Heil.'' In '*...denn ich bin bei Euch' (Mt. 28, 20): Perspektiven im Christlichen Missionsbewusstein heute*. Ed. Hans Waldenfels. Einsiedeln: Benziger, 75-84.

Müller, Karl, Theo Sundermeier, Stephen B. Bevans, and Richard H. Bliese, Ed. 1997. *Dictionary of Mission: Theology, History, Perspectives*. Maryknoll, NY: Orbis Books.

Murphy, Edward 1962. 'The Concept of Mission: Popes and Theologians.' In *Global Mission of the Church*, Ed. J. Franklin Ewing, II-1-II-5. New York: Fordham University Institute of Mission Studies.

Mushete, A. Ngindu 1994. "An Overview of African Theology." In ed. Rosino Gibellini, *Paths of African Theology*, 9-25 (Maryknoll, NY: Orbis Books)

Mutiso-Mbinda, John 1983. 'The 6th Assembly.' *International Review of Mission* 72:288, 568.

Mveng, Engelbert 1987. *Afrique dans l'Église*. Paris: L'Harmattan.

NA 1965. Vatican Council II. Declaration on the Relation of the Church to Non-Christian Religions *Nostra Aetate*. http://www.vatican.va/archive/hist_councils/ii_vatican_council/documents/vat-ii_decl_19651028_nostra-aetate_en.html.

National Catholic Education Commission Data Committee 2009. *Australian Catholic Schools 2009*. Canberra: NCRC.

Nazir-Ali, Michael 2009. *From Everywhere to Everywhere*. Eugene, OR: Wipf and Stock Publishers.

NMI 2001. John Paul II. Apostolic Letter *Novo Millennio Ineunte*. http://www.vatican.va/holy_father/john_paul_ii/apost_letters/documents/hf_jp-ii_apl_20010106_novo-millennio-ineunte_en.html.

National Conference of Bishops 1986. *To the Ends of the Earth: A Pastoral Statement on World Mission*. Washington, DC: United States Catholic Conference of Publication and Promotion Services.

_____ 1984. *The Hispanic Presence: Challenge and Commitment. A Pastoral Letter on Hispanic Ministry*. Washington, DC: United States Catholic Conference.

ND 2001. Joseph Neuner and Jacques Dupuis, Ed. *The Christian Faith in the Documents of the Catholic Church*. Seventh Revised and Enlarged Edition. Staten Island, NY: Alba House.

Neil, Stephen 1966. *Colonialism and Christian Mission*. London: Lutterworth Press.

Nemer, Lawrence 2003. 'Mission and Missions.' In *New Catholic Encyclopedia*. 2nd ed. Volume 9. New York: Thomson-Gale, 683-89.

'New Encyclical' 1951. 'The New Encyclical on the Missions.' *The Clergy Monthly* 15, 321-29.

Nissen, Johannes 2002. *New Testament and Mission: Historical and Hermeneutical Perspectives*. 2nd ed. Frankfurt am Main: Peter Lang.

Noort, Gerrit 2011. 'Emerging Migrant Churches in the Netherlands: Missiological Challenges and Mission Frontiers.' *International Review of Mission* 100:1, 4-16.

Notitiae 1988. 'Le Missel Romain pour les Diocéses du Zaire.' *Notitiae*, 24, 454-72.

Nwachukwu, F. 1994. *The Birth of Systematic Theology in Contemporary Black Africa*. Rome: Domenici-Pécheu.

OA 1971. Paul VI. Apostolic Letter *Octagesima Adveniens*. http://www.vatican.va/holy_father/paul_vi/apost_letters/documents/hf_p-vi_apl_19710514_octogesima-adveniens_en.html.

Obi, C. A., Ed. 1985. *A Hundred Years of the Catholic Church in Eastern Nigeria 1885-1995*. Onitsha, Nigeria: Africana-Fep Publishers.

Oborji, Francis A. 2008. 'The Mission *ad gentes* of the African Churches.' *Omnis Terra* 336: 37, 155-64.

_____ 2007. 'Le vie del dialogo nel contesto africano.' In *Nel convivio delle Differenze: Il Dialogo nelle Società del Terzo Millennio*. Ed. E. Scognamiglio and A Trevisiol. Rome: Urbaniana University Press, 67-89.

_____ 2006. *Concepts of Mission: The Evolution of Contemporary Missiology*. Maryknoll, NY: Orbis Books.

_____ 2005. *Towards a Christian Theology of African Religion: Issues of Interpretation and Mission*. Eldoret, Kenya: Gaba Publications.

_____ 2001. 'Missiologia Contemporanea: Storia e Nuove Sfide.' *Euntes Docete* 54:1, 143-57.

_____ 2001b. 'Towards African Model and New Language in Mission.' *African Ecclesial Review* 43:3, 109-33.

_____ 1998. *Trends in African Theology since Vatican II: Missiological Orientations*. Rome: Liberit SRL Press.

Ocaña, Martín 2007. 'Los Extranjero en la Missio Dei: Apuntes Biblicos para una Misionología con y hacia los Emigrantes.' http://www.lupaprotestante.com/redsocial/index.php/teologia/800-los-extranjeros-en-la-missio-dei-apuntes-biblicos-para-una-misionologia-con-y-hacia-los-emigrantes.

O'Connell, James 1952. 'Some Notes on the Missionary Encyclical: *Evangelii Praecones*.' *The Irish Ecclesiastical Record* 77, 409-20.

O'Farrell, Patrick 1992. *The Catholic Church and Community in Australia: A History*. Kensington, NSW, Australia: New South Wales University Press.

O'Malley, John W. 2008. *What Happened at Vatican II*. New York: Oxford University Press.

_____ 2006. 'Vatican II: Did Anything Happen?' *Theological Studies* 67:1 (March), 3-33.

O'Sullivan, Dominic 2005. *Faith, Politics, and Reconciliation: Catholicism and the Politics of Indigeneity*. Wellington, New Zealand: ATF Press, Huia Publishers.

Ohm, Thomas 1962. *Machet zu Jüngen alle Völker: Theorie der Missiin*. Freiburg: Wevel Verlag.

Okoye, James Chukwuma 2006. *Israel and the Nations: A Mission Theology of the Old Testament*. Maryknoll, NY: Orbis Books.

Okure, Teresa. 1988. *The Johannine Approach to Mission: A Contextual Study of John 4:1-42*. Tübingen: J. C. B. Mohr.

Ommerborn, Jürgen 2008. 'Arnold Janssen's Understanding of Mission in the Context of His Times.' *Verbum SVD* 49, 241-66, 369-93.

Orobator, Agbonkhianmeghe E. 2005. *From Crisis to Kairos: The Mission of the Church in the Time of HIV/AIDS, Refugees and Poverty*. Nairobi: Paulines Publications Africa.

D'Orsa, Jim 2000. *The Catholic Missionary Movement in Australia: Past, Present, and Future*. Columban Research Project on Mission.

D'Orsa, Jim and Therese 2010. *Explorers, Guides and Meaning-Makers: Mission Theology for Catholic Educators*. Mulgrave: John Grant.

_____ 2012. *Catholic Curriculum: A Mission to the Heart of Young People*. Mulgrave: John Grant

Pacelli, Emilia Paolo, Ed. 2007. 'Proceedings of the International *Fidei Donum* Congress.' *Omnis Terra* (English) 41:379, 1-120.

Palomino, Miguel A. 2004. 'Latino Immigration in Europe: Challenge and Opportunity for Mission.' *International Bulletin of Missionary Research* 28:2, 55-58.

Parrat, J., Ed. 1995. *Reinventing Christianity: African Theology Today*. Grand Rapids, MI: William B. Eerdmans Publishing Company.

Parolin, Gaetano 2010. *Chiesa Postconciliare e Migrazioni: Quale Teologia per la Missione con i Migranti*. Tesi Gregoriana. Serie Missiologia 6. Roma: Editrice Pontificia Università Gregoriana.

_____ 2010b. 'Quale Missione con i Migranti?' *Studi Emigrazione* 47: 178, 377-408.

_____ 2011. ''Missione dei Migranti Paradigma della Nuova Missione.' *Ad Gentes* 30, 227-42.

Paventi, Saverio 1967. 'Étapes de l'Élaboration du Texte.' In Schütte, Ed. 149-81.

PCPCU 1998. Pontifical Council for Promoting Christian Unity. *Directory for the Application of Principles and Norms on Ecumenism*. Origins 23:9 (entire issue).

_____ 1998. 'The Ecumenical Dimension in the Formation of Pastoral Workers.' *Origins* 27:39, 653-61.

Pepinster, Catherine 2010. 'The Green Pope.' *The Tablet* (4 September), 10-11.

Phan, Peter C. 2010. 'The World Missionary Conference, Edinburgh 1910: Challenges for the Church and Theology in the Twenty-first Century.' *International Bulletin of Missionary Research* 34:2, 105-08.

_____ 2008. 'Dialogo Interreligioso.' In Battistella, Ed. 365-71.

________ 2003. *In Our Own Tongues: Perspectives from Asia on Mission and Inculturation*. Maryknoll, NY: Orbis Books.

Philpott, Daniel 2012. *Just and Unjust Peace: An Ethic of Reconciliation*. New York: Oxford University Press.

Piedra, Arturo 2002. *Evangelización Protestante en América Latina: Análisis de las razones que justificaron y provovieron la expansion protestante*. Quito: CLAI.

Pieper, Josef 2000. 'Bemerkungen über die Missionsituation der Kirche in Deutschland' (1935). In Joseph Pieper, *Werke in acht Bänden*, Vol. 7: Hamburg: Religionsphilosophische Schriften, 1-9.

'Pius XII' 1951. 'Pius XII on the Missions.' *America* 85, 321.

Pohl, Christine 1999. *Making Room: Recovering Hospitality as a Christian Tradition*. Grand Rapids, MI: William B. Eerdmans Publishing Company.

Poling, James N. and Donald E. Miller 1985. *Foundations for a Practical Theology of Ministry*. Nashville: Abingdon Press.

'Pope' 1952. 'The Pope and the Missions.' *The Catholic Mind* 50, 373-74.

Pope, Stephen J. and Charles Hefling, Eds. 2002. *Sic et Non: Encountering Dominus Iesus*. Maryknoll, NY: Orbis Books.

Portes, Alejandro and Rubén G. Rumbaut 2006. *Immigrant America: A Portrait*. 3rd ed. Berkeley: University of California Press.

PP 1967. Paul VI. Encyclical Letter *Populorum Progressio*. http://www.vatican.va/holy_father/paul_vi/encyclicals/documents/hf_p-vi_enc_26031967_populorum_en.html.

PP 1959. John XXIII. Encyclical Letter *Princeps Pastorum*. http://www.vatican.va/holy_father/john_xxiii/encyclicals/documents/hf_j-xxiii_enc_28111959_princeps_en.html.

Puebla 1979. Third General Assembly of the Conferences of Latin American Bishops. John Eagleson and Philip Sharper, Eds., *Puebla and Beyond: Documentation and Commentary*. Maryknoll, NY: Orbis Books.

Putenpurakal, Joseph 2008. *Evangelizing Mission*. Shillong: DBCIC Publications.

________ 1997. *Mission in the Documents of the Catholic Church*. Shilong, India: Vendrame Institute Publications.

Quigley, Tom 2009. 'The Great North-South Embrace.' *America* 201:18, 17-21.

Raguin, Yves 1947. *Théologie Missionaire de l'Ancient Testament*. Paris: Éditions du Seuil.

Rahner, Karl 1979. 'Towards a Fundamental Theological Interpretation of Vatican II.' *Theological Studies* 40:4, 716-27.

________ *The Trinity* 1974. New York: Seabury Press.

Ramirez, Bishop Ricardo 1990. 'Hispanic Peoples of the United States and the Church from 1865-1985.' *U. S. Catholic Historian* 9.1:2, 165-80.

Rausch, William G. and Jeffrey Gross 1998. *Deepening Communion: International Ecumenical Documents with Roman Catholic Participation*. Washington, DC: United States Catholic Conference.

RE 1926. Pius XI. Encyclical Letter *Rerum Ecclesiae*. http://www.vatican.va/holy_father/pius_xi/encyclicals/documents/hf_p-xi_enc_28021926_rerum-ecclesiae_en.html.

Rétif, A. and Paul Lamarche 1966. *The Salvation of the Gentiles and the Prophets*. Baltimore and Dublin: Helicon Press.

RH 1979. John Paul II. Encyclical Letter *Redemptoris Hominis*. http://www.vatican.va/holy_father/john_paul_ii/encyclicals/documents/hf_jp-ii_enc_04031979_redemptor-hominis_en.html.

Rigoni, Flor Maria 2004. 'Retos y Desafíos de la Migración a la Misión.' http://www.sedosmission.org/site/index.php?option=com_docman&task=cat_v iew&gid=53&Itemid=59&lang=it.

Robert, Dana L. 2011. 'Mission in Long Perspective.' In *Edinburgh 2010: Mission Today and Tomorrow*. Eds. Kirsteen Kim and Andrew Anderson. Oxford: Regnum Books International, 55-68.

_____ 2011b. 'Cross-Cultural Friendship in the Creation of Twentieth-Century World Christianity.' *International Bulletin of Missionary Research* 35:2, 100-07.

_____ 2006. 'World Christianity as a Women's Movement.' *International Bulletin of Missionary Research* 20:4, 180-88.

_____ 1996. *American Women in Mission: A Social History of Their Thought and Practice*. Macon, GA: Mercer University Press.

Rogers, Anthony 2008. 'Globalizing Solidarity with Faith Encounters in Asia.' In Baggio and Brazal, Ed. 203-18.

Ross, Kenneth 2009. *Edinburgh 2010: Spring Board for Mission*. Pasadena: William Carey International University Press.

_____ 2005. 'Non-western Christians in Scotland: Mission in Reverse.' *Theology in Scotland* 12:2, 71-89.

Rouse, Ruth and Stephen Neil, Eds. 1954. *A History of the Ecumenical Movement, 1517-1948*. London: SPCK.

RM 1990. John Paul II, Encyclical Letter *Redemptoris Missio*. http://www.vatican.va/holy_father/john_paul_ii/encyclicals/documents/hf_jp-ii_enc_07121990_redemptoris-missio_en.html.

Ruether, Rosemary Radford 1992. *Gaia and God: An Ecofeminist Theology of Earth Healing*. New York: HarperCollins.

Rusch, William, Harding Meyer and Jeffrey Gros, Eds. 2000. *Growth in Agreement II*. Geneva: World Council of Churches.

Rütti, Ludwig 1972 *Zur Theologie der Mission: Kritische Analysen und neue Orientierungen*. Munich: Chr. Kaiser Verlag.

Sjada, Peter 2001. 'Ecclesiology and Mission: A Roman Catholic Perspective.' *International Review of Mission* 90:359, 417-26.

Sanneh, Lamin 2009. *Translating the Message: the Missionary Impact on Culture*. Revised and Expanded. Maryknoll, NY: Orbis Books.

_____ 2003. *Whose Religion Is Christianity? The Gospel Beyond the West*. Grand Rapids, MI: William B. Eerdmans Publishing Company.

Saraiva, Martins José 1994. *La Missione Oggi: Aspetti teologico-pastorali*. Rome: Urbaniana University Press.

Saturnino Dias, Mario 2005. *Rooting Faith in Asia*. Quezon City, Philippines: Claretian Publications.

SC 1963. Vatican Council II. Constitution on the Sacred Liturgy. *Sacrosanctum Concilium*. http://www.vatican.va/archive/hist_councils/ii_vatican_council/ documents/vat-ii_const_19631204_sacrosanctum-concilium_en.html.

Scalzotto, Tiziano 1977. 'On the Twentieth Anniversary of Publication of the Encyclical *Fidei Donum*.' *L'Osservatore Romano* (English) 10:21, 10.

Scherer, James A. and Stephen B. Bevans, Eds. 1992 / 1994 / 1999. *New Directions in Mission and Evangelization: 1: Basic Statements 1974-1991; 2: Theological Foundations; 3: Faith and Culture*. Maryknoll, NY: Orbis Books.

Schillebeeckx, Edward 1983. *Christ: The Experience of Jesus as Lord*. New York: Crossroad.

Schmidlin, Joseph 1933. *Catholic Mission History*. Techny, IL: Mission Press.
_____ 1931. *Catholic Mission Theory*. Techny, IL: The Mission Press.
_____ 1917. *Einführung in der Missionswissenschaft*. Münster: Aschendorff.
Schneiders, Sandra M. 2005. "Christian Spirituality: Definitions, Methods and Types."
    In ed. Philip Sheldrake. *The New Westminster Dictionary of Spirituality*. 1-6.
    Louisville, KY: Westminster John Knox Press.
Schreiter, Robert J. 2011. 'Cosmopolitanism, Hybrid Identities, and Relgion.'
    Exchange 40: 1-16.
Schreiter, Robert J. 2005. 'Reconciliation and Healing as a Paradigm for Mission.'
    International Review of Mission 94.372: 74-83.
_____ 2005b. 'The Changed Context of Mission Forty Years after the Council.'
    Verbum SVD 46.1: 75-88.
_____ 2001. 'Globalization and Reconciliation: Challenges to Mission.' In
    Mission in the Third Millennium. Ed. Robert J. Schreiter. Maryknoll, NY:
    Orbis Books.
_____ 1999. 'The Impact of Vatican II.' In *The Twentieth Century*. Ed. Gregory
    Baum. Maryknoll, NY: Orbis Books, 158-72.
_____ 1994. 'Changes in Roman Catholic Attitudes toward Proselytism and
    Mission.' In *New Directions in Mission and Evangelization 2*. Ed. James A.
    Scherer and Stephen B. Bevans. Maryknoll, NY: Orbis Books, 113-25.
_____ 1992. *Reconciliation: Mission and Ministry in a Changing Social Order*.
    Maryknoll, NY: Orbis Books.
Schreiter, Robert J., Ed. 2001. *Mission in the Third Millennium*. Maryknoll, NY:
    Orbis Books.
Schroeder, Roger P. 2008. *What Is the Mission of the Church? A Guide for
    Catholics*. Maryknoll, NY: Orbis Books.
Schütte, Johannes, Ed. 1967. *Vatican II: L'Activité Missionaire de l'Église*. Unam
    Sanctam 67. Paris: Editions du Cerf.
_____ 1967b. *Mission nach dem Konzil*. Mainz: Matthias-Grünewald-Verlag.
SD 1992. Fourth General Assembly of the Conference of Latin American Bishops.
    Alfred T. Hennelly, Ed. *Santo Domingo and Beyond*. Maryknoll, NY: Orbis
    Books. Printed 1993.
Senior, Donald and Carroll Stuhlmueller 1983. *The Biblical Foundations for
    Mission*. Grand Rapids / Maryknoll, NY: William B. Eerdmans Publishing
    Company / Orbis Books.
Seumois, André 1993. *Teologia Missionaria*. Bologna: EDB.
_____ 1973-1981. *Théologie Missionaire* (5 Vols.). Rome: OMI Bureau de
    Presse.
Shah, Timothy, Alfred Stepan and Monica Duffy Toft, Eds. 2012. *Rethinking
    Religion and World Affairs*. New York: Oxford University Press.
Sheard, Robert 1987. *Inter-religious Dialogue in the Catholic Church since Vatican
    II: A Historical and Theological Study*. Lewiston, NY: Edwin Mellen Press.
Sheen, Fulton J. 1951. 'A Commentary on *Evangelii Praecones*.' *Worldmission* 2,
    3-13.
Sheldrake, Philip 1998. *Spirituality and History: Questions of Interpretation*.
    Maryknoll, NY: Orbis Books.
Shenk. Calvin E. 1993. 'The Demise of the Church in North Africa and Nubia and
    its Survival in Egypt and Ethiopia.' *Missiology: An International Review* 21:2,
    131-54.

Shenk, Wilbert R. 2002. *Enlarging the Story: Perspectives on Writing World Christian History*. Maryknoll, NY: Orbis Books.

Shorter, Aylward 1988. *Toward a Theology of Inculturation*. Maryknoll, NY: Orbis Books.

_____ 1972. *Theology of Mission*. Cork, Ireland: The Mercier Press.

Smith, Christian 2005. *Soul Searching: The Religious and Spiritual Lives of American Teenagers*. New York: Oxford University Press.

Sobrino, Jon and Juan Hernandez Pico 1985. *Theology of Christian Solidarity*. Maryknoll, NY: Orbis Books.

Spencer, J. S. 1962. *A History of Islam in West Africa*. Oxford: Oxford University Press.

SRS 1987. John Paul II. Encyclical Letter *Sollicitudo Rei Socialis*. http://www.vatican.va/holy_father/john_paul_ii/encyclicals/documents/hf_jp-ii_enc_30121987_sollicitudo-rei-socialis_en.html.

SS 2007. Benedict XVI. Encyclical Letter *Spe Salvi*. http://www.vatican.va/holy_father/benedict_xvi/encyclicals/documents/hf_ben-xvi_enc_20071130_spe-salvi_en.html.

St. Thomas Aquinas. *Summa Theologiae*. Various Editions.

Stanley, Brian 2009. *The World Missionary Conference: Edinburgh 1910*. Grand Rapids, MI: William B. Eerdmans Publishing Company.

_____ 2006. 'Defining the Boundaries of Christendom: The Two Worlds of the World Missionary Conference, 1910.' *International Bulletin of Missionary Research* 30:4, 171-76.

Stransky, Thomas 1990. 'From Mexico to San Antonio.' *International Review of Mission* 79:313, 40-53.

_____ 1981. 'A Roman Catholic Reflection.' *Missiology: An International Review* 9:1, 41-52.

_____ 1980. 'Mission in Power in the 1980s.' *International Review of Mission* 69:273, 40-48.

_____ 1966. 'Roman Catholic Missions 1964-1965.' *International Review of Mission* 55.217: 81-85.

Strynkowski, John J. 2006. "Spirituality and the Triune God." In ed. Richard W. Miller, II. *Spirituality for the 21ˢᵗ Century: Experiencing God in the Catholic Tradition*. 6-22. Ligouri, MO: Ligouri Publications.

Stoeger, William 2007. 'Reductionism and Emergence: Implications for the Interaction of Theology with the Natural Sciences.' In *Evolution and Emergence: Systems, Organisms, Persons*. Eds Nancy C. Murphy and William R. Stoeger. Oxford: Oxford University Press, 229-47.

Suess, Paulo 2011. *Introduçao à Teologia da Missao. Convocar e enviar: servos e testemunhas do Reino*. 3ʳᵈ ed. Petropolis: Vozes, 2011.

_____ 2010. 'Pobres.' *Dicionário de Aparecida. 42 palavras-chave para uma leitura pastoral do Documento de Aparecida*. 3ʳᵈ ed. Sao Paolo: Paulus.

_____ 1988. *Queimada e semeadura. Da conquista espiritual ao descrobrimento e uma nova evangelizacao*. Petrópolis: Vozes.

_____ 1982. 'Rodolfo Lunkenbein (1939-1976). Asesinado por oponerse al exterminio de los indios.' In *Testigos de la fe en America Latina desde el descubrimiento has nuestros dias*. Ed. Emil Stehle. Navarro: Verbo Divino, 142-46.

Swartley, Willard M. 2006. 'The Relation of Justice/Righteousness to Shalom/Eirene.' *Ex Auditu* 22, 29-54.

Synod of Bishops 2009. *II Special Assembly for Africa. Message.* Nairobi: Paulines
    Publications-Africa.
Synod of Bishops 1994. *Special Assembly for Africa. Relatio Ante-Disceptationem.*
    Vatican City: Libreria Editrice Vaticana.
Synod of Bishops 1994b. *Special Assembly for Africa 1994b. Relatio Post-
    Disceptationem.* Vatican City: Libreria Editrice Vaticana.
Synod of Bishops 1994c. *Special Assembly for Africa. 'Message.' L'Osservatore
    Romano.* Special English Edition May 11.
Synod of Bishops 1993. *Special Assembly for Africa. Instrumentum Laboris.*
    Vatican City: Libreria Editrice Vaticana.
Synod of Bishops 1994. *Special Assembly for Africa. Lineamenta.* Vatican City:
    Libreria Editrice Vaticana.
Tan, Jonathan 2004. "Missio Inter Gentes: Towards a New Paradigm in the Mission
    Theology of the Federation of Asian Bishops' Conferences (FABC)." *Mission
    Studies.* 21. 1: 65-95.
_____ 2003. 'Mission and Evangelization, Papal Writings on.' *New Catholic
    Encyclopedia.* 2nd ed. Volume 9. New York: Thomson-Gale, 680-82.
"These Living Waters: Common Agreement on Mutual Recognition of Baptism." A
    Report of the Catholic Reformed Dialogue in the United States 2003-2007."
    http://www.pcusa.org/media/uploads/worship/pdfs/these-living-waters.pdf.
Thomas, Norman 2010. *Missions and Unity: Lessons from History. 1792-2010.*
    Eugene, OR: Wipf and Stock Publishers.
_____ 1995. *Classical Texts in Mission and World Christianity.* Maryknoll, NY:
    Orbis Books.
Thoppil, James 2005. *Towards an Asian Ecclesiology: The Understanding of
    Church in the Documents of the FABC (1970-2000).* Shillong: Oriens
    Publications.
TMA 1994. John Paul II. Apostolic Letter *Tertio Millennio Adveniente.*
    http://www.vatican.va/holy_father/john_paul_ii/apost_letters/documents/hf_jp-
    ii_apl_10111994_tertio-millennio-adveniente_en.html.
Tomko, Jozef 1994. 'The Situation of the Church in Africa and Madagascar – Some
    Aspects and Observations.' *L'Osservatore Romano.* (27 April), 17-21.
Torres, Segio and Virginia Fabella, Eds. 1976. *The Emergent Gospel: Theology
    from the Underside of History.* Maryknoll, NY: Orbis Books.
Tutu, Desmond 1999. *No Future without Forgiveness.* New York: Doubleday.
Üffing, Martin 1994. *Die Deutsche Kirche und Mission.* Nettetal, Germany: Steyler
    Verlag.
United States Catholic Conference of Bishops 2003. *Strangers No Longer:
    Together on the Journey of Hope.* Pastoral Letter on Migration issued jointly
    by the United States Catholic Conference of Bishops and the Conferencia del
    Episcopado Mexicano. Washington, DC: United States Conference of Catholic
    Bishops.
_____ 2003. *Native American Catholics at the Millennium.* Washington, DC:
    United States Conference of Catholic Bishops.
_____ 2001. *A Call to Solidarity with Africa.* Washington, DC: United States
    Conference of Catholic Bishops.
_____ 2001. *Asian and Pacific Presence.* Washington, DC: United States
    Conference of Catholic Bishops.

UR 1965. Vatican Council II. Decree on Ecumenism *Unitatis Redintegratio*.
http://www.vatican.va/archive/hist_councils/ii_vatican_council/documents/vat-ii_decree_19641121_unitatis-redintegratio_en.html.
UUS 1995. John Paul II. Encyclical Letter *Ut Unum Sint*.
http://www.vatican.va/holy_father/john_paul_ii/encyclicals/documents/hf_jp-ii_enc_25051995_ut-unum-sint_en.html.
Uzukwu, E. E. 1997. *Worship as Body Language – Introduction to Christian Worship: An African Orientation*. Collegeville, MN: Liturgical Press, Pueblo Book.
Vadakumpadan, Paul 2006. 'The Catholic Understanding of Mission, 1911-1962.' In *Missionaries of Christ: A Basic Course in Missiology*. 23-33. Shillong, India: Vendrame Institute Publications.
_____ 1992. 'Paving the Way for *Redemptoris Missio*: A Brief Survey of Modern Mission Documents.' *Indian Missiological Review* 14: 6-14.
van Engen, Charles 2010. 'Biblical Perspectives on the Role of Immigrants in God's Mission.' *Evangelical Review of Theology* 34.1: 29-43.
Vethanayagamony, Peter 2010. 'Mission from the Rest to the West: The Changing Landscape of World Christianity and Christian Mission.' In Kalu, Vethanayagamony, and Chia, ed. 59-70.
Villanova, Evangelista 2000. 'The Intersession (1963-1964).' In Alberigo and Komonchak, ed., 347-490.
Volf, Miroslav 2006. "Spirituality and the Triune God." In ed. Mirosalv Volf and Michael Welker. *God's Life in Trinity*. 3-12. Minneapolis, MN: Fortress Press.
Volunteer Missionary Movement 2006. 'What is VMM's History?' http://www.vmmusa.org.
Walldorf, Friedemann 2002. *Die Neu-Evangelisierung Europas*. Giessen: Brunnen Verlag.
Walls, Andrew F. 2008. 'Afterword: Christian Mission in a Five-Hundred Year Context.' In *Mission in the Twenty-First Century: Exploring the Five Marks of Global Mission*, Andrew F. Walls and Cathy Ross, ed., 193-204. London: Darton, Longman, and Todd; Maryknoll, NY: Orbis Books.
_____ 2005. 'Mission and Evangelization: The Gospel and Movement of Peoples in Modern Times.' *Covenant Quarterly* 63. 1: 3-28.
_____ 2002. *The Cross-Cultural Process in Christian History*. Maryknoll, NY: Orbis Books.
_____ 2002b. 'Mission and Migration: The Diaspora Factor in Christian History.' *Journal of African Christian Thought* 5. 2: 311.
_____ 1996. *The Missionary Movement in Christian History: Studies in the Transmission of Faith*. Maryknoll, NY: Orbis Books.
Walzer, Michael 1983. *Spheres of Justice*. New York: Basic Books.
Warneck, Gustav 1906. *Outline of a History of Protestant Missions*. Edinburgh: Oliphant, Anderson Ferrier.
_____ 1892-1905. *Evangelische Missionslehre*. 5 Volumes. Gotha: Perthes.
Warner, Stephen 2004. 'Coming to America.' *Christian Century*. February 10: 20-23.
Werner, Dietrich 2011. 'Theological Education in the Changing Context of World Christianity – an Unfinished Agenda' *International Bulletin of Missionary Research* 35.2: 96: 92-100.

White Lance, Francis 2000. 'My Friend – the Rev. Dr. Claude Marie Barbour.' In
    The Healing Circle: Essays in Cross-Cultural Mission, ed. Stephen Bevans,
    Eleanor Doidge, and Robert Schreiter, 24-29. Chicago: CCGM Publications.
Wiest, Jena-Paul 1999. 'The Legacy of Vincent Lebbe.' *International Bulletin of
    Missionary Research* 23:1, 33-37.
Wolanin, Adam 1989. *Teologia della Missione: Termi Scelti.* Casale Monferrato:
    Piemme.

LIST OF CONTRIBUTORS

Claude Marie Barbour has served as Professor of World Mission at Catholic Theological Union in Chicago since 1976. She is an ordained minister in the Presbyterian Church (USA) and served as missionary in South Africa. She has been in a ministry of dialogue and accompaniment with Lakota (Sioux) on the Rosebud and Pine Ridge Reservations, SD for the past 30 years.

Stephen B. Bevans, SVD is Louis J. Luzbetak, SVD Professor of Mission and Culture at Catholic Theological Union, Chicago. He is past president of the Association of Professors of Mission and the American Society of Missiology. He has published *Models of Contextual Theology* (Orbis, 1992, 2002), *An Introduction to Theology in Global Perspective* (Orbis, 2009), with Jeffrey Gros, *Evangelization and Religious Freedom* (Paulist Press, 2009), and, with Roger P. Schroeder, *Constants in Context: A Theology of Mission for Today* and *Prophetic Dialogue: Reflections on Mission Today* (Orbis, 2004 and 2011).

Maria Clara Luchetti Bingemer is Professor of Theology at the Pontifical CatholicUniversity, Rio de Janeiro in Brazil. Her publications include *Mary: Mother of God, Mother of the Poor* (with Ivone Gebara, Orbis, 2004), *A Face for God: Reflections on Trinitarian Theology for Our Times* (Convivium, 2013), *Cuerpo de mujer y experiência de Dios. Sentir y experimentar a Dios de un modo femenino* (San Benito, 2007), *Simone Weil: una mística en los límites* (Ciudad Nueva, 2011). She has also published many articles in English and in Spanish and Portuguese.

Gioacchino Campese, CS, formerly an instructor at the Scalabrini International Migration Institute (SIMI) of the Pontifical Urbaniana University in Rome, presently researches on migration and theology in Southern Italy. He is the editor of *Migration, Religious Experience, and Globalization* (with Pietro Ciallella—Center for Migration Studies, 2003), and *A Promised Land, A Perilous Journey: Theological perspectives on Migration* (with Daniel G. Groody—Notre Dame, 2008)

Edmund Kee Fook Chia is Senior Lecturer at Australian Catholic University in Melbourne, where he is also the co-director of the Centre for Inter-religious Dialogue. Until 2011 he was Associate Professor of Theology at Catholic Theological Unoin, Chicago and had served eight years as the executive secretary of the Federation of Asian Bishops' Conferences' Office of Inter-religious Affairs. He has published widely, including *Schillebeeckx and Inter-religious Dialogue* (Pickwick, 2012).

Eleanor Doidge, LoB recently retired as Associate Professor of Cross Cultural Ministries at Catholic Theological Union in Chicago. She is a member of the Vrouwen van Bethanië (Ladies of Bethany). She has served in ministry in the inner-city in the U.S. and has co-lead traveling seminars to the reservations in South Dakota since 1983. She has edited, with Stephen Bevans and Robert Schreiter, *The Healing Circle: Essays in Cross-Cultural Mission* (Wipf and Stock, 2000).

Angelyn Dries, OFM is Danforth Professor of Theological Studies, Danforth Chair in the Humanities Emerita at St Louis University. She is past president of the American Society of Missiology and author of *The Missionary Movement in American Catholic History* (Orbis, 1998).

Denis Edwards is Professor of Theology at Flinders University, Adelaide, Australia. Among his many publications are *Jesus the Wisdom of God: An Ecological Theology* (Orbis, 1995), *The God of Evolution: A Trinitarian Theology* (Paulist: 1999); *Breath of Life: A Theology of the Creator Spirit* (Orbis, 2004), and *How God Acts: Creation, Redemption and Special Divine Action* (Fortress, 2010).

William P. Gregory is Assistant Professor of Religious Studies at Clarke University in Dubuque, Iowa, USA. From 1994-1996 he taught in The Gambia, West Africa. He has also taught in the Religious Studies Department of the University of Dayton. From 2010-2011 he served as president of the Association of Professors of Mission in the United States.

Jeffrey Gros, FSC is Distinguished Professor of Ecumenical and Historical Theology at Memphis Theological Seminary, Emeritus, and has served as Kenan Osborne Visiting Professor at the Franciscan School of Theology, Graduate Theological Union, Berkeley, California. He is past president of the Society for Pentecostal Studies. For ten years he directed the Faith and Order Commission for the National Council of Churches, USA and for fourteen years was associate director of the Secretariat for Ecumenical and Inter-religious Affairs at the United States Conference of Catholic Bishops. Among his many publications is *Evangelization and Religious Freedom*, written with Stephen Bevans, SVD.

Madge Karecki, OFM-TOSF is director of the Office for Mission Education and Animation for the Archdiocese of Chicago. She was on mission in South Africa for 21 years. She holds a DTh in Missiology from the University of South Africa (UNISA) where she taught Missiology. In 2004 Sr Madge was the recipient of the UNISA excellence in teaching award. Her interests are in the theology of mission praxis, prayer and mission and cultural issues related to mission. She is a member of the American Society of Missiology and the International Association of

Catholic Missiologists. Sr Madge is part of the adjunct faculty of the University of St Mary of the Lake/Mundelein Seminary.

James H. Kroeger, MM is Professor of Systematic Theology, Missiology, and Islamics at the Loyola School of Theology in Manila and regular professor at the Mother of Life Catechetical Center. He has served in Asia (Philippines and Bangladesh) since 1970. Currently, he is President of the Philippine Association of Catholic Missiologists (PACM), Secretary-Convenor of the Asian Missionary Societies Forum (AMSAL), and consultant to both the Asian Bishops' (FABC) Office of Evangelization and the Philippine Bishops' (CBCP) Commission on Mission. His recent publications include: *Theology from the Heart of Asia: FABC Doctoral Dissertations I-II* (Claretian Publications, 2008), *Migration: Opening Pathways of the Church's Mission* (Scalabrini Migration Center, 2010), and *A Fiery Flame: Encountering God's Word* (Claretian Publications and Jesuit Communications, 2010).

José M. de Mesa is Professor of Theology, Emeritus, and a Lifetime Fellow at de la Salle University, Manila, Philippines. He serves as Louis J. Luzbetak, SVD Visiting Professor of Mission and Culture at Catholic Theological Union, Chicago and has published widely. Recent publications include *Why Theology is Never Far from Home* (DLSU Press, 2003), *The Prayer Our Lord Taught Us* (CCM, 2005), *Bakas: Retrieving the Sense of Sacramentality of the Ordinary* (DLSU-Anvil, 2008) and *Mabathalang Pag-aaral: Ang Pagteteolohiya ng Pilipino* (DLSU-Vibal, 2010).

Mary Motte, FMM directs the Mission Resource Center of the Franciscan Missionaries of Mary in North Providence, Rhode Island. She is past president of the American Society of Missiology, former provincial of the Franciscan Missionary of Mary in the United States, and editor, with Joseph Lang, of *Mission as Dialogue: The Sedos Research Seminar on the Future of Mission* (Orbis, 1982).

Lawrence Nemer, SVD is senior lecturer in church history and missiology at Yarra Theological Union of the Melbourne University of Divinity in Melbourne, Australia. He is past president of the Missionary Institute London and past president of the Australian Association for Mission Studies. He is the author of *Anglican and Roman Catholic Attitudes on Missions: An Historical Study of Two English Missionary Societies in the Late Nineteenth Century* (Steyler Verlag, 1981).

Francis Anekwe Oborji is Professor of Missiology at the Pontifical Urban University, Rome. Originally from Nigeria, he is the author of *Concepts of Mission: The Evolution of Contemporary Missiology* (Orbis, 2006), *Towards a Christian Theology of African Religion: Issues of Interpretation* *and Mission* (Gaba Publications, 2005), and *Trends in African Theology since Vatican II: Missiological Orientations* (Liberit SRL Press, 1998).

James Chukwuma Okoye, CSSP is director of the Spiritan Institute at Duquesne University in Pittsburgh, Pennsylvania, USA. Until 2012 he was Carroll Stuhlmuller Professor of Old Testament at Catholic Theological Union, Chicago. A Nigerian by birth, he is former member of the Spiritan general council and member of the International Theological Commission for the Catholic Church. Okoye as published numerous articles and *Israel and the Nations: A Mission Theology of the Old Testament* (Orbis, 2006).

Jim and Therese D'Orsa are noted Australian Catholic educators. James is senior lecturer at the Broken Bay Institute in Sydney, and Therese is Head of Mission and Culture at the Borken Bay Instiute and an honorary fellow of Australian Catholic University. They have published *Explorers, Guides and Meaning-makers: Mission Theology for Catholic Educators* (Broken Bay Institute and Garratt Publishing, 2010), and *Catholic Curriculum: A Mission to the Heart of Young People* (Broken Bay institute and Garratt Publishing, 2012). Their latest book, *Leading for Mission: Integrating Life, Culture and Faith in Catholic Education* is scheduled for publication in 2013.

Joseph Puthenpurakal SDB is a member of IAMS (International Association for Mission Studies), IACM (International Association of Catholic Missiologists), FOIM (Fellowship of Indian Missiologists), AND is presently director of DBCIC (Don Bosco Centre for Indigenous Cultures). He teaches missiology at Sacred Heart Theological College, Shillong, India. Fr Joseph has been the South Asia Mission Delegate for Salesian Provinces for nine years. He has been serving in North East India for over four decades.

Robert J. Schreiter, CPPS is Vatican II Professor of Theology at Catholic Theological Union, Chicago. He is past president of the American Society of Missiology and the Catholic Theological Society of America. His many publications include *Constructing Local Theologies* (Orbis, 1985), *Reconciliation: Mission and Ministry in a Changing Social Order* (Orbis, 1992), *The New Catholicity: Theology between the Local and the Global* (Orbis, 1997), and *The Ministry of Reconciliaton: Spirituality and Strategies* (Orbis, 1998).

Roger P. Schroeder, SVD is Bishop Francis X. Ford Professor of Catholic Missiology at Catholic Theological Union, Chicago. Former president of the Association Professors of Mission and the American Society of Missiology, he is the author of *What is the Mission of the Church? A Guide for Catholics* (Orbis, 2008), and, with Stephen Bevans, *Constants in*

Context: A Theology of Mission for Today and *Prophetic Dialogue: Reflections on Mission Today* (Orbis: 2004 and 2011).

Susan Smith, RNDM is retired Senior Lecturer at the Catholic Institute of Theology at the University of Auckland, New Zealand. She has vast experience in mission work and is the author of *Women in Mission* (Orbis, 2007). She has recently published *Call to Mission: The Story of the Mission Sisters in Aotearoa New Zealand and Samoa* (David Ling, 2010), and has edited *Zeal for Mission: The Story of the Sisters of Our Lady of the Missions 1861-2011* (David Ling, 2012).

Paulo Suess was the co-founder of the Postgraduate Department of Missiology at the Pontifical University of Our Lady of the Assumption in São Paulo, Brazil and was for many years the secretary of the Indigenous Christian Mission in Brazil. He is a renowned missiologist and liberation theologian in Latin America and past president of the International Association for Mission Studies. His many publications include *Introduçao à Teologia da Missao. Convocar e enviar: servos e testemunhas do Reino* (Vozes, 2011) and *Queimada e semeadura. Da conquista espiritual ao descrobrimento e uma nova evangelizacao* (Vozes, 1988).

Jonathan Y. Tan is Senior Lecturer in the Faculty of Theology and Philosophy of Australian Catholic University in Sydney. He is the author of *Introducing Asian American Theologies* (Orbis, 2008) and more than fifty essays, articles, and book chapters on a wide range of theological issues in Asian and Asian American theologies, missiology, inter-religious dialogue, contextual theology, and comparative theology.

Martin Üffing, SVD is director of the Steyler Missionswissenschaftliches Institute and Professor of Missiology at the Theologische Hochschule, Sankt Augustin, Germany. A former missionary to the Philippines, he is author of *Die Deutche Kirche in Mission* (Steyler Verlag, 1994), *Non-European Missionaries in Europe: A Missiological Reflection* (Steyler Missionswissenschafliches Institut, 2011), and *Mission seit dem Konzil* (Steyler Verlag, 2013).

REGNUM EDINBURGH CENTENARY SERIES

David A. Kerr, Kenneth R. Ross (Eds)
Mission Then and Now
2009 / 978-1-870345-73-6 / 343pp (paperback)
2009 / 978-1-870345-76-7 / 343pp (hardback)

No one can hope to fully understand the modern Christian missionary movement without engaging substantially with the World Missionary Conference, held at Edinburgh in 1910. This book is the first to systematically examine the eight Commissions which reported to Edinburgh 1910 and gave the conference much of its substance and enduring value. It will deepen and extend the reflection being stimulated by the upcoming centenary and will kindle the missionary imagination for 2010 and beyond.

Daryl M. Balia, Kirsteen Kim (Eds)
Witnessing to Christ Today
2010 / 978-1-870345-77-4 / 301pp (hardback)

This volume, the second in the Edinburgh 2010 series, includes reports of the nine main study groups working on different themes for the celebration of the centenary of the World Missionary Conference, Edinburgh 1910. Their collaborative work brings together perspectives that are as inclusive as possible of contemporary world Christianity and helps readers to grasp what it means in different contexts to be 'witnessing to Christ today'.

Claudia Währisch-Oblau, Fidon Mwombeki (Eds)
Mission Continues
Global Impulses for the 21st Century
2010 / 978-1-870345-82-8 / 271pp (hardback)

In May 2009, 35 theologians from Asia, Africa and Europe met in Wuppertal, Germany, for a consultation on mission theology organized by the United Evangelical Mission: Communion of 35 Churches in Three Continents. The aim was to participate in the 100th anniversary of the Edinburgh conference through a study process and reflect on the challenges for mission in the 21st century. This book brings together these papers written by experienced practitioners from around the world.

Brian Woolnough and Wonsuk Ma (Eds)
Holistic Mission
God's Plan for God's People
2010 / 978-1-870345-85-9 / 268pp (hardback)

Holistic mission, or integral mission, implies God is concerned with the whole person, the whole community, body, mind and spirit. This book discusses the meaning of the holistic gospel, how it has developed, and implications for the church. It takes a global, eclectic approach, with 19 writers, all of whom have much experience in, and commitment to, holistic mission. It addresses critically and honestly one of the most exciting, and challenging, issues facing the church today. To be part of God's plan for God's people, the church must take holistic mission to the world.

Kirsteen Kim and Andrew Anderson (Eds)
Mission Today and Tomorrow
2010 / 978-1-870345-91-0 / 450pp (hardback)

There are moments in our lives when we come to realise that we are participating in the triune God's mission. If we believe the church to be as sign and symbol of the reign of God in the world, then we are called to witness to Christ today by sharing in God's mission of love through the transforming power of the Holy Spirit. We can all participate in God's transforming and reconciling mission of love to the whole creation.

Tormod Engelsviken, Erling Lundeby and Dagfinn Solheim (Eds)
The Church Going Glocal
Mission and Globalisation
2011 / 978-1-870345-93-4 / 262pp (hardback)
The New Testament church is… universal and local at the same time. The universal, one and holy apostolic church appears in local manifestations. Missiologically speaking… the church can take courage as she faces the increasing impact of globalisation on local communities today. Being universal and concrete, the church is geared for the simultaneous challenges of the glocal and local.

Marina Ngurusangzeli Behera (Ed)
Interfaith Relations after One Hundred Years
Christian Mission among Other Faiths
2011 / 978-1-870345-96-5 / 338pp (hardback)
The essays of this book reflect not only the acceptance and celebration of pluralism within India but also by extension an acceptance as well as a need for unity among Indian Christians of different denominations. The essays were presented and studied at a preparatory consultation on Study Theme II: Christian Mission Among Other Faiths at the United Theological College, India July 2009.

Lalsangkima Pachuau and Knud Jørgensen (Eds)
Witnessing to Christ in a Pluralistic Age
Christian Mission among Other Faiths
2011 / 978-1-870345-95-8 / 277pp (hardback)
In a world where plurality of faiths is increasingly becoming a norm of life, insights on the theology of religious plurality are needed to strengthen our understanding of our own faith and the faith of others. Even though religious diversity is not new, we are seeing an upsurge in interest on the theologies of religion among all Christian confessional traditions. It can be claimed that no other issue in Christian mission is more important and more difficult than the theologies of religions.

Beth Snodderly and A Scott Moreau (Eds)
Evangelical Frontier Mission
Perspectives on the Global Progress of the Gospel
2011 / 978-1-870345-98-9 / 312pp (hardback)
This important volume demonstrates that 100 years after the World Missionary Conference in Edinburgh, Evangelism has become truly global. Twenty-first-century Evangelism continues to focus on frontier mission, but significantly, and in the spirit of Edinburgh 1910, it also has re-engaged social action.

Rolv Olsen (Ed)
Mission and Postmodernities
2011 / 978-1-870345-97-2 / 279pp (hardback)
This volume takes on meaning because its authors honestly struggle with and debate how we should relate to postmodernities. Should our response be accommodation, relativizing or counter-culture? How do we strike a balance between listening and understanding, and

at the same time exploring how postmodernities influence the interpretation and application of the Bible as the normative story of God's mission in the world?

Cathy Ross (Ed)
Life-Widening Mission
2012 / 978-1-908355-00-3 / 163pp (hardback)
It is clear from the essays collected here that the experience of the 2010 World Mission Conference in Edinburgh was both affirming and frustrating for those taking part - affirming because of its recognition of how the centre of gravity has moved in global Christianity; frustrating because of the relative slowness of so many global Christian bodies to catch up with this and to embody it in the way they do business and in the way they represent themselves. These reflections will - or should - provide plenty of food for thought in the various councils of the Communion in the coming years.

Beate Fagerli, Knud Jørgensen, Rolv Olsen, Kari Storstein Haug and
Knut Tveitereid (Eds)
A Learning Missional Church
Reflections from Young Missiologists
2012 / 978-1-908355-01-0 / 218pp (hardback)
Cross-cultural mission has always been a primary learning experience for the church. It pulls us out of a mono-cultural understanding and helps us discover a legitimate theological pluralism which opens up for new perspectives in the Gospel. Translating the Gospel into new languages and cultures is a human and divine means of making us learn new 'incarnations' of the Good News.

Emma Wild-Wood & Peniel Rajkumar (Eds)
Foundations for Mission
2012 / 978-1-908355-12-6 / 309pp (hardback)
This volume provides an important resource for those wishing to gain an overview of significant issues in contemporary missiology whilst understanding how they are applied in particular contexts.

Wonsuk Ma & Kenneth R Ross (Eds)
Mission Spirituality and Authentic Discipleship
2013 / 978-1-908355-24-9 / 248pp (hardback)
This book argues for the primacy of spirituality in the practice of mission. Since God is the primary agent of mission and God works through the power of the Holy Spirit, it is through openness to the Spirit that mission finds its true character and has its authentic impact.

REGNUM STUDIES IN GLOBAL CHRISTIANITY

David Emmanuel Singh (Ed)
Jesus and the Cross
Reflections of Christians from Islamic Contexts
2008 / 978-1-870345-65-1 / 226pp
The Cross reminds us that the sins of the world are not borne through the exercise of power but through Jesus Christ's submission to the will of the Father. The papers in this volume are organised in three parts: scriptural, contextual and theological. The central question

being addressed is: how do Christians living in contexts, where Islam is a majority or minority religion, experience, express or think of the Cross?

Sung-wook Hong
Naming God in Korea
The Case of Protestant Christianity
2008 / 978-1-870345-66-8 / 170pp (hardback)

Since Christianity was introduced to Korea more than a century ago, one of the most controversial issues has been the Korean term for the Christian 'God'. This issue is not merely about naming the Christian God in Korean language, but it relates to the question of theological contextualization - the relationship between the gospel and culture - and the question of Korean Christian identity. This book demonstrates the nature of the gospel in relation to cultures, i.e., the universality of the gospel expressed in all human cultures.

Hubert van Beek (Ed)
Revisioning Christian Unity
The Global Christian Forum
2009 / 978-1-870345-74-3 / 288pp (hardback)

This book contains the records of the Global Christian Forum gathering held in Limuru near Nairobi, Kenya, on 6 – 9 November 2007 as well as the papers presented at that historic event. Also included are a summary of the Global Christian Forum process from its inception until the 2007 gathering and the reports of the evaluation of the process that was carried out in 2008.

Young-hoon Lee
The Holy Spirit Movement in Korea
Its Historical and Theological Development
2009 / 978-1-870345-67-5 / 174pp (hardback)

This book traces the historical and theological development of the Holy Spirit Movement in Korea through six successive periods (from 1900 to the present time). These periods are characterized by repentance and revival (1900-20), persecution and suffering under Japanese occupation (1920-40), confusion and division (1940-60), explosive revival in which the Pentecostal movement played a major role in the rapid growth of Korean churches (1960-80), the movement reaching out to all denominations (1980-2000), and the new context demanding the Holy Spirit movement to open new horizons in its mission engagement (2000-).

Paul Hang-Sik Cho
Eschatology and Ecology
Experiences of the Korean Church
2010 / 978-1-870345-75-0 / 260pp (hardback)

This book raises the question of why Korean people, and Korean Protestant Christians in particular, pay so little attention to ecological issues. The author argues that there is an important connection (or elective affinity) between this lack of attention and the other-worldly eschatology that is so dominant within Korean Protestant Christianity.

Dietrich Werner, David Esterline, Namsoon Kang, Joshva Raja (Eds)
The Handbook of Theological Education in World Christianity
Theological Perspectives, Ecumenical Trends, Regional Surveys
2010 / 978-1-870345-80-0 / 759pp

This major reference work is the first ever comprehensive study of Theological Education in Christianity of its kind. With contributions from over 90 international scholars and church leaders, it aims to be easily accessible across denominational, cultural, educational, and geographic boundaries. The Handbook will aid international dialogue and networking among theological educators, institutions, and agencies.

David Emmanuel Singh & Bernard C Farr (Eds)
Christianity and Education
Shaping of Christian Context in Thinking
2010 / 978-1-870345-81-1 / 374pp

Christianity and Education is a collection of papers published in *Transformation: An International Journal of Holistic Mission Studies* over a period of 15 years. The articles represent a spectrum of Christian thinking addressing issues of institutional development for theological education, theological studies in the context of global mission, contextually aware/informed education, and academies which deliver such education, methodologies and personal reflections.

J.Andrew Kirk
Civilisations in Conflict?
Islam, the West and Christian Faith
2011 / 978-1-870345-87-3 / 205pp

Samuel Huntington's thesis, which argues that there appear to be aspects of Islam that could be on a collision course with the politics and values of Western societies, has provoked much controversy. The purpose of this study is to offer a particular response to Huntington's thesis by making a comparison between the origins of Islam and Christianity.

David Emmanuel Singh (Ed)
Jesus and the Incarnation
Reflections of Christians from Islamic Contexts
2011 / 978-1-870345-90-3 / 245pp

In the dialogues of Christians with Muslims nothing is more fundamental than the Cross, the Incarnation and the Resurrection of Jesus. Building on the *Jesus and the Cross*, this book contains voices of Christians living in various 'Islamic contexts' and reflecting on the Incarnation of Jesus. The aim and hope of these reflections is that the papers weaved around the notion of 'the Word' will not only promote dialogue among Christians on the roles of the Person and the Book but, also, create a positive environment for their conversations with Muslim neighbours.

Ivan M Satyavrata
God Has Not left Himself Without Witness
2011 / 978-1-870345-79-8 / 264pp

Since its earliest inception the Christian Church has had to address the question of what common ground exits between Christian faiths and other religions. This issue is not merely of academic interest but one with critical existential and socio-political consequences. This study presents a case for the revitalization of the fulfillment tradition based on a recovery and assessment of the fulfillment approaches of Indian Christian converts in the pre-independence period.

Bal Krishna Sharma
From this World to the Next
Christian Identity and Funerary Rites in Nepal
2013 / 978-1-908355-08-9 / 238pp

This book explores and analyses funerary rite struggles in a nation where Christianity is a comparatively recent phenomenon, and many families have multi-faith, who go through traumatic experiences at the death of their family members. The author has used an applied theological approach to explore and analyse the findings in order to address the issue of funerary rites with which the Nepalese church is struggling.

J Kwabena Asamoah-Gyada
Contemporary Pentecostal Christianity
Interpretations from an African Context
2013 / 978-1-908355-07-2 / 194pp

Pentecostalism is the fastest growing stream of Christianity in the world. The real evidence for the significance of Pentecostalism lies in the actual churches they have built and the numbers they attract. This work interprets key theological and missiological themes in African Pentecostalism by using material from the live experiences of the movement itself.

Isabel Apawo Phiri & Dietrich Werner (Eds)
Handbook of Theological Education in Africa
2013 / 978-1-908355-19-5 / 1110pp (hardback)

The *Handbook of Theological Education in Africa* is a wake-up call for African churches to give proper prominence to theological education institutions and their programmes which serve them. It is unique, comprehensive and ambitious in its aim and scope.

Hope Antone, Wati Longchar, Hyunju Bae, Huang Po Ho, Dietrich Werner (Eds)
Asian Handbook for Theological Education and Ecumenism
2013 / 978-1-908355-30-0 / 675pp (hardback)

This impressive and comprehensive book focuses on key resources for teaching Christian unity and common witness in Asian contexts. It is a collection of articles that reflects the ongoing 'double wrestle' with the texts of biblical tradition as well as with contemporary contexts. It signals an investment towards the future of the ecumenical movement in Asia.

David Emmanuel Singh and Bernard C Farr (Eds)
Inequality, Corruption and the Church
Challenges & Opportunities in the Global Church
2013 / 978-1-908355-20-1/ 217pp

This book contains papers from the Oxford Centre for Mission Studies' quarterly journal, Transformation, on the topic of Christian Ethics. Here, Mission Studies is understood in its widest sense to also encompass Christian Ethics. At the very hearts of it lies the Family as the basic unit of society. All the papers together seek to contribute to understanding how Christian thought is shaped in contexts each of which poses its own challenge to Christian living in family and in broader society.

Martin Allaby
Inequality, Corruption and the Church
Challenges & Opportunities in the Global Church
2013 / 978-1-908355-16-4/ 228pp

Why are economic inequalities greatest in the southern countries where most people are Christians? This book teases out the influences that have created this situation, and concludes that Christians could help reduce economic inequalities by opposing corruption. Interviews in the Philippines, Kenya, Zambia and Peru reveal opportunities and challenges for Christians as they face up to corruption.

REGNUM STUDIES IN MISSION

Kwame Bediako
Theology and Identity
The Impact of Culture upon Christian Thought in the Second Century and in Modern Africa
1992 / 978-1870345-10-1 / 507pp

The author examines the question of Christian identity in the context of the Graeco–Roman culture of the early Roman Empire. He then addresses the modern African predicament of quests for identity and integration.

Christopher Sugden
Seeking the Asian Face of Jesus
The Practice and Theology of Christian Social Witness
in Indonesia and India 1974–1996
1997 / 1-870345-26-6 / 496pp

This study focuses on contemporary holistic mission with the poor in India and Indonesia combined with the call to transformation of all life in Christ with micro-credit enterprise schemes. 'The literature on contextual theology now has a new standard to rise to' – Lamin Sanneh (Yale University, USA).

Hwa Yung
Mangoes or Bananas?
The Quest for an Authentic Asian Christian Theology
1997 / 1-870345-25-5 / 274pp

Asian Christian thought remains largely captive to Greek dualism and Enlightenment rationalism because of the overwhelming dominance of Western culture. Authentic contextual Christian theologies will emerge within Asian Christianity with a dual recovery of confidence in culture and the gospel.

Keith E. Eitel
Paradigm Wars
The Southern Baptist International Mission Board Faces the Third Millennium
1999 / 1-870345-12-6 / 140pp

The International Mission Board of the Southern Baptist Convention is the largest denominational mission agency in North America. This volume chronicles the historic and contemporary forces that led to the IMB's recent extensive reorganization, providing the most comprehensive case study to date of a historic mission agency restructuring to continue its mission purpose into the twenty-first century more effectively.

Samuel Jayakumar
Dalit Consciousness and Christian Conversion
Historical Resources for a Contemporary Debate
1999 / 81-7214-497-0 / 434pp
(Published jointly with ISPCK)

The main focus of this historical study is social change and transformation among the Dalit Christian communities in India. Historiography tests the evidence in the light of the conclusions of the modern Dalit liberation theologians.

Vinay Samuel and Christopher Sugden (Eds)
Mission as Transformation
A Theology of the Whole Gospel
1999 / 978-18703455-13-2 / 522pp

This book brings together in one volume twenty five years of biblical reflection on mission practice with the poor from around the world. This volume helps anyone understand how evangelicals, struggling to unite evangelism and social action, found their way in the last twenty five years to the biblical view of mission in which God calls all human beings to love God and their neighbour; never creating a separation between the two.

Christopher Sugden
Gospel, Culture and Transformation
2000 / 1-870345-32-0 / 152pp
A Reprint, with a New Introduction,
of Part Two of Seeking the Asian Face of Jesus

Gospel, Culture and Transformation explores the practice of mission especially in relation to transforming cultures and communities. - 'Transformation is to enable God's vision of society to be actualised in all relationships: social, economic and spiritual, so that God's will may be reflected in human society and his love experienced by all communities, especially the poor.'

Bernhard Ott
Beyond Fragmentation: Integrating Mission and Theological Education
A Critical Assessment of some Recent Developments
in Evangelical Theological Education
2001 / 1-870345-14-2 / 382pp

Beyond Fragmentation is an enquiry into the development of Mission Studies in evangelical theological education in Germany and German-speaking Switzerland between 1960 and 1995. The author undertakes a detailed examination of the paradigm shifts which have taken place in recent years in both the theology of mission and the understanding of theological education.

Gideon Githiga
The Church as the Bulwark against Authoritarianism
Development of Church and State Relations in Kenya, with Particular Reference to the
Years after Political Independence 1963-1992
2002 / 1-870345-38-x / 218pp

'All who care for love, peace and unity in Kenyan society will want to read this careful history by Bishop Githiga of how Kenyan Christians, drawing on the Bible, have sought to share the love of God, bring his peace and build up the unity of the nation, often in the face of great difficulties and opposition.' Canon Dr Chris Sugden, Oxford Centre for Mission Studies.

Myung Sung-Hoon, Hong Young-Gi (Eds)
Charis and Charisma
David Yonggi Cho and the Growth of Yoido Full Gospel Church
2003 / 978-1870345-45-3 / 218pp

This book discusses the factors responsible for the growth of the world's largest church. It expounds the role of the Holy Spirit, the leadership, prayer, preaching, cell groups and creativity in promoting church growth. It focuses on God's grace (charis) and inspiring leadership (charisma) as the two essential factors and the book's purpose is to present a model for church growth worldwide.

Samuel Jayakumar
Mission Reader
Historical Models for Wholistic Mission in the Indian Context
2003 / 1-870345-42-8 / 250pp
(Published jointly with ISPCK)

This book is written from an evangelical point of view revalidating and reaffirming the Christian commitment to wholistic mission. The roots of the 'wholistic mission' combining 'evangelism and social concerns' are to be located in the history and tradition of Christian evangelism in the past; and the civilizing purpose of evangelism is compatible with modernity as an instrument in nation building.

Bob Robinson
Christians Meeting Hindus
An Analysis and Theological Critique of the Hindu-Christian Encounter in India
2004 / 987-1870345-39-2 / 392pp

This book focuses on the Hindu-Christian encounter, especially the intentional meeting called dialogue, mainly during the last four decades of the twentieth century, and specifically in India itself.

Gene Early
Leadership Expectations
How Executive Expectations are Created and Used in a Non-Profit Setting
2005 / 1-870345-30-4 / 276pp

The author creates an Expectation Enactment Analysis to study the role of the Chancellor of the University of the Nations-Kona, Hawaii. This study is grounded in the field of managerial work, jobs, and behaviour and draws on symbolic interactionism, role theory, role identity theory and enactment theory. The result is a conceptual framework for developing an understanding of managerial roles.

Tharcisse Gatwa
The Churches and Ethnic Ideology in the Rwandan Crises 1900-1994
2005 / 978-1870345-24-8 / 300pp
(Reprinted 2011)

Since the early years of the twentieth century Christianity has become a new factor in Rwandan society. This book investigates the role Christian churches played in the formulation and development of the racial ideology that culminated in the 1994 genocide.

Julie Ma
Mission Possible
Biblical Strategies for Reaching the Lost
2005 / 978-1870345-37-1 / 142pp

This is a missiology book for the church which liberates missiology from the specialists for the benefit of every believer. It also serves as a textbook that is simple and friendly, and yet solid in biblical interpretation. This book links the biblical teaching to the actual and contemporary missiological settings with examples, making the Bible come alive to the reader.

I. Mark Beaumont
Christology in Dialogue with Muslims
A Critical Analysis of Christian Presentations of Christ for Muslims
from the Ninth and Twentieth Centuries
2005 / 978-1870345-46-0 / 227pp

This book analyses Christian presentations of Christ for Muslims in the most creative periods of Christian-Muslim dialogue, the first half of the ninth century and the second half of the twentieth century. In these two periods, Christians made serious attempts to present their faith in Christ in terms that take into account Muslim perceptions of him, with a view to bridging the gap between Muslim and Christian convictions.

Thomas Czövek,
Three Seasons of Charismatic Leadership
A Literary-Critical and Theological Interpretation of the Narrative of
Saul, David and Solomon
2006 / 978-1870345-48-4 / 272pp

This book investigates the charismatic leadership of Saul, David and Solomon. It suggests that charismatic leaders emerge in crisis situations in order to resolve the crisis by the charisma granted by God. Czovek argues that Saul proved himself as a charismatic leader as long as he acted resolutely and independently from his mentor Samuel. In the author's eyes, Saul's failure to establish himself as a charismatic leader is caused by his inability to step out from Samuel's shadow.

Richard Burgess
Nigeria's Christian Revolution
The Civil War Revival and Its Pentecostal Progeny (1967-2006)
2008 / 978-1-870345-63-7 / 347pp

This book describes the revival that occurred among the Igbo people of Eastern Nigeria and the new Pentecostal churches it generated, and documents the changes that have occurred as the movement has responded to global flows and local demands. As such, it explores the nature of revivalist and Pentecostal experience, but does so against the backdrop of local socio-political and economic developments, such as decolonisation and civil war, as well as broader processes, such as modernisation and globalisation.

David Emmanuel Singh & Bernard C Farr (Eds)
Christianity and Cultures
Shaping Christian Thinking in Context
2008 / 978-1-870345-69-9 / 271pp

This volume marks an important milestone, the 25th anniversary of the Oxford Centre for Mission Studies (OCMS). The papers here have been exclusively sourced from Transformation, a quarterly journal of OCMS, and seek to provide a tripartite view of Christianity's engagement with cultures by focusing on the question: how is Christian thinking being formed or reformed through its interaction with the varied contexts it encounters? The subject matters include different strands of theological-missiological thinking, socio-political engagements and forms of family relationships in interaction with the host cultures.

Tormod Engelsviken, Ernst Harbakk, Rolv Olsen, Thor Strandenæs (Eds)
Mission to the World
Communicating the Gospel in the 21st Century:
Essays in Honour of Knud Jørgensen
2008 / 978-1-870345-64-4 / 472pp (hardback)
Knud Jørgensen is Director of Areopagos and Associate Professor of Missiology at MF Norwegian School of Theology. This book reflects on the main areas of Jørgensen's commitment to mission. At the same time it focuses on the main frontier of mission, the world, the content of mission, the Gospel, the fact that the Gospel has to be communicated, and the context of contemporary mission in the 21st century.

Al Tizon
Transformation after Lausanne
Radical Evangelical Mission in Global-Local Perspective
2008 / 978-1-870345-68-2 / 281pp
After Lausanne '74, a worldwide network of radical evangelical mission theologians and practitioners use the notion of "Mission as Transformation" to integrate evangelism and social concern together, thus lifting theological voices from the Two Thirds World to places of prominence. This book documents the definitive gatherings, theological tensions, and social forces within and without evangelicalism that led up to Mission as Transformation. And it does so through a global-local grid that points the way toward greater holistic mission in the 21st century.

Bambang Budijanto
Values and Participation
Development in Rural Indonesia
2009 / 978-1-870345-70-4 / 237pp
Socio-religious values and socio-economic development are inter-dependant, inter-related and are constantly changing in the context of macro political structures, economic policy, religious organizations and globalization; and micro influences such as local affinities, identity, politics, leadership and beliefs. The book argues that the comprehensive approach in understanding the socio-religious values of each of the three local Lopait communities in Central Java is essential to accurately describing their respective identity.

Alan R. Johnson
Leadership in a Slum
A Bangkok Case Study
2009 / 978-1-870345-71-2 / 238pp
This book looks at leadership in the social context of a slum in Bangkok from a different perspective than traditional studies which measure well educated Thais on leadership scales derived in the West. Using both systematic data collection and participant observation, it develops a culturally preferred model as well as a set of models based in Thai concepts that reflect on-the-ground realities. It concludes by looking at the implications of the anthropological approach for those who are involved in leadership training in Thai settings and beyond.

Titre Ande
Leadership and Authority
Bula Matari and Life - Community Ecclesiology in Congo
2010 / 978-1-870345-72-9 / 189pp
Christian theology in Africa can make significant development if a critical understanding of the socio-political context in contemporary Africa is taken seriously, particularly as

Africa's post-colonial Christian leadership based its understanding and use of authority on the Bula Matari model. This has caused many problems and Titre proposes a Life-Community ecclesiology for liberating authority, here leadership is a function, not a status, and 'apostolic succession' belongs to all people of God.

Frank Kwesi Adams
Odwira and the Gospel
A Study of the Asante Odwira Festival and its Significance for Christianity in Ghana
2010 /978-1-870345-59-0 / 232pp

The study of the Odwira festival is the key to the understanding of Asante religious and political life in Ghana. The book explores the nature of the Odwira festival longitudinally - in pre-colonial, colonial and post-independence Ghana - and examines the Odwira ideology and its implications for understanding the Asante self-identity. Also discussed is how some elements of faith portrayed in the Odwira festival can provide a framework for Christianity to engage with Asante culture at a greater depth.

Bruce Carlton
Strategy Coordinator
Changing the Course of Southern Baptist Missions
2010 / 978-1-870345-78-1 / 273pp

This is an outstanding, one-of-a-kind work addressing the influence of the non-residential missionary/strategy coordinator's role in Southern Baptist missions. This scholarly text examines the twentieth century global missiological currents that influenced the leadership of the International Mission Board, resulting in a new paradigm to assist in taking the gospel to the nations.

Julie Ma & Wonsuk Ma
Mission in the Spirit:
Towards a Pentecostal/Charismatic Missiology
2010 / 978-1-870345-84-2 / 312pp

The book explores the unique contribution of Pentecostal/Charismatic mission from the beginning of the twentieth century. The first part considers the theological basis of Pentecostal/Charismatic mission thinking and practice. Special attention is paid to the Old Testament, which has been regularly overlooked by the modern Pentecostal/Charismatic movements. The second part discusses major mission topics with contributions and challenges unique to Pentecostal/Charismatic mission. The book concludes with a reflection on the future of this powerful missionary movement. As the authors served as Korean missionaries in Asia, often their missionary experiences in Asia are reflected in their discussions.

Allan Anderson, Edmond Tang (Eds)
Asian and Pentecostal
The Charismatic Face of Christianity in Asia
2011 / 978-1870345-94-1 / 500pp
(Revised Edition)

This book provides a thematic discussion and pioneering case studies on the history and development of Pentecostal and Charismatic churches in the countries of South Asia, South East Asia and East Asia.

S. Hun Kim & Wonsuk Ma (Eds)
Korean Diaspora and Christian Mission
2011 / 978-1-870345-89-7 / 301pp (hardback)

As a 'divine conspiracy' for Missio Dei, the global phenomenon of people on the move has shown itself to be invaluable. In 2004 two significant documents concerning Diaspora were introduced, one by the Filipino International Network and the other by the Lausanne Committee for World Evangelization. These have created awareness of the importance of people on the move for Christian mission. Since then, Korean Diaspora has conducted similar research among Korean missions, resulting in this book

Jin Huat Tan
Planting an Indigenous Church
The Case of the Borneo Evangelical Mission
2011 / 978-1-870345-99-6 / 343pp

Dr Jin Huat Tan has written a pioneering study of the origins and development of Malaysia's most significant indigenous church. This is an amazing story of revival, renewal and transformation of the entire region chronicling the powerful effect of it evident to date! What can we learn from this extensive and careful study of the Borneo Revival, so the global Christianity will become ever more dynamic?

Bill Prevette
Child, Church and Compassion
Towards Child Theology in Romania
2012 / 978-1-908355-03-4 / 382pp

Bill Prevett comments that "children are like 'canaries in a mine shaft'; they provide a focal point for discovery and encounter of perilous aspects of our world that are often ignored." True, but miners also carried a lamp to see into the subterranean darkness. This book is such a lamp. It lights up the subterranean world of children and youth in danger of exploitation, and as it does so travels deep into their lives and also into the activities of those who seek to help them.

Samuel Cyuma
Picking up the Pieces
The Church and Conflict Resolution in South Africa and Rwanda
2012 / 978-1-908355-02-7 / 373pp

In the last ten years of the 20th century, the world was twice confronted with unbelievable news from Africa. First, there was the end of Apartheid in South Africa, without bloodshed, due to responsible political and Church leaders. The second was the mass killings in Rwanda, which soon escalated into real genocide. Political and Church leaders had been unable to prevents this crime against humanity. In this book, the question is raised: can we compare the situation in South Africa with that in Rwanda? Can Rwandan leaders draw lessons from the peace process in South Africa?

Peter Rowan
Proclaiming the Peacemaker
The Malaysian Church as an Agent of Reconciliation in a Multicultural Society
2012 / 978-1-908355-05-8 / 268pp

With a history of racial violence and in recent years, low-level ethnic tensions, the themes of peaceful coexistence and social harmony are recurring ones in the discourse of Malaysian society. In such a context, this book looks at the role of the church as a reconciling agent, arguing that a reconciling presence within a divided society necessitates an ethos of peacemaking.

Edward Ontita
Resources and Opportunity
The Architecture of Livelihoods in Rural Kenya
2012 / 978-1-908355-04-1 / 328pp
Poor people in most rural areas of developing countries often improvise resources in unique ways to enable them make a living. Resources and Opportunity takes the view that resources are dynamic and fluid, arguing that villagers co-produce them through redefinition and renaming in everyday practice and use them in diverse ways. The book focuses on ordinary social activities to bring out people's creativity in locating, redesigning and embracing livelihood opportunities in processes.

Kathryn Kraft
Searching for Heaven in the Real World
A Sociological Discussion of Conversion in the Arab World
2012 / 978-1-908355-15-7 / 1422pp
Kathryn Kraft explores the breadth of psychological and social issues faced by Arab Muslims after making a decision to adopt a faith in Christ or Christianity, investigating some of the most surprising and significant challenges new believers face.

Wessley Lukose
Contextual Missiology of the Spirit
Pentecostalism in Rajasthan, India
2013 / 978-1-908355-09-6 / 256pp
This book explores the identity, context and features of Pentecostalism in Rajasthan, India as well as the internal and external issues facing Pentecostals. It aims to suggest 'a contextual missiology of the Spirit,' as a new model of contextual missiology from a Pentecostal perspective. It is presented as a glocal, ecumenical, transformational, and public missiology.

Paul M Miller
Evangelical Mission in Co-operation with Catholics:
Pentecostalism in Rajasthan, India
2013 / 978-1-908355-17-1 / 291pp
This book brings the first thorough examination of the discussions going on within Evangelicalism about the viability of a good conscience dialogue with Roman Catholics. Those who are interested in evangelical world missions and Roman Catholic views of world missions will find this informative.

REGNUM RESOURCES FOR MISSION

Knud Jørgensen
Equipping for Service
Christian Leadership in Church and Society
2012 / 978-1-908355-06-5 / 150pp

This book is written out of decades of experience of leading churches and missions in Ethiopia, Geneva, Norway and Hong Kong. Combining the teaching of Scripture with the insights of contemporary management philosophy, Jørgensen writes in a way which is practical and applicable to anyone in Christian service. "The intention has been to challenge towards a leadership relevant for work in church and mission, and in public and civil society, with special attention to leadership in Church and organisation."

Mary Miller
What does Love have to do with Leadership?
2013 / 978-1-908355-10-2 / 100pp

Leadership is a performing art, not a science. It is the art of influencing others, not just to accomplish something together, but to want to accomplish great things together. Mary Miller captures the art of servant leadership in her powerful book. She understands that servant leaders challenge existing processes without manipulating or overpowering people.

Mary Miller (Ed)
Faces of Holistic Mission
Stories of the OCMS Family
2013 / 978-1-908355-32-4 / 104pp

There is a popular worship song that begins with the refrain, 'look what the Lord has done, look what the Lord has done'. This book does exactly that; it seeks to show what the Lord has done. Fifteen authors from five different continents identify what the Lord has indeed been doing, and continues to do, in their lives. These are their stories.

GENERAL REGNUM TITLES

Vinay Samuel, Chris Sugden (Eds)
The Church in Response to Human Need
1987 / 1870345045 / xii+268pp

Philip Sampson, Vinay Samuel, Chris Sugden (Eds)
Faith and Modernity
Essays in modernity and post-modernity
1994 / 1870345177 / 352pp

Klaus Fiedler
The Story of Faith Missions
1994 / 0745926878 / 428pp

Douglas Peterson
Not by Might nor by Power
A Pentecostal Theology of Social Concern in Latin America
1996 / 1870345207 / xvi+260pp

David Gitari
In Season and Out of Season
Sermons to a Nation
1996 / 1870345118 / 155pp

David. W. Virtue
A Vision of Hope
The Story of Samuel Habib
1996 / 1870345169 / xiv+137pp

Everett A Wilson
Strategy of the Spirit
J.Philip Hogan and the Growth of the Assemblies of God Worldwide, 1960 - 1990
1997 /1870345231/214

Murray Dempster, Byron Klaus, Douglas Petersen (Eds)
The Globalization of Pentecostalism
A Religion Made to Travel
1999 / 1870345290 / xvii+406pp

Peter Johnson, Chris Sugden (Eds)
Markets, Fair Trade and the Kingdom of God
Essays to Celebrate Traidcraft's 21st Birthday
2001 / 1870345193 / xii+155pp

Robert Hillman, Coral Chamberlain, Linda Harding
Healing & Wholeness
Reflections on the Healing Ministry
2002 / 978-1- 870345-35- 4 / xvii+283pp

David Bussau, Russell Mask
Christian Microenterprise Development
An Introduction
2003 / 1870345282 / xiii+142pp

David Singh
Sainthood and Revelatory Discourse
An Examination of the Basis for the Authority of Bayan in Mahdawi Islam
2003 / 8172147285 / xxiv+485pp

For the up-to-date listing of the Regnum books visit
www.ocms.ac.uk/regnum

Regnum Books International
Regnum is an Imprint of The Oxford Centre for Mission Studies
St. Philip and St. James Church
Woodstock Road
Oxford, OX2 6HR